Remaking the
Middle Ages

Remaking the Middle Ages

The Methods of Cinema and History in Portraying the Medieval World

ANDREW B.R. ELLIOTT

McFarland & Company, Inc., Publishers
Jefferson, North Carolina, and London

LIBRARY OF CONGRESS CATALOGUING-IN-PUBLICATION DATA

Elliott, Andrew B.R.
    Remaking the Middle Ages : the methods of cinema and history
in portraying the medieval world / Andrew B.R. Elliott.
        p.   cm.
    Includes bibliographical references and index.

    ISBN 978-0-7864-4624-7
    softcover : 50# alkaline paper ∞

    1. Middle Ages in motion pictures.   2. Historical films —
History and criticism.   I. Title.
    PN1995.9.M52E44   2011
    791.43'65840902 — dc22   2010040481

British Library cataloguing data are available

On the cover: Sean Connery as King Arthur in *First Knight*,
1995 (Columbia Pictures/Photofest)

Manufactured in the United States of America

*McFarland & Company, Inc., Publishers
    Box 611, Jefferson, North Carolina 28640
    www.mcfarlandpub.com*

For Mae

Table of Contents

Acknowledgments

I would first like to acknowledge the help and support given to me by Dr. Claudio Canaparo, who after an initial exchange of emails at 3 A.M. has helped me from the very outset to formulate, develop, defend and (perhaps no less importantly) source funding for my research. Both he and Dr. Emma Cayley have patiently read and reread my thesis, papers and articles; they have given me constant support and encouragement, toned down my outrageous ideas, bolstered my weaker ones and have painstakingly tried to fully remove all the split infinitives from my work (and of which I am so inexplicably fond). A third academic pillar has been Professor Jane Taylor, who first introduced me some time ago (via a certain Dennis the Peasant) to the recreation — and subversion — of the Middle Ages, and has indulgently supported my efforts ever since. Similarly, I am grateful for the support of many of the "masters of medieval film" for their warm welcome into the folds; most notable among these are Elizabeth Sklar and Donald Hoffman, whose interest and encouragement meant a great deal to me at the outset of my career. Finally, an enormous debt of gratitude is owed to Professor Kevin J. Harty for all of his cheery help and encouragement in the preparation of these pages, and for his unrivalled knowledge and insight into the world of medieval film. I can only hope to repay him by recognizing his contribution to my work, and by "paying it forward," to use his expression.

Beyond the academic sphere, my thanks must also go to my parents, Brian and Pat, and to Alastair, Louise and Lorna, who will probably never read this book, but whose support, respect and sofa-beds have helped me to write it in ways which I don't think they realize. A similar debt is owed to all of my friends who have supported me and hosted me (and endured my obsession with medieval films); most especially among these must be Dr. Antonella Liuzzo Scorpo, who has been present at almost all of my papers, criticized my posture, and constantly reminded me of what a *real* medievalist does; so too, in their own warm way, have Abigail and Daniele been invaluable friends, not least for rescuing me from midnight ready meals. My other friends and colleagues have been a source of constant support, most especially Dr. Ulrike Zitzlsperger, Isabelle Rodrigues, Dr. David Houston Jones, Dr. Stephanie Darrie, Cécile Maudet (my Rennes host and tour guide), Fréderique Ozanam, Giorgio Tartari and Anna-Maria Mazza (these latter two for their kindness), and those who have been there from the beginning: Matthew, James, Cassian and Alex. My final thanks must of course go to Sara, who has been by my side throughout everything, patiently tolerated my own "medieval mess," and without whom none of this would make any sense.

Preface

"France ... the fifteenth century, the Dark Ages.... The people were still gripped by ignorance and superstition...." So begins the title sequence of Leslie Megahey's 1995 film *The Advocate*, introducing us to a world characterized by accordingly ignorant and superstitious peasants who, we discover when the camera pulls back, are at present gathering to witness the public hanging of a man and a donkey for "unnatural carnal relations." There is dirt and mud everywhere. Straw lies scattered around the scene of the trial. An angry crowd has assembled hastily, the sort of ad hoc rent-a-mob armed with pitchforks and moral outrage which Hollywood seems to permanently keep on standby, on the off-chance that someone makes a historical film. The defendant stares blankly out at his persecutors. His charges are read aloud amid the hushed condemnation of the gathered crowd. At the fatal moment, local priest Father Lucien runs up to the gallows with a last-minute reprieve testifying to the "previous good character of the beast." The "she-ass" is freed; the crowd cheers. The human defendant swings grotesquely from a noose, and the mob stares impassively as a close-up of the hanged man's feet fills the screen.

There is no doubt about it; we are back in the Middle Ages. It is the world of barbarity and squalor, in which dark forces sweep unchecked through defenseless villages, storm monasteries and ransack their way into the annals of history. It is the world of superstition and religious zeal, too, in which the earth is still flat and all phenomena — from comets to rainbows — are instantly ascribed to the ineffable Divine. As *The Advocate*'s prologue continues, the people were "mortally afraid of the power of Satan, daily expecting God's punishment — the plague that was sweeping Europe." It is of course a familiar world to us; we know its signs, we know how it operates, and we know — thanks to years of conditioning — vaguely what to expect from the dark primitivism of the Middle Ages.

Yet we look again at another screen and are confounded. A procession

1

of knights in glistening armor and bright, spotless raiments gallops through the verdant forests, in search of adventures. We are back in the fourteenth century again; the sun shines down on a warm spring morning, and the wind is light enough to make the colorful flags adorning the castles flutter playfully in the breeze. A princess emerges from a turret on the castle walls, beneath which beautiful damsels in trailing dresses sit patiently on docile palfreys awaiting their gallant champions. The whole pageant — filmed in glorious Technicolor to bring out its richest hues — rides nobly out of sight into the dignified and refined MGM castle.... And we have no need to follow them there, for we know already what happens next. We have seen its tournaments, its loud declamations of loyalty to the king and obeisance to the beautiful queen; its honor and chivalry, and the frisson of delight stemming from the clash of duties when *noblesse oblige* encounters personal desire, but Love's persistence permits no refusal.

So which medieval world is it to be? The dirty or the clean one? And what about those who inhabited those worlds? Were they the brutal simpletons of *Le Bon Roi Dagobert* and of *Dragonslayer*, terrified by the portentous and diabolic machinations of Twain's Sir Boss which blot out the sun? Were they the devious intellectuals of *The Name of the Rose*? Or were they the devout, God-fearing folk of *El Cid* and Camelot? Perhaps they were cruel and merciless, invoking the institutionalized — though almost certainly fictitious — "right of the first night" on a whim in order to satisfy their barely repressed primal urges; or else the refined, courtly knights whose sexual advances were deemed shameful if they progressed beyond a midnight serenade or the occasional dance at a May Day festival?

And here lie the two problems with which this book will be chiefly engaged: on one hand the creation of medieval people, and on the other the worlds which they inhabit. As tempting as it might be to try to do so, this book will not seek to uncover the "truth" about the Middle Ages, since — as I will argue in chapter 1 — the "truth" of this problematic era lies very much in the eyes of the beholder. Instead it will ask some more probing questions concerning how we go about reconstructing history in the cinema, how each of these disparate and often contradictory concepts has arisen in film, where they have come from, what they mean to contemporary audiences, and in what capacity they are being used.

It is to the first of these questions that I address my two introductory chapters, in which I highlight a fundamental rupture between the retrospectively created neo-medieval period and what it is realistically possible to understand about the era. To this end I use criticism of narrative, montage and ideology (traditionally cinematographic terms here used to critique Historical enquiry) to examine the problems we have with our reliance on historical methods, before moving on to look at recent historiographic criticism and its effect on historical films. My examination of the fields of historiography and cinematography — fields which I have argued to be convergent and not contradictory — thus tries to show that rather than being at loggerheads, the means by which we reconstruct medieval History on the page is broadly similar to those by which we re-imagine that same history on film. In other words, the process of filmmaking and the process of writing History bear a number of similarities. In response to challenges from Rollins, Aberth and others about the *inevitable* inaccuracy of filmic history, I show that *all* Historical inquiry is plagued by a similar range of problems, in terms of limitations of our knowledge, the conflation of temporal planes and what Sobchack and White have called the "Modernist Event."

Consequently, I argue in chapter 2 that when it comes to recreating history on film, we are in reality trying to construct a medieval world whose formal signs are determined by two concerns: first, to try to represent as close an approximation to the "Historical" Middle Ages as is possible, and second, to decide whether to *retain the form at the risk of the concept, or to retain the concept while forsaking the form*, a concept I call a semiotic paradox." Using my arguments from chapter 1, I examine step by step the processes at work in "constructing the Middle Ages," and try to outline some of the major theoretical issues involved in the process. In this attempt, I have used François Amy de la Bretèque's *L'Imaginaire médiéval* as a starting point, a monumental work in which he has developed an inductive theoretical summary of the means by which we reattach the history to the film by a close reading of a staggering range of "medieval films." As a methodology, it is indubitably thorough, but one whose reproduction would be impossible, for reasons of space and direction, in the present study. Instead, I build on his results in order to focus more deeply on the ontological process itself by which we construct these worlds: hence the observation that we "construct" the era in place of "rediscovering" it. In this endeavor, in chapter 2 I put forward the theory which will be discussed throughout the remainder of this book, that there exist two dominant modes by which we attempt to bridge this gulf between the two eras. These are, briefly, by an iconic recreation (which seeks to recreate the vertical relationships between iconic images which we have of the period itself), or by a paradigmatic representation (which aims to reproduce the Middle Ages horizontally, by assimilating its form to other, more recognizable and familiar models).

The first, iconic recreation, occurs when the filmmaker tries to use various aspects (predominantly visual, but not exclusively so) to explain the medieval referent. This might be to refer to iconographic images (from statues, museum pieces, illustrations from *Children's Illustrated*, and other films, to name only a handful), or else to use visual symbols to anchor the character in the appropriate milieu, an approach which is, I will suggest, far more prevalent in the European filmmaking tradition than in its North American counterpart, perhaps for the reason offered by Airlie that in Europe the Middle Ages still exist alongside us, and "monuments of medieval civilisation still survive."[1]

The second option, however, is not to look vertically back into the past, but to use a horizontal assimilation, which I have called paradigmatic association. In this scenario, the filmmaker does not try to recreate the visual iconic or indexical signs of "medieval-ness," but instead seeks to draw a comparison with a modern equivalent (or, at best, an approximation). In this case, the structural relationships of the Middle Ages are brought forward into the present, and re-imagined as modern relationships.

Given chapter 1's assertion that the Middle Ages cannot be accessed *directly*, my argument is that these two modes (paradigm and icon) function *indirectly*, acting in two different ways in order to conjure up a picture of the medieval period in the mind of the spectator in the absence of a concrete referent, the former by a wholesale translation (in the geometric sense), the latter by a piecemeal, mosaic form.

Having tried to discredit the belief in such an authoritative, empirical approach to the subject in the first two chapters, Part two therefore moves on to analyze how medieval people are represented in film, providing a demonstration of these iconic and paradigmatic processes at work in the field of medieval film. Adopting a cross-section of society drawn from medieval understanding, the four chapters deal with the representation of "those who fight, those who rule, those who pray, and those who work." Each chapter begins with a brief synopsis of the medieval referent, before moving on to identify some of the ways in which filmmakers have attempted to represent them. In this respect, I am acutely mindful of Nickolas Haydock's warning against inherently flawed attempts to establish a real (as opposed to reel) Middle Ages, which makes the assumption of an underlying historical reality (and consequently a falsity in its "reel" reflection).[2] In answer to this charge I make constant reference to my arguments for the rejection of a single Historical record in chapter 1, and to the work's overall hypothesis that the "real" medieval referent is only the sum of all beliefs that we, as a society, hold (or perhaps *held*) about the Middle Ages. We might usefully borrow a term here from the title of François Amy de la Bretèque's study of the field, in calling this sum of beliefs our "medieval imaginary,"[3] thereby evoking images of the Lacanian collective unconscious which is ably discussed in turn by Haydock himself.

The third section on "medieval worlds" represents an attempt to draw the focus away from the characters on our medieval "stage," and rather to turn attention to that stage itself, and how these medieval worlds have been constructed. The arguments brought into play here reflect merely the surface of a great deal of scholarship which remains to be done on the subject of the initial worlds (or, as I come to call them, forums). In this respect I am the fortunate inheritor of a good deal of thinking about neo-medievalism, and take as my starting point a series of types or forms of Middle Ages which others have bequeathed to posterity: Paden, for example, offers us three such medieval worlds, Williams advances us to five, Airlie contributes three more and Eco notoriously — at the beginning of our first forays into neo-medievalism — offered us no fewer than ten.[4] The changes made to these schemas have been to view them not as restrictive typologies, but as "starting points" from which filmmakers go about trying to re-imagine the medieval period. Looking at them in this way, as chapter 9 will argue, offers the secondary advantage that it goes some way to answer another of the important questions facing medieval films; namely, to what extent do accuracy and authenticity diverge? In this last chapter, then, far from offering a comprehensive theory about these medieval worlds, I have tried to open the field up to further works, by calling into play some useful questions which — it is to be hoped — later scholarship will address in more depth.

This work is geared, consequently, to three audiences in particular. The first is the academic medievalist who, confounded and distressed by the perpetual errors and anachronisms in medieval-themed films, might be persuaded to pause and see things from the other side. In this respect, there have been one or two recent studies which have begun to apply this thinking with great success; most notably Haydock's *Movie Medievalism*, which uses film theory and psychoanalysis to delve more deeply into how we construct our "medieval imaginary," along with Finke and Shichtman in their excellent *Cinematic Illuminations*, who have applied their extensive knowledge of the field to examine how medieval films "work," and propose a useful methodology for doing so. In my own work I have tried to use the same approach to make us think twice before condemning medieval films out of hand: when we stop to think about the filmmaker trying to make sense of what is essentially an interminable academic debate, perhaps we might forgive them for going ahead and doing it their way, ignoring what might on the surface seem to be fussy, academic preciosity.

The second audience is also perhaps an academic one, but one drawn from across the field of history on film; it stretches from the student of historical films to the historian or the film specialist, each dissatisfied with the other's intrusion into their discipline. Some truly admirable scholarship has emerged over the last three or four decades, written by specialists working on historical films, and I hope over the course of this work to offer them some more ideas about how we transfer this specific — and deeply problematic — period of our past onto the silver screen.

My third audience, though by no means any less important, is the non-academic who, for whatever reason, seeks to discover in a little more detail the reasons behind decisions taken in respect of historical films. Why Robin Hood, for example, is always associated with a jolly, round friar; why knights look like cowboys, or why the best of Camelot speak so often with a distinctly New York accent. For the sake of this audience, I have tried as far as possible to make my work accessible, avoiding unnecessary jargon and academic buzz-words, to ensure that my arguments make sense beyond the ivory towers. After all, in my view, if a theory is to be of any use in the real world it must make sense beyond the narrow confines of disciplines and academic departments.

Outside the text itself, there remains of course both a great deal of excellent scholarship already in print and a great deal of work which remains to be done. Of inestimable value in establishing the validity of medieval films in the first place has been the work of Kevin J. Harty, and in particular his pioneering work *The Reel Middle Ages*, for which he has tirelessly sourced, listed and evaluated a staggering corpus of films with medieval themes, whose enormity took us all — and, one suspects, Harty himself— by surprise. I have been fortunate enough in the preparation of this book to benefit from both his encyclopedic knowledge of medieval film, as well as his generosity in reading and critiquing a substantial part of my theory. Equally invaluable has been the work of François de la Bretèque, to whose masterly oeuvre I freely confess an unpaid debt in the preparation of these pages. My only attempt to repay him has been, in the continued wait for an English-language translation of his chef-d'oeuvre, to try to introduce readers unfamiliar with French to his truly excellent scholarship in the field. Finally, I must recognize my debt to a great deal of interesting thinking in terms of historical film which has emerged over the past few years, and which has helped to pave the way for such reassessments of the field. Certainly Robert Rosenstone has earned his place as an authority in the field, since the freedom of his intellectual curiosity, bolstered by his solid historical training, has provided the backbone for renewed criticism, and has afforded me the freedom to impudently challenge the findings of the master medievalists in the first place.

As for the work remaining to be done, if the theoretical basis of this text should prove to be even half as useful to future scholars as the existing scholarship has been to me, I shall consider it to have been successful in its quest. After all, like the original quest for the grail, it is not in providing all the answers, but in simply asking the right questions that the greatest revelations are most often to be found.

PART I

PROBLEMS

1

History, Historiography and Film

*We try to reproduce the reality, but the harder we try, the more we find the pictures that make up the stock-in-trade of the spectacle of history forcing themselves upon us.... Our concern with history ... is a concern with pre-*formed images already printed on our brains, *images at which we keep staring while the truth lies elsewhere, away from it all, somewhere as yet undiscovered.*[1]

Over twenty years ago, in his much-quoted essay "Revisiting the Middle Ages," Umberto Eco famously noted the continued interest in — and retransmission of — the medieval period, claiming simply that "people seem to like the Middle Ages."[2] Yet when it comes to film versions of that same medieval period, we find an almost immediate resistance, principally (but by no means exclusively) among scholars: in one article, David Williams observes that for many medievalists "medieval movies at first appear to reveal a disappointing or frustrating scene,"[3] and a few years further on we meet Stuart Airlie's warning that "movies can be dangerous for medievalists."[4] In another volume devoted to the issue of history in film in general, however, Mark C. Carnes indicates that this frustration is not limited to the Middle Ages but is endemic among *all* historical films, musing (with tongue firmly in cheek), "Historians love movies about the past."[5] So what precisely changes in the process of transforming the medieval history which popular culture finds so pleasing on the page to an equally subjective version of events on the screen, especially when filmmakers are frequently drawing their ideas from the same pool, that which Sorlin defines, in terms distinctly reminiscent of Bourdieu, as a society's "historical capital"?[6] The question, then, might be reframed as follows: if people seem to like films as a whole, and they seem to like the Middle Ages in general, why are they so frequently dissatisfied with films made about the Middle Ages in particular?

Without perhaps going as far as Williams and Airlie in their wholesale condemnation of medieval films, it must be admitted that there remains a general dissatisfaction among audiences and scholars alike with the ways that the Middle Ages have been brought to life on the big screen. While in the historical fictions of Walter Scott and Thomas Costain, the most egregious wanderings from the accepted versions of written history are tolerated, very often from the outset the feature film is felt to have overstepped itself in trying to "do history." What is on the page at least bears a surface similarity to written History, the stern elder sibling of the historical novel. Film, on the other hand, is to serious historians often "classed simply as a medium of the trivial and ephemeral popular entertainment."[7] As Rosenstone suggests:

> To accept film, especially the dramatic feature film, as being able to convey a kind of serious history (with a capital H), runs against just about everything we have learned since our earliest days at school: History is not just words on a page, but pages ... and film, why that's just entertainment.[8]

One cannot help but feel that part of the hubris of historical film — especially Hollywood film — comes not from the inaccuracies nor from the liberties taken with the subject matter, nor even from the re-writing of history (for as we shall see below, these are all charges which have been brought against history itself at one time or another), but is instead provoked by a disapprobation of a filmmaker's audacity to infringe on the serious scholarly domain of "History with a capital H" in the first place (see Glossary: History). Defending the Hollywood "historicals," Fraser remarks that "one sometimes wonders what critics are looking for in a film of this kind, how they think it should have been made, and if their real objection is not simply *that it was made at all*."[9] Furthermore, in his 2003 study of the corpus, John Aberth offers the useful suggestion that it is perhaps not purely because some of them are bad *medieval* films that we dismiss them, but because they are simply bad films in the first place. "Movie magic (and disaster)," he argues, "remains elusive. The best we can do, perhaps, is dissect how a particular film got things right or wrong after it was made."[10]

While it is not my intention to provide an extensive guide to criticisms of historical films, in order to be able to understand where and why filmmakers are deemed to "get things wrong," the following section will briefly outline some of the major objections raised. The three "problems" of history on film, I will argue, are that the narrative, the montage and the ideologies of films serve to distort the historical record and reveal the inherent inaccuracies made along the way. Part of this argument, however, is that these three problems may equally be applied to History per se, meaning that both filmmakers and historians are besieged by similar accusations of distortion and inaccuracy.

Three Problems of History on Film

> *"It is a pleasant thing to see, but the chances are very great that it will be a far pleasanter thing to remember, when this and that detail have been forgotten and imagination joins with memory to create something that the literalness of a book-page or a movie screen could never bring to life by itself."*[11]

One of the first major problems we broach in the criticism of historical film is that with only a very few exceptions, the overwhelming majority of scholars working in the area of history and film have approached the issue from the a priori assumption that there is somehow a conflict between film as a medium for entertainment and History as a discipline, and have as a consequence often unwittingly placed themselves into gradations along a spectrum of interpretation. The supposed conflict between filmmakers and historians is often construed as a polarization between two camps, built on a "relationship of constrained anxiety," in which historians react to the "bastardization" of their art by rejecting it out of hand, claiming rather grandly that "Clio's aesthetic impulse has tended to ignore the screen."[12] On one extreme we find the conservative viewpoint of critics such as Hughes, whose underlying argument seems to reject films as *inevitably* inaccurate, suggesting that their usefulness only demonstrates how mankind leaves his mark on history with each rewriting of it: "Film, like other artifacts, is an article produced or shaped by human workmanship. In its form and function it reflects the economic and technological impulses of the culture that brought it forth."[13] Such a criticism is echoed by Rollins' position that far from "doing History," Hollywood's function is to serve merely as "an unwitting recorder of national moods."[14]

At the other extreme, we move to the more liberal Ferro, for example, who observes that even while committing factual errors, historical films may usefully be seen as a kind of document chronicling the way that man understands his own history. He argues that some, albeit few, might even make an actual contribution to the process of writing history, being "no longer merely a reconstruction or a reconstitution, but really an original contribution to the understanding of past phenomena and their relation to the present."[15] Yet by describing the majority of these films as inevitably inaccurate, both of these positions are still working from the tacit assumption that there is somehow a single version of events from which these films are deviating; an assumption which is no longer afforded even to written History as a discipline.[16]

Moreover, one of the rarely recognized details which is only now beginning to creep into analyses of historical film is that the relative accuracy or inaccuracy of a film is by no means the only yardstick by which we should be measuring a "good" or "bad" medieval film. It seems unlikely, for example, that a book reviewed in a Historical journal would be dismissed simply as "inaccurate" or "bad" history without at least considering the writer's methodology or argumentation or without trying to understand its aim and audience. It would be deeply unfair, for instance, to hold le Goff's *Le Moyen Âge expliqué aux enfants* (*The Middle Ages Explained to Children*) up to the same degree of scrutiny as his more academically orientated works, since they clearly go about accessing the period in markedly different ways.

Likewise, a film may be "bad" for any number of reasons — its mise-en-scène, script, direction, camerawork — or it may be "good" for a whole host of others; nevertheless, in his article on Arthurian melodrama, Nickolas Haydock remains one of the few critics to recognize that in our criticism of these historical films we must be sure about whether we are remarking on the film *qua* film, or as historical document, in which case we must carefully moderate our inquiry accordingly. He rightly observes that, for example, "contemporary films about the Middle Ages made within the Hollywood system are best approached as products of that system rather than as attempts to approximate the interpretations of professional medievalists."[17] Perhaps this is in part because the appreciation of a film's "qualities" is a great deal more subjective and personal than the criticism of a historical account. Furthermore, historical film occupies what seems to be a more confused position in modern culture, broaching the gap between "serious" academic study and "frivolous" pop culture a lot less categorically than its written counterpart, which opens it up to armchair criticism more readily than written historical works.

Rosenstone, too, warns us that when historians write about film, "judgments are made about historical value on widely divergent grounds — accuracy of detail, use of original documents, appropriateness of music, the looks or apparent suitability of an actor to play someone whose body language, voice and gestures we can never know from the historical record."[18] Our criticism should therefore be applied in equal measure across the field, for as Umland observes with regard to the historical novel, "to admire a writer for his originality but to castigate a film-maker for his failure to produce a 'faithful' representation [...] is surely unfair."[19] Rosenstone equally criticizes the tendency for historians to dismiss film as "bad history," for if we "ask what we expect a film to be or do, basically we historians don't know, other than to insist that it adhere to the facts. Our basic reaction is to think that a film is really a book somehow transformed to the screen, which means that it should do what we expect a book to do: get things right."[20] In fact, it is a part of the very problem of examining history through film that there are no real concrete guidelines by which we are measuring their success or failure. We tend consequently to dwell on one or another single aspect, meaning that "a reading of the film interested exclusively either in an historical aspect (i.e., in the sources and in the cultural implications) or in a cinematographic one (direction, settings, music, costumes, etc.) is partial and therefore incomplete."[21] If we as critics and analysts do not know specifically what we are looking for in these films, then how is it possible for any film to "succeed" in providing it?

Perhaps one way around the issue is to examine the situation from the opposite perspective. When we ask whether film can do history, in most cases it seems to me that we are *actually* unconsciously asking whether film can do *written* History, which is basically asking whether one medium is able to ape another effectively. It seems, however, that this is as ineffective and wrong-headed a question as to ask whether written History can do filmic history, or whether we can use an apple to make orange juice, a comparison borne out by Paul Halsall, the online "curator" of the Fordham University medieval film database, who observes, "I once taught a course on medieval literature into film and discovered that film and things medieval are apples and oranges."[22]

Even to ask *what kind of history* film is able to do can lead us into the same dead end, since the most obvious answer would be "filmic history" (as Ferro discovers in his seminal study),[23] a response which gives us no further clues about what kind of history this might be, nor whether it can ever be "accurate," objective or Historical in its inquiry. To use the wrong criteria to examine a film can only ever result in the wrong conclusions, and "evaluating films against non-fiction history books thus makes about as much sense as evaluating historical monographs based on their popular entertainment value."[24]

Instead, perhaps we ought to examine the differences between the two types of historical records, asking, "if it *could* exist, then what might the formal elements of a filmic writing of history be?" My proposition, which I will demonstrate below, is that when we examine the "formal elements" of "doing history" (that is, looking at exactly what it is that historians "do"), there are marked similarities with what filmmakers "do." After all, both are working from a selected series of "known facts" to elaborate a believable narrative; like the written text, on occasion the film must by necessity depart from the written record to sustain credibility, or else introduce fabrications to cover gaps in the historical record. In this way "both written history and films invoke the authenticity (or reality) that comes from using those traces, that documentary evidence we call 'facts,' and then go on to employ a literary or filmic vocabulary to create 'History.'"[25]

Bearing this proposition in mind, I will outline below three specifically cinematic "formal elements" which have been frequently criticized as means by which film can approach or distort history in general: narrative, montage and ideology. What I hope to show is that none of these three is limited to "filmic" history, but they are in fact the same accusations which may be levied at traditional History, too, in one way or another.

PROBLEM 1: NARRATIVE

"My name is Lester Burnham. This is my neighborhood; this is my street; this is my life. I am 42 years old; in less than a year I will be dead. Of course I don't know that yet...."[26]

The opening narration of Sam Mendes' *American Beauty*, quoted above, presents in a remarkably explicit way one of the problems of assembling narrative, namely the authority of the narrator to be able to explicate the past. In this (albeit extreme) case, if we know that the narrator is dead, or about to die, our faith in their omniscience is of course challenged in the most fundamental way.

This is one example, therefore, of the first "formal element" of filmic history; its almost exclusive use of the narrative form, a form of history discussed in depth most notably by Hayden White and Paul Ricoeur.[27] The use of historical material to anchor an exercise in storytelling is of course as old as culture itself, from the poet or griot's [see Glossary] campfire tales of mythical history to newsreels and live TV coverage of current affairs, and in our examination of medieval history we find no exception. If we are defining "History" as simply "an account of past events," then in this period it might find itself recorded in a wide variety of means, both "factual"— chronicles, genealogies, annals, yearbooks, etc.— and creative, or narrative — the songs of troubadours, lais, romances, poems, allegories, sermons, plays, and so on. The range and diversity of these media may be largely divided, however, by what we construe their purpose to have been, since it would be easy to claim that the first four, "factual" types of history were consciously written as historical records, while the others recognize themselves as fictions drawing on popular reworkings of past events. It is easy to claim, perhaps, but far more difficult to justify. Where, for example, does this leave Geoffrey of Monmouth's fictionalized *Historia Regum Britanniae*, or Chaucer's Franklin in his claim to be recounting his story from a historical work?[28] Upon closer examination of the narrative form in history, the distinctions between these "purposes" become less easily delineated, and "the distinction between history and fiction cannot, in its modern clarity, be applied to medieval books or to the spirit in which they were read."[29]

Despite the variance of forms of historical records, and our presumptions about historical intentions, each of the above "accounts of past events" is in fact united mainly by its need for a beginning and an end — even if this is only a point at which the story begins and a point at which it ends. Herlihy's criticisms of the documentary film are true of the narrative cinema too, since they both "force the events into a narrative scheme — with a beginning, a middle, and an end; with crisis and resolution. In contrast, authentic history is always a continuum."[30] In other words, they foreground the process of narrative, for it is in the retelling (sjuzhet) that the subject matter (fabula) is given this narrative form. This means that — regardless of what we think their purposes were, or even perhaps of what the chronicler himself thought it was — in our ways of writing and recording History we are not slavishly recording "just the facts, ma'am" (as Rosenstone would have it), but we are giving form to them, shaping them, and placing them within a narrative scheme.[31]

We are reminded here of those classical Greek orators whose audiences were able to choose which mode of expression they preferred, between *mythos* or *logos* (myth or logical argumentation), which implies that the same "fabula" may be narrated in at least two different ways, and by extension intimates that both could legitimately be classified as "Historical." The narration of history in mythic form, obviating by this rationale any duty to logical causality, thus engenders a certain conflict between traditional (predominantly written, scientific, objective) methods of representing History (*logos*) and overtly narrative representations (*mythos*) such as the historical novel, myth or film in one sense. The conflict is exposed by White's remark that historians might naturally object to this subjective account of the past, given that they "do not have to report their truths about the real world in narrative form."[32] If this is the case, we might ask, does it imply that the narrative form will affect the retelling of History? To allude to the title of White's influential work, does the form affect the content?

Sidestepping the question about the form *of* the content, a convincing argument is that as far as the narrative is concerned, the form *is* the content, since the narrative is in fact an element of the récit itself (see Glossary). By undertaking a retelling of history, the narrator is assuming from the outset that they have sufficient authority and knowledge of the period to tell the story. The whole notion of representation, therefore, is not a part of the real world, but is a part of the fiction itself; even within a "factual" documentary, for example, there is still a need for a narrator, who is equally as fallible as anyone else. Thus, "representation in its narrative form, as with other forms which we will discuss, is not added from outside of the documentary or explicatory phase, but rather accompanies them and carries them [both]."[33] If this were true, and the use of narrative form could be shown to weaken the objectivity of written History, we would expect to see at least some surface similarities between narrative and documentary History. If we try to bolster the authority of the narrative form by demonstrating its similarity to the documentary form, however, we risk — rather than strengthening the veracity of the narrative form — placing in doubt the authority of the "documentary or explicatory phase." Rather than both becoming objective historical accounts, both become subject to our historiographic criticism.

Clearly, it is therefore not the film's use of narrative itself which is under discussion (for how else are we to narrate?), but what is under attack is rather the inclusion of a human agent to "assemble" the narrative. We ought logically then to negate all narrative forms as equally suspicious and prone to this "re-shaping," for narrative (in our definition of it since the nineteenth century, in any case) inevitably involves some form of narrator placed "outside" of the events so as to appear in some way objective. In this respect, we find Lacan's assertion of the illusory omniscience of the narrator:

> What is imaginary about any narrative representation is the illusion of a cen-
> tred consciousness capable of looking out on the world, apprehending its
> structure and processes, and representing them to itself as having all of the
> formal coherency of narrative itself. But this is to mistake a "meaning" (which
> is always constituted rather than found) for "reality" (which is always found
> rather than constituted).[34]

To follow this line of logic through, however, forces us to enter into something of a circular argument, for if we criticize the narrative form in filmic history as inherently inaccurate because of its "assembled" nature, we must have recourse to the presumed accuracy of an objective documentary form, which equally demands a form of assembly of the facts which presupposes a "centred consciousness" capable of ordering them in this way. On the other hand, to criticize both starts to seem a little like sawing through the branch on which we are standing. How then might we escape this vicious circle?

For our purposes we can feel on much safer ground if we accept that all written history assumes *at least some* of the formal elements of narrative, inasmuch as we impose on the historical record the same formal coherency as we would normally for narrative fictional events. Such a proposition obviates any criticism of the narrative form itself, but allows us at least to recognize that some element of "shaping" is allowed — even necessary — in order for us to understand it. Thus if we accept, at least to some extent, that a degree of a narrative form is inevitable, we can more readily acknowledge that these accounts are in one sense "shaped" histories (to borrow a word from Rosen-stone),[35] but without being forced necessarily to deny their factual reliability. Indeed, if we trace back the argument far enough, we find Aristotle using such criticism of the narrative as its chief virtue. In his *Poetics* he places the triumph of the narrative — the deviations from the "official story" — far above the factual retelling of verifiable events, claiming that:

The poet and the historian differ ... [in that] one relates what has happened, the other what may happen. Poetry therefore is a more philosophical and a higher thing than history, for poetry tends to express the universal, history the particular.[36]

Perhaps we need to resign ourselves to the idea that in order to recount a universal history, then, we *must* impose a certain degree of the narrative's "formal coherency," since this coherency is precisely the device which allows us to make sense of our past.[37] When we look again at our criticism of these narratives, then, we realize that what we are *actually* criticizing, rather than the narrative, is the authority of the human agent to shape them — which is quite a different thing altogether.

Within the narrative form, we can see further points of convergence between film and History, such as when we view history as a closed process, or as cinema defines its narratives, "a closed series of events."[38] To reduce it to its simplest definition, film tries to use images to tell a story that might or might not have taken place, but which draws on a line of logic inferred from the images or soundtrack which culminates in a sense that a story has been told and completed. The participation of the historical event in the grand narrative of history replicates this, so that "the plot places us at the crossing point of temporality and narrativity: to be historical, an event must be more than a singular occurrence, a unique happening. It receives its definition from its contribution to the development of a plot."[39] A "plot," here, and not a story, but a sense that — when we read a Historical account — we are able to see in that work both the events and the causes of those events, and at the end of which we feel that same sense of a story which has been told and completed.

Re-presenting history in narrative form, however, of course has its difficulties — particularly when it comes to the attribution of those causes. While it usefully "fills irritating gaps in the historical record and polishes dulling ambiguities and complexities,"[40] it also risks using that same license to distort events to fit them into the specific narrative. In order that the plot runs smoothly, for example, we might have recourse to those "invented dramatic elements that all historians judge fictional."[41] Napoleon's farewell speech to the Convention, for example, might be invented by Abel Gance only to service a narrative need and not to relate the historical record faithfully; Sofia Coppola's numerous historical oddities are excused on the grounds that she "wanted to make it fun and involve life and what it would really be like to be there at that time [...] and not looking at it from a distance as a history lesson."[42] Furthermore, as we are reminded above, we must be careful not to adopt a Manichean view which paints all invention as bad and all "accuracy" good, for if we scorn the attempt to render history into a coherent narrative in a form palatable for the public to absorb instantly, we would logically have to reject the "Fathers of History" too, from Herodotus to Thucydides, as well as Procopius' contradiction of his own historical records.[43] In these early "histories," the dialogues and famous speeches are often "retold" centuries after they allegedly took place, and therefore cannot realistically be considered as anything other than "shaped" versions of history in their own right. Even when writing about events taking place within his own lifetime, Thucydides — in what might be the first example of historiographic criticism — admits that:

> In this history I have made use of set speeches some of which were delivered just before and others during the war. I have found it difficult to remember the precise words used in the speeches [...] so my method has been [...] to make the speakers say what, in my opinion, was called for by each situation.[44]

Yet we must not view this as a betrayal, but rather a self-consciously "shaped" narrative. History begins, after all, where for every narrative there is an equal and opposite "anti-narrative"; "unless at least two versions of the same set of events can be imagined, there is no reason for the historian to take upon himself the authority of giving the true account of what really happened."[45]

So what may we establish from these conjectures? Above all, that when we apply historiographic criticisms of narrative history to film, we must remember that in their formal elements — as far as narrative is concerned — these same criticisms can often be applied to both film and the written record, on two grounds. First, that the presence of a narrator — even if not a character narrator but Lacan's illusory "centred-consciousness" — is not only necessary, but in some senses inevitable in the process of rendering our historical past into a palatable and comprehensible form. Even while accusing our medieval chroniclers of distorting the historical record, we must equally recognize that without them we would be left with no (or at least one fewer) record of our past at all. Second, we can propose that this fashioning of historical events into a narrative form imparts a largely unavoidable subjectivity to the account, but one that does not necessarily compromise the fidelity of the account. If Froissart offers support for the French at the Battle of Crécy, this does not mean that there was no battle, nor that it is impossible to believe in any one of the details he provides; rather that we must acknowledge the viewpoint of the narrator in his account, and perhaps (to adopt the stratagem of Atticus Finch) if we "remove the adjectives we might be left with some of the facts."[46]

Thus, the area of most obvious convergence between History and film comes when we consider the personal involvement of the historian/filmmaker in composing (shaping) their history/plot, a process of assembly which establishes a dialogue with the historical past/the story.[47] It is, in fact, precisely in the acknowledgment of this element of selection in narrative that we come to the second area, montage, since narratives are construed not only by the choice of the original material but by the way that they are pieced together.

PROBLEM 2: MONTAGE

"This feeling of adventure definitely does not come from events. It's rather the way in which the moments are linked together."[48]

In 2004, during the furor surrounding Michael Moore's documentary *Fahrenheit 911*, the controversial filmmaker launched a contest, offering $10,000 to anyone who could disprove any fact in his film. Three years later, according to an interview in *Time* magazine, he has not had to pay out any of his prize money at all, since he claims that "every fact in my films is true."[49] How is it then possible that his films can continue to cause such controversy if the facts he presents are (or, to use the terms we have outlined above, if the narrative he selects is) incontestable? The answer lies in his admission in the same interview that "the opinions in the film are mine. They may not be true, but I think they are." It is latent in the acceptance that it is not necessarily the "facts" which can lie, but the way in which they are pieced together, for historical events can be "distorted" by far more than the "content of the form" and its need for narrative "closure."

If History consists of a selection of facts, then the Histories which we are engaged in writing depend not only on which facts have been selected, but also the way in which they are pieced together. To give one illustration, Sartre's phenomenology of events in constructing an adventure makes two equally useful suggestions: first that the event depends not on its objective existence (which is of course subject to his existentialist doubt) but on its being retold ("for the most banal event to become an adventure, you must [...] begin to recount it");[50] second, that it is created from its montage or, as the epigraph suggests, "the way in which the moments are linked together." As an example, we might use two axiomatic historical certitudes to demonstrate how the rather innocuous-sounding "telescoping of history" can severely distort the historical record:

1. "Caesar crossed the Rubicon."
2. "Caesar died."

Both individual statements, of course, are true, verifiable, and beyond the doubt of even the most mischievous of historians. Nevertheless, by placing them together as though in sequence — even in the written form — and taken in isolation, we have imparted a sense of causality, implying that Caesar died both *immediately after* and *precisely because* he crossed the Rubicon, which is of course a patent fallacy.[51] This argument about the representation of verifiable history, though somewhat oversimplified, is not entirely incompatible with the arguments raised by Bazin, Vertov, Eisenstein and others over the so-called "montage or bust"[52] controversy, in which the Kuleshov Effect demonstrates exactly the same sequence at work, though in reverse.[53] In Kuleshov's famous experiment, a test audience was shown exactly the same stock footage of the famous actor Mozhukin;

> [Kuleshov] then intercut a perfectly neutral close-up of an actor with a shot of a plate of soup; then the same close-up with a dead woman in a coffin; then with a little girl playing with a doll. Audiences raved about the actor's sensitive projection of hunger, grief and paternal joy, his subtle shifts of emotion depending on what he was looking at. Kuleshov proved that the order of shots in a sequence influenced the perception and meaning of any given action.[54]

In both instances, from Caesar to Mozhukin, the placing of sequences together is playing on an imagined line of causation, which Kuleshov has shown is able to court an association of images in order to link sequences together, causal sequences which were not present at source. Strictly speaking, like Moore's "facts" the individual fragments are not lying, but the meaning is divined, rather than presented: the idea of reality produced by any given sequence is produced "not according to what it adds to reality but what it reveals of it."[55] If we apply Bazin's principle of "total cinema" to the representation of historical records within a narrative sequence, then we find that we must side with the critics of historical film who lament the betrayal of the "official version" of history.[56]

In a sense, of course, they are right, for the montage can be used to lead the audience to apply an entirely fictitious causal sequence to an event. If, for example, a friend reproaches me, saying, "You borrowed my pen, and now it doesn't work," he is doing exactly the same thing — the accusation is not explicit but inheres in the causal sequence of the two events (borrowing the pen, the pen being broken). I might, consequently, feel utterly betrayed if I discovered that a third event, the pen being dropped in a puddle, had deliberately been omitted, since its inclusion would have both exonerated me and completed the causal sequence. In Bergman's *The Seventh Seal*, if we see a series of shots of the knight and his squire asleep (dead? unconscious?) on the shore of the sea juxtaposed with a shot of the sea itself washing against the stones, then we are right to assume that this is an elliptical way of intimating to the audience that they have been washed up on the shore after a voyage, even if in the long run this is not true (or at least not relevant, which to Bergman is more or less the same thing). Furthermore, we can assume both from the iconic indications (the absence of ship, the lack of movement) and from paradigmatic association (memories of Homer's *Odyssey* or *Robinson Crusoe*) that the knight and his squire have been shipwrecked. This is no accidental causal sequence, but in fact Bergman is consciously playing with the montage as a way of isolating the audience by denying them the possibility of associating events in the way to which we are accustomed.

In a different example, however, such assumptions at the level of montage lead us to infer a more deleterious association of the images, which works over and above authorial intent. Reading between the lines, a film such as Annaud's *In the Name of the Rose* can be made to reinforce the rather modern vogue of portraying the Church (especially the Catholic Church) as a wholly malevolent and sadistic institution, which I do not believe to have been intentional.[57] When we cut from the empty pyre of Remigius and Salvatore to Bernardo Gui's attempt to escape, we begin to associate by the same processes the concatenation of charges of cruelty, authoritarianism, etc., levied against the Catholic Church.[58] We do this again by a combined process of both iconic (the warning "signs" of the Red vestments, the expressionless cruelty of F. Murray Abraham) and paradigmatic association (the Spanish Inquisition of a later period, the witch hunters of *Witchfinder General*, Imperial Storm troopers of the *Star Wars* trilogy, the Nazi troops of Hollywood's imagination).[59] Nevertheless, the association is made, and the resultant sequence of images results in a narration of facts infused with ideological concerns.

These ideological concerns are not caused by the montage, of course, in exactly the same way as Moore's documentary "facts" do not cause their controversies. Rather, it is that the montage — and here I am talking about both film and the Historical document — appeals to a pre-existent belief, and above all a willingness on the part of the audience to attribute causal meaning to the images. The influence of montage on the editing level, as well as a process similar to Eisenstein's "montage-association" on the symbolic and intertextual level, is in fact a testament more to the power of the narrative cinema, than to a deliberate infusion of ideology on the part of the filmmaker. "It implies, consequently, both a more active mental attitude on the part of the spectator and a more positive contribution on his part to the action in progress."[60] When Annaud cuts between Remigius and Bernardo Gui in *The Name of the Rose*, he is of course making his point (that Gui is unaffected by the suffering of his fellow humans) by what Griffith terms "montage by contrast."[61] The power, however, of the sequence comes from a public willing to assimilate those ideas paradigmatically on the ideological level over and above the film's specific utterance; it is not only that Gui is unaffected by the suffering but by extension, the argument might go, that the medieval Church (of which Gui becomes the symbol) is blind to the suffering of its poorest servants (here Remigius, Salvatore and the unnamed peasant girl).

It is here that we begin to see the grey areas around Kuleshov's experiment, for we must recognize that the association of the ideas was not *only* the result of careful editing (and therefore a product of authorial intention), but it also depended for its power on the willingness of the subjects to connect the images in a causal sequence (and is therefore equally a product of the audience's predisposition to associate images in this way).[62] In another of Kuleshov's experiments, a handful of shots of a man, a woman, a meeting and a house, are sufficient for an audience to assimilate some form of plot (or at least a story). Yet, of course, this "story" depends for its existence on an observer to connect the signifier to signified, an observer who must therefore be familiar enough with this succession of images so as to be able to formulate a plot from these disparate images.

Here again, then, we can see that the element which we are really criticizing is not only the misrepresentation of history by the film in narrative form, but a mis-association (whether willful or unintended) of the signifiers (the means used to produce the message) with the signifieds (the "true" events themselves) as interpreted by the observer (the audience, the reader, etc). In each instance they are unable to access directly the histories which are being retold, and are therefore led to form a narrative sequence of causation by associating the images produced. It is not only by the selection of facts in the narrative, then, that both cinema and history can distort a form of "pure" historical record: at the level of the montage, we have seen that, be it Caesar crossing a river or the medieval Church burning Christians, there is a possibility that audiences themselves will play a part in understanding causal sequences of events. This possibility can even work over and above authorial intent, allowing the audience to assimilate ideas by following the impression gained by this juxtaposition of images.

PROBLEM 3: IDEOLOGY/MODE OF APPROACH

The final factor which affects our re-presentation of history through film relates to what I have loosely termed "ideology." Here, I am thinking less of the Althusserian sense of an ideology as the corollary of the Real, nor of the overt encoding of feature films with a specific, propagandistic program imposed on the director from outside (e.g. Eisenstein or Tarkovskii) but rather the reverse, wherein the subjective perception of events and the individual mode of approach of the filmmaker affects the histories which are being told. In this process, filmmakers trying to bring to life a historical past are frequently prone to reflect the cultural, political and social trends most prominent in the climate of the film's production.

There is, of course, a strongly identifiable link between the past and the present (see also: The Present in the Past, below), for "it is difficult to think of any historical film which does not tell more about the society and circumstances in which it was made than about those which it is supposed to represent."[63] When we come to apply the tenets of the historiographic tradition to film as a cultural product, we find Sorlin's proposition that "History is a society's memory of the past, and the functioning of this memory depends on the situation in which the society finds itself."[64] Sorlin, Smith and Rollins all seem to perceive the film as a historical document of the time of its production rather than a genuine attempt to narrate history, which leads to the potentially patronizing position on account of which "instead of listing historical inaccuracies, we should be praising a description of 'how men living at a certain time understood their own history.'"[65] Such a proposition, however, relies on a fundamentally flawed argument — that records of the past are no more than documents of present beliefs — which could logically see us praising a given historian's understanding of his or her own contemporary world but hinting that he or she knows next to nothing about his or her area of specialization. Nevertheless, we must recognize that we can no more experience or access the past purely and objectively than we can escape our own shadow, for "we cannot interpret medieval culture or any historical culture except through the prism of the dominant concepts of our own thought world."[66]

It is on this ideological level that — most frequently without realizing it — most critics are prone to attack films made about the medieval period, for the way in which a filmmaker perceives the period underpins the approach he or she takes to the film, and often indirectly dictates its montage and narrative organization. Thus when Richards claims of *El Cid*, for example, that "the whole film has the feel of the Middle Ages about it, not the Middle Ages as it was but as the troubadours saw it,"[67] we are not dealing with its accuracy vis-à-vis the period itself, but rather a comment on the approach undertaken by Mann, that is, on Mann's particular perception and understanding of the medieval period. After all, objections to Richards' reading of the film could be raised about our ability to identify precisely what is the "feel" of the Middle Ages "as it really was."

But is this ideological influence restricted to looking at history through film? In trying to answer this question, we might first bear in mind the influences which individual "Schools" of history can have, or the classifications which are often unthinkingly applied to individual historians: Whig, Positivist, Social, Political, Marxist and so on. It would seem absurdly naïve to pretend that the worldview of a given historian has nothing to do with the histories which they are engaged in writing. Can we find a link between these "starting positions," then, and the ideological approaches of filmmakers? One of the most useful critical positions in this respect can be found in Marc Ferro's landmark *Cinéma et Histoire*, and this most notably in his response to the apposite question "can a filmic writing of history exist?"[68] In his conclusions, he advances the theory that "statements about society come from four impulses"[69]:

1. Dominant institutions and ideologies
2. Those opposed to this vision. Now is the time for all good men to come to the aid of their country.
3. Social or historical memory
4. Independent interpretations

Following on from these "modes of approach," he proceeds to draw a similarity with films dealing with history which are "no longer merely a reconstruction or a reconstitution, but really an original contribution to the understanding of past phenomena and their relation to the present." He proceeds, then, to surmise that there exist four distinct ways of looking at history through film: *from above, from below, from inside and from outside.* Thus, siding with Rosenstone that cinematography can play a specific — but not yet crucial — role in the writing of history, Ferro has unwittingly subjected the historical film to the same criticism which he was seeking to avoid in the first instance. In recognizing the ideological influence in each filmmaker's specific mode of approach, he has argued convincingly that film can be seen as a kind of document, which has as its logical sequitur that as a document, it is therefore subject to the same sort of historiographic criticism as its written counterpart.

While there is scarcely space within this study to pursue traces of such ideologies, we can usefully turn to Norman Cantor's *Inventing the Middle Ages* to see how the Middle Ages have been continuously constructed and reconstructed throughout the twentieth century. In this work, Cantor argues that a great deal of the differences encountered have been based not on "the facts," but on interpretations of them, arguing that:

> The ideas of the Middle Ages articulated by the master medievalists vary substantially one from another. The libretto and the score they are working from — the data of historical fact — are the same. The truth, therefore, is ultimately not in the textual details but in the interpretations.[70]

It is, therefore, these "impulses" or "modes of approach" which contain once again, in the kernel of the criticisms levied at filmic history, the criticism of the individual human agent in organizing the histories they tell. That there exist any number of dissident voices in the retelling of history is in itself a reinforcement of Veyne's statement that "because everything is historical, history will be that which we choose."[71]

One final notion ought to be at least mentioned here, which is that, in all of our thinking and writing about historical films, it is often taken for granted that the filmmaker is earnestly trying to "do history." Two excellent books in particular have recently confronted this assumption; in *Using History*, Jeremy Black argues that in the public forum (that is, outside of the walls of academia), history is very often not the measured, footnoted and written form, but rather that public history and collective memory have begun to merge at what were once clearly divided tangents. "In considering public history," he argues, "it is not generally easy, or indeed helpful, to distinguish between history and memory: the public use of history is frequently a matter of collective memory and its uses."[72] Similarly, in an excellent chapter called "Selling History," Hughes-Warrington reminds us that films very often serve an economic — not academic — function,[73] and "commercial imperatives most often fuel cinematic rewrites of history. Complex economic and social issues are puréed into easily digestible bits of information intended for consumption by Hollywood's most sought-after demographic: the lowest common denominator."[74]

Over the course of this first section, I have been trying to demonstrate not that filmic history ought to be permissible as a kind of History (since — as the following chapters will demonstrate — I do not believe this to be the case), but rather that the criticisms which are raised about historical film *are equally applicable to written History*, provided that we rigorously and uniformly apply them. When, therefore, we criticize the way in which a particular filmmaker perceived the Middle Ages, we ought to be clear that what we are criticizing is consequently not their use of the "facts," or their set of "known cultural values," but rather we are objecting to the authorial choices made by the human agent involved in trying to reconnect our signifying Middle Ages on screen to the idea of the Middle Ages which we ourselves hold. Things may, of course, be simply and categorically wrong or right, but we must recognize that this is equally true of written History. What can be of more use to us in evaluating the filmic Middle Ages is trying to understand *why* they have chosen to create the Middle Ages in this way. The use of the narrative form, or of montage and ideology can therefore be a useful way to recognize exactly those elements which we are criticizing.

History and Historiography

> GILBERT: *My humble life is indebted to your exalted prowess, your dauntless courage, and your superb, swift sword!*
> BOWEN: *You have the poet's gift of exaggeration.*
> GILBERT: *Oh, sir, you should read my histories.*[75]

It is at this point, having identified three ways in which the narrative cinema can be accused of distorting history, that we can apply those same objections against Historical enquiry in and of itself. Within this short section, then, I will examine the historiographic movement within traditional academic History, to show how it has recognized its own shortcomings. My purpose here is, of course, not to criticize History itself, but rather to demonstrate that many of the criticisms of history on film are based on those same gray areas within the historical record. Consequently, my argument runs, we should not be too reliant on the innate superiority of academic history when criticizing filmic visions of the past, since both are subject to the same flaws, namely the conflation of temporal planes ("The Present in the Past"), and the collapse of temporal "distance" in what has been called the Modernist Event ("Historiography and the Modernist Event").

However, the three subsections which follow will serve merely as an outline of those aspects of historiographic criticism most immediately relevant to our purposes. Given the rapid growth of this field of academic enquiry, here I have tried to disentangle a few threads in order to show that the works of theoreticians have, over the course of decades, begun to unravel the objectivity and perceived "Truth" of the historical record in the sense that most popular audiences understand such historical truth to be. Without wishing to engage in an internecine war between academic disciplines, I aim to elaborate some of the evidence in support of Sorlin's claim that "Historians often think that their conception of history is the only valid one. Very few of them accept that what they regard as historical truth has nothing in common with what other people think of as truth."[76]

This being the case, I will first introduce some of the claims raised by Droysen and Veyne against this historical "truth" in general, before examining the way in which the traces of the past era which were to be explicated can be found in the present, and vice versa. These two arguments will lead me on to examine one of the more recent phenomena evinced by technological advances in reportage and the narration of events, a temporal distortion which Hayden White has termed "historiophoty."

THE LIMITATIONS OF HISTORICAL INQUIRY

"If it's Truth you're interested in, Dr. Tyree's philosophy class is right down the hall."[77]

We left the last section by posing the relatively straightforward question about whether film can "do" History; it seems fair, therefore, to begin this new one with a similar, albeit a touch impertinent, question: can History itself "do" history? Over the course of the last two centuries, there has been a phenomenal amount of ink spilled over this simple question, beginning with Ranke's canonical assertion in 1824 that the task of the historian is "to show how it really was (*wie es eigentlich gewesen*)," and revolutionized by the series of lectures published by E.H. Carr under the title *What is History?* almost a century and a half later in 1961.[78]

So what, then, is History? One of the most illuminating summaries of the historian's craft comes from Droysen's authoritative *Historik* as early as 1868; according to whom

> The historian's principal task cannot be simply to resurrect the past; rather it is to explicate (*erschliessen*) the past through an unveiling (*Erhebung*) of the present that was latent within it, or conversely, to enrich (*bereichen*) the present through explication and illumination (*Aufklärung*) of the past that inheres within it.[79]

Droysen's position, therefore, recognizes at least the interweaving, or, as he terms it, the "latency," of the present in each attempt to understand the past. What we are decidedly not dealing with, however, is any idea that the historian is engaged in a search for Truth, which can be dismissed as "an idealist approach to historiography."[80] The tacit recognition that the purpose of History is not necessarily to "resurrect" but to "explain" can be useful when it comes to medieval History in particular. With modern History (by which I mean historical research recounting events much closer to our present day rather than the period we designate as "Modern," "Early Modern," etc.), we are facing a number of different problems, such as the proliferation of documents, the increased number of photographic or cinematographic sources which serve to foster a sense of immediacy of the most recent past. With medieval History, however, we are already working from the premise that we can no longer resurrect a period which has been defined predominantly by negation of other eras, and once we acknowledge its alterity, we can only explain the period by "unveiling the present that was latent" within it. As we shall see in chapter seven ("Necessary Invention"), we enter therefore into the domain of "necessary anachronism,"[81] which affords to the writer of history (and consequently to the filmmaker) a reworking of themes which conform to our values and beliefs.

If we fast forward through another century from Droysen, we can find Marc Bloch extending this uncertainty to the records themselves, defining the titular historian's craft as the reconstruction of events in the present based on encounters with the tracks of people in the past,[82] a claim which emphasizes further the historian's role in reconstructing (and tellingly not "resurrecting") the histories from the sources with which he or she is working. As Carr explains:

> History consists of a corpus of ascertained facts. The facts are available to the
> historian in documents, inscriptions, and so on, like fish on the fishmonger's
> slab. The historian collects them, takes them home, and cooks and serves
> them in whatever style appeals to him.[83]

Continuing Veyne's aphorism that there is an element of selection in the
historical record,[84] the selection and "arrangement" (to use Le Goff's celebrated
term) can even be extended to the titles of books, since "a historical book is
made out to be something very different to that which it seems to be: it doesn't
deal with the Roman Empire, but rather what we can possibly know today
about that Empire."[85] This idea finds support in Carr's contention that:

> No document can tell us more than what the author of the document
> thought — what he thought had happened, what he thought ought to happen
> or would happen, or perhaps only what he wanted others to think he thought,
> or even only what he himself thought he thought.[86]

All of which brings us to something of an impasse, since for every interpretation we might offer about a given historical event, the authority of that
interpretation is undermined on three counts: first — the sources — that our
primary sources are not to be trusted as objective (Bloch); second — the narrative — that the existence of an alternative interpretation of that event is sufficient to place both under suspicion (White); third — the ideology — that the
influence of the present has become so intertwined with our views about the
past that our viewpoint can be nothing but subjective (Droysen).

So where do we proceed from here? We have seen in section one that a
great number of the criticisms which can be levied at historical analysis are
reflected by a criticism of a similar process in film (narrative, montage, ideology, etc). Yet here we may take this argument further, for Carr, Croce, Ankersmit, et al. have all launched their attack on History from within, i.e., by
analyzing historical writings using historical methods of criticism. By the
time, then, that we arrive at the present day, we find not only that these once
revolutionary ideas are now by and large accepted as limitations to that same
craft, but also that these acknowledged limitations have caused thinkers to
consider the epistemological limitations on the knowledge *that we can ever
have*. The privileged position of History as the official record has in many
ways been undermined, and replaced by an acknowledgement of those same
distortions of which "filmic history" stands accused, undermining "the ability
of academics to act as priests of Clio (the muse of History), or as intercessors
with past wisdom."[87] By recognizing that the histories which we write consist
of a constant (and constantly evolving) dialogue between the historian and
his or her facts, we can see the importance of recognizing that — no matter
how carefully, how astutely or how painstakingly attentive we might be — we

are always recreating, rewriting or reproducing those factual past worlds within the domain of the present.

THE PRESENT IN THE PAST

With the twofold recognition within historiographic criticism not only of the naivety of Ranke's past "as it really was," but also that Droysen's "unveiling" of the past works on the basis of the present which inheres within it, we can further identify two trends which occur as a result of writing history during the widening gap between the events and the reportage of them.

The first is that the process of creating a meaningful history (in addition to creating the form of narrative closure which I proposed in problem 1 above) imparts a sense of meaning to the historical events, which in turn suggests a retrospectively implied sense of causation. It is meaningful for us, perhaps, but we must be wary of assuming that this is the same as a meaningful history for the eras about which we are writing. It is this process, in fact, to which Carr dedicates an entire chapter of his seminal work, in observing that the attribution of fictitious and often private causes (offered under the innocuous sounding, and pseudo-objective guise of "motivations") can lead to "the total disintegration of the human personality, which is based on the [twin] assumption that events have causes, and that enough of these causes are ascertainable to build up in the human mind a pattern of past and present sufficiently coherent to serve as a guide to action."[88]

It is again this process to which Veyne is objecting when he cites the goal of ideal History "to describe, and to presuppose nothing else; not to presuppose that there exists a goal, an objective, a material cause."[89] When we begin retrospectively to attribute causes and effects, he argues, we allow our history to be infused with the ideologies of the present, for we are attributing motives, ethics and values of our own era to one of the past. When, for example, we encounter Sir Gawain appearing before the Green Knight to conclude the beheading competition, we are wont to ascribe his opponent's refusal to strike Gawain to a twentieth-century sense of compassion and mercy — a compassion which was not, in all probability, present in the original (and tellingly, when Stephen Weeks makes his film of this narrative, it is precisely this compassionate reading of it which he employs).[90] Given the sacred position of "trowthe and honour" in the period, the sense of mercy and pity which we hold works against the fulfillment of duty: thus it seems less comprehensible to us if it is not compassion that leads the Green Knight to spare Gawain but a belief that he has fulfilled his pledge. As Martha Driver and Sid Ray remark on the same topic, "in medieval film we are more likely to encounter a medievalized Marlboro Man than a faithful representation of the *Pearl* poet's Sir

Gawain [...] whose idea of a day's work is vastly different from the work ethic promoted in modern-day America."[91] We should not criticize this as a peculiarly modern invention, however, since we can also see it at work in medieval representations of Biblical History, in which the values and truths of medieval society are exposed in the mystery plays rather than those properly belonging to the peoples of the Bible itself. Thus we see in certain mystery plays a distinctly "un–Biblical" Herod recreated as a fifteenth-century magnate[92] offering "grith" (a medieval form of asylum) to his loyal followers, along with medieval rewards such as "ye knights of ours / Shall have castles and towers / Both to you and yours / For now and evermore," and pronounces his judgment that "a hundred thousand pound is good wage for a knight / Of pence good and round....."[93] The morality of one era, then, begins to finds its echo in the apparently motive-less actions of another era when we attribute a causation to the histories we are telling. "Consequently," it could be argued, "the Middle Ages in the movies are often modernity in drag. The subject of medieval films is 'the present, not the past.'"[94]

The second trend is this: if film collapses the temporal distance between the past and the present, then it follows that the "récit" which the historian is creating becomes as much a commentary on the present as it is on the past (reflecting, by a neat symmetry, those same criticisms raised by Smith and Rollins about films trying to "do" History). As Pugh neatly terms it, "the Middle Ages undergoes continual rebirth as each succeeding generation turns back to history to consider issues directly relevant to the present, and Hollywood Arthuriana offers an especially fertile field for studying such mythopoeic cultural appropriations."[95] To give an example, when we encounter Schramm and Kantorowicz writing their treatises on medieval kingship against the backdrop of nascent national socialism, Cantor reminds us not to ignore the influence of the two far-right historians on the construction of medieval kingship — particularly given that they were working in the 1930s, and that Schramm later became official historian for the Nazi regime.[96]

However, this is to forget that one of the technical processes involved in narrating historical events in a meaningful way involves precisely this entangling of temporal planes, making use of White's "formal coherency."[97] When it comes to making sense of our past we come up against a certain paradox. In order to escape the subjectivity of narrating history as though it were a present tense happening, we are obliged to immerse ourselves into the past, placing ourselves in that past world and trying to make sense of it according to their perspective. This latter course, however, is equally to intertwine the past and the present, the only difference being that instead of bringing their past into our present, we take our present into their past.[98] In both instances, "past and present are conflated, as contemporary concerns are superimposed on earlier historical periods in the process of reconstruction."[99] Both worlds, in the last analysis, are constructed worlds.

If they are both constructed, however, then in the cinema we can tentatively propose a third theory, which proceeds from a negation of the two above: the constructed world is made neither of the present projected into the past, nor of the past made imminent in the present, but represents a virtual temporal plane in which the past "facts" and the present "meanings" are commingled. As Pasolini (who was by no means a stranger to the recreation of history through film) comments: "I have come to realize that the time of a film is always an ideal time."[100] The creation of an "atemporal" world in which the past is recreated through the modes of expression belonging to the present therefore leads us into another quite different area, that which Vivian Sobchack has proposed as the "persistence of history," and one which has as a byproduct "collapsed the temporal distance between past, present and future," producing instead a spatially delineated historical plane instead of one which is aligned along traditional chronological parameters.[101]

HISTORIOPHOTY AND THE MODERNIST EVENT

These arguments therefore bring to the fore one of the more complex subsidiaries of history on film, namely the difference of temporal planes when dealing with history. These arguments present us with three timescales: the time of the film's narrative (when the film was set), the time of the film itself (when the film was made) and the time of énonciation (the time in which the narrative unfolds).[102] It follows that when we are looking back at a particular film about the Middle Ages, say Eisenstein's *Aleksander Nevskii*,[103] the initial question posed earlier about whether film can do history raises itself again; we are dealing simultaneously with a problem of accessing the culture of production (Russia in the late 1930s), as well as those of accessing the Middle Ages (from the twenty-first century) and those problems which Eisenstein encountered when trying to access that same medieval period during his own lifetime and political context (the Middle Ages seen from Russia in the 1930s as opposed to Tarkovskii in the 1970s, or the USA in the 1950s, etc).[104] We are therefore left with three issues of communication (and consequently three potential barriers to our understanding of the history as presented to us in film). Yet these criticisms of course are no less applicable to written history than they are to filmic history. When, for example, we try to understand Gibbon writing about the demise of one empire while writing at the height of another, how can we understand that same fall in the light of new evidence thrown up in the last century? How, too, can we begin to understand Gibbon when we are looking at him after the demise of the British Empire? Thus the history provided by Gibbon becomes itself a historical document. The commingling of temporal planes consequently poses some significant problems in terms of representation, particularly if we are no longer (post Walter Benjamin and Bazin) to accept the belief that the cinema is a means of "mechanical," slavish reproduction of reality.

Recognizing this precise problem, Hayden White holds to account "the Modernist Event," claiming that "modernist literature, and by extension modernist art in general, dissolves the trinity of event, character and plot which provided the staple both of the nineteenth-century realist novel and of the historiography from which nineteenth-century literature derived its model of realism."[105] That event which he calls modernist, he asserts, was defined as an event by being both observable and observed. Yet, given the proliferation of twentieth-century means of reportage, we have not only lost any sense of an independent observer, but (as we saw in Problem 1) we have also begun to attack the notion of an extraneous narrator, with the result that that same event is reported within a "ceaseless dialectic of past, present and future."[106] This new reportage is thus as reliable as its original because it is directly reported, but also — being no longer directly observable nor observed — it cannot therefore be deemed as certain as a present event of which we can have direct observation.

Christian Metz offers the useful example (albeit for a slightly different purpose) of a man who is participating in a demonstration while listening to the coverage of that same event on a portable radio. The reportage of the event brings into account a double temporal sequence, "the time of the thing told and the time of the telling,"[107] both of which are being related simultaneously to the "time of the thing happening" itself. The question therefore arises: which of the two narrations is more real — that which is observed or that which is observable? The one which perceives the demonstration from the outside, from the boundaries of the real, who is permitted to see and interpret all of the events but who has no direct observation of nor participation in them? Or the one who has actually observed the event (from below and inside) by participating in it, but who lacks the narrator's ability to step outside (above) the demonstration to see the whole? Whose account is most reliable? The eyewitness, the policeman, the politician or the TV helicopter?

If this is true for the "Modernist Event," then how may we apply it to the medieval era? If we stretch this analogy to its limits, imagining that the medieval past is a foreign country, we might approximate (for argument's sake) the medieval film to a report on a demonstration taking place in another country, outside of our immediate environment. The reportage, then, would serve as a guide to the events (of which there is more in chapter eight). This reportage, consequently, can take one of two forms:

1. Following Droysen's contention that there is a past which inheres in the present, we can choose to try to report on the demonstration "from above and outside" to use Ferro's terminology, as though an anchor in the newsroom, and in doing so we accept the limitations of our possibility of knowing it in depth, and treat it like a foreign (past) event being related in the present (in our country and according to our narrative style). This is the paradigmatic reconstruction which I will propose in chapter two, using what we know to explain by metaphor that which we do not.

2. Alternatively, we might try to report on the events via a reporter "live at the scene," in which case we are looking at those same events "from below and from inside." The objectivity which we lose in this process may be compensated for by the increase in immediacy, so to speak, which results in the feeling that we are experiencing true events, foregrounding the immediate "present," and making it seem closer to our own country, at the expense of the alterity of the past. The drawback of this approach is that by listening to a reporter on the scene, he or she becomes a "foreign object," and we are liable to misunderstand him. This is the iconic reconstruction, which uses specific signifiers to communicate the significance of the specific over the general.

As we will see below, we are therefore left with potentially two different ways in which we can — via the medium of film — try to access our medieval past. The first is mediate, the second immediate: the first depends for its authenticity on a familiarity with the present, through which we interpret our past, and therefore uses paradigmatic associations with concepts familiar to present audiences; genre films, stars, intertextual references, popular culture associations, etc. The second uses precisely the "foreign-ness" of the past in order to unfold its story, drawing, so to speak, its authority by a closer affinity to medieval sources. In this way it uses iconic associations in order to reconstruct consciously that immediate reality outside of our familiar domain.

All of which, however, is based on the presupposition that we are willing, or able, to access the Middle Ages in order to obtain our reliable accounts of the era. Over the course of the next chapter it is to this question, therefore, that I will turn.

Conclusions

Here then, we can come to offer some tentative conclusions. Over the course of this chapter I have tried to evaluate three major problems of historical inquiry involved in accessing our medieval past, and demonstrated that such problematic issues are equally applicable to History in and of itself. In my first section, I looked at the theoretical objections leveled at History on film in general, and argued that there were, in most cases, assumptions that historically themed films *inevitably* got things wrong. However, given that we have yet to develop any form of standard criticism, I suggested that perhaps the two processes of historical reconstruction — that is, filmic and written history — were in fact more similar than had been assumed. To this end, I showed how the three main areas from which criticism of historical films were launched fell into three main categories: narrative, montage, and ideology. In examining these three areas, I hope to have shown that in all three, though fabrications, assimilations, or other alterations of the "facts" do inevitably occur, they are in principle similar to the reconstruction of known facts in academic History.

In my second section, therefore, having asked whether film could "do history," I turned to historiographic criticism to ask whether, in fact, History itself could do so. After a brief summary of recent historiography, I re-examined these three limitations examined above from the point of view of historiography. The limitations uncovered in this section revealed the ways in which the temporal planes (the time of the events and the time of their retelling) began to be intertwined, since retelling the past brings out a certain aspect of it which "inhered in the present," just as re-examining past events must inevitably take place in the present, and thus risk being infused with the present. This process was further complicated by what White calls the Modernist Event, which I showed removed the illusion of an external consciousness altogether, ultimately collapsing the different timeframes. Thus when it comes to *any* form of narrative concerning our past, the historian is faced with the same problems as the filmmaker, which equally disbar him or her from total accuracy, purity and impartiality. They are obliged to use narrative to attribute motivations; they must concede that the structure of each historical element or fact is influenced by its context, in a process not entirely unlike montage; they are also influenced by the approach they themselves use, or the beliefs which they hold about the past, which comes to form their ideology.

The crucial argument, then, to emerge from all of this is that we are forced to accept that there is no real, single *truth* about the Middle Ages. While it is difficult to access the period unambiguously, even the term itself is highly dubious, and thus when we try to recreate history on film — as we shall see in the next chapter — we are constrained to concede a great deal of "accuracy" from the outset. What emerges from such Historical inquiry, therefore, is not a single, *absolute* version of the Middle Ages, but a concatenation of beliefs and known facts, from which we extrapolate an imaginary version of the period. In the next chapter, then, I will turn to examine how this imaginary is constructed, and its consequences for medieval film.

2

"One Big Medieval Mess": Accessing the Middle Ages

In *The Sword in the Stone*, Merlin — acting as our somewhat befuddled guide to the Middle Ages — bemoans the lack of coherence and organization of the period, eventually coming to dismiss it in its entirety as "one big medieval mess." It is a somewhat harsh generalization, admittedly, yet when it comes to analyzing the disparate and often contradictory "versions" of the Middle Ages in film, we could be forgiven for agreeing with him. We have seen in the previous chapter that the task both of the filmmaker seeking to recreate the past on film and of historians approaching their chosen period is beset on a number of fronts by a variety of technical and theoretical obstacles which must be, if not overcome, then at least consciously recognized before any earnest attempt can be made to understand History. If, as I argued in the previous chapter, we have no definitive versions of the Middle Ages which films are trying to recreate on the screen, then this next chapter will introduce and explore some of the ways in which filmmakers seek to evoke any number of disparate medieval worlds by relying on a medieval imaginary. Cognizant of the limitations discussed in the previous chapter of both historical inquiry and filmic history, then, I will examine two principal problems inherent in the recreation of the Middle Ages in film: first, the process of accessing the period and constructing the imaginary, and, second, the process of reconstruction based on the recollections from this same imaginary "historical capital."

Accessing the Middle Ages

Over the course of this book so far, I have been trying to demonstrate that one of the main conflicts derives from both the assumed inaccuracy of historical film on the one hand, and the assumed accuracy of History as an infallible documenter of the past on the other. In our attempt to arrive at a sort of "degree zero" before reproducing the Middle Ages in film, therefore, I will offer below a survey of the difficulties inherent in accessing the Middle Ages in particular via the "accepted" historical route. One of the most pertinent works in this regard has been Norman Cantor's *Inventing the Middle Ages*, whose central premise may be found in his opening chapter, revealingly titled "The Quest for the Middle Ages":

> The Middle Ages as we perceive them are the creation of an interactive cultural process in which accumulated learning, the resources and structures of the academic profession, the speculative comparing of medieval and modern worlds, and intellectualisation through appropriation of modern theory and society, personality, language, and art have been molded together in the lives, work, and ideas of medievalists and the schools and traditions they have founded.[1]

Coming to the rather poetic conclusion that "the memory of the Middle Ages lingers like the air of a clear, windful day in the collective mind of the West,"[2] Cantor elucidates a number of the problems which face most medievalists in their respective research, and which I will address below.

First, there is the problem of accessing the period in a physical sense in terms of the material culture, a problem which is compounded by both the impossibility of obtaining absolutely reliable records, and by the abundance of records itself, whose contradictions and ambiguities preclude any categorical assertions. In recognizing the need to reinterpret these data, we thus come to recognize equally that the adjective "medieval"—an elusive term at the best of times — comes equally to be constructed as an imaginary set of beliefs which the current data support. Using precisely this ambiguity, in the second section of this chapter, "Constructing the Middle Ages," I will put forward the initial conclusions which will form the theoretical basis on which my subsequent chapters will rely. These are, in their simplest form, that we do not (and perhaps cannot?) access the period directly, and consequently our attempts to "explicate the past," as Droysen calls it, involve a twofold process of recreation or re-appropriation by icons or paradigms. Before we can go about trying to recreate it, however, let us first begin by looking at how we try to access the period itself in a physical sense.

THE MATERIAL CULTURE

When it comes to dealing with the relics of medieval culture, as far as literature is concerned, "contemporary readers never experience medieval texts directly, unambiguously, or ahistorically. Their reading is always mediated in highly complex ways by the scholarly activities that make these texts accessible:

the editions, glosses, textual notes, manuscript facsimiles, transcriptions, and translations through which medieval literature is filtered and transmitted."[3] If this is true for those extant works of literature which might otherwise give us insight into a culture so far removed from us, it seems doubly true for any material objects, artifacts or relics, for these require a double interpretation: first, we must understand what meaning these objects represent to us, and then extrapolate from this hypothesis any meaning which they might have held for medieval culture (or, indeed, vice versa). A brooch, for example, may have any range of functions, from a keepsake or love token to an everyday commonplace object, or might even have spiritual/religious significance; and this is not to mention the difficulties of dating objects, for if the brooch was a family heirloom, then its cultural and personal meaning would change significantly over time (from everyday object to personal memento to museum piece, for example).

Though dire and pessimistic for our concerns, this double interpretation does support the idea that we can only ever theorize about the culture either from its material remains or from the texts handed down to us. Aside from the theoretical obstacles mentioned in the previous chapter, there are indubitably physical barriers existing alongside them. For once, these are not due to a lack of material evidence for, thanks in part to the preference toward durable parchments over the more perishable paper, we in the twentieth century are able to lay our hands on between ten and twenty times more written medieval than Classical material.[4] In fact — in contrast to modern history's abundance of documentation — all of the sources of these periods may be treated as equally valid, since

> one of the fascinations of ancient and medieval history is that it gives us the illusion of having all the facts at our disposal within a manageable compass: the nagging distinction between the facts of history and other facts about the past vanishes, because the few known facts are all facts of history.[5]

This relative abundance, however, is by no means all good news. One of the main physical barriers arises precisely because of abundance rather than scarcity: it is perhaps rather perversely by the existence of two contradictory texts that these problems of historicity are brought to the fore. Where two extant manuscripts disagree over specific details, for example, our attempts at "history" are removed one stage back, so that instead of critiquing the society by its material remains, we are first forced to evaluate the reliability of the documents themselves. The ambiguity of conflicting reports — rather than deepening our knowledge of the period — once again places us at a further remove from the text, for we must first go through an explicatory phase before we are able to engage directly with the work.

Thus the advancement of "general theories" about the Middle Ages becomes increasingly frail, for in order to propose any idea of the Middle Ages we must first establish to what extent we can talk about the reliability of our primary sources, and second propose another theory based on the first hypothesis, trusting to faith that our theories developed from these sources are an adequate reflection of them. For medievalists, thus, "it is extremely important to consider the broader picture, the world of the Middle Ages, because the Middle Ages in particular survive only in fragments, as a ruined castle here, a charter there, a music manuscript there."[6] Consequently, as soon as we begin to criticize the credibility of the materials themselves, we run the risk of undermining our theories built on that evidence. As Marcus Bull observes, instead of approaching material as a solid and reliable document per se, "a great deal of a medieval historian's effort is directed towards the reinterpretation of material that is already in the scholarly domain."[7]

THE "IMAGINARY" MIDDLE AGES

In addition to these difficulties in accessing the material relics of medieval culture, and the impossibility of advancing any incontrovertible theories about the period as a whole, we are also faced with one further paradox, familiar to all medievalists; that the Middle Ages did not exist during the Middle Ages — neither in the form that we "know" them now, nor as a period of time.[8] That is to say, the period of roughly one thousand years which we conveniently stretch between Roman domination at one end and the Renaissance at the other was not occupied by people who considered themselves to be living in a middle period.[9] Such confusion is reflected even in the terminology; the term "Middle Ages" was of course invented long after the age, and would be unrecognizable to those living within the period.[10] Furthermore, the term carries with it a certain value judgment which has accrued over the course of time.

> The Middle Ages aren't what they used to be. When the term was coined in the sixteenth century, it was not only in Latin but also in the singular (*medium aevum*), and it referred to a thousand-year-long period, the Middle Age, largely undifferentiated, separating Classical Antiquity from the Renaissance. Moreover, this period bore the stigma of a value-judgement so negative that its adjectival form "medieval" came to be used by some as a synonym for "dark," "ignorant," "barbaric," or the like.[11]

To simplify matters, therefore, we might observe that if the Middle Ages did not exist during the period which we ascribe to it, but exist now as a familiar enough term to require no historical clarification, then it logically follows that the term must at some point have been "invented" ex post facto.

Furthermore, if the term belongs to us (or at least to those living outside of the historical period), then it is a fiction of ours, and not a statement of historical fact belonging to the medieval period. We are therefore confronted with something of an irony; we have in our contemporary and cultural vocabulary, a term with a strong and fixed meaning which, when we come to apply it rigidly to its referent, becomes distinctly blurred around the edges. We know exactly what we mean when we describe someone's attitude as "medieval," and have no difficulties in conjuring up an idea of "medieval dress," for example (however inaccurate this might be in point of fact), yet if we ask about concrete issues such as medieval attitudes to war or religion, then we have to concede a great deal of ground. The terms "Middle Ages" and "medieval" therefore come to "refer to a set of cultural forms sufficiently remote from us in time to be totally outside our experience as twentieth-century people. At best we can pick up here and there a fossilized image of them, preserved among the debris of pre-industrial civilisations that mingle with our own."[12]

The corollary of this invented term is found in the referent itself. One of the primary obstacles to our understanding of the Middle Ages as a whole comes from our treatment of it precisely as a "middle" — a medium aevum, as later commentators described it — in other words, as an era defined precisely by a negation of two neighboring periods.[13] Moreover, attempts to define it by opposition force a unity upon this overriding (and retrospectively applied) term, which have as a more problematic consequence the pigeon-holing of a vast tract of history into one, coherent whole. This "pigeon-holing" is exacerbated by the singularity of the terminology which implies that we can speak of "THE Middle Ages"[14] when in reality we are talking about moments within this period, for "medieval culture, even if more homogeneous than our own, was by no means monolithic."[15] Convenient as it might be, we cannot realistically talk of a thousand-year period as a rational whole characterized by one or two overriding interests, for this would be to force on the period a characterization which we would scarcely accept for ourselves over the last decade or so.

The problem of periodization, therefore, is a particularly thorny area, not least because of the ideological judgments to which such a way of dividing history is prone. As we have seen, "the division of history into periods is not a fact, but a necessary hypothesis or tool of thought, valid in so far as it is illuminating, and dependent for its validity on interpretation. Historians who differ on the question of when the Middle Ages ended differ on the interpretation of certain events."[16] We must also take into account the loaded preconceptions which have embedded themselves into our very terminology, for "Middle Ages and Renaissance by the usage of half a century have become terms which call up before us, by means of a single word, the difference between two epochs, a difference which we feel to be essential, though hard to define."[17] The problem of knowing and accessing the Middle Ages, for Marcus Bull, is that of the relationship between words and things, so that "the label becomes shorthand for the values that are associated with a particular period."[18]

One solution, of course, is simply to recognize them as issues of terminology, and to reassert that "if we abolish the terms 'medieval' and 'Middle Ages' tomorrow, the important thing would be not to find alternative labels that simply filled the same mental spaces."[19] We must, however, recognize from the outset that the "Middle Ages" as such did not exist except as our way of labeling the period (and therefore by extension must be a modern, and not medieval, invention). So when did they come into existence? Maurice Keen is by no means alone in arguing convincingly the conventional wisdom that

> It was the men of the Renaissance who first called the period which preceded their own "the Middle Ages." For them this was a term of opprobrium, a label for the centuries of ignorance, barbarism and obscurantism, which they saw as intervening between the end of the classical age and the revival of classical learning.[20]

We might also turn to Cantor, le Goff or Eco among others to lend weight to the proposition that the Middle Ages exist only as a product of the Renaissance.[21] Yet even this might not go far enough, for if the term "Renaissance" is dependent for its existence on its opposition to the term "the Middle Ages," and we have demonstrated above that the meaning of this latter term is subject to a sufficiently wide interpretation as to call its accuracy into question, then perhaps we might equally turn our suspicion on the term "Renaissance" itself, challenging thereby the "Early Modern Triumphalism" against which Nancy Partner was objecting? Either way, that is perhaps another discussion. For the purposes of my argument here, it is sufficient to recognize the abstract nature of the labels, on the condition that its logic be followed through thoroughly. If we acknowledge that the Middle Ages began to be "rebranded" during the Renaissance period, it is not unreasonable to suggest that the evolution of the "capital" which we associate with that period has continued in the popular imagination, for otherwise we would only have one way of imagining the medieval world today.

As Marcus Bull comments, today the term "medieval" triggers a range of meanings, calling up notions of "primitiveness, superstition, small-worldism, bigotry, fearfulness, irrationality, superficiality, inflexibility, and intolerance," many of which could convincingly be traced back to a "knee-jerk" reaction of the sixteenth-century humanists.[22] Such a range of meanings stand, therefore, as a testament to the polysemy of the period in the modern understanding. What is especially noteworthy, however, is that alongside this first, negative conception of the Middle Ages as a dark world, a bifurcation of ideas about the period has produced its polar antithesis in a nostalgic, halcyon Middle Ages. Thus, as we will see in Part III on medieval worlds, "two images are superimposed: a 'dark' Middle Ages and an idealized one."[23]

Neither is this process of reinvention limited to the sixteenth century. The reconstruction of the Middle Ages over the past four centuries has led us to the point that there now exists a multiplicity of "medieval worlds," so that "l'Ailleurs remplace l'Autrefois."[24] The choice we make in our interpretation of the period depends on a number of factors for, as Cantor reminds us, "everyone carries around a highly personal view of the Middle Ages. For most people this is extremely vague or grossly simple and dogmatically crude, although not thereby to be held in contempt."[25] Or, to borrow from Eco's conclusions:

> before rejoicing or grieving over a return of the Middle Ages, we have the moral and cultural duty of spelling out *what kind of Middle Ages we are talking about.* To say openly which of the above ten types we are referring to means to say who we are and what we dream of....[26]

In which case the ideas which we have about the Middle Ages can no longer be pinpointed to a specific (and immediate) reinvention after the "official ending" of the period, but rather have come down to us over the course of a continued evolution through time. As multifarious, contradictory, and above all as *imaginary* as they are, it is precisely those different reinventions of the Middle Ages which have governed and promoted these disparate medieval worlds.

Constructing the Middle Ages

> *"The cinema — and not only the cinema — has neither the duty to reproduce, nor the intention to explain, the Middle Ages: on the contrary,* it reinvents them, it recreates them *by reconstructing without philological ties and using a powerful and unrivalled imagery"*[27]

When it comes to reconstructing the Middle Ages, then, we can see that filmmakers wishing to reinterpret the Middle Ages are already forcibly removed from the period by historiography, cinematography and the problems inherent in accessing the period; we are consequently dealing not with the recreation of history, but with the construction of the period based on a cinematic (and, perhaps, cultural) "imaginary." In his landmark essay "Living in the New Middle Ages," Umberto Eco observes that in trying to recreate a new Middle Ages we are essentially "trying to formulate a 'hypothesis of the

Middle Ages' (as if we were setting out to fabricate the Middle Ages and were deciding what ingredients are required to make one that is efficient and credible)."[28] It is an analogy which may be quite useful for our present purposes. In cinematic form, in a sense we *are* trying to fabricate the Middle Ages, or at least a version of them, and in so doing, we are obliged to consider which elements are going to allow us to do so most credibly. Furthermore, it is a curious "recipe" for their recreation, since we as audiences are in many ways like those awkward diners who demand specific exclusions and inclusions to their dish, and thus insist on dictating the recipe to the chef, instead of accepting the recipe which is placed before them, even if— and this is so often the case for us — the original is the one which "works." Small wonder, to continue the metaphor, that when faced with such a meal, critics will instinctively turn on the chef.

The construction of the period is further complicated by the consideration that (despite what academics and medievalists might imagine) not all filmmakers begin with the intention of recreating an "efficient and credible" Middle Ages.[29] Films for children, especially, are prone to using such a "fairy-tale" Middle Ages, not as a lesson in History but instead as a vague backdrop against which to expound the moral values which tales of Arthur and Robin Hood embody in the popular imagination. Elsewhere, taking a film like Helgeland's *A Knight's Tale* it is clear that concerns about Historical accuracy are hardly at the forefront of the creators' minds; what they seek is instead to make the past "come alive" in a way that is immediately understandable to a modern viewer — by deliberate anachronism if necessary. Working within the context of this imaginary medieval period, "we now play with the past, treating it like a giant shopping mall, full of images, motifs and ideas which we can consume in whatever combinations we choose."[30] Thus, "in an extreme form, films bring home the distance between the historical Middle Ages and reconstructions of that period."[31] For every genuine attempt to construct the medieval world from the source material, as the epigraph indicates, there is equally an example of a filmmaker fabricating his or her own world from other twentieth-century imaginations of the period, creating a twentieth-century iconography — a stock series of symbols, icons and sequences "without philological ties" which for us stand for the Middle Ages — which exists independently of actual recreations of the period. The explanation for this, of course, lies in the previous section, in which we saw that the period is mostly reconstructed according to present concerns and hypotheses, coming to form a medieval imaginary. Such a fabrication, therefore, means that any given medieval period in film is always to some extent constructed, and its construction is most often informed not by meticulous academic research, but by the individual imaginations of a given filmmaker.

We should consequently be aware that if this process of retransmission and re-use of the period is not Historical in intent, then it cannot be seen as a direct link spanning the centuries between their time and ours as though it were an unbroken thread, and that somehow tying the two ends of the string back together would reveal no great difference all along. The cinematic, imaginary Middle Ages belongs more to the twentieth century than it does to the fourteenth, which means that we must acknowledge a difference between the two eras. We should rightly be wary of assuming either at one extreme a continuous, contiguous presence of the Middle Ages (which asserts that nothing much has changed from the medieval period to the twentieth century), or at the other a sudden, jarring rupture (such as the Renaissance, or the "waning" of civilization in the later medieval period).

The reality lies somewhere between the two extremes. On the one hand, we are surrounded by direct remnants of the medieval period, so that "the Middle Ages besiege and provoke us on all sides,"[32] and many of the practices and habits of twentieth-century Europe reflect the still potent influence of our medieval antecedents. On the other hand, in many instances the original significance of these remnants has now been largely lost (consider, for example, the continued use of the military salute despite the disuse of helmets with visors), transforming many of these medieval relics — and particularly many of the practices — into what Barthes terms "empty signifiers,"[33] that is a signifier with no continued "signified." Such empty signifiers more often reveal the "untraversable abyss"[34] between then and now than any idea of an unbroken tradition, highlighting the "vast and unbridgeable gap between us and the Middle Ages."[35]

From the point of view of the spectator, then, we can see that we are in a sense chasing a ghost of the Middle Ages. Such a pursuit of the imaginary consequently raises questions about the reliability and credibility of this period, which — as we will see in chapter 9 — is often more about authenticity than accuracy *in stricto sensu*. In order to depict any form of Middle Ages, then, both filmmaker and viewer (sender and receiver, to adopt a communicative model) must agree on the theoretical authenticity (though not necessarily the accuracy) of the images being shown to them.[36] These are based on two prerequisites, or a belief contract[37] between filmmaker and spectator, that (1) it is a representation, because the referential reality has disappeared, and (2) it is invented, because we are discussing fictional works which "are inserted in the 'gaps' of History: [a fictional work] has as its function to overcome the interstices of the real."[38]

If the problem, then, can be seen as one of signification, it is to semiotics that we might turn to elucidate it more clearly, observing first the traditionally accepted view of the three elements of the sign which make up a triad of signification: the signifier/representamen, the signified/interpretant and the referent/object.[39] If we are no longer able with any certainty or authority to connect with the referents, or material objects, of the Middle Ages, then we can no longer posit the existence of a completed "triad of signification"— in short, if one of the components is missing, then we are no longer able to summon up a direct signifying link to our medieval past.

To clarify how this works in practice, let us use the example of a knight, who will be studied in more depth in the next chapter. In the twentieth century, we have no longer any familiarity with the sort of striated feudal society which produced and even necessitated the concept of a warrior class, and consequently, we have no understanding of the everyday meaning of the object "knight." Though, of course, we may know what a knight is, and most of us would have a good idea of what a knight does, we no longer have any direct equivalent in our societies, and therefore no *direct* knowledge. Which means that, on a day-to-day level, it has no directly equivalent meaning.[40] This means that in order to construct a cinematic knight, we must have recourse to a manufactured link — a representation, and not a recreation — to that same referent; we saw above that we can do so either by explaining the concept of knighthood to imply the object (paradigmatic), or by explaining the object to imply the concept (iconic). In the first case, we are forsaking some of the accuracy to the form in order to preserve fidelity to the concept (a cowboy knight may not look like a real knight, but he might behave like one); in the second, we do the reverse, forsaking the concept in order to preserve the form (the knight looks like a credible knight, even if he may not behave like one).

As Lévi-Strauss observes about science, although it has equal value for our present concerns, when it comes to representation there are "two ways of proceeding: it is either reductionist or structuralist. It is reductionist when it is possible to find out that very complex phenomena on one level can be reduced to simpler phenomena on other levels.... And when we are confronted with phenomena too complex to be reduced to phenomena of a lower order, then we can only approach them by looking at their relationships, that is, by trying to understand what kind of original system they make up."[41] Here we can see that cinema — in trying to reach popular audiences, is acting in the same way; when we encounter studio systems such as MGM, for whom the historical record is deemed to be unnecessarily complex, it is reduced to comparable paradigms in our own culture (the Western, the detective genre, the World War II epic). Where the historical record is considered to be primordial, however, the original relationship is retained and filmmakers try to reconstruct the original significance of those events like a ship in a bottle, by reproducing those structural relationships with other iconic elements, keeping the whole at arm's length.

ICONIC RECREATION

"There is in the narrative cinema a medieval world whose images are famil-iar...."[42]

One of the most fruitful demonstrations of these iconic recreations can be seen in Eric Rohmer's attempt to slavishly reconstruct the medieval sense of space and stylized representation in his *Perceval le Gallois,* which in reality seems to be more successful in adhering to a forgotten sense of space than communicating that sense to a modern audience.[43] While receiving mixed critical reception, the words of one commentator seem particularly apposite when he claims that it "does not transport the spectator to the Middle Ages but jarringly reveals the gulf between medieval conventions of representation and ours."[44] Simply by filming even highly faithful reproductions of the period we cannot thereby assume that we have unrestricted access to that era, for we are rather trying to use one medium to connect to a tradition rightly belonging to another, using conventions which are by now alien to our culture. What has happened instead is that we recognize the film's importance as a repre-sentation of those objects which were comprehensible to the medieval audi-ence. It is consequently by and large accepted among historians working on films that the camera cannot simply act like a time machine, as though going back to the twelfth century and filming things "as they really were,"[45] but rather it functions most effectively by a process of approximation, establishing conventions which the spectator may recognize as being "medievalesque" in intent, or "vaguely medieval."[46] In short, it may well be the closest cinema has ever been to reproducing the Middle Ages, but the whole film cannot help but remain inaccessible, remote and more of a museum curio than a liv-ing, breathing Middle Ages.

In our ideas about the period, then, we must also recognize that this approximated image is by no means a true and accurate representation of the period, but it is simply a mediated concatenation of preconceived ideas which we hold about things relating to the period. Crucially, it belongs as much — if not more — to the period in which it was produced as to the period which it is trying to recreate; especially given that it is dependent on a contemporary audience to unravel its significance. The form of a given historical represen-tation, then, is not necessarily a carbon copy, but is predicated on a mutual acceptance of its visual representation by both spectator and observer, given that "we may re-present something by presenting a substitute of this thing in its absence,"[47] which means that both the represented and representation belong to, are drawn from, and have meaning in the contemporary world of its production *even if not the world of its putative origins.*

Using Peirce's definitions of the qualities of a sign, we might illustrate this point with another example of the iconography of the knight. The horse and rider, as the figure *per antonomasia* of the medieval knight, has become — as much by repetition as anything else — a staple figure in the chivalric medieval film, and therefore can be seen as both an iconic and a symbolic sign (iconic because it is a direct copy having resemblance to its original, and symbolic because it is predicated on a conventional agreement that /horse+ rider/ signifies more than it initially seems to be, i.e., /fantasy hero/, /cowboy/, /knight/ and so on). Of course, when we examine the finer details, we are almost certain to find any number of inaccuracies, in dress, in weaponry, in the size, shape, breed, color or any other aspect of the horse (including whether or not they ought to be wearing horseshoes, have stirrups, use a looped bridle and so on). Even so, no matter how much we might criticize the formal aspects of the signifier (for that is, of course, what the horse and rider have become), we unfailingly recognize its function as an exact replica of what we believe to be medieval, irrespective of its historical veracity. Therefore, we can observe in embryo one of the arguments which I will later develop: that even if something of the concept might be lost, it clearly retains some of its formal relationship with the object. Thus, although the iconic sign is by no means "accurate" in its capacity of signifier, it can nevertheless adequately signify a meaningful, "authentic" referent.

PARADIGMATIC REPRESENTATION

"On the other hand, do you think Hollywood might be ready for The Song of Roland? *The ultimate buddy movie. Action, scenery, high stakes, and the love of fair women. Bruce Willis as the grizzled Roland, Mel Gibson as the fabled Oliver...."*[48]

Paradigmatically, on the other hand, we might take a film like Richard Thorpe's *Ivanhoe*,[49] which presents us with a hero whose values, codes and actions resemble nothing so much as a Western in medieval garb, which supports Williams' claim that "the imagery of Hollywood dominates the cinema's Middle Ages."[50] The strong, silent, mysterious stranger arriving into town becomes in this respect a prototype of the Eastwood/Leone "man with no name," who reinforces standard Hollywood Western codes by eschewing the advances of the dark-haired, Jewish Rebecca (the Native American "other") in favor of the blonde, Anglo-Saxon princess, and heralds the reign of "civilization" over the rule of lawless gangs.[51] The laic removal of overtly Christian values aligns the film's moral code with that of Manifest Destiny over the divine right of kingship, the latter being a premise which would be less well received in North America than in a country with strong monarchic heritage. In so doing, Thorpe's film replicates the paradigms familiar to contemporary

North American audiences, rather than imbuing each individual object with "medievalized" values.

The reprisal of a paradigm borrowed from another culture is, of course, by no means a one-way process. Films as varied as Godard's *A Bout de Souffle* to *The 51st State* pay homage to Hollywood's influence by borrowing elements from visual aesthetics developed in the mainstream cinema in order to imbue their own films with a sense of familiarity. To this end we can even read of Kurosawa — a director whose own medieval film, *The Seven Samurai*, was famously remade as a Hollywood Western, *The Magnificent Seven*— that *Hidden Fortress* represents his appropriation of Hollywood techniques in the endeavor to make his historical setting suitably "foreign"; it is "really a John Ford Western, with Japanese and feudal overtones."[52]

Therefore, we may not dispense with our Peircean triadic unit of signification just yet. What is happening here is that we are no longer loading the signifier with meanings which refer backwards in time to their original signified (as the iconic sign does), but we are in fact bringing forward the signified to identify it with paradigms which are more familiar from our own era. In this aspect, what is being stressed is not the original, visual meaning of the knight, for example, but the position of that knight in medieval society, so that — to us at least — the knight operates in much the same way as the cowboy, the detective, the policeman, or the action hero, and it is therefore the relationship and interaction with other elements of the world which are being communicated. This is what Greta Austin classifies as the "third problem with medieval films [...] that they usually tell stories not about the Middle Ages, but about Modern Western life in a period dress."[53] It is again Rosenstone who responds to this most convincingly, suggesting that these paradigmatic "normalizations" (as he terms them) do not *have to be* problems as such. Discussing the tournament scene in *A Knight's Tale* which is constructed as a modern Superbowl, he asks:

> Don't they [the anachronisms] violate what we know about tournaments in the fourteenth century? Yes and no.... The film, after all, is made for a twenty-first century audience, for people to whom such a tournament, however exciting, seems no more than a distant, exotic, and bizarre spectacle. To normalize it, to show that in the thirteenth and fourteenth centuries such tournaments were wildly popular spectator sports [...] the filmmaker utilizes anachronisms that are so blatant that nobody could mistake them for an actual historical reference. Yet they do help to communicate something that would otherwise be difficult for that audience to comprehend, and they do so precisely by using contemporary imagery and language.[54]

When films begin to cast their nets a little wider, consequently, drawing on a range of mythological and quasi-historical sources, we begin to see:

with what aptitude a very good commercial film is able to use a sort of syn-
cretism, a mythology in which can be found at once both the archetypes of
a collective imagination nourished by centuries of popular tales, legends,
myths, simplified hagiographies, superstitions and emblematic figures remod-
elled by circumstance. [It is] an idea which Americans have used in order to
create a medieval alibi, marvellous, fantastic and timeless in which fairy tales
can come back to life and rediscover their form...[55]

An inchoate secondary theory therefore begins to emerge, which will be
tested throughout the remainder of this study. In the two examples outlined
above (*Perceval le Gallois* and *Ivanhoe*), it is possible that the choices are not
arbitrary: given the tendency for Hollywood and popular "blockbuster" cinemas to conceive, accept and perpetuate genres and typologies, we might
wonder whether the paradigmatic approach is more suited to a more mainstream mode of film production and, more forcefully, whether it might not
hold more appeal to audiences who have no immediate links with a tangible
Middle Ages (at least, lest Western triumphalism impugn my arguments here,
there are no immediate links with a *European* Middle Ages). Furthermore,
this conforms neatly with a division between Hollywood studios and European
auteurs recently proposed by Veronica Ortenberg, according to which studio
productions are more likely to use staple themes from already successful films
than to experiment with Historical films.[56] Though such a distinction is somewhat generalized, and certainly does not do justice to the diversity either of
Hollywood films or of European mainstream production, it does nevertheless
go some way to explaining the stark similarities between studio-backed
medieval films and their preference for paradigmatic representation over iconic
recreation. Is there, then, equally a stronger tendency to revert to the iconic
image in European cinemas, for whom the Middle Ages are still present alongside us as material relics? Over the course of the examples which I give in
chapters 3 to 6, it will consequently be worthwhile to bear this second theory
in mind.

Conclusions

Having advanced the argument in chapter 1 that there can be no single,
incontestable version of History in general and the Middle Ages in particular,
the purpose of this last chapter has been to offer some suggestions about
how — in theory — we go about accessing and constructing a medieval world.
The first division which we encountered was to discover that in the fabrication
of a film which deals with the Middle Ages, there is a fundamental problem
in trying to explain the period to a twentieth-century spectator, since many

of the most central elements of the period are either totally unfamiliar (like the meaning of a given knight's coat of arms), or have a very different meaning in the modern imagination (like the knight himself). This, we have seen, gives rise to two possible approaches: we can use a paradigm as something of a metaphor, to suggest that the knight is like a cowboy, or a policeman, and so on, or we might otherwise use an icon to suggest the importance of a knight in the mind of a spectator (so that, in this instance, the depiction of a man with a horse, a sword and some armor would suffice to conjure up images of knight).

PART II

PEOPLE

3

When Knights Were Bold:
Those Who Fight

"Irresistible force meets immovable object."[1]

To a given filmmaker, who needs quickly to assimilate a diverse range of traits in the creation of a credible character, the medieval knight is undoubtedly a difficult figure to understand unambiguously. There is an inherent contradiction between the "gentil" courtly knight and the "irresistible force" of the warrior, a contradiction which arises because "the image of the knight [...] best represents our mixture of awe at the barbaric splendor of the Middle Ages and revulsion at its violence and hierarchy."[2] Even if we look at the knight as a literary construct, we can find little more clarity; in the lais and romances of Marie de France and Chrétien de Troyes we find knights clad in shimmering armor, rescuing damsels, restoring property and dispensing justice, while in *La Chanson de Roland* and *Beowulf*, we meet a warrior carving out his existence on the frontiers of civilization and fighting against the dark forces of evil which ravage a peaceful society. Lest we be inclined to attribute these differences to a merely temporal evolution, the thirteenth-century *Queste del San Graal* gives us deeply spiritual, gallant knights engaged on sacred quests, which contrast starkly with the blustering, bumbling aristocrats of the fabliaux which emerged during the same period. Among the various representations, however, one overriding trend is that the literary knight more often than not represents a fusion of belligerent tenacity infused within an inescapably romantic ideal, a fundamentally violent nature scarcely concealed beneath the highly polished veneer of a courtly knight.

In practical terms, too, the evolution of the figure of the knight is by no means straightforward. At the societal level, knighthood is based on a fundamental paradox: as one who fights for right,[3] the knight is both a lover and a fighter, responsible for both protection and aggression, peace and violence, honor and villainy. As a distinct fighting class brought into being by necessity, they represent a form of institutionally sanctioned violence which is perennially viewed uneasily by those who recognize the fine line between protection and oppression. This, then, is perhaps why the literary incarnation of the knight was equally ambiguous, since the code of chivalry which it imposes on its fighting class represents an attempt to combine these fissiparous forces which both forestalled and inaugurated the "violent tenor" of medieval life, as Huizinga describes it.[4] This same literature served as an outlet designed to elaborate the codes which governed life, so that just as sexual passion was regulated by a code of love, so too was war "(in intention) formalised by the art of heraldry and the rules of chivalry."[5]

When we consider that between these two extremes lies a range of possible interpretations, over the course of this chapter we will see that the evolution of the role of "those who fight" has been — perhaps more than any other individual medieval figure, given its frequent association with, and elision into, the difficult concept of the "hero" — subjected to a relentless reshaping and remolding from its inception through to the modern day. As Martha Driver and Sid Ray observe, "in order to appeal to a contemporary audience, film must reinvent the Middle Ages and create in the medieval hero a hodgepodge of traits derived from a mixed understanding of what is medieval and of traits we value in the heroes of postmillennial Western culture."[6]

The Medieval Referent

> "A knight ther was, and that a worthy man, That from the tyme that he ferst bigan, To ryden out he loved chyvalrye, Trouthe and honour, fredom and curtesie.... He was a verray parfit, gentil knight."[7]

We began by observing a central paradox in terms of the modern understanding of the medieval knight, torn between a fundamentally violent nature designed to vouchsafe the emerging medieval society, and a chivalric aspect which is geared to the preservation of peace and the eschewal of warfare. At the same time, however, even within the period attempts were made to temper these two extremes by the introduction of a more spiritually orientated form of knighthood designed to play down the violence of "those who fight," using concepts like the *miles Christi*, the Knights of Christ.[8] Nevertheless, it must be acknowledged that this third form of knighthood was not destined to dispense with violence altogether, for the necessity of a fighting class was more or less universally recognized throughout the Middle Ages; while "not all medieval thinkers saw a triple division of society into orders ... what matters is that fighting men are frequently seen as a separate and important order in society."[9] The aspect of the medieval referent which *did* change, however, was the *extent* to which that violence was concealed, for "the Church's attitude was still guarded: it encouraged knighthood, but only in order to control and tame the warrior instinct."[10]

Though somewhat simplified for our purposes, broadly speaking, the medieval knight did undergo a gradual evolution throughout the Middle Ages, with only few major exceptions. In knighthood's earliest literary form, heroes like Beowulf, Cuchulain and Roland, all the way through to *Njals Saga* and *El Cantar del mio Cid*, were perceived and construed predominantly as warrior-knights rather than the courtly hero more familiar from later romances. Such warrior-heroes — given that their status as hero is predicated precisely on their martial prowess — have a notable tendency to transform into mythic, or epic heroes, of the *mythos* mode whose heroes are, to use Frye's terminology for their literary cousins, "superior in kind to men and nature."[11] Thus early medieval knights are often lauded for their superhuman strength — and unrestrained violence — which surpasses both their peers and Nature herself. When, for instance, Roland strikes one unfortunate pagan, his forcefulness reveals an aggression quite excessive for modern tastes:

> Ço sent Rollant que s'espee li tolt,
> Uvrit les oilz, si li ad dit un mot;
> "Men escïentre, tu n'ies mie des noz!"
> Tient l'olifan qu'unkes perdre ne volt,
> Si l'fiert en l'elme ki gemmét fut a or;
> Fruisset l'acer e la teste e les os,
> Amsdous les oilz del chef li ad mis fors
> Jus a ses piez si l'ad tresturnét mort.[12]

> Now Roland feels the pagan take his sword.
> Opening his eyes, he says but this to him,
> "I do not think you can be one of ours."
> Seizing the horn he never hoped to lose,
> He strikes the pagan on his golden helm;
> Smashing the helmet's steel, his head and bones,
> He drives the pagan's eyes out of his head
> And knocks him over dead right at his feet.

The problem with such warriors, however, is that they were originally conceived as a fighting force designed to repel invaders and put down local rebellions, attacks and the genre of military threat which characterized the late ninth and early tenth centuries in Europe. Their literary representation, accordingly, emphasizes such violence to the extent that it becomes a distinguishing characteristic. When we move through to the late eleventh and early twelfth centuries, however, the raw aggression which once gave comfort to villages and kingdoms frequently begins to jar alarmingly with new ideas about peaceful coexistence within a civilized society. It is this incongruity, in fact, which might go some way to explaining why in film, as we shall see, these early warriors most often evolve into epic heroes celebrated in "Heroic Fantasy," in which "in contrast to the hero of the Middle Ages, who is most often (always?) a noble, powerful by birth, our heroes are men of the people ... Made in the USA."[13]

As we move away from the early medieval era, then, we begin to see that the concept of chivalry becomes increasingly prominent, reflecting the importance placed in the early twelfth century on clemency and temperance,[14] that in short *chivalry* comes to be separated from *knighthood*, the former governing *sapientia*, the latter more concerned with the hero's *fortitudo*.[15] Here, then, chivalry becomes more concerned with the comportment of these men in peacetime than belligerence in war, placing them into the Romance mode, making of them heroes who are "superior in *degree* to men [for it is after all, a closed rank] and environment," but no longer superior in *kind*.[16] While we still find them engaged in astonishing feats of human prowess — from breaking iron window bars, crawling across sword-bridges and defeating giants[17] — their superiority comes from a level of training (and not an innate superiority) and their endearingly human faults render them by no means divine. Such human failings include Lancelot's inability to track down Guinevere in *Le Chevalier de la charette*, which lays him open to unguarded mockery,[18] and Yvain similarly comes unstuck when he realizes he has promised to be in two places at once or must be rescued mid-fight by the titular lion.[19]

As we move again through to the later medieval period, with the eminence and emergence of the *miles Christi*, the soldier's pugilistic prowess and bellicose nature "was to be channelled into the maintenance of peace and the defence of the weaker members of society."[20] They become, therefore, a product of the environment itself, who are promoted to an elite order whose duty it is to protect the weak and defenseless. We enter therefore into the high mimetic mode, which demands only that its heroes be "superior in *degree* to man, but not to environment."[21] Such a progression, fortuitously, together with the increasing accretion of human values and concerns, reflects Frye's general proposition that "European fiction, during the last fifteen centuries, has steadily moved its centre of gravity down the list."[22]

This complex interpolation of issues leads me to that which I am proposing in my attempt to explore the medieval knight on screen; that the concept of knighthood and its relationship to chivalry is by no means *betrayed* by the narrative cinema, since it has been a rather synthetic construct from its very inception, leaving us with a confusing inheritance, a "chivalry [which] owes more to the pen than to the sword."[23] Furthermore, we must again be wary of general accusations of infidelity to a historical reality since, even leaving aside the arguments in chapter 1 against a fixed idea of History, I hope to have shown even in this brief summary that the notion of the knight was a far from concrete and stable entity throughout the medieval period itself.

One interesting suggestion for our purposes, however, comes from Huizinga's suggestion that *already* within the Middle Ages, the "Age of Chivalry" was recognized as an idealized construct, and its acceptance as such is the predominant reason behind its perpetuation. Toward the end of the period, he argues, there began a sort of nostalgic reverence of its own glorious ancestry; "this hero worship of the declining Middle Ages finds its literary expression in the biography of the perfect knight."[24] Leaving aside the problematic assertions of waning and decline, we are left with a provocative postulation, that already within the period of literary production there was an impossible romanticism involved in the literary knight which found no reflection in reality.

Possible support for this notion of a nostalgic recollection of the knight comes from the suggestion that the "waning" does not describe the period, but the function of the knight in everyday society. The introduction of gunpowder and longbows is traditionally accredited to be one of the major causes for the downfall of the knight in battle,[25] while at the same time their unassailable position in "feudal society" was under threat by a shift to judicial trials over trial by sword. "The substitution of an inquisitory procedure for battle transformed the archaic test of martial strength into a test of intellectual strength"[26] leading late medieval society to "verbalize physical conflicts, in a society increasingly aware of the power of the spoken or written word and in the light of a failing feudal system."[27] Pastoureau reminds us, in the same spirit, that such an idealization is normal, and that there must by necessity exist a distance "between the dazzling luminescence of dreams and the drab greys of everyday existence."[28] Thus, Huizinga concludes that "reality gives the lie to the ideal, and accordingly the ideal will soar more and more towards the regions of fantasy, there to preserve the traits [...] too rarely visible in real life."[29]

So we can see that, even within the medieval period itself, there emerge visions of a codified — and probably idealized — paradigm of the perfect knight.[30] To condense what might be a long argument, then, throughout a great deal of literary visions, there are a number of enduring qualities which seem to govern all actions of the idealized knight and which find their way even into modern conceptions of the knight. These qualities, despite the individual focus of medium or text, are invariably concerned with the notion of service: service to women, service to society, retaining honor in one's conduct, protection of the innocent, and so on. Barber, for instance, reminds us that in origin "service is nonetheless an essential element of knighthood," especially considering that the Old English word *cniht* corresponds to something like "servant," from the West Saxon *cneoht,* meaning simply "boy." These obligations can be — when treated well — subsumed into a visible sign when the knight is shown fulfilling his duty, a duty which we have reformed into societal expectations, from Cub Scouts assisting the elderly to charity work: "obligation was the key factor in the life of early medieval man, and under the pyramidal structure of the feudal system, *everyone* was subject to it. In epic terms, obligation became transformed into a moral quality."[31]

Iconic Recreation

"The knight, he's the man who owns a horse."[32]

In this section, therefore, we can use these arguments to examine the ways in which the knight is iconically constructed in cinema. I have argued above that even within the medieval period itself there emerged an idealized form of knighthood which retrospectively romanticized the ideal knight in the face of its imminent disappearance. This idealized form, despite the surface differences, was largely united by abstract concepts like preserving honor, respect for one's enemies and service to women, notions which are difficult — though not impossible — to translate into visual and iconic signs.

So how does the cinema iconically portray medieval knighthood? To answer this we must first work backwards from what we have identified as "the medieval referent" of service, ability to fight, and the recognition of the importance of honor. In order to demonstrate those same abstract notions, medieval writers and artists were in a similar predicament, meaning that they would either have to explicitly state those values (which was by no means uncommon), or have to have recourse to a secondary model of heroism (a paradigm) or a symbol of heroic values (an icon). Thus the model of the knightly hero was imbued with the values of the period, becoming, in a sense, a metonym for those values.

In the same way, then, although modern cinematic evocations of the medieval knight are (as we shall see) frequently drawn from paradigms which existed already in the cultural domain, my theory of iconographic conventions asserts that an alternative approach might draw on conventions at work within the cinema itself (such as visual signals, interfilmic comparisons, historicons [see Glossary], loaded images, passages obligés and "iconogrammes").[33] These, of course, are fairly simple in one respect, when it comes to visual conventions: the knight is the man with the sword, clothed in armor from head to toe, carrying such iconic weapons as to identify his status as a man of war — shield, lance, axe, mace — together with flags, pennants, crests or other insignia designed to single him out. Further, as the epigraph suggests, he is the one with the horse, a medieval attribute which one contemporary chronicler in particular insists upon:

> Men call the knight the man who, of custom, rides upon a horse. He who, of custom, rides upon another mount, is no knight; but he who rides upon a horse is not for that reason a knight.... Knights have not been chosen to ride an ass or a mule...."[34]

Yet when we examine these conventions from a semiotic perspective, we can see that there is more at work; the signifier of man + horse does not *have to* signify a knight. It could be a mounted policeman, Royal Guard, or even a master of the hounds (in a British aristocratic hunt), for instance. The sign also encounters resistance because of unwitting iconic meanings, since the cost of keeping a horse prompts an association with wealth, placing the man + horse signifier into a specific socio-demographic grouping. Reading backwards, we can see the same thing, that a knight must have had a certain degree of wealth and status, an automatic sense of privilege to which modern audiences frequently take exception, and which thus risks alienating a modern viewer.

Further complications arise from the other visual aspects, too. The sword — the symbol par excellence of the medieval knight — connotes notions of that same violence which later evocations of knighthood were at pains to play down. To us, excluding the niche markets of extreme or hardcore violence, the notion of unchecked violence is largely repugnant, and our modern heroes must walk a very fine line between cowardice and aggression. When deconstructed semiotically, then, almost everything associated with the knight has an ulterior and contrary significance: armor, traditionally designed for personal protection, becomes threatening when it conceals identity; a collection of weapons including a shield, axe, mace and lance would almost certainly be construed as a deeply disturbing — if not psychotic — characteristic in today's society; spurs indicate cruelty, service to a lady risks a feminist interpretation as patronization; unwavering obedience is often a trope used to hint at a somewhat inferior intelligence (cf. Sancho Panza, Obelix, or a host of cartoon and comic-book sidekicks).

We can see, then, that things are not quite as simple as they might initially seem. Even when recreating the medieval knight in meticulous detail (which, thanks to modern museums and archaeological finds, is more or less possible), a filmmaker is still forced to negotiate a whole series of indexical values which risk alienating audiences, subverting characterization, or imparting an unwanted character flaw below the level of the narrative. Just as the codes of chivalry were added to later medieval imaginations of knights to play down their violence and emphasize their servitude, even while attempting to "faithfully" render the medieval knight, a modern film must try to convey these same values in order to align the knight with a modern understanding of a hero. In this section, we will briefly turn to look at how modern film-makers have tried to evoke the medieval knight on screen.

TAMING AGGRESSION

"We'll make a new Order of Chivalry! We'll make it a great honour. Very fashionable, all the knights will want to join. Only now, the knights will whack only for good."[35]

One of the first problems of representing medieval knighthood on film comes from the essential difficulty of deciding what kind of violence is justified, and how much of it can be shown. Just as "chivalry was an ideal which aimed to soften the rough ways of the soldier,"[36] so too have films made noticeable attempts to downplay the raw aggression of the heroic warrior and reinsert a form of "legitimated violence" back into their medieval societies. In the continued attempt to sanitize the bloodshed of medieval battle, a range of cinematographic and thematic devices have come into being — most especially in recent years, in which the gradual relaxation of censorship (and the introduction of the straight-to-DVD/VHS markets) have brought about a subculture of video-nasties, or films containing extreme violence from which mainstream films understandably wish to distance themselves.

One way in which they have done so is by a simple act of opposition, in which the filmmakers first associate the villains with unchecked aggression, and then place their heroes in opposition, neatly avoiding the necessity to pass judgment on the justification of violence. Harnessing the shocking power of raw, unrestrained violence, these qualities are transferred to the villains who as a result come to embody its negative elements. This functions in *First Knight*, for example, by polarizing the pacifist Arthur ("There's a peace only to be found on the other side of war. If that war should come, I will fight it"[37]) with the distinctly unhinged, and one-dimensional Malagant, in order to paint Arthur as the ideal, pacifist hero. Elsewhere, in *Dragonheart*, the henchmen of the villainous Prince Einon are constructed as evil because of their aggression towards "the weak villagers" (see chapter 6), which includes not only unarmed men but also women, children and the elderly. Using a reliance on iconic signs, the film juxtaposes the cold metal of the villains' swords with the fragility of human flesh, exposing their arms and legs in order to emphasize their vulnerability. This trope is further reinforced by using the icon of the man + horse, too, by placing the villains on horseback which raises them above the level of the villagers, so as to emphasize their power; the subtext therefore communicates a total abuse of physical power which we have come to associate with moral cowardice. *Dragonheart* further compounds this unrestrained violence by playing down any justification for such aggression. In one scene, one of the villagers speaks out against the newly crowned King Einon, and is instantly cut down by an arrow to the chest; a rapid shot/reverseshot between the villain and villager emphasizes the speed with which the "punishment" is enacted, which takes the villagers (and us) wholly by surprise. By editing out any explanatory phases, the violence seems not only unwarranted, but unchecked brutality symptomatic of an oppressive and immoral regime.

By constructing the "evil" knights as an oppressive and brutal force, therefore, *Dragonheart* simply needs to place its hero, Bowen, into the opposite role of Redeemer/Deliverer for him to represent all of the positive values which the anti-hero lacks. If killing is generally frowned upon, killing a killer is deemed as a noble act — forestalling further violence. Despite being initially construed as a mercenary dragon-slayer who is more interested in money than honor ("your honor has a price, Sir Knight?" "It has *expenses*. Honor won't feed my belly nor shoe my horse"), Bowen gradually learns the values of honor and service in order to be reborn as a chivalric hero who is ultimately able to apply his superior martial prowess to "whack only for good" (as White and Logan describe it) and not for purely selfish pursuits. In the final showdown between Einon and Bowen, therefore, when Bowen has risked his own life in order to rescue the kingdom, protect the girl and exact revenge, the editing slows noticeably in order to demonstrate — by the pace of the film — the longer distance between provocation and reaction which suggests that violence here is treated as a last resort and not a knee-jerk reaction. Before delivering the fatal blow, the director Cohen uses slow motion, and extends the same sequence of shot/reverse-shot to a total of 13 shots, which cut backwards and forwards between Bowen, Einon and Draco (the titular Dragon), dragging the whole sequence out to 19 seconds, and a total of 42 seconds (and 21 shots) before the real conclusion of the scene. Furthermore, Bowen's "necessary" violence to resolve the film and deliver the kingdom is directed towards the dragon, and not to the human, which softens its impact on modern audiences who, in the main, find it difficult to feel compassion for an unjustifiably violent hero. Furthermore, the editorial decision to play the scene in slow motion gives the impression that the violence is considered necessary, and that the hero has the time to formulate a measured, controlled reaction, motivated by cold reason and not impulsive, unchecked aggression.

This leads us onto another manner of taming the violent edges of knighthood, which is the vengeance theme, a theme which is designed to depict any violence used as a necessary, justified and (what would nowadays be termed) "reasonable" force. Where in *Dragonheart*, Bowen's quest is ostensibly undertaken selflessly (and thus becomes a sort of "social" justice), in a film like *First Knight* (though many other examples could be adduced) the vengeance is wholly personalized. On the surface level, Camelot, "Arthur, and Lancelot exemplify a democratic, non-interventionist-but-get-tough-if-we-have-to attitude of foreign policy and set themselves up against the enemies of democracy and free will,"[38] which posits a selfless service of the public good; nevertheless, such an altruistic purpose does not expiate Lancelot's prior existence outside of Camelot as an itinerant swordsman. As the film progresses, Lancelot's violence is eventually explained away as a medieval form of survivor's guilt, making of him "the product of a symbolic, ideological Holocaust that he must exorcise in order to embrace a new, redeemed self,"[39] all of which places his violence and general nihilism (to be a good swordsman, "you have to care little whether you live or die") in the context of a personal vendetta which will ultimately legitimize his aggression. Immediately before one battle, for instance, the image of a burning village seen from a distance (the perspective of the young Lancelot) flashes across the screen, recalling the initial violence exacted on his loved ones as a child. Thus, the unjustified aggression towards the helpless serves to frame Lancelot's own actions in war, playing on a rather cheap moral relativism to excuse his own rampage. A similar use of childhood trauma comes to underpin (and exonerate) a whole host of medieval figures, from Joan of Arc to Tristan, from Grendel to fellow itinerant swordsman Inigo Montoya.[40]

Finally, the martial prowess of the knight is underscored and tamed by a cinematographic form of distancing from the naked aggression of battle. Given the prominence given to restraint and self-control here, it is interesting to see that camera angles, editing and the use of space often, perhaps unwittingly, contribute to distance the knight from the conflict. To give an example, a rather literal interpretation of this distance can be seen in the knight's use of the sword, which becomes the symbol of his power and his ability to defend, attack, subdue and provoke; it is for this reason, we may assume, that cinema insists on infuriating weapons experts by staging swordfights as blade-to-blade affairs, since the blade thus becomes simultaneously a defensive and offensive device. While a sword and shield affair would have been more likely in single combat,[41] the introduction of a shield means that each has a function — sword for attack, shield for defense — which means that the man with only a sword becomes exclusively a belligerent force. Furthermore, the sword is able to offer a greater distance (and therefore restraint) in that it places the hero further away from the specific site of conflict. Cawelti, discussing the even greater distance achieved by the cowboy's gun, observes that:

> The hero often fights with his fists, but he never kills in this kind of direct, hand-to-hand combat ... since knives and clubs suggest a more aggressive and uncontrolled kind of violence which seems instinctively wrong.... [The distance and mastery of his weapon] not only symbolises his masculine potency, but indicates that his violence is disciplined and pure.[42]

The sword itself, then, acts as a device used to distance the knight from his opponent, and thereby to tame the raw aggression.

A similar distance is ensured by the absence of blood, which can here serve as an indexical sign. Given that bloodstains serve both literally and metaphorically as an indexical sign of involvement in a violent event, filmmakers — and especially matinee filmmakers of the 1950s, governed by Hollywood codes which forbade the depiction of blood[43] — were often at pains to avoid calling up images of such a primitive form of conflict. On a purely thematic level, therefore, the absence of blood serves to hint that the violence, like that of the cowboy, is disciplined and pure, and that the knight was not transported by pure rage or fury, but — as is appropriate when the violence is suitably motivated — was enacted "humanely," and only to a degree which is justifiable and sufficient. The net effect of all of this controlled violence, then, is that it creates a medieval world in which "battles are vigorously fought, people are wounded and die, but they shed little visible blood; the sun shines as on a May morning, and the colourful costumes seem to be of a stuff that repels dirt."[44]

Blood also serves as a reminder of the underlying humanity of the antagonist, meaning that even the most unredeemable villain, like *First Knight*'s Malagant, is still only human, and as such his quick dispatch might become necessary, but should by no means be conducted with relish. When the antagonist is finally "dispatched," then, one of the most common tropes is to have him fall from a great height or die as a result of fatal wounds, for example, which are both indirect means and hint that the intention was not to kill but to restrain (and, by extension, it is the villain's inherent weakness which prevents him from surviving a wound that a hero like Lancelot would doubtless have dusted off before plunging back into the fray). On the other hand, a film like *Excalibur* is no stranger to bloodshed, and uses its presence in a deeply symbolic way.[45] In the final showdown, the warfare which destroys the Round Table confraternity is represented visually by staining the shimmering armor with blood, to imply that the spilling of blood represents the end of the idyllic reign of Camelot (a bathetic reflection of which can be seen in the pre-lapsarian utopia of *Erik the Viking*, in which a drop of blood causes the island to sink). Arthur's fatal blow to Mordred is shown in a very tightly framed close-up, denying the bloodlessness of the historical epics, and placing the audience right at the center of the action. The resultant bloodbath, then, serves to remind the audience that in Boorman's reading of the Arthurian plot, each and all are individually and collectively guilty.

These attempts to distance the knight from the epicenter of aggression find support even at the level of the cinematography, the most straightforward of which is to translate metaphorical distance into distance in a very real sense. In Gabriel Axel's *Prince of Jutland* (Les Films Ariane/Woodline, 1994), the Danish Prince Amled (on which Hamlet was later to be based) becomes a very difficult character to portray, since his feigned "madness" ostensibly exonerates his aggression, yet his underlying sanity holds him ultimately to account for any wrongdoings. At the level of the mise-en-scène, Axel therefore constructs two ways of viewing him: from a close-up and from a long shot. During his "madness," there comes a point at which Amled (Christian Bale) is shown attempting to kill another man with his bare hands; the camera tightly frames the two in their desperate struggle, with Bale's face in the direct center of the frame, mere inches from that of his adversary. Towards the end of the film, however, before a final showdown with his uncle's henchman, his sanity is revealed, thereby disbarring him from the same "excusable" impassioned fury. In this second shot, framed by the overhanging branches of a tree and backlit by a heavy mist, Amled is once again placed at the center of the frame, only this time his back is turned, and the focus of the shot is no longer his facial expression, but his calm composure. His slightly hunched figure recalls the tree which demarcates the combat zone (thus connoting stability, calm, etc.), and his legs are slightly apart with his sword held in both hands before him, exuding an air of measured aggression, balance and expertise. His opponent appears at the extreme left of the frame, and wielding an axe in his right hand; his stance is much less composed, with his legs wide apart, arms outstretched and even fingers splayed, all of which give him an air of unchecked aggression and lack of composure. The crucial detail, however, is that the camera is placed so far back that the two actors' bodies occupy only half of the height of the frame, with the result that the opponent's face is this time almost wholly obscured, diminishing his humanity and precluding any form of audience identification.

EARNING KNIGHTHOOD

"This Wallace, he doesn't even have a knighthood. But he fights with passion, and he inspires..."[46]

If untamed aggression represents one of the more contentious connotations of the knightly fighting class, then to a modern audience there is also a second aspect involving the adherence to a feudal hierarchy. Returning to our semiotic model of knighthood above, I argued that the signifier "knight" conjures up images of an unfair and exploitative feudal structure, in which the privileged are born into their rank rather than being seen to *earn* their privileged position. A similar effect occurs with man + horse, too; because of the costs involved in stabling, etc., it is often seen (and reinforced through film) as the preserve of an elite, based on genetic happenstance — rather than meritocratic election — which renders the concept of a hereditary knighthood somewhat disagreeable to audiences (and most especially North American audiences). The emphasis on training, service and merit, which I have grouped together here as aspects of "earning knighthood," may well be a natural response to such a doubly contentious issue and might even go some way to explaining its prevalence within the codes of the Middle Ages.

One of the most common devices used to "earn knighthood" in medieval films has been a delay in narrative, rather than any specifically iconic elements, that which Amy de la Bretèque terms a "pattern of integration," "the democratic and liberal version of the chivalric myth."[47] For example, in *Kingdom of Heaven*, one of the major subtexts is that knighthood — like the Crusades themselves in intention — is not an automatic right, nor an unwelcome byproduct of an exploitative regime, but it is instead an opportunity to serve one's fellow men, respect one's enemies, and protect the weak. Director Ridley Scott makes clear efforts to distance himself from the notion of knighthood as a privileged and oppressive stratum of society — and thus he subscribes to a modernized view of the Middle Ages in which knighthood is *earned* and not *inherited*. Rather than relying on an automatic conferment of knighthood, it is made clear to Balian that he must train both physically and mentally, yet, at the same time his actual accession to his father's barony (as an illegitimate child and the widow of a suicide) runs counter to the sacred institution and his later position of *miles Christi*. In this case, knighthood becomes neither the preserve of an elite nor the reward for loyal service, but along with service in the Holy Land, becomes a way of allowing Balian to atone for his past sins as well as those of his father.

The undercurrent running through the film supports this reading, emphasizing that the past itself does not matter as much as the future one carves out for oneself; Godfrey de Ibelin, Balian's father, receiving Extreme Unction, professes his repentance for all his sins, but staring at his illegitimate son recants, "all but one." For his part, too, Balian's "relic" to his deceased wife is conveniently a crucifix, thus his meditation upon it corresponds to the iconography of devout prayer, recalling the requisite vigil for adepts awaiting knighthood. His meditations therefore create an unresolved ambiguity over whether he is praying for the future or is unrepentant about past sins; thus the recidivism of the two knights serve to reveal their underlying humanity.

This absolution of past transgressions does indeed present a parallel with the "spiritual cleansing" of the Crusades against which the film is set, a religious fervor already apparent in Urban II's proclamation at the council of Clermont that:

> All who die by the way, whether by land or by sea, or in battle against the pagans, *shall have immediate remission of sins*.... Let those who have been accustomed unjustly to wage private warfare against the faithful now go against the infidels and end with victory this war which should have been begun long ago. *Let those who for a long time have been robbers now become knights.* Let those who have been fighting against their brothers and relatives now fight in a proper way against the barbarians. Let those who have been serving as mercenaries for small pay now obtain the eternal reward. Let those who have been wearing themselves out in both body and soul now work for a double honour.[48]

Thus Scott manages to fuse the global narrative of the Crusades (in part, one suspects, to draw comparisons with current events) with the personal quest for absolution, all the while appealing to a democratic audience for whom an elitist caste of society has become rather unsavory.[49] Rather than being a reward which places the newly dubbed knight above his peers, Balian's admittance to the Order of Chivalry helps to construct it solely as an inauguration into the institution which will afford him the possibility of spiritual atonement through service.

This notion of knighthood thus has its roots in the perception of the knight as servant — rather than the more popular image of the privileged, baronial landlord of popular imagination. Nowhere is the servile nature of knighthood more explicitly brought out in the film than in Balian's dubbing ceremony, in which the duties of protection and the necessity of *earning* a higher status are explicitly underlined by the oath recited by his father:

> Be without fear in the face of your enemies. Be brave and upright that God may love thee. Speak the truth, always, even if it leads to your death. Safeguard the helpless. Do no wrong. That is your oath.[50]

In addition to the spoken oath (which, incidentally, is not repeated by Balian himself, lending support to his humbled position, since it implies instruction more than consent), the scene is populated by a number of visual clues to suggest the master/servant relationship over and above the natural father/son dialectic.

On his entrance, clad in penitential vestments, Balian is instructed to kneel. A close-up shot placed at the same level as Balian shows him looking upwards at his father, with fill lighting behind him to emulate the candles of the "sanctum," casting a shadow behind him and isolating him in the foreground. The short focal depth blurs the background into a homogeneous pale color which matches the robes worn by the knights, supported by strong key lighting from above, which recalls messianic imagery of illumination and religious enlightenment. By constructing Balian as a quasi-religious naïf, Scott undermines the notion of an unelected and unworthy fighting class, replacing it with an earned knighthood imparted only to those willing to serve. The shot bears a strong resemblance with other "conventional" dubbing ceremonies, which Amy de la Bretèque would term a *passage-obligé* of the chivalric film. Joshua Logan's *Camelot*, for example, uses exactly the same mise-en-scène and even lighting (high-angle key lighting emanating from the right of the camera) in order to show the initiation of Lancelot into the court. The main difference, however, is that in this instance that Lancelot wears an ornate silver suit of armor which risks undermining any sense of servitude, intimating a degree of wealth and riches. This aspect is, however, countered by placing the camera not at the level of the adept, but at the level of the king (in gold), in an effort to humble the newly dubbed knight and fix his place within a visual hierarchy, in which the knight visibly ranks higher than "the people," but nevertheless remains subservient to his king.

Another interesting notion is the position of the dubbing ceremony in the narrative sequence. In *Kingdom of Heaven*, the scene occurs about one-third of the way through the film, meaning that we do not meet Balian as a knight (which would imply that he is *already* worthy), but we see his training, placing us in a position to judge his merit. In *Camelot* the dubbing takes place almost exactly at the midpoint of the film, signaled overtly (and conveniently) for us by the insertion of a theatrical "entr'acte." In formally recognizing Lancelot as knight at this stage of the film, we are introduced to Lancelot as knight of the Round Table only after the initial set-up of the film's plot has been established, and the "starting positions" of the film's characters have already been subjected to a number of transformations. The bestowal of an elevated position within a social hierarchy thus ceases to resemble a feudal system which tends to be regarded as an antiquated, retrograde system based on unfairly conferred privilege, and instead resembles more than anything else the realization of the American Dream through the hard work and determination of the self-made man, that which Aronstein and Coiner have termed the "Democratisation of the Middle Ages."[51]

This meritocratic interpretation of knighthood finds its final support in a common topos in both medieval-themed films and elsewhere — that of the "reluctant hero."[52] Such a hero, drawn from the people, is a lowly underdog who is driven by circumstance, persuasion, coercion or exigency to rise up against an oppressor; having been driven to take a stand, his opposition comes to represent the convergence of private and public causes, which engenders popular support and places them inevitably (but unwillingly) into the power vacuum which their opposition creates. While by no means exclusively reserved for medieval films (the archetypal reluctant heroes like Spartacus and Ben-Hur — or their avatar General Maximus in *Gladiator*— belong, after all, to the classical period), the topos is perennially invoked in films set in the Middle Ages, perhaps because the popular version of the Middle Ages is made from an ideal balance of its constituent parts.

The feudal pyramid, for example, provides us with clearly demarcated lowly "underdogs," and itself represents (again, in the public mind) an oppressive regime; popular support comes from the perception that medieval peasants were at any moment ready to down tools and form ad-hoc angry mobs, rising up against their ideological oppressors. Thus not only does *Kingdom of Heaven*'s Balian represent a popular, post-colonial revolution in the Middle East (as well as his own expiation of guilt), but in the same way *Braveheart*'s Wallace combines a masculist vendetta with a rejection of Mother England's imperial yoke, *A Knight's Tale* conjoins William's dream of knighthood with a battle against unfair elitism, and even the Arthurian myth can be rewritten as a truly democratic royal appointment in *The Sword in the Stone* and again in Steve Barron's *Merlin*.

The reluctant hero therefore becomes a means of transmuting the formerly elitist and exclusive ranks of knighthood into something accessed only by those who have "taken a stand" and demonstrated the courage required to justify their status as a knight.

KNIGHTHOOD AS INSTITUTION

"But behold now ... I lay upon you all the Order of Chivalry.... Do no outrage nor murder nor any cruel or wicked thing; Fly from treason and all untruthfulness and dishonest dealing; Give mercy unto those that seek it."[53]

When Godefroi de Papincourt, the time-traveling knight of *Les Visiteurs*, is mistaken for a mentally imbalanced cousin of the former countess Béatrice, the CRS (the French equivalent of riot police) are called in. Finding and engaging the knight in the garden, the camera is pulled upwards and outwards into a long crane shot overlooking the "riot"; the policemen uniformly raise their shields, draw their batons, lower their helmet visors, and form a tightening circle around the knight. The scene draws a direct comparison between the two, evidently favoring the bravery and nobility of the knight who battles until the end (France, and the theatre group Le Splendid who were behind the film, would certainly have mixed memories of the riot police dating back to 1968, and immortalized in films like *Tout va bien* and later *La Haine*). Most crucially it places the camera far enough back to obscure the individuality of each policeman, emphasizing their part in the subjugation of the knight.

While this scene is intended to compare, for the benefit of a modern audience, the medieval knight with a modern armored policeman, in order to do so it is somewhat ironically using conventions codified — if not established — during the Middle Ages themselves. By masking the policemen and dressing them in black, they are playing on a trope even older than the black hat/white hat trope of the Western, because

> the Hero, who normally is also the star, not only has to ride a white horse wherever possible, but also has to wear an open-face helmet, in order to make absolutely sure that the audience gets a good look at the star's radiant brow, while the villain is hiding his sinister countenance behind a closed visor.[54]

Such use of darkness and concealment is a prominent motif in medieval literature,[55] most especially in an era which placed a great deal of emphasis on names and outward signs of identity,[56] and for whom anonymity can be tantamount to guilt or shame. In contrast to the antagonist's closed visor, the hero's identity is assured by his open helmet, which explains, for instance, the much criticized scene in *First Knight* in which Lancelot rides into battle without helmet: not only are we as an audience able to identify him more easily (though, it is true, this could be achieved by the use of identifying armor, as our medieval forebears have done, and as, say, *Excalibur* does, using the fleur-de-lys motif on Lancelot's shield), but it is also the telos of a chain of symbolic logic. By exposing their identity, the knights align themselves with the Good and the Just, rather than becoming the masked henchmen of an evil regime.

So how do films go about associating their knights with institutions? Reprising our example of the *Kingdom of Heaven*'s dubbing ceremony, in addition to the first two characteristics of this knighting process (taming aggression and meritocratic knighthood), we also notice that the ceremony bears remarkable liturgical overtones. Though overt references to God are pared down to the expression "so that God may love thee," there are many elements which highlight the rite of the original ceremony, which "implied both ritual and a non-military status."[57] These in turn reflect the problematic "militant knight-service" which characterized the knight's obligations during the period of the Second Crusade, under which "the knight was now expected to live by the ethical and religious standards formerly required only from the ruler, and to assume the ancient and royal obligations of protecting the poor and weak, including women."[58] The ceremony thus marked an initiation into more than a simply violent feudal order, but into a confraternity to which were appended a series of ethical and moral values. If we accept Kaeuper's postulation that "belief in the *right kind of violence* carried out vigorously *by the right people* is a cornerstone of [medieval chivalric] literature,"[59] then in medieval films we can see that by adding liturgical — or at least ritual — elements to the initiation ceremony, the filmmaker has fixed the concept of knighthood within the legitimizing aegis of the institution, which comes to represent the "right people."

A similar process can be seen at work in Robert Bresson's minimalist masterpiece, *Lancelot du Lac*, in which the knights representing the institution (and its concomitant battles and bloodshed) are masked to the point that they are seen as automata, merely enacting the will of the state ideology.[60] Conversely, when their more human failings are invoked (Lancelot's affair with Guinevere, for example), Bresson divests the characters of their restrictive armor and uncovers their faces to bring out the human (all too human?) side of his *modèles*.[61] By paring down his cinematography to frame only that which is strictly necessary, he obscures the faces and individuating features of his characters, with the result that the whole "army"—and indeed knighthood as a whole—has been subsumed into the institution, so that when the state self-destructs, the knights must ineluctably fall along with it.

As ever, the final word on such an iconic construction can be found with parodies of the genre. Though appearing well before many of the films under discussion, the knighting ceremony of Hubert Hawkins (Danny Kaye) in *The Court Jester* bears witness to the power of these iconic signs already by 1955.[62] Having been selected for knighthood purely to warrant his immediate dispatch in the lists, a storm brings forward the timing, forcing them not to abandon the ceremony but rather to speed it up, a suggestion enacted literally within the cinematography. In a masterful sequence which follows, Hawkins is knighted in double time, going through the sacred motions is a carefully choreographed ritual in which the knights (moving at double speed) are all filmed from a long shot, and move together in time to the drumbeat, whisking the unwitting adept along with them as they go.

Hawkins' involuntary participation in this ritual, losing individuality to be subsumed into the legitimizing institution, serves as a testament to the importance of the ritual to cinematic representations of knighthood and chivalry, since even for a parodic film designed to send up the grandiose pomp of the historical epics of the time, the institution of knighthood is deemed to be sufficiently important as both a plot device and a "passage obligé" to merit inclusion and, ipso facto, derision. The ritualization of the dubbing ceremony can thus be seen to impart a sense of legitimacy to a potentially wayward icon, establishing the knight as an unambiguous force for good.

Paradigmatic Influences

If we remember that the medieval referent gave us a complex range of attributes pertaining to the medieval knight, then we can instantly see that trying to translate such qualities directly into paradigms to be reflected in film is far from straightforward. In terms of any overt exhibition of them, we are immediately faced with any number of difficulties in trying to prove whether the modern cinema has managed to successfully convey any, let alone all, of these qualities through its various knights, not least of these problems being that such "qualities" must by necessity be demonstrated through actions (either affirmative to assert the hero's innate superiority, or else by their absence in order to upbraid a villain's "unchivalric" qualities). In the latter case, one such device is the paradigm of *knighthood by contrast*, which foregrounds "heroic qualities" by placing them in parallel with a villain who most evidently lacks these, a device which as we shall see in the next chapter is used to an even greater extent in medieval kingship on film.

Another way to demonstrate these qualities is to explicitly state what is expected of the knight, what we might call the paradigm of *prescribed knighthood*. This explication of knightly qualities is most often found in the dubbing ceremony, since one of the most common features of medieval chivalric films, as we have seen, involves the *training* of the knight. The acceptance of the adept into the ranks of chivalry thus becomes one of the "traditional ingredients of the knighthood epic" listed as "training of the youth, defence of the faith and loyalty to the crown."[63] Nevertheless, even this scene becomes relatively rare when we consider that, as I maintained in the section above, the dubbing ceremony has slipped into mainstream convention as a reward for having *already* performed the duties of a knight. Consequently, being a reward, it comes further and further towards the *close* of the film, and therefore obviates the need to explain its required values to the audience, which leads to the second characteristic, that knighthood is the reward for having *already* demonstrated those virtues without requiring them to be formally stated.

A third means, and the method which we will be examining in most depth here, is to align those qualities with another concept which is borrowed from elsewhere in the cinema. In this process, as I mentioned in chapter 2, instead of trying to use visual qualities to describe what the medieval knight was like, cinema uses a paradigmatic comparison to suggest that they showed certain similarities to another concept; instead of explaining the object, they connote the concept. In neither case do we access those traditions *directly*, but via a *mediated form* of these same fundamental tenets. In this respect, we will turn now to look at how cinema has borrowed from other paradigmatic structures, as well as from other films in order to understand the medieval knight. Retaining those notions of courage, respect, honor, self-sacrifice and service, we will see that films have often communicated these by recourse to two other, ready-made "chivalric" figures in the western cinema, namely the swashbuckling hero and the cowboy, which have both subsequently been moderated after the emergence in the 1990s of the "all-action hero."

THE SWASHBUCKLER KNIGHT

To anyone familiar with medieval-themed films made before the 1950s, it scarcely seems to be an exaggeration to say that one of the most influential models to which filmmakers have turned for inspiration has been the swashbuckling hero. It is a borrowing not without a certain degree of irony, since Jeffrey Richards has observed that the values of the swashbuckling gentleman hero are, in the first place, "the values of the knightly class, as embodied in the chivalric code."[64] Nevertheless, the confluence of the two trends (knight and swashbuckling hero) can certainly be traced back in film at least to Douglas Fairbanks' portrayal of Robin Hood which engendered "a heroic, bounding, sportive, chivalric hero who owes more to American-style dynamism than to specific European traditions."[65] The lasting influence of this film can thus go some way to explain why the appropriation of this swashbuckling paradigm should subsequently become attached, in particular, to Robin Hood more than any other medieval figure (and most especially, one who is "not exactly a knight," to quote Indiana Jones).[66] Nevertheless, a second reason lies in the physical advantage which Robin has over his armored counterparts, given the frenetic pace of the early swashbucklers (such as Fairbanks' and Flynn's *Robin Hood* films), the general athleticism of its heroes is incompatible with the heavy, restrictive armor of the medieval knight (particularly by the fifteenth century, the era most favored by Hollywood). It therefore makes much more practical sense for "those who fight" to be incarnated by Hood's outlaw in green tights rather than by the heavy "human tanks" familiar to us from storybooks and general historical memory.

The advantages of agility over the unwieldy suit of armor have been, in fact, overtly asserted throughout a range of medieval films. In films as diverse as *Prince Valiant*, *Ladyhawke* and *The Adventures of Robin Hood*, the outlaw heroes can be seen outwitting their heavily armored adversaries by leaping over them, crawling under them, diving through windows, or else slipping through gaps. Such an obviously comic effect has been used elsewhere in Disney's medieval cartoon *Knight for a Day*,[67] in which the chivalric hero wins the day by hiding in a suit of armor, or in *Robin Hood: Men in Tights*, where Robin fights a series of guards simply by knocking over the first one, which sets in motion a domino effect.[68]

It is a trope seized with relish by a number of filmmakers who sought to emphasize the "everyday hero" type of narrative, a modern avatar of the Bel Inconnu myth.[69] These include films like *Prince Valiant*, Navarre in *Ladyhawke*, and *The Black Shield of Falworth*, among others, in which the filmmaker goes to extraordinary lengths to demonstrate that the central protagonist contains all of the gentlemanly qualities of the knight by nature, but needs to be tempered on the surface by the acquisition of a courtly code, a trope parodied to excellent effect (as we saw above) in the dubbing scene of *The Court Jester*. These films (as with *Prince Valiant* and *Black Shield*) are most prone to following what we might call a "delayed knighthood" model, in which the characters are knighted at the dénouement in order to show that knighthood is a reward and not the preserve of an elite, superannuated feudal order.

Thus we are presented with a new type of knight which is a long way from the metal-clad battle machines we saw in the literary construct, but who is more often a scantily armed hero dueling energetically up staircases and swinging from chandeliers, or like *Prince Valiant*'s first cinema outing, diving out of windows, jumping drawbridges or any number of stunts during the course of their knightly duties. Such a re-imagination of knighthood, of course, seems to be less based on any historical interpretation of the Middle Ages or on any attempt to recreate the period in earnest, but rather on the iconography of Hollywood's swashbuckler instead. In Errol Flynn's immortal incarnation of *Robin Hood*, for example, "although its opening credits proclaim it to be based upon ancient Robin Hood legends, [the signs] tell us that we are in the land of the Hollywood swashbuckler."[70]

The drawback of such a visual code is that it creates something of a restrictive paradigm, so that "by 1938 [the release of *The Adventures of Robin Hood*], audiences knew what to expect of a costume drama featuring Flynn, de Havilland and Rathbone and the studio continued to mine this profitable genre."[71] In fact, so engrained did the two archetypes become that by the 1950s slew of epics it was almost to be expected, so that they in turn became combined with the Romantic hero, "perpetuating the convention of a thinly-moustachioed knight who is simultaneously a sort of Robin Hood figure [...] as well as his romantic descendents which are more or less conditioned by a re-reading of Breton themes mediated by nineteenth-century Anglo-Saxon sensibilities."[72] Thus the "bounding hero" ("l'héros bondissant") of the silent era represented the re-introduction of the swashbuckling model to the Middle Ages, giving birth to a new, Romantic medieval hero. Presiding over this birth was, of course, Walter Scott, for it was his "nineteenth-century Anglo-Saxon sensibilities" more than anything else which helped to both sanitize and reinvent a more palatable Middle Ages, furnishing it with a new idiom for subsequent generations. "Scott apprehended the Middle Ages on their spectacular, and more particularly, their military side. He exhibits their large, showy aspects; battles, processions, hunts, feasts in halls, tourneys, sieges and the like.... It was the literature of the knight, not of the monk that appealed to him."[73]

The one stable characteristic throughout the swashbuckling tradition, however, has been the hero's unbending adherence to a moral code, born of nobility of conduct, since "the singlemost common characteristic of the swash-buckling hero was that he was a gentleman."[74] Though this temporarily closed the circle of knighthood which Hollywood was subsequently at pains to demo-cratize, the conflation of the two archetypes of knight and gentleman was not without some historical advantages. The figure of the swashbuckler entered Hollywood's vocabulary as a stock figure of the gentleman swordsmen (Fair-banks, Flynn, (etc.), whose triple duties are to serve the crown, preserve one's honor and protect the girl. Thus, although they were formulated during the emergence of a different paradigm (particular the Musketeers of Dumas and the courtiers of a later age), these threefold duties of the gentleman swordsmen are also the chief duties of the romanticized medieval knight in the first place, which I have outlined above in Part I. As a result, the fusion of the two (gen-tleman swordsman and swashbuckling knight) allows Hollywood to achieve its original goal: by using a swashbuckling mold, their hero is already infused with the ideals of chivalry, and they have no longer to contort the narrative in order to display to an audience whether or not their hero is "knightly" enough.

The type of hero produced by a fusion with the swashbuckler is often, like Robin Hood, aristocratic (and therefore nominally superior in degree), but despite his boundless enthusiasm, his vulnerability to traps and pitfalls, and underlying humanity prevent him from being anything other than equal in kind to his fellow men. We can see instantly here (perhaps by happy coin-cidence) a rapport with the heroes of the romances mentioned above, whose feats of derring-do placed them equally within the high mimetic mode. It is by no means, of course, an accurate depiction of the Middle Ages, but it does reflect a certain serendipitous similarity to the archetypal knight found in Chrétien's *Lancelot* and *Yvain*, and whose counterpart I have been trying to locate in the cinema. The hero therefore becomes idealized while equally sweeping away any of the negative consequences. As Williams observes:

> In Hollywood's Middle Ages, until the end of the fifties, there persists a kind of idealization deriving more from the romantic gloss through which the swashbuckling past is viewed than from an understanding of the idealism inherent in the medieval material.[75]

It was during the 1950s, however, that the dominance of this romanticized "gloss" was to fade, and even when it did so, it was only the surface of the medieval knight which was to change in order to avoid the same fate as the swashbuckler was to face. With the rise of the epics, and the concomitant evolution of new technologies available to shoot them even more spectacularly, the "glories of Babylon and Rome" could not provide enough raw material to fuel the audience's desire for bigger and brasher spectacle.[76] Thus the knight found himself once again quite literally in the spotlight, since "chivalric epics figure prominently in the cinema of the 1950s and 1960s because Cinema-Scope, Technicolor and casts of thousands were perfect vehicles for the reconstruction of feasts, jousts and battles,"[77] of which three, naturally, the knight is the sole protagonist. Despite its codes being formalized during the silent era, then, "medieval cinema came into its own most of all in the 1950s."[78] By this period, however, the wane of the swashbuckler forced a new reference point for the knight, from the boundless energies of the men in tights to the laconic loner of the Western.

THE COWBOY KNIGHT

If the swashbuckler of the first half of the last century was to serve as a celebration of the body of the knight, for its values and ethics, mainstream cinema (and to some extent the already burgeoning independent or national cinemas in Italy and France) was to turn to the cowboy of the plains rather than the forests of the Middle Ages. It is a move which makes sense, after all, for the tastes and mores of the cowboy had been, for a decade at least, carefully cultivated to appease those same tastes and mores of its contemporary American audiences, thus establishing already a rapport between audience and hero.

Second, the rapport between knight and cowboy is surprisingly neat, since both figures share a number of similarities: martial prowess, obligation to aid women, self-sacrifice, a rigid code of honor and unfailing courage. Furthermore, although it is relatively rare to find an explicit exposition of the chivalric code within medieval-themed films (other than by the use of a "delayed knighthood" reward or by using the dubbing ceremony to outline those values), the cowboy/gunslinger is seldom reticent when it comes to expounding exactly those themes of courage and honor. Evidence of the palatable humility of the knights of the Wild West can be found in the lone gunman Shane's denial of prowess and refusal to take pride in his almost supernatural quick-draw — "A gun is a tool, Marian; no better or no worse than any other tool: an axe, a shovel or anything. A gun is as good or as bad as the man using it."[79] Equally, we find meditations on bravery in O'Reilly's refusal of praise for his "courage" in *The Magnificent Seven*, "you think I am brave because I carry a gun; well, your fathers are much braver because they carry responsibility.... I have never had this kind of courage. Running a farm, working like a mule every day with no guarantee anything will ever come of it. This is bravery."[80]

The final advantage offered by the appropriation of genre convention from the Western is that it comes pre-packaged with a host of subsidiary characters which find a natural rapport with medieval counterparts; the sheriff/king, the villain, the native/barbarian as Other, and both knight and cowboy serve as pioneers into the unknown and uncivilized to instill justice and uphold social order, if necessary by the force of their weapons and their supernatural expertise in using them. In its simplest terms, "the most basic definition of the hero role in the Western is as the figure who resolves the conflict between pioneers and savages," just as the knight is often called upon to reconcile the extremes of the castle and the forest, representing civilization versus lawlessness in the medieval world.[81] Unlike the classical epics with their mythical heroes and gargantuan, *Conan*-inspired wastelands, "the cinematographic Middle Ages evokes instead a precisely defined space, like the Western,"[82] intimating that both the archetypes and the physical spaces are sufficiently clear and defined to provide the filmmaker with an "oven-ready" Middle Ages, replete with its own rules and conventions. These conventions can, by repetition, devolve into archetypes:

> When it comes to filmmaking, *the medieval period can bear comparisons with a Western. The archetypes are really clear.* You know where you are. There's a hierarchy; a King, the serfs, and you can play with these.[83]

Whereas I have argued above that the swashbuckling knight conforms much more closely to the courtly, chivalric notion of knighthood held by modern audiences, it is in the cowboy knight that we find many more of the qualities of the *miles Christi*—if only we are prepared to separate out its overtly religious qualities. Given the generally laic mood of Hollywood in the 1950s, such a distillation of the more obvious Christian elements of knighthood would leave us with a hero who works in service to an (unspecified) higher power, and who uses this higher power in order to justify and uphold a particular social or moral code — if necessary by resorting to physical violence. Adopting this non-denominational definition of Christian knighthood, then, we are able to see a remarkable similarity between the cowboy archetype outlined above and that of the Crusading knight. These similarities can be seen more openly if we consider the oaths sworn by Arthur's knights in *Knights of the Round Table*[84] — to fear God, to honor the king, and to defend the kingdom — which Bretèque argues resemble more the Scouts' honor than the medieval knight:

> In form, this oath seems to repeat what Romantic medieval novels spoke of regarding the spiritual mission of chivalry. But it is coloured, in fact, by a democratic, laic and moralizing ideology, which is that of the United States.[85]

Both represent fundamentally violent men (since both the Western and the medieval film genre are distinctly male-oriented) who operate on the very extremes of society (what are, in effect, the frontiers between the known world and the Other), who operate according to a sharply delineated sense of right and wrong with very little ambiguity. Both invoke a higher power in order to ratify their actions, either in God ("God wills it") or honor ("a man's gotta do..."), but function in practice as the earthly agents of such a force, and uphold these codes of action with violence.

With a sufficient body of research already undertaken demonstrating a general acceptance that "the qualities ascribed to the cowboy are identical to those of the English [*sic*] knight [...] in fact, the cowboy can be seen as the American incarnation of the knight,"[86] it seems unnecessarily repetitive to explore this assertion in too much depth within the present study.[87] Furthermore, if such a connection is accepted between the two archetypes, we are also able to claim that — with regards to the "mode" of the cowboy — the democratization which mollifies a mainstream audience serves in the second instance to re-open the ranks of knighthood to any and all. If the sole criterion of technical prowess is harnessed in the service of a moral and social code of conduct, then it logically follows that all may join its ranks, irrespective of background, "station" and (perhaps even) merit. Significantly, for films made under the shadow of McCarthyism and accusations of un–American activities, the sole pre-requisite for both cowboy and knight is the protection of national interests, represented either by the town and its law code or by the castle and its lord. Such an unconditional acceptance into what had previously been represented as an elite stratum of society, of course, bears a strong resemblance to the ideological concerns which seek to represent knighthood as a self-justifying institution.

The second consequence comes when we consider the demise of the Western genre. If we accept the symbiotic interdependence of the cowboy/ knight archetypes, then its use ought more or less to coincide with the rise and fall of the cowboy in Hollywood mainstream cinema. Thus at the point when the potent cowboy icon fell out of favor (which Cawelti situates at some point in the late 1950s), we would expect to find that the paradigmatic knight/ cowboy rapprochement would equally disappear.[88] This is an assertion which is true in the main, for certainly at this point in Hollywood's history we can see that the lavish widescreen epics which so dominated the '50s and '60s were far less prevalent from 1964 onwards,[89] yet this downturn did not necessarily signify the wholesale abandonment of the archetype. With films throughout the '70s, '80s and '90s, such as *Excalibur*, *Dragonheart* et al., we can see in the pioneering myths and the gritty stoicism of their knightly heroes traces which have proved difficult to shake off. Furthermore this is to forget that the same process happened to the cowboy figure as happened to the swashbuckler; rather than simply disappear, the archetypal knight/cowboy enacted a slow transmutation from one character type to another, even though the essential values remained the same, causing "old-fashioned heroic virtues like courage and duty [to] give way to new ones like irony and detachment."[90] By the time we reach the mid–'90s *First Knight*, then, we find that instead of drawing from the codes of the Western, "Lancelot's character (like [*Top Gun*'s] Maverick) is drawn almost whole-cloth from the gun-for-hire exile of American Westerns."[91]

THE ALL-ACTION HERO

Thus as we move through the ages, we are able to see that the ways in which filmmakers have recast the figure of the medieval knight have often been influenced by dominant models drawn from parallel genres. It is interesting to note, therefore, that during the period of the 1970s and early '80s which saw the waning of archetypal masculine paradigms, there seems equally to be a marked paucity of chivalric films in the Hollywood tradition.[92] It is not until we reach the late '80s and early '90s, in fact, that medieval filmmakers are furnished with another sufficiently established male paradigm through which to view the concept of the knight, by means of films like *Braveheart* and *Robin Hood: Prince of Thieves*, which show their knights cast in the same mold as the dominant cultural paradigm of this new era: the all–American action hero. Even at first viewing, for example, it is hard to miss the similarities between *Braveheart*'s William Wallace and Gibson's earlier *Payback* or *Die Hard*'s John McClane; both are constructed as superhumanly strong, reluctant heroes (superior in *degree and kind*), operating at the fringes of a society which rejects and dispossesses them, and tolerating both excruciating physical levels of pain and stoically repressing emotional ties in their personal struggle against a corrupt system. Even Lancelot, the paragon of chivalry, subverts the received code of chivalry which highlights the concepts of honor and fidelity, being recast in *First Knight* as a merely itinerant swordsman who spurns the values of emotional attachment, a reincarnation applied unanimously to the "Knights" of *King Arthur*.[93] Consequently, a degree of interdependence emerges, with somewhat deleterious effects. If in trying to recreate our medieval knights we harness the audience appeal of the late nineties action hero which is in turn infused with every step by a reassertion of masculinity, then this machismo begins to rub off on the recasting of the medieval knight, which has a lasting effect on the mold by which they are subsequently cast.

To compare two scenes based on the same character, here the Robin Hood of *Ivanhoe* with that of Reynolds' *Prince of Thieves* (20th Century–Fox, 1991),[94] we can see the effect of the paradigm in action. In the first of these two films, Robin is presented as a minor figure within a panoply of group affiliations (outlaws, Saxons, Normans, Jews and peasants), who is situated outside of the main character arcs until he is drawn into the narrative at the tournament at Ashby, in which he volunteers his services to Ivanhoe.[95] What is interesting here is his motivation for pledging an allegiance; impressed by his martial prowess and stoical tolerance of pain, he advances from the stand in order to offer his services to the hero. His motivation, therefore, is to serve Ivanhoe in a battle against a corrupt establishment, expressing solidarity not based on values of courtly prowess and honor, but on the ongoing conflict fought at the frontier between right and wrong within a clear moral spectrum. While *Ivanhoe*'s Robin is visibly impressed by the hero's skill at the joust, his solidarity is based not on a reassertion of masculinity but by recognizing the hero's willingness to operate outside of normative societal values in service of a higher power — be it moral, religious or a sense of social duty.[96]

If we compare this to Robin's outing in 1991, we can see instantly that he is operating on a wholly different set of values. Robin's personal motivation to overthrow the sheriff (and, by extension, the usurper Prince John) is predicated not on a sense of moral or social injustice, but rather by a personal sense of vengeance for the murder of his father and the confiscation of the lands which were his rightful inheritance. This already male-dominated competition is exacerbated by the introduction of Marian as a female "object" over which the two rivals are fighting. More than simply a moral issue of right or wrong, then, the conflict becomes an attempt to establish male dominance as both a fearless fighter and an unsurpassed lover, creating a virile reflection of the "perfect" knight's mastery of both love and death: regardless of Mel Brooks' famous jibe, we are a long way away from men in tights. The reinterpretation of the knight as a virile, powerful warrior somewhat ironically serves to turn the knighthood paradigm back to its literary origins outlined in the introduction to this chapter; having begun as a bellicose warrior surviving by his wits and martial prowess, the all-action hero delivers the knights from their gentlemanly, chivalric code (demonstrated in the swashbuckler) and returns them back to the Dark Ages.

The second difference here, which equally reflects their similarities to Beowulf and Roland, is in the way in which these "knights" redress the balance. Where Robin and Ivanhoe join forces to storm the castle by a combination of sheer numbers, persistence and bravery, Costner's Robin attacks the castle of Nottingham by individual cunning, stealth, trickery and a supernatural skill with a bow and arrow, shearing through the ropes of the hangman's noose, igniting barrels of gunpowder or firing in quick succession at a rate equaled only by the Elven warrior Legolas in the *Lord of the Rings*.[97] Thus the twin forces of motivation and skill become most susceptible to change as we move across the paradigms. Where once the much-vaunted medieval values of service, righteousness and prowess were sufficient, in the action-hero we may well see these same societal needs being redressed, but we must *also* be faced with a personal motivation for our hero to be drawn forth from the crowd. The hero's masculinity, therefore, is reasserted not by being the "born hero" in the first place, but by being the character who has the courage to emerge from the general populace in order to redress the wrong done to him: a wrong which often serves in the narrative cinema to indicate that somehow the hero wasn't "man enough" to prevent its occurrence in the first place. Robin Hood as action hero, then, no longer protects the weak because he feels he should, but rather he pursues the villain because he had not protected the weak in the first place, and must consequently atone for his emasculation by reasserting his virility. William Wallace, too, embarks on his quest to avenge his wife's death in part because of his powerlessness at the time of the attack; it is therefore significant that part of this revenge consists of cuckolding the prince, a recapitulation of both Wallace's virility and the prince's lack of it. By the time that we arrive at Fuqua's high-octane repackaging of the Arthurian legend, we have less of a Round Table of chivalry than a beefed-up posse, and our "knights" owe rather more to *The Magnificent Seven* than the *Siete Partidas*.

As we move into the twenty-first century, however, this mood changes again. The divorce from spirituality and the generally ambivalent mood of post-modernity begins to replace the lost spiritual motivation of the Crusader in *Kingdom of Heaven*, infusing the hitherto dichotomous "anti-infidel" ideology with a sense of vendetta. Such a heightened sense of personalized revenge thus reduces the tension of the film to a polarization of protagonist vs. antagonist, emptying in the process the service to society which was present in the medieval hero.[98] It is a motif which finds a great deal of sympathy with *King Arthur*, and *Tristan and Isolde*: no longer able to conjure up a feudal order imbued with a twofold chivalric duty to king and to courtly love, the film instead paints King Mark as simply a rejected, powerful suitor, playing up the relationship between Tristan and Mark as more of a surrogate father and son, and thereby subsuming the loyalty motif to a form of Oedipal struggle. This same vengeance motif strikes such a chord with a contemporary film audience — perhaps reflective of a more tit-for-tat sentiment in an increasingly litigious society — that it has spread to other subjects, coloring even the resurrection of the sister genre to the Middle Ages, the sword and sandals epic as seen in Ridley Scott's *Gladiator*, whose unfailing adherence to duty and the ideal of Rome is undermined only by a sense of personal vengeance for the murder of Marcus Aurelius, cast in the film not as a moral issue, but as the loss of a father figure.[99]

Conclusions

The semiotic construction of knighthood — in the chivalric sense identified above — is thus achieved by a mediation of a field of established signs.

In the first section of this chapter, I established that in terms of a medieval referent, we are confronted with two problems: one of the concept (that the "knight" was a paradoxical and permanently evolving notion throughout the Middle Ages) and one of the sources (that its reflection in literature, since the literary knight seems to have risked an idealization creating a notion of "chivalry [which] owes more to the pen than to the sword"[100]). When it comes to representing these in film, the absence of a clear, stable referent means that filmmakers are placed already at one remove from the medieval knight and consequently have frequent recourse to a series of paradigms and icons in their attempts to reconnect to this notion.

The first process was an iconic one, in which the characteristics which are most readily identifiable with chivalry are incorporated into a visual framework. These, I have argued, function to provide a specific "ideal" of knighthood, which is established by qualifying a number of aspects of knighthood. First, I argued that the raw aggression which may well have brought knighthood into existence had to be pared down for the big screen, by the use of vengeance themes to justify them, and by increasing the delay between action and retaliation. Secondly, since the elitism of knighthood risks alienating modern viewers, I argued that modern films had a tendency to represent knighthood not as a closed circle but an open rank attained as a reward for good service. In this respect, for example, dubbing ceremonies are often delayed to the end of films, in order to stand for the typical dénouement in which the just are rewarded and the evil are punished. The final iconic aspect examined was to impart a sense of legitimacy to the knight by presenting knighthood into an institution.

The paradigms, drawn from parallel genres (the swashbuckler and the Western), often serve to provide a familiar framework which audiences can use as an "analogy" for medieval society. Where the Western provides the ideals, the threat of the externalized Other, and contextualizes the violence of a society living on a dangerous frontier, I have shown that the swashbuckler on the other hand works on an assimilation of the athletic, martial, and gentlemanly conduct of its stars into the post-medieval re-imagination of chivalry. These two paradigms were ultimately to find their way into the emergent paradigm of the action hero, providing the knight with almost (but not quite) superhuman skill and a vendetta as a personal motivation, in order to present the knight as a perfect version of ourselves, who is dedicated to the service and honor which we nostalgically assign to the Middle Ages.

It is, however, in the notion of service that we find some particular difficulties for a modern audience, since it belongs within a feudal paradigm at once familiar and foreign, idealized and yet vilified. It is made familiar both by its gradual codification in films from the 1950s onwards as well as by the continued popularity of its literary descendant, the chivalric romance or epic; yet it is also foreign because the arrangement of society into strict social strata is largely considered to be anathema to a modern audience. Nevertheless, ranking among the most prominent characteristics of the extensive chivalric body of literature (both within and beyond the Middle Ages), duty, honor and service have frequently been painted as noble and praiseworthy qualities in the feudal era. Yet when these notions of service and honor come to be applied to the higher and lower echelons of medieval society, we find them to be more difficult to ennoble than in the creation of the knight. The place of the peasant, for example, being bound to a life of servitude, is often used to provoke an unthinking, antagonistic reaction to the Middle Ages, giving support to the modern uses of the term "medieval" to indicate something primitive, barbaric or unflinchingly cruel.[101] At the other extreme, however, the king presents us with a similarly unstable referent which can also conjure up an image of an unjust society, based on heredity and unfair usurpation. It is, then, to this latter problem of the representation of kingship that we will next turn.

4

The Power and the Glory: Those Who Rule

Philippe: "I am no man's boy. I am a King."[1]

Given the subtlety of the vassalatic links, the intermingling of political allegiances, and the complexity of medieval civilization in Western Europe, as well as its perpetually changing nature throughout the Middle Ages, when examining the category of "those who rule," some very specific parameters are here necessary to avoid becoming caught up in the intricacies of medieval power structures. To this end, I have chosen to focus exclusively on the figure of the king as he appears in cinema, although as we will see many of the arguments I put forward are equally valid, *pars pro toto*, when applied to the various lords, barons, liege-men, manorial knights, sub-kings, regents, princes, officers, sheriffs and so on.

A second — but no less important — exclusion has been made on the basis of gender, since the examples which I adduce are almost without exception male. The reasons for such a decision are twofold; first, although there have been some excellent studies on the subject already undertaken, much that could be said about medieval queenship has little to do with the cinema,[2] and second, within the corpus studied I have uncovered very few films which directly engage with the issue of the medieval queen (perhaps precisely because of the complexities of understanding queenship in the first place).[3] As a rule, "with the exception of one or two very recent developments, female protagonists in films and novels set in the Middle Ages are seen as objects to be seized or used, or else as treasures to steal or fight over."[4] However, my exclusions can to some extent be justified by noting that the various depictions of medieval kings studied here serve to create a paradigm of kingship, which is recalled in the depiction of queens, lords or minor rulers (which I will discuss as "sub-kings" in Part III). The argument *ex silencio* which emerges is therefore one which I believe may be borne out by an examination of other films —

that when trying to depict the varied and numerous subordinates throughout medieval society (including queens), filmmakers have very often resorted to precisely those tropes elaborated in respect of kingship (along with those of the sub-king) described below.

My third exclusion is one of nationality, since I focus chiefly on English monarchs. It is true that certain French kings do appear over a number of films (the Dauphin and future King Charles VII of France in Joan of Arc movies, Louis XI in the series of films featuring François Villon),[5] as do sporadic instances of individual kings such as Dagobert I, Louis VI or Philippe I; nevertheless, with the exception of the parodic depiction of Dagobert, these kings most frequently play supporting roles, ceding the limelight to Joan of Arc, Villon, Godefroi and Henry II.[6] English kings, on the other hand, have fared much better, with the result that "in medieval film, the kings *par excellence* are the Kings of England," perhaps because for French audiences the 1789 revolution created a rupture in continuity which is not reflected in their English counterparts.[7] A second explanation can be found in the lingering influence of Shakespearean models of kingship which leave their mark on the way in which filmmakers come to re-imagine their monarchs (with which, for example, Zeffirelli, Rohmer, Rossellini and Donner are certainly familiar, having produced their own Shakespearean film adaptations). The immediacy and longevity of Shakespearean kings thus proves an enormous temptation for a filmmaker struggling to produce a verisimilar version of a medieval king; consequently "the cinema, when it wants to film the political aspects of a given historical period, turns readily to a theatrical mould."[8]

The Medieval Referent

"Commonwealths would be blessed if they were guided by those who make wisdom their study, or if those who guided them would make wisdom their study...."[9]

In order to examine individual influences in filmmakers' conceptions of medieval kingship, however, we must first try to get an idea of what the concept of the medieval king actually was, what it meant in the Middle Ages, and therefore which elements are most important to retain. Turning to scholarship, we find that significant studies in this field, such as Kantorowicz, Figgis and Brooke, are fundamentally (and frustratingly) at odds in their conclusions about the exact nature of kingship in the periods in which they each specialize.[10] Throughout the wealth of criticism, however, it is precisely this disagreement which helps to make clear one fundamental truth: that there was certainly never any fixed and clear typology of medieval kingship. Many of these histories are eventually forced to conclude that there is a great deal of scope to "fill in the gaps," such as Brooke's appropriate metaphor in which he resigns us to the fact that "we are constantly tantalised by problems we cannot solve; our early kings appear before us like a row of unfinished portraits."[11]

We might, however, identify at least three overriding notions of kingship which emerge from these studies, as well as those coming from general ideas held about kingship/leadership among lay audiences. The first is overwhelmingly that *the king is wise*, and that it is his wisdom over and above his ability to fight which differentiates a good leader from a bad one. Such a notion has roots traceable as far back as Biblical models of good governance in the form of Solomon and David, in which support for kingship came from Old Testament models,[12] which meant that medieval kings were often keen to consolidate their positions by appeal to Biblical models in terms of practices (such as anointing) and politico-theology (using Jeremiah 1:5 as support).[13] Nevertheless, when drawing evidence from Biblical comparisons, Sawyer and Wood remind us that "it is not always easy to discern whether kings acted in a particular way because of the Bible, or whether priests described what kings were doing in Biblical terms, because the Bible provided appropriate language."[14]

The second is that certainly by the twelfth century, medieval society "organises itself strongly around two principles of order: the King and the feudal pyramid."[15] The consequence of this to the medieval referent is that the idea of the king cannot be imagined without also taking into account the various substrata of the feudal pyramid. "For the King, as for his subjects, the whole power of the State was concentrated in the monarch."[16] One can be a king only over a kingdom, and thus in the minds of medieval society at large *the king functions as the lynchpin for society and sits at the head of a feudal pyramid.* Should the king fall, or be challenged, then the entire social order can be seen to falter, as the Hundred Years' War and the War of the Roses in the fourteenth and fifteenth centuries were to show.

This second aspect leads to the third; *the king becomes a metonym for the whole nation over which he presides.* In just the same way as we still talk metonymically about the power of "the crown," so too "in the later Middle Ages the idea was current that in the Crown the whole body politic was present — from king to lords and commons down to the least liege-man."[17] The idea of the king becoming a symbol for the entire nation finds a correlation with Macrobius' claim that, in general, "the world is man writ large, and man is the world writ small."[18] Such a conception of kingship means that when it comes to representing nationhood as a whole, it can occasionally suffice to talk only of the king of that nation (as indeed Shakespearean plays were later to demonstrate), meaning only the kings of those nations and not, for obvious reasons, the entire populace.

Iconic Recreation of Kingship

It is, then, this threefold conception of kingship which dominates the medieval referent as we, in the twentieth and twenty-first centuries, go about understanding it. To imagine a medieval king, we might conclude, is to imagine not the complex totality of relations, of internecine political wrangling, nor even of the two bodies and contentious struggle for power between the secular and the religious, but it is rather *to imagine someone who is wise, powerful and the head of a nation.* When a given filmmaker therefore tries to reconnect a signifier to the medieval signified, he or she is by necessity trying simply to demonstrate that these three notions — fundamental to the audience — are all sufficiently clear to enable us to identify him as a king.

In order that these internal aspects of kingship might be converted into iconic signs, however, they must find an appropriate range of outward signs which communicate them to a modern audience. We are looking for, consequently, a range of *indexical signs*, which will lead a viewer to associate the visible sign to a specific image or concept, and it is to these signs that we will next turn.

WISDOM

"Knowledge and wisdom are the real power."[19]

With regards to the first of these signs, wisdom, fortuitously we have inherited from a range of cultures (Biblical, classical, mythological and medieval) a traditional association of age with sagacity. Thus the ideal king is often portrayed as a middle-aged, or even elderly, man — the subtext suggesting, of course, that after the accumulation of a lifetime's wisdom, he is in the position to rely on experience and learning — whose other signifiers in film have often been a beard, gray hair, and a Stoic, impassive temperance.[20] By relying on a direct link with these other cultures, these signifiers were slowly developed within the cinema by a similar process of accretion which we have seen elsewhere. They were, however, most notably consolidated in the modern cinema by the MGM historicals of the 1950s, a franchise which normally makes more use of a paradigmatic return to the period than by carefully reconstructing its signifiers.[21] In these medieval epics, as well as in the Classical and Biblical epics churned out in their droves by the Hollywood industry in the second half of the twentieth century, we can see the gradual evolution of a stock character: the sagacious old man, who often also appears in the capacity of what I have labeled a "sub-king."

The series of "sub-kings" and kingly figures, having been established through their perpetuation and constant repetition, became almost interchangeable, as we see with the example of Finlay Currie's Alfgar in *The Black Rose*,[22] where he plays a Saxon chieftain displaced by the Norman "invasion."[23] Two years later, in *Ivanhoe*, we find Currie reprising the same role as Cedric, the Saxon chieftain and father of the eponymous hero, and equally making use of a partnership with Felix Aylmer, each of whom perpetuate a series of intertextual models which gave birth to our idea of an aged king.[24] As bearded, graying figures, they impart the sagacity of traditional images of authority, established by an intertextual paradigm which equates age with wisdom, inherited from literary topoi and artistic trends witnessed in artworks as diverse as the Nine Worthies and Pre-Raphaelite depictions of Apostles, Saints and — most importantly here — Old Testament kings and prophets, from Noah and Abraham down to Solomon. This partnership of Aylmer and Currie then continued in *Saint Joan*, with Currie playing a host of other kingly figures in later films, coming almost single-handedly to become a stock symbol of "wise authority" — and thus establishing the topos which later films were to reprise. Comedies and low-budget pepla films — whose ideas about history often draw not on scholarship, but on *other films* — have proved to be particularly reliant on such visual shortcuts; to take only one example, we can see that the Pharisees in Monty Python's *Life of Brian* are visibly indebted to Charlton Heston's Moses in *The Ten Commandments*.

Thus in the creation of a series of iconic symbols of wisdom, a vast number of films — and even those which traditionally rely more heavily on paradigmatic association — have made use of the star-system, which allows them to import into one film something of the characterization built up in another. Currie and Aylmer, by their continued appearances in a number of similar roles, were therefore able to do two things. First, they could bring to any new film a certain air of sagacity lent to them by their previous roles; secondly, they established for posterity a very clear image of the wise counselor/king to which later generations of actors might appeal. One more recent instance of an appeal to this sagacious model of the ideal king comes in the form of Sean Connery, "the reigning king of Hollywood's Middle Ages ... [and] the emblem of a benign paternalism overseeing a young man's transition into adulthood."[25] Having played both of cinema's preferred medieval kings — King Arthur and King Richard — in addition to a host of paternalistic figures drawn from the Middle Ages,[26] Connery comes to symbolize the wisdom and experience of his most famous role as William of Baskerville, continuing the symbolism inherited from "stock actors" like Currie and Aylmer which we expect from our medieval kings.

One interesting iconic construction of the ideal king comes when we look at cinematic depictions of King Richard I. Despite appearing in more than fifty feature productions, he often occupies a marginal position, such as in Robin Hood or Ivanhoe treatments, whose plots usually unfold during his captivity or absence on Crusades. Thus there does appear to be some evidence to support the notion of a continued symbolism which remains unchallenged, since the relegation of the kingly figure to the sidelines does not require any form of character transformation. In one sense, then, we can argue that here the exception is made because his ideal kingship is established simply by default, using quasi–Aristotelian logic of the excluded middle; if Prince John — as we all *know*— is wicked, then anyone who is not John is an immediate improvement. Richard, consequently, is not only "not John," and therefore not present to make the kinds of unpopular decrees to which John is held to account, but he is also the Crusading hero, a paragon of chivalric exploits which we will encounter in the "king as knight" paradigm below. The use of Richard — though he has seen a decline in his importance in recent films (to the point that he is scarcely mentioned in Ridley Scott's *Kingdom of Heaven*, and is sometimes evoked only in name in Robin Hood productions) — has become a useful symbol of even, just and rightful kingship, based solely on a reputation of courage and martial acclaim, having almost never been depicted as an actively governing king. He is thus notable mainly by his absence from the screen, yet instantly recognizable when he returns, usually to signal to us that the film is over (and that service will shortly resume as normal).

His character is, however, only explored in a very few films. In *King Richard and the Crusaders*,[27] we find the filmmakers opting to emphasize the physical strength of the king over the sense of wisdom which comes with age, most notably when the titular hero provokes a blacksmith into an exchange of blows simply to prove that his is the more powerful arm.[28] We must acknowledge that the film version falls squarely in the Hollywood pageantry tradition, if only for its ridiculous romp through history under the ambitious tagline "The Mighty Story of Richard the Lion-Hearted!" including lines not without a certain homely appeal, lying as far from MGM mock-medieval as possible, from Richard's "Go squat on your Alps" to Saladin's claim that "these strange pale-eyed Goths show their hearts like bumps on a pomegranate." The reframing of international diplomacy as a domestic spat culminates in Lady Edith's (Virginia Mayo) immortal reproach: "war, war, war. That's all you ever think about, Dickie Plantagenet!"

Nevertheless, as the only film dedicated exclusively to Richard himself, it remains one of the very few films seriously to pose any challenge to his cinematic hegemony as ideal king and can also, owing more to the sheer length of screen-time devoted to him than any artistic merit, be credited as one of the most prevalent influences in creating a more rounded, cinematically "acceptable" image of the Coeur-de-Lion. This is bolstered by Butler's reading of the "Lionhearted" epithet itself—which was later parodied by Wolfgang Reitherman who depicts him quite literally as a lion—an epithet which is garnered to reinforce a sense of nobility and quintessential "Englishness," as well as a degree of fierceness. The lion iconology works, of course, on two levels: it emphasizes his martial prowess and war-loving status, but it also appeals to the folkloric notion of the lion as king of the jungle, traceable at least as far back as Aesop, and perpetuated throughout numerous literary incarnations such as *Le Roman de Renart*, the fables of La Fontaine and— more recently—animations such as Disney's *The Lion King* and *Madagascar*. Thus by courting this epithet of "Lionheart," films such as *King Richard and the Crusaders* compound his status as a bearded, appropriately leonine symbol of power and rectitude, unfailingly living up to his iconography in the popular imagination as the rightful king by the lion painted on his chest—"the obligatory attribute of anyone holding power"—or by the red cross of a Crusader.[29]

Even a casual glance at the various incarnations of Richard reveals not only the continued potency of this crusader/lion iconography, but also that despite a gap of over 50 years, filmmakers' ways of imagining the lionhearted king have scarcely varied at all. These images may be reduced further to three underpinning attributes: a beard, a lion/cross, and the color red, which consequently denote wisdom, courage/fortitude, and danger/passion. A second, and more telling, observation also arises in support of my claim above, regarding the equation of wisdom with age. Looking at a range of cinematic Richards in chronological order by film, the progression of the images reveals that, despite the fact that the events they recall all take place in the 1190s, as we go from the 1950s to 1991, Richard himself has steadily grown older.

To explain this disparity, we can see that it lies in the conflict between accuracy and authenticity which I will discuss in chapter 9. Though in reality Bloch makes the claim that the medieval world was a world "governed by young men," the cinema, for reasons outlined above, prefers the traditional wisdom of an older monarch.[30] This is, then, an example of the semiotic paradox (see Glossary), in which in order to communicate the concept faithfully, the filmmaker must betray the object; that is, in order to suggest the wisdom of the king (the concept), they must contradict the historical likelihood that the king was young (object). Given that to a medieval world "old age seemed to begin very early, as early as mature adult life with us,"[31] Richard I would have been considered well into his middle age (ruling from the age of 32 to 42); yet to a modern world for whom it is not unusual to see an accession to the throne after the age of fifty, an accurate portrayal of his age would make him seem a relatively young monarch. Consequently, in order to preserve fidelity to the idea and not the fact—that is, to authenticity and not accuracy — filmmakers often adjust his age accordingly, so that in Robin Hood films, when he would be around 32 to 35,[32] his cinematic counterparts are almost always played by older actors, such as Ian Glenn at the age of 44, Richard Harris at 46, George Sanders at 48, Peter Ustinov at 52, Patrick Stewart at 55, and even Sean Connery at 61.[33]

The reverse process happens when, in *The Lion in Winter*, Peter O'Toole plays Henry II; while Henry would have been 50 in 1183 (the film's explicit setting), O'Toole himself would have been only 35 at the time of filming. It is in this situation that we see the iconic process most potently, in that in order to make O'Toole *seem* like a fifty-year-old medieval king, the film's designers resort to precisely this iconography by adding a false beard and graying hair, historically symbols of age and therefore wisdom. Thus the outward symbols of this age and wisdom (long beard, gray hair, underscored by empowering low-angle camera shots) make use of the visual language which dominated the second half of the twentieth century as a way of signifying that a given character has the requisite experience, patience, fairness and sagacity to rule a kingdom. It is no surprise, therefore, that when searching to evoke the idea of wisdom and respectability requisite to the medieval referents, filmmakers have been quick to reprise this well-established iconography.

KING AS HEAD OF FEUDAL ORDER

"England is a ship. The King is Captain of that ship."[34]

This second notion of kingship is, evidently, a far more problematic one to convey using symbols of appearance alone. However, as far as the perpetuation of an iconic "language" is concerned, there is one way in which the cinematography helps to anchor the king within such a hierarchical societal structure, which is by manipulating of the architecture of the film space. Where the physical appearance of the king may lend an air of sagacity to the idea of kingship, and where even his extravagant clothing might suggest to us his riches, in order to fix the king firmly at the head of the feudal pyramid, we must turn to the cinematography, and most specifically the layout of the set, and the way in which the camera broaches and navigates the film space. The most poignant example of this can be seen in what we might call the "Great Hall" establishing shot, a visual trope employed in numerous films and which comes — perhaps without us even realizing it — to signify the grandeur of the king as the head of the feudal order.

In such a sequence, the standard establishing shots used to introduce the king in his court begin to follow a recognizable pattern. Beginning from a high-angle establishing shot which usually encompasses the Great Hall, we see it from either the point of view of a balcony (and therefore that of a spatially detached observer but one who is intimate enough to be granted access to the balcony) or from a visitor coming through the door (and therefore an outsider). The camera frequently either tracks downwards and sweeps through the hall or makes the same transition by a series of correlated camera angles, eventually coming to rest at the king's table. The symbolism here is unmistakable, placing the king at the head of his court, and converging all of the lines of the physical architecture to the camera's vanishing point places the king as the focal point of the mise-en-scène. Borrowing from religious iconography (including depictions of the Last Supper, the Crucifixion, and nativity scenes), the traveling shot is coupled with a low camera angle so as to emphasize the king's status as the hierarchical authority as well as — by extension — to highlight his spiritual importance as God's representative on earth. To the same ends, the camera uses the modern audience's understanding of the significance of a raised table, which implies that those physically closest to the king are also closest metaphorically speaking, and constructs the king as the pinnacle of these subjects.

This is precisely the case in the dubbing scene in Joshua Logan's *Camelot* mentioned in the previous chapter. Here the camera follows Arthur and Guinevere in a long tracking shot from their entrance to the Great Hall until they reach the top of the stairs. Clearly, by navigating the film space in this way, the camera assumes the perspective of a member of the royal retinue, placing us below, behind and at some distance away from the royal pair. The logical corollary of this is that we get a sense of the grandeur of the state occasion (in this case the dubbing of Lancelot); more importantly we can see that the status of the monarch is firmly fixed at the head of the state. The king and queen are placed at the center of the frame, and consequently form the apex of a triangle formed by both the lines of the architecture and by the rows of knights lining each side of the hall. They are further individualized (and therefore given a heightened sense of importance) by their appearance: golden, flowing robes to emphasize richness and luxury against silver armor, giving a sense of rich warmth against cold pallor; both monarchs' heads are uncovered, separating them from the closed helmets of their knights; their position in front of the elaborate window further individualizes them, for while they are in silhouette against the backlighting, the highly polished armor of the other knights intimates that they themselves are the source of light, while all others merely reflect their luminescence.

As we move through the twentieth century chronologically, it is interesting to find that despite the innumerable technological advances on other fronts, this hierarchical division of the film space is so powerful that it remains unchallenged. Even in a film like Gil Junger's *Black Knight*[35] which makes no real attempt at Historical veracity, we find that even though practically every other "medieval-esque" element of the cinematography is evoked only to be subverted, the establishing shot is still used unchallenged to identify and valorize the king (and even reprised to establish the rebel queen as an icon equal to the king in a later scene). Framed by both the arched entrance and the symmetry of the court, the lines once again converge on the central, raised, royal figures. These figures, once again, are individualized by the colors of their robes, their seated positions and the fact that they are the only figures who face the approaching camera.

Thus in order to connect to the medieval referent of a hierarchical order, we can see that cinematography, by a reappropriation of iconographic details from the fine arts, has been able to create a series of indexical signs which serve to translate this vertical hierarchy into a horizontal, spatial extension. Through the construction of a "Great Hall shot" the audience is able — by the creation and perpetuation of a generic "horizon of expectations" — to assign a respective importance to the characters framed within it.[36]

KING AS SYMBOL OF NATIONHOOD
"On your knees ... lower. I am Jerusalem."[37]

The final aspect of the medieval notion of kingship which films must try to interpret in the modern cinema is to present the king as a symbol of the nation, a distinctly problematic notion for the studio epics which pay less heed to an identifiable nation's history, preferring instead a more general "Olde Worlde" Middle Ages. It is noticeable, however, that after the general surfeit of historical epics was brought to a catastrophic close with the box office flop of, rather appropriately, *The Fall of the Roman Empire* in 1964, medieval-themed films began to adopt a far less grandiose scope in their portrayals, and in general became — as we have seen with *Camelot*— more personal character studies with a historical theme than the grandiloquent spectacle of their predecessors. This scaling down gave birth to a series of character films such as *Alfred the Great, The Lion in Winter, Becket* and *The War Lord,*[38] all made within an five-year period (1964–1969), yet which all pose a semiotic problem, since their focus is on reducing the highest echelons of the feudal order to the level of the everyman, thereby losing their iconic construction as "higher beings" explored in the previous section. How then might filmmakers communicate this new approach while still reminding viewers that the consequences of human failure have much wider ramifications when that human happens to be king? The answer, as the title of this subsection indicates, is that the king must be transformed into a symbol of the whole nation, making them "the world in small."[39]

The first noteworthy element among these films is the period chosen to be represented, with *Alfred the Great* and *The War Lord* representing two of the very few films which address the early medieval period (the ninth and eleventh centuries respectively). One explanation which offers itself is that their use of the king as a symbol for their nation finds a much more striking rapport with the earlier medieval period, since the personal character transformations are set against the backdrop of the era in which national states began to emerge in the form in which we know them today. Consequently these large-scale conflicts offering an inchoate form of national identity can be much more easily transferred to the concept of a king as personification of the nation over which he reigns.

When switching from the ostensibly twelfth- or fifteenth-century settings of the Arthurian world[40] to the early medieval period settings, the Middle Ages seem then to be painted in much more somber colors, moving from a stage of what Lindley describes as mythical "Beckett-time"[41]— the "temporally abstract Middle Ages" mentioned in chapter 2 — into real, datable history. Such a move into a "real," tangible historical period was not only restricted to the Early Medieval, either, since by situating one end of the period in a historical context, films made after the late 1960s depicting later periods were obliged to construct their worlds as chronologically sequential, representing real worlds in history rather than dream worlds in a mythological land far, far away. In *The Lion in Winter* and *Becket*, for example, the emphasis on place names (Chinon, the Vexin) and historical people (Henry II; Eleanor of Aquitaine; their sons Richard, Geoffrey and John; William Marshal; and Philip II) serves to place the two films firmly in a datable historical period. Furthermore, when kings needed to become symbols of the countries they rule, it was impossible to return to the mythical treasure chests in search of an ideal kingship, because such a movement would necessitate the invention of entire countries, thereby placing the whole film outside "real history" and into mythical no-time. With King Arthur already loaned to Hollywood, too, the confluence of these two trends meant that real nations began to be represented by "real" kings.

One secondary outcome, however, of the turn towards more personal biopics of the kings was that the films produced in the early to mid–1960s, such as *The War Lord*, *Alfred the Great*, and *A Walk with Love and Death*[42] — while still deeply representative of the decade of their production (and perhaps far more than the era they were trying to reproduce) — seemed to get much closer to the subjects of the Middle Ages than their epic counterparts, and can certainly be seen to situate their narratives around verifiable historical kings or events. Eschewing the grandiose gestures and mock-medieval speech which characterized the latter, they also began to turn away from the reinvented epics which were haunted by the specter of nineteenth-century Romanticism. While not exactly returning to medieval sources themselves, they did at least turn to a twentieth-century perception of the era, through plays (*The War Lord, The Lion in Winter, Camelot*) or through modern novels (*The Sword in the Stone, The Name of the Rose, A Walk with Love and Death*).

Thus, rather simply, the king himself comes to be constructed as an indexical sign for his country, in the same way as a Shakespearean character like Wessex or Cornwall refers properly to the area governed, for which the duke or earl has become a symbol. Donner's *Alfred the Great* in particular further highlights this association by choosing the troubled young king Alfred during a period in which the kingdom of Wessex was equally "young and troubled," following a mythological Fisher King motif which suggests that the fates of the nation are tied to the fate of the reigning monarch (reprised by Boorman's assertion that the king "and the land are one").[43] Throughout the film, the events in Alfred's life become mirrored by the realpolitik of the nation he represents — when he abandons the priesthood, Wessex too abandons God; when the king marries without love, the kingdom enters into loveless allegiances. Serving as a nexus through which the forces of circumstance and international intrigue are brought into sharp conflict, Alfred thus becomes the meeting point of national heroicism and a deeper, more personal struggle for identity.

From the very opening of the film we are presented with a model of kingship separated between Alfred the man and Alfred the king, a tension which is overcome in one bold stroke by having Ethelred die on his wedding night, making Alfred both king and husband in the same moment, marrying Aelswith for land and for the Land Herself. This tension between priesthood and kingship (though elaborately reconciled by Alfred's own writings in later life)[44] finds its visual expression in a close-up of Hemmings' dilemma: on the verge of taking his holy vows to enter the priesthood, he is called away to repel a Danish invasion. In the short but startling sequence which follows, this perceived dichotomy between priest and king is made explicit, as is the hasty decision spurred on by national expedient. A close-up of Alfred the priest staring out at camera from the extreme left of frame dissolves to a blood-red background, before turning to face a crowned Alfred the king, right of frame, who repeats the process by turning to stare back out again, this time on the extreme right of the frame.

By painting him as *either* priestly king *or* warrior-king, Donner risks the same Manichean oversimplification of which Alfred himself falls foul when he sulkily claims that he has been tricked by the council "to get me to renounce the priesthood and be a warrior-king." Furthermore, the metonymy which binds king to nation is perpetuated to the extent that when priest becomes warrior, the nation follows suit in this polarization. With no standing army, Alfred's attempts to "militarize" Wessex mean that monasteries become prisons, marshes become training grounds, peasants are scantily armed and drawn from the churches and lands in order to go to war, an effect supported by the use of grays, drab lighting, exterior locations and reducing the color palette to the same stark red as the transition scene described above.

The resolution of the conflict between king as priest/king as warrior is ultimately illustrated by a third close-up towards the end of the film, adopting exactly the same proportions, when at last he learns that the ideal kingship towards which he strives is based neither on a total "priestly" abnegation of his passion, nor from a "warlord's" expression of cruelty and demand for absolute obedience, but — as with many ideals — lies in a compromise between the two. In an exact recreation of the shot sequence above, a low-angle shot in the marshes paints him once again as a true king and national hero, placing him in direct center of the frame divested of all symbols of both priesthood and kingship. The blood-red background of the earlier sequence is here replaced by the marshes, indexically signifying the land over which he governs, thereby tying together the final maturity of the man as king and the land as a united front without bloodshed.

Paradigmatic Construction of Kingship

Having established the iconic symbols which cinema has used to connote the key elements of a modern understanding of kingship, here I will turn to the ways in which the cinema has reproduced it by paradigmatic association. In doing so, however, we uncover a certain difficulty, for in terms of the paradigms used themselves, there is a marked paucity of models of kingship available to the filmmaker, which can be partially explained by my earlier suggestion that the paradigm is far more frequently used by Hollywood than by other national cinemas. One plausible explanation for this is that, given the lack of monarchy in North America and the resistance of audiences everywhere to forms of autocratic rule, it seems unlikely that Hollywood and mainstream filmmakers would therefore possess any such model within their cinematic "vocabulary."

The overwhelming convention, therefore, for a paradigmatic association is to rely on the existing paradigm of medieval knighthood examined in the last chapter, and to highlight the pugilistic capacity of the king in order to imply a democratically *worthy election* rather than an automatic inheritance.[45] As we have seen, a modern audience tends to object to an automatic assumption of superiority, preferring to believe that our leaders are elected, and that, as Monty Python would have it, "supreme executive power derives from a mandate from the masses" instead of the dynastic subjugation which films so often imagine. Thus we have two major paradigms which this section will explore, both predicated on worthiness within a meritocracy rather than a natural deference to the prominence of an aristocracy: the king as a kind of knight, and the king as a worthy *senex*, a concept in turn inherited from a classical Roman model.

THE KING AS KNIGHT

"All the bravest and noblest of them rejoiced exceedingly that they had such a king, one who would risk his life in an adventure as other ordinary knights did."[46]

Turning first to the paradigm of the king as a kind of knight, we can see from the epigraph that what distinguishes a king in this respect is his continued ability (and volition) to fight to uphold justice and laws of the land, interpreting a regal power as a physical one. This paradigm is once again most evident within the current corpus in the 1950s and early '60s, dominated by the MGM–backed Richard Thorpe films *Ivanhoe*, *The Knights of the Round Table*, and *The Adventures of Quentin Durward* (MGM, 1955), each of which starred Robert Taylor, sparking a Taylor/Thorpe partnership which lasted throughout the decade and confirming Taylor's status as a matinee idol. Developing this partnership, these films succeeded in establishing a visual language from film to film which almost sets the standard for a whole range of subsequent medieval films, and gave birth to a legendary medieval world of vibrant Technicolor, sumptuously dressed sets populated by all–American knights of Olde England.

On the one hand, Taylor's successive portrayal of Lancelot, Ivanhoe and Quentin Durward created a codified system of knighthood, "perpetuating the convention of the knight with a thin moustache similar to the figure of Robin Hood [...] and his Romantic descendants."[47] This "convention" forms part of a visual language almost exclusively drawn from the later end of the Middle Ages, enabling them to conflate their nominal sixth-, twelfth-, and fifteenth-century settings[48] by reliance on the same set of historicons (and frequently even the same physical cinema sets) in order to communicate quickly and effectively the "historical" (if not necessarily specifically medieval) nature of the films, prompting Goimard to observe wryly that "medieval," to Hollywood at least, means "fifteenth-century."[49] The reason for this, according to Amy de la Bretèque, is that "the cinema loves to show the rituals and codes of chivalry as they were once they had been formalised at the end of the Middle Ages, because they are more spectacular."[50]

On the other hand, the figure of kingship established with this triptych of medieval historical epics is influenced by two factors. First, that these films are all derived from literary predecessors, namely Walter Scott and Malory (neither of whom wrote contemporaneously nor with any intention of seriously reproducing the period in which their works were nominally set) or else their imagination of the "real Middle Ages" has been filtered through romanticized notions of the period in terms of wardrobe, set-dressing or mock-medieval speech, or influenced by contemporaneous trends in the conventions outlined above. Such conceptions of the medieval period often represent a concatenation of neo-medieval beliefs, artifacts and nostalgic whimsy, since "the Middle Ages of the Nineteenth Century in the cinema deals not with the Middle Ages, but the idea of the Middle Ages as reconstructed during the Nineteenth Century."[51]

Second, being adaptations, the three films deviate marginally from their sources by placing their narrative focus on the knights of the film, motivated primarily by a love triangle, thereby relegating the figure of the king to a more secondary role.[52] The effect of this is that by foregrounding the convention of the late medieval knight, the king is placed in a subservient position with respect to the narrative, and the characters of the monarchs are not required to undergo any serious form of character transformation in order to bring the plot to its resolution. Equally, stressing the role of the knight over that of the king, to a 1950s and '60s audience the king becomes (as the epigraph suggests) simply an elevated kind of knight who is expected to behave exactly as his subjects do. This betrays a deep-rooted democratization of the Middle Ages, for what this suggests is that the right of kingship is due neither to designation nor inheritance, but rather hints that the king's authority is indebted to his superior physical ability.[53]

One advantage of portraying the king as a kind of knight in a logical extension of his chivalric court is that it creates a much closer rapprochement with his people, so that he can dine alongside them at court (*Lancelot and Guinevere, King Arthur*), joust alongside them in peace time (*King Richard and the Crusaders, A Knight's Tale*), and in certain cases fight alongside them in battle (*Knights of the Round Table, Excalibur, King Arthur*), and therefore appealing to an audience for whom the concept of an autocratic king who interferes directly with affairs of state is almost entirely foreign.[54] This is seen in *King Arthur*'s internal debate about national identity, for example, which depicts the Once and Future King as a Romano-Britain drawn from the plains of Sarmatia.[55] While Historically questionable in the extreme,[56] Bruckheimer's Arthur does have the advantage that in the climactic denouement of the film, when he symbolically removes his Roman-plumed helmet and dismounts in battle to join the ranks of the un-armored Woads, we are so attuned to this iconic convention that despite the illogicality of removing a helmet *before* engaging in battle, the paradigm of king as knight underscores his symbolic rebirth as hero of his people.[57]

In a similar vein, we patiently sit through five minutes of the first act of *Knights of the Round Table* watching Mel Ferrer and Robert Taylor battering each other with broadswords over the trifling matter of whose privilege it is to rescue their equally patiently waiting damsel, an episode repeated with only a little more flair in Boorman's *Excalibur* some twenty years later.[58] Yet *Knights of the Round Table* is by no means standard Hollywood fare, and highlights one disadvantage of imagining the king through the prism of chivalry. That the Arthur of Hollywood is here more knight than king is undeniable, but its logical inverse — that a knight is therefore a kind of king — produces some interesting results. Reprising his role in *Ivanhoe* as upholder of morality, honesty and decency, Robert Taylor in the role of Lancelot *already* manifests the attributes that we might otherwise expect rather from the model king than his worldly knight. By placing the adulterous knight in the forefront, and sanitizing the affair which brings about the downfall of Camelot, Thorpe's second collaboration seems to cast doubt on Arthur's legacy as an ideal (if impossible to reproduce) model of kingship. Given that he is never overtly cuckolded, Arthur's punishment of his best knight seems, like the equally chaste "adultery" of *First Knight*, to be mere jealousy, over-protectiveness and a churlish abuse of power, rather than representing a serious threat to the court.[59] Moreover, with the king no longer representing nationhood, the adultery loses the urgency of Malory, or of *La Queste del Saint Graal*, in which the betrayal of the king is a fourfold sin: betraying a friendship, infringing sacred marital vows, violating vassalatic vows of knighthood and posing a threat to the stability of the nation. Never does there emerge the same dilemma on which *Camelot, Excalibur,* and *The Sword of Lancelot* are all predicated: that for Arthur to be the perfect king he must recognize that the law extends to all men, kings and peasants alike.

The fourfold sin brings into the foreground a visual (though largely unrecognized) exemplification of the king's two bodies. Of Lancelot's four sins, two are against the man, and two against the king; in the same way, Guinevere's actions have betrayed the sacred bond of marriage to Arthur the man, but the serious crime (for which the death penalty is invoked) is the treason against the institution of the king. Joshua Logan in particular has Arthur forced to watch through a window overlooking the courtyard as Jenny (Guinevere) is to be burned, while David Hemmings' Mordred (cinema's former Alfred) watches Arthur in turn to ensure that the law is upheld to the point of the destruction of the king by the perpetuation of the King. This double spatial significance sees the elevation of the king (commoner courtyard / elevated window) against the psychological closure (open, cold exterior /

enclosed, warm interior), and leaving the rest of the film to play out these themes. There is no such personalization, however, in the Thorpe version of the story: Mel Ferrer's Arthur instead suffers stoically like the man-with-no-name cowboy ("a man's gotta do..."), reflecting Albert Johnson's claim of early medieval films that "it was obviously popular then [in the '30s] as now [in the '50s] to make historical monarchs assume many of the characteristics and codes of the traditional Western hero."[60]

A more difficult implication of the "king as knight" paradigm is that these kings must therefore be relatively young, in direct contrast to the iconic aspect of wisdom discussed above. These fighting kings are all in their twenties or mid-thirties at most (reflecting again the dictum that the medieval world was governed by young men),[61] a threefold indication of their virility, vitality and continued ability to fight. This idea of kingship reflects more the demands of the audience (who sought in their matinee idols a reassertion of masculinity, of power and of justice) than a logical or coherent appeal to the medieval referent outlined above. Clearly, by relying on a tradition which places young men on the throne — while also making use of an iconography whereby old age signifies wisdom — brings to the fore a certain contradiction: if the king is young, he can fight but does not symbolize sagacity; on the other hand, however, older kings might be wise, but are no longer able to fight. By highlighting the physical body of the king (over that of the political Body of the King), this series of films manages to sidestep any of the complex debates which plagued the institution of kingship — from the Investiture controversy to the Dissolution of the Monasteries — during the Middle Ages, and rage in both history and cinema today.[62]

The knights and the barons of cinema, however, have a much more clearly delineated temporal sphere of power over men and land, and are therefore comparable in the popular mind to statesmen, senators and politicians, kept clearly apart from issues of control on the spiritual plane, and as such bow unapologetically to the superiority of the Church.[63] Just as the knight (as Chrysagon ably demonstrates in *The War Lord*) is lord only in a strictly temporal sense over a specific area of land or body of men (hence his war caused by invoking the *ius primae noctis*, another highly dubious post-medieval construct), and is ultimately subject to a higher authority, so the king as knight may easily be made to sit on a purely temporal throne in the cinema, and subjected to a higher spiritual power, which in the laic world of film becomes the code of chivalry.[64]

In contrast to the previous section, which sees the crown as a metonym for the nation, the king as human becomes divested of all national symbolism, which has as a consequence the further distancing of the space of "the medieval" to a mythical no-place as well as no-time; England simply becomes

Olde England, and therefore is temporally disconnected to ideas we might have about the English nation today.[65] This kind of king is given over to knightly pursuits, and relieved of any obligation to legislate, govern or sit in state; all of the niceties (and therefore complexities and moral ambiguity) of actual governance are limited to the knightly, and not judicial, sense of right and wrong held by the literary construction of chivalry. Punitive measures are swiftly enforced by either *iudicium Dei* (*Knights of the Round Table, Ivanhoe*), by the sword (*Sword of Lancelot*), and by honor (*The War Lord*) or, less commonly, by legal trial (*First Knight, Saint Joan, Ivanhoe*, although the latter does resolve its trial by combat in any case); but not, in this vision of the king as knight, by any recourse to spiritual or Divine designation.[66]

So if, as we have shown, the paradigm of the king most favored by Hollywood has been to highlight his continued vitality and in turn his knightly status, we must therefore ask about where this second paradigm has come from. I have demonstrated in chapter 3 that when it comes to imagining knightly heroes, Hollywood has often turned to the Western genre to re-interpret their knights as medieval cowboys, fighting on the frontiers of society against the Other. In constructing the king as simply a knight elevated in degree to the throne, then a very neat comparison may be drawn between the sheriff of the Western and the medieval king. Both figures are raised up from the ranks of the cowboy to assume the responsibility of government by an overtly meritocratic process, engendering an essential tension which comes from a duty to uphold the law as it applies to all, constantly challenged by the need to enforce the law by violent means. This tension is based upon the paradox that the sheriff must be *capable* of physical violence, but in order to remain a sheriff he must refrain from resorting to it unless absolutely and unequivocally necessary.

It is scarcely surprising to find that films have re-appropriated this paradigm in two ways; first, by highlighting the vitality and virility of the king by constructing him as a knight, and second, by then removing him from the domain of physical and violent exertion of power. In *Excalibur*, this has even been interpreted visually, so that although he is dressed in plate armor (signifying his capacity for violence), it is both noticeably clean, polished (and therefore unused, as well as metaphorically blameless), and visibly ceremonial, and the heavy plates noticeably inhibit his movements, implying his excision from the physical enforcement of power.

THE SUB-KING

The use of a young king, therefore, has been shown to characterize kingship as a more palatable and democratic institution, which I have likened to the promotion of a frontier sheriff of the Western genre. However, when comparing this to the iconography of the wise old king, we find something of a paradox, since if the king is young he can fight but cannot symbolize sagacity, whereas older kings might fulfill the need for wisdom and temperance but are no longer able to fight. It is here, then, that many of the films relying on paradigmatic representations of the Middle Ages have killed two birds with one stone, so to speak, reconciling the need for democracy with the capacity for violence by introducing the concept of a "sub-king." In the example given, we see that *Excalibur* risks a compromise on both fronts, since all the signs point to a king too young to be "wise," and yet at the same time too "regal" to fight. This dilemma is resolved by the introduction of two subordinate models which each symbolize the perfection of the two extremes: for simplicity's sake, perhaps we might call them Merlin and Lancelot roles.[67] The ideal form of kingship in films relying on a paradigmatic ruler (and therefore not requiring a character transformation, or at the very least only a limited one) becomes thus a triumvirate comprising:

1. Arthur, a ruler who is drawn from the ranks of knighthood and therefore removed from violence but also too young to be considered wise;
2. Merlin, whose evolution in both literature and cinema alike has served to make of him an icon of sagacity, but who is too elderly to be able to enforce the law by violence;
3. Lancelot, whose function as a "sub-king" is precisely the reverse of Merlin's role as "counselor," in that he provides the requisite virility and violence in order to uphold the laws promulgated by "the wise."[68]

In *Knights of the Round Table,* for example, Thorpe has drawn on a clearly defined section of the Arthurian saga — the passage from newly crowned king to *rex quondam rexque futuris,* the embodiment of ideal kingship. Nevertheless, my comments about the impossibility of a cinematic ideal king notwithstanding, Thorpe cannot emphasize the two poles, but only the journey in between, and in doing so he provides us with precisely these two guides; Merlin represents the perfect embodiment of wisdom and sagacity of an elderly "king" figure (not to mention otherworldly magician, recalling John's Gospel),[69] while the perfect physical body of the king is upheld by Lancelot. His transition between the two, therefore, comes from two moments in the film in which Arthur is placed in parallel first with Lancelot (their duel which proves their equality in martial prowess) and the second in which Arthur re-enacts Merlin's ritual at Stonehenge and thus demonstrates that he has learned to reconcile the head with the body. The culmination of these two seemingly incompatible traits (wisdom and violence) is seen in the final battle between Arthur and Mordred which takes place at the close of the film, in which his use of violence is reluctant, but efficient — a perfect demonstration of that much-sought balance of "reasonable force." Lest we feel too confident, however, that this culmination ultimately paints Arthur as the ideal king, we must remember that concomitant with the tragedy of the Arthurian saga is also the necessity that Arthur achieves this ideal balance between the two extremes precisely at the moment in which the kingdom itself falls apart.

A similar process occurs within another of Richard Thorpe's "medieval epic" series, his version of *Ivanhoe* in 1952, which presents us with an interesting way of measuring the notion of an ideal kingship by explicitly foregrounding the close parallels between four "monarchical" figures, which may be loosely aligned with the three categories of the sage "Merlin" function, the actively ruling "Arthur" function, and the strong "Lancelot." In the first category we find Isaac of York, the Jewish banker and patriarch of the banking community in England, disenfranchised leader of a "tribe" living outside of society, who is placed in parallel with Cedric, the ousted Saxon king representative of the supplanted regime. In the second category lie the "rulers"; King Richard the Lionhearted is the ousted — but ideal — king of the new regime juxtaposed with Prince/King John, the usurper and tyrannical ruler, disbarred from legitimacy as ruler by laws of succession. Finally, in the third category, the two fighters are symbolized by Ivanhoe himself, the returning Crusader, and by Robin Hood, the ousted leader of a group of outlaws, living outside societal norms. The parallel between each of these figures of authority (in the first two categories) is supported by a number of narrative devices which divide them into two groups united under the old regime and the new.

As representatives of the "old," and the "Merlin" function, Isaac and Cedric are placed in parallel by their situations: both represent tribal leaders of a displaced and persecuted regime, both have young and beautiful wards in a typically constructed "princess" role, but to which royal positions neither can aspire any longer owing to racial barriers and not by dint of any personal actions. Both royal "families," then, are disinherited by events beyond their immediate control, and represent a displaced kingship, a confused position in the social hierarchy. Visually, these parallels are supported most prominently in the tournament at Ashby, in which Ivanhoe (the nexus through which these varied social networks are united) rides in the name of Richard, while championing the Saxon cause (naming Rowena the Saxon "princess" as the Queen of Beauty), lowering his lance in deference to Rebecca "the Jewess," and forming an allegiance with the outlaw Robin Hood. All four causes constitute challenges to the hegemony of John's usurpation, thereby establishing Ivanhoe as the symbol of the coalition of previously heterogeneous strata against the common enemy.[70] While the royal box shelters John sitting uneasily in his throne, a lesser "royal box" places Cedric (Finlay Currie) and Rowena (Joan

Fontaine) opposite the king (reinforced by the shot-reverse shot montage between the two royal units), and in the commoners' enclosure we find Isaac standing next to his daughter Rebecca, which three parallels reflect a certain "Lordship" over three social divisions based on overtly claimed preconceptions of racial superiority.

An interesting parallel overlooked in the film adaptation places Robin of Locksley as a further figure of kingship. In Scott's novel this parallel is more overtly crafted, and reinforced by Robin's claim that "in these glades I am monarch: they are my kingdom; and these my wild subjects could reck but little of my power, were I, within my own dominions, to yield place to mortal man," establishing him as leader of the outlaws, a further social grouping whose alienation from "civilized society" constitutes a further challenge to John's rule.[71] Yet this is a different marginalization, the outlaws being displaced by legal, not racial, discrimination; the racial outcasts can be portrayed as innocent victims of a social prejudice, rather than by legally dubious actions, whatever received wisdom may tell us about John's arbitrary sense of justice. In Thorpe's adaptation, however, the dubious legal status of Robin Hood (bearing in mind a community-minded 1950s audience in Middle America) potentially serves to detract from the heroicism of Ivanhoe himself; the convergence, then, of the major characters in the tournament is the only instance where there is any hint to this parallel, in a brief cut to Robin conferring with a Little John figure, which sketches his position only by rapprochement with the other groups of dissidents.

The social divisions are most effectively manifested by spatial separation; each figurehead is placed in a separate enclosure around the arena on a series of podia, each reflecting the elevated status of John and the prevalent hierarchical structures of society. Such spatial separation finds some sympathy with le Goff's (albeit simplified) argument that "during the Middle Ages, the opposition between the high and the low was 'projected in space': highly visible towers and walls were built, in order to demonstrate that one wanted to escape from lowliness."[72] The iconographic details support this spatial division by decking both John and Cedric in emblems of regal paraphernalia: both wear a form of crown, are seated on 'thrones' and are decked in blue (though the "dynastic colour of the Capetians," its significance as royal color found sympathy in England's monarchy)[73] with red trimmings, finished with chains of office. Their paired opposition is compounded by their position to each side of the tournament lists, John and his retinue looking out of the frame to their left, and Cedric to his right, fixing the line of sight on something lower than, and between, the two pairs.

The use of a closed frame reinforces the general sense of claustrophobia of the delicately composed long shot, which poignantly complements a film whose protagonists spend the majority of the running time either locked in castles or held prisoner in some other way, and whose central figurehead, the king, spends all but the very beginning and very end of the film chained up in an Austrian prison. The consequently tight, closed frames of the camera produce an altogether more intimate feel than the wide establishing shots which the anamorphic lenses of CinemaScope later offered, and which would become characteristic of the burgeoning Hollywood costume epic. Throughout the scene, the retention of fixed frames, long static takes and preference of low-angle shots, representing the point of view level of horseback on the field, visually underscore the narration from Ivanhoe's perspective, and the positioning of the two pairs poses a striking similarity which could scarcely be coincidental.

Thus despite its reduction to a dichotomous opposition of "goodies and baddies," *Ivanhoe* is a particularly interesting example here as, even if we reduce it to its structural polarity, when we think about the aims of the plot — namely the restitution of King Richard to his rightful throne — we can see that even by winning the tournament itself, the plot is no further advanced. All that has taken place is a public insult and act of defiance, setting in motion a united popular opposition to the current ruling establishment. While using the paradigmatic construction of a king himself in order to construct a series of "sub-kings," the actual manifestation of the king as an ideal ruler is noticeably absent. Thus it does not hold Richard up to be the paragon of good kingship either (an argument which would be difficult to uphold historically, with him having only spent nine months of his short reign actually resident in the country which he so publicly disdained), and it is here that *Ivanhoe* differs from the Robin Hood model which simply accepts and perpetuates the dichotomous Good King Richard/Bad King John so prevalent in popular opinion, while equating these with the plot device introduced by Scott of pitting Norman against Saxon, a trend carried through historically to the thirteenth-century in films such as *The Black Rose* (1950) and in cinema to 1991's *Robin Hood*.[74] *Ivanhoe*, then, rather than constructing an ideal king, raises a legitimate question about Richard which is equally applicable to other cinematic rulers: what happens when there *is no ideal king*?

The Land Without a King

"The King without a sword! The Land without a King!"[75]

This last section is devoted to an aspect of the paradigmatic and iconic interplay which is central to the concept of medieval kingship; it concerns what happens when the king is not ideal. What is interesting about this last series of films is that they avoid the arduous and difficult process of recreating an ideal medieval king by choosing to depict a king who is unfit to rule, the throne having been taken either by usurpation, by unsuitable inheritance or by an unpopular appointment. These are interesting because here we see that the attempts to depict an unfit, or non-ideal, ruler reflect not necessarily twentieth-century antipathy but are — whether consciously or not is impossible to assert — direct reversals of the investiture requirements of medieval kings, based on "inheritance, election, and designation [given that] in some way or another each of these three elements entered into most acts of king-making in western Europe in the Middle Ages."[76]

Here, then, we will explore three trends in the cinematic "lands without a king," which each subvert the models outlined in the two sections above. In the first case, in which the *throne is usurped*, the character transformation (the move towards an ideal king) is achieved not by the reform of one character, but very frequently by its contrast with the ideal. In the second model the king's accession to the throne is legitimate, but he is not — or is no longer — a suitable ruler. Finally, we have a number of films based on the "Lear principle": the succession disputes of a king, each of which raise the question of how to replace a displaced "good king," seen in films such as *The Lion in Winter, Braveheart, Edward II,* and *The Siege of the Saxons.*[77]

USURPATION OF THE THRONE

"Is it not also illegal to sit on the king's throne and usurp his power in his absence?"[78]

The first of these three subversions of ideal kingship, then, comes as a direct negation of the King's divine right to rule, by insinuating (or establishing directly) that this power has not been accessed in a legitimate fashion. Here, in films such as *Prince Valiant, The Court Jester* and *Black Knight,* the king is rejected on grounds of illegitimacy, which is often communicated on-screen by a reversal of the icons of kingship outlined in the section above on iconic kingship. Where the king stands as the lynchpin of the feudal order, we see in these three films that "the people" who make up this feudal order are noticeably divided into factions, such as "loyalist," rebels, troops and "outlaws." This last group, the outlaws, use the medieval topos of the forest as opposition to civilization, so that each group raises its anti-monarchic momentum from *outside* the castle walls in order to remove the king from his usurped throne — and thereby demonstrate that the recognizably pyramidal structure of medieval society is decidedly lopsided. The forest as a place of refuge for outlaws is, of course, one of the primary attributes of the Robin Hood legend, whose Prince John represents the "unconstitutional usurper" *per antonomasia*. The necessity to enforce an illegitimate and oppressive regime, then, takes its cue not from an iconic recourse to medieval records of usurpers (who would, for obvious reasons, be careful to expunge references to their unlawful claim to power from the historical record in any case), but from a paradigmatic borrowing from twentieth-century coups, replete with their rhetorical assertions of legitimacy and the maintenance of power by the use of militia. Danny Kaye's dubbing ceremony in *The Court Jester*, for example, uses its knights as automata to parody cinematic representations of this faceless oppression, since the cowardice (and intertextually assured malevolence of its usurper king, Vincent Price) and inhumanity of the king is reflected by the facelessness and dehumanization of his knights/militia. In this way, then, we see that the usurper becomes painted in the same colors as a military dictator, whose hollow claims to authenticity are hyperbolically simulated by the blanket oppression of his feudal subjects.[79]

The second way of implying illegitimacy of rule is by the reversal of the trope which I have labeled "king as symbol of nationhood." The emphasis here is to subvert both the ruler himself and thus, according to nationalist precepts, disbar him from legitimate succession by presenting him as "foreign" at best, or at worst a traitor to the nation.[80] In one sense, this is already achieved by the presentation of the populace as disparate (and antagonistic) factions instead of the united front of, say, *Alfred the Great*. In another sense, it is achieved by subverting the intended national "image" which the individual filmmaker is trying to communicate. Continuing with our Robin Hood example, we can see that where King Richard represents the lion-hearted, brave, courageous and proud King of Hollywood's Olde England, its diametric opposite would be found in John's serpentine, cowardly, calculating Prince.[81] This representation is made most clearly, once again, in comedic approaches to the legend, in which Reitherman's zoomorphic portrayal interprets them respectively as a full-maned lion and a somewhat more effete lion cub in the 1973 Disney version. Mel Brooks' parody goes even further here, by using national and cultural stereotypes to represent the Prince as an all-American with neatly coiffed hair and a matinee idol's "wholesome" smile, depicting him as an effete coward who, in his only showdown with Robin, hides under the table to protect his hairdo and new clothes.

Thus the usurped throne causes, by extension, a rift with the country instead of uniting its people under a single national banner, as the ideal kings of the cinema have been shown to do. It also makes use of the absent king as an idealized version, a sort of absent parallel with the usurper king, which serves continually to undermine the unlawful monarch, while at the same time obviating the necessity to demonstrate the actual ruling capacity of the idealized rightful king. As I have mentioned above, Richard becomes ideal simply by virtue of *not being John*.

Unsuitability for the Throne

"If you're a prince, there's hope for every ape in Africa."[82]

In this respect, we can see that in trying to depict the ruler as somehow unfit to rule, many of the same techniques are used as for the usurper motif, since at base they reflect a similar concern — namely to cast doubt on the legitimacy of the ruler. The major difference between the two, however, is that the usurper is placed in *parallel* with the ideal king, while the unsuitable ruler is shown to be inferior by a *linear* comparison with the previous king (as in *Dragonheart*) or — more commonly — by simply undermining the iconic and paradigmatic tropes we have already seen. We will briefly adduce two opposing examples here to demonstrate how this iconoclastic approach works, in the hope that, *pars pro toto*, a sufficiently recognizable pattern will emerge which can be applied to other films.

In the first film, Rob Reiner's *The Princess Bride*,[83] we can find not only an example of flawed succession in the form of Prince Humperdink — a cowardly and unsavory character whose inadequacy is brought out by a juxtaposition with our brave (and distinctly swashbuckling) hero, Wesley — but also a subversion of the "wise king" iconography outlined earlier in this chapter. This works on a traditional association of age with wisdom, but merely extends the lines to their logical conclusion: that there must exist a point at which old age becomes a handicap to effective government. Thus the king (Willoughby Gray, who is given no character name in the film), is constructed according to exactly the same iconic signals as other wise kings examined above (gray/white hair and beard, and kindly, avuncular appearance).[84] Nevertheless, in place of the requisite wisdom and stoicism expected of a medieval king, it is immediately obvious that the king is more senile than sagacious, and his deafness and lack of orientation make of him a puppet ruler in the hands of his malevolent son.[85]

In *The Black Shield of Falworth*,[86] we again find the combination of flawed heir and unsuitable ruler in the form of Dan O'Herlihy's Prince Hal and Ian Keith's Henry IV respectively. In this respect, however, we find a more explicit use of the twin flaws since in the case of the current ruler, we are led to understand that his bad government comes as a result of corrupt counselors, and thus (like Arthur and King Marc of Cornwall) their fault is not bad leadership but misplaced trust, which is a more human and instantly amenable vice. In the case of Hal — the future Henry V — we find both metatextual and intra-diegetic explanations for his seeming unsuitability to succeed. On the one hand, we know of Henry's later heroic status from a slew of Shakespearean films, if not from the play, while on the other hand we discover as we progress through the film that Hal's apparent drunken ineptitude is in fact a clever ruse to avoid suspicion from the vipers of the court. Here, then, the king is shown to be only temporarily "unsuitable" to rule; the *real* shortfall is the ability of the "sub-king," which keeps the legitimacy intact. Like the removal of Grima Wormtongue in *Lord of the Rings*, the removal/unmasking of the corrupt counselor is sufficient to immediately expiate the king and relieve the populace from the yoke of oppression.

FLAWED SUCCESSION

"An heir can be as much a threat as a comfort...."[87]

A third means of generating conflict by the presentation of a flawed successor is by slighting the political body of the actual or potential heir. In this instance, the prince is often painted as inefficient, malevolent, tyrannical or even maniacal; in short as one whose accession to the throne places a threat to the nation in terms of policy. This is the model adopted by films such as *Dragonheart*, whose Prince/King Einon (David Thewlis) is portrayed from an early age as one preoccupied with his own superiority and who manifests seemingly sociopathic behavioral traits in his evident delight at indiscriminate killing, his tantrum when defeated in swordplay and his selfishness manifested by his ill-concealed pleasure at the death of his father. After a short early episode in which we witness his training by the knight Bowen (Dennis Quaid), we fast-forward several years into the future and find much darker sets used, a prevalence for low fill-lighting and almost total absence of key-lighting, creating a shadowy, subterranean feel reflective of his Dark Age "heart transplant" with the dragon (a plot point which veers noticeably into the sword-and-sorcery genre). In an inversion of the sub-king model posed above, the degeneration of the kingdom into chaos and lawlessness is marked by Bowen's own degeneration into introspection and selfishness as he is reinvented from chivalrous knight into soldier of fortune, outlaw and conman, borrowing heavily from the man-with-no-name Western tradition, sidestepping moral and social responsibility in a world which he sees as unfair and lawless in itself. Indeed, in the final act, the film makes use of a redemption quest in order to mark the demise of the king and kingdom, as a result of Bowen's transformation into chivalric knight, and consequently possessor of those ideal qualities of kingship which are lacking in the real king. The end result, of course, is that the knight ends up functioning as a contrast to the king, and a moral "yardstick" by which we are able to measure the ineptitude of King Einon.

A secondary way of slighting the capacity of the would-be king can be seen at the intertextual level. Even before the opening credits begin, there is a degree of interplay in the construction of the character of Prince Einon, drawing on Thewlis's previous major cinematic roles in, for example, Mike Leigh's *Naked*, playing a down-and-out rapist running from social culpability by hiding in the murky depths of London's criminal underbelly.[88] In a similar way, in Paul Matthews' *Merlin: The Return*, Craig Sheffer is able to use his portrayal of Mordred (in which he spends most of the film merely snarling and sneering menacingly) to export this malevolent prince motif to a role as a Berserker in a later collaboration with Matthews, the marginally less dreadful (despite the title) *Berserker: Hell's Warrior*.[89] We can see this interplay at work at the mythological level, too, in the casting of Robert Addie — Mordred in *Excalibur*— as Sir Guy of Gisbourne in the television series *Robin of Sherwood*.[90] The influence of these external factors creates a very potent and effective way of conferring character traits by an appeal to archetypes established during the first "act" or "setup," usually taking place within the first ten minutes of the running time, and integrates these into the extratextual typecasting of individual actors (in precisely the same way as Sean Connery imparts a sense of dignity and sagacity).[91] When we learn, therefore, that these unpleasant characters are destined to be king, our antipathy toward the intertextual model ensures that we understand the threat which the kingdom faces.

Although in many of these examples the interplay works at the level of characterization and does not, as we mentioned, directly concern their capacity to rule as king, this depiction of unsympathetic personal behavior is often extended to their imagined political capacity. It is by this process that a given character's unsuitability for the throne is established, by tarnishing the personal character of the prince, frequently playing on social prejudices and a feeling of inevitability, which dictate that a prince with a weak personal character must equally become a king with a weak political character. A number of films, in fact, go one step further, translating these personal weaknesses into physical 'imperfections,' for "physical handicap — as an aspect of characterization — is a theatrical convention."[92] These include physical disabilities (such as Richard III's hunchback), speech impediments (*The Messenger*'s Dauphin;[93] Einon in *Dragonheart*), or by the cinematic tendency to depict medieval princes as weak (*Braveheart*, *The Princess Bride*, a number of versions of *Robin Hood*), cowardly (*Dragonslayer*, *Edward II*), or otherwise unfit to rule.

A natural corollary of this is found in *The Lion in Winter*, for example, which lengthens the shadow of the existing king, Henry II, by a more "manly," powerful depiction, which therefore pits the gruff, masculine king against an effete, weakling Prince John by a process of caricatured polarization. This is parodied by Monty Python's King of Swamp Castle and his lisping, musical heir, and also repeated throughout historical dramas (such as *The Madness of King George*) and twice resurrected in earnest by Brian Blessed as King Mark of Cornwall in *King Arthur the Young Warlord* (1975) and as Lord Locksley in *Robin Hood: Prince of Thieves*. Even now, however, the trope is showing no signs of decline, having been re-used in Rufus Sewell's King Mark (*Tristan and Isolde*).[94]

Finally, the challenge to the succession of the throne can also be effectuated precisely by avoiding both of the above, and by presenting the initial "lack" (again to use Propp's morphology) as a lack in a very real sense; by the absence of a legitimate heir.[95] To return to Arthur, this is one of the few areas which has resisted the plundering of centuries; regardless of the liberties which have been taken with the Matter of Britain over the years, the addition of a legitimate heir to the throne (and thereby disinheriting Mordred and obviating the ensuing civil war) has never found any real support. Where an heir is evidently absent, therefore, the sense of urgency is naturally engendered by the prospect of a vacant throne and a power vacuum.

What is more interesting here, however, is that even in those cases when heirs *are* provided to Arthur, they are invariably female, which to a modern mind conditioned to view the period as misogynistic and patriarchal, is the same as not having any heirs at all. Within the corpus examined, Nathan Juran's *The Siege of the Saxons* remains one of only three films to provide Arthur with a child, in this case Princess Katherine,[96] to whom the kingdom is expected to pass after the murder of King Arthur by Saxons (in rather incongruous horned helmets).[97] Yet even in what might have become an interesting step towards a progressive re-casting of a male-orientated mold, she is represented as little more than a walking dowry seeking protection from Juran's other curious addition, the character of Robert Marshall.[98] Towards the end of the film — even having courted and won over the princess, Marshall's inevitable succession to the vacant throne is finally assured by invoking the supernaturally assisted sword in the stone ritual, both of which sidestep the necessity for Marshall to actually prove himself worthy of inheritance, and relegates Katherine's importance to little more than "royal baby-maker" to forestall a repetition of the absence of a male heir which caused the problem in the first place.[99]

At least one version of the Connecticut Yankee adaptations, *A Kid in King Arthur's Court*, has — by way of romantic sub-plot rather than any particular musing on the dynastic continuation of the ideal monarchy — replaced the Alisande figure by giving two daughters to Arthur, retaining the idea of a Princess Katherine (here Katey) and adding a Princess Sarah, who disguises herself as the invincible Black Knight. Yet even this attempt to display her skill as a knight and present something of an empowered female character is ultimately derailed, since her claim to the throne tacitly requires her fairy tale marriage, in this case to Daniel Craig's Master Kane. Such attempts to subvert the "male-oriented medieval world" can be seen to have found their greatest rapport with the rise of the "girl power" action heroine prominent in the mid- to late '90s,[100] giving rise to at least three other Arthurian action heroines within the mainstream Hollywood tradition: *Quest for Camelot*'s Kayley, *Prince Valiant*'s Princess Ilene and Sandy (from Alisande) in *A Knight in Camelot*, in which Paloma Baeza draws heavily on her former role as Princess Katey in *A Kid in King Arthur's Court*. However, rather disappointingly, none of these films actually makes any real effort to explore the possibilities which such gender subversions might promise, preferring instead to simply create a positive — but largely ephemeral — teenage girl role model within a tired and unimaginative repetition of other depictions of the period.

The automatic rejection of a female heir, however, indicates that even within the post-feminist twentieth-century mentality, the prospect of a female being a suitable heir is an untenable proposition to modern audiences, who seem to believe in a primitive, misogynistic Middle Ages which would not have permitted it. This rejection, as even a cursory glance at the historical record will show, is demonstrably insupportable since, despite the exigencies of the Salic law, there were in reality a number of females who have succeeded to the throne upon the death of the king, though, admittedly, their power was not quite on the same plane.[101] What we see here, therefore, is evidence of the belief in the modern mentality that such female heirs could not have existed, which is subsequently borne out by the films made about the medieval era (and which therefore in turn causes such a situation to seem less likely in future films, according to Jauss's ideas about the horizon of expectations). Such gender bias becomes therefore yet another example of a situation in which actual fidelity to received historical evidence (i.e., what we have termed "accuracy") is overlooked in favor of an appeal to a modern audience's concept of plausibility (i.e., authenticity).

Conclusions

The difficulties encountered in Part I, in the attempt to understand medieval kingship, demonstrate that the cinematic depiction of kingship — let alone ideal kingship — is in one sense deeply problematic, beset on all sides by ideological ramifications of even seemingly innocent details, but can also be seen to conform to a certain, limited number of conventions. In the first section, we observed that there was certainly no consensus among scholars on the qualities required from an ideal king. There were, nevertheless, three distinct characteristics on which most authorities seem to agree: 1) wisdom, 2) that the king must be the head of a feudal order, and 3) that the king was construed as a metonym for the nation as a whole.

These three assertions brought us into Part II, in which we examined the ways in which certain films tried to signify these three qualities using iconic signs, so that wisdom was suggested by an association with age, and that a sense of hierarchy was achieved by a manipulation of the architectural film-space which established the king as the head of the court. Finally, we saw that in order to represent the king as a symbol of nationhood, films have often turned to the early medieval period to reflect a time when Europe was "in its infancy," and nation-states were only then beginning to be formed; consequently, by showing a king at the beginning of his own reign, it was possible to tie the two processes together, uniting the king and the land as one.

The paradigmatic processes of representing medieval kingship examined in the final section showed that two processes were invoked to help recreate the structures of medieval feudal society: depicting the king as a kind of knight, and by the introduction of sub-king paradigm, which necessitated two subordinate "guides" for the king (the "Lancelot" and "Merlin" roles). The introduction of two such sub-kings symbolizing virility and wisdom allowed filmmakers to construct the notion of an ideal king as a compromise between the two extremes, incorporating elements from each in order to mark character transformation.

However, we saw that even throughout all of these iconic and paradigmatic constructions, the lack of scholarly (and, to some extent, audience) unanimity about what exactly constitutes ideal kingship led to the problem that we are rarely, if ever, privy to a cinematic representation of an ideal king. This absence was established in three ways: by a direct reversal of the three iconic attributes of the ideal king (usurper king), by slighting the character's ability to rule (unsuitability), or by depicting them as unfit heirs using a direct parallel with the existing (and de facto ideal) king (flawed succession).

All of this leaves us at an interesting point in our study of medieval society as reflected through the cinema, in which we have seen a number of flawed humans who strive for perfection (in knighthood, in kingship, etc.), yet who are permanently disbarred from achieving it. The unbridgeable gap between the ideal and the reality is equally one of the principal problems faced by filmmakers seeking to represent the class of medieval society for whom the fallen status of humans was most acute: the priests, monks and saints which were loosely grouped as "those who pray." It is, therefore, to this next class of society that we will now turn.

5

Clergy and Saints: Those Who Pray

"Where's a priest? Somebody dig me up a priest! You, fetch me a bishop."[1]

In this section, having proposed a range of themes and motifs which cinema has used to recreate the nature and function of kingship and knighthood in the cinema, we will move on to look at a third section of society, characterized simply as "those who pray." I have here used this term in the same way as the medieval thinkers understood it, to designate only those who *lead prayer*, rather than any member of the populace who might simply have prayed, since when we imagine the sheer diversity of characters embraced by the latter, it becomes immediately clear that some restrictions are needed. Among these former, then, the first figure which we will examine is that of the priest; as we shall see, one of the problems involved in the iconic construction of priesthood within a twentieth-century context is that its referent — the medieval priest — still survives, but in a very different form. My study of the priest will accordingly examine two iconic attributes, wealth and feudal status, which were particularly associated with the priesthood in general, which recurrently appear in criticisms of priests' worldly concerns. I will then move on to a central figure within medieval religion, the monk, and look at the monk-scholar and the monk-reveler as two distinct paradigms of monasticism in film. In the final section, I will turn to what Kozlovic has called "Saint Cinema," analyzing the way in which St. Francis has been treated in film to try to establish some conventions in this area.[2] In this first section, however, we must first examine the medieval referent of those who pray, in order to gain an overview of how this stratum of society was seen by others, and to establish what are the most salient features which must be communicated in cinematic depictions of the priesthood.

The Medieval Referent

When it comes to the medieval concept of priesthood and "those who pray," we immediately encounter a difficulty at the level of signification. The problem is that the continued existence of priests, monks, nuns, popes, ministers and so on means that — in one sense — a modern audience is by no means unaware of their notional position within modern society. Nevertheless, the practical function of many of these to a medieval audience is undoubtedly alien to a modern viewer, since a medieval priest operated within a society which formed itself centrally around the Church. So great, in fact, was the priest's involvement in day-to-day life, that "medieval thought in general was saturated in every part with the conceptions of the Christian faith,"[3] meaning that medieval men and women "had therefore a sense of belonging to the same ensemble of institutions, beliefs and customs: Christianity."[4]

There is one scene in *The Advocate* which ably demonstrates our failure to understand this level of involvement. Richard Courtois (Colin Firth), the newly arrived lawyer, pays a visit to the local priest (Ian Holm) in order to seek advice on the case assigned to him. During their meeting, they begin to discuss the finer legal points of the case, and a number of clarifications are proposed by the priest himself, on the basis of the profound local knowledge which he is in a position to impart. Such a scene, both on the surface and quite possibly in intent, seems to highlight the superstition and stupidity of the medieval people, whose lawyers, the argument would run, would be so credible and easily influenced. Such a view would seemingly align Megahey's vision of the period with Eco's notorious dirty, barbaric Middle Ages, and could easily continue an attitude (seemingly established from the beginning of the film) of laughing behind our hands at the credulity of a village who would try animals as though they were humans, and mocking any lawyer worth his salt who would need to take advice from a non-expert. It only, in fact, makes any sense to a modern viewer because Megahey constructs this scene as an attempt to obtain information about the *pastoral* care of the village, which the priest is more naturally expected to administer. In this way, then, the village priest is safely confined to his modern position, tending to his flock and serving their spiritual needs, and leaving the lawyers and functionaries to their own area of expertise.

This path is certainly a good deal easier than trying to explain within the film's narrative that the local priest would *indeed* have been expected to fulfill a variety of legal, medicinal, administrative and judicial duties in addition to ensuring his congregation's spiritual salvation, in a time of rather less extensive literacy (even within the fourteenth century of the film's setting) and within the spectrum of a far greater influence of the church. After all, if an entire chapter of Coulton's own summary of *The Medieval Scene* is required merely to sketch the function of the village priest,[5] it hardly seems realistic either to expect mainstream directors to be sensitive to the nuances of this role, or — even if they were aware of it — to be able to explain its intricacies in one short scene.

Similar proof of the narrative disruption which such an explicatory note would cause can be found in Peter Tremayne's *Our Lady of Darkness* in which the reader may find a seven-page "historical note" in order to explain how it could be that Sister Fidelma as a *dálaigh*, like Peter Ellis's Cadfael as a Benedictine monk, might be in a position to hear and rule on cases of a judicial nature as well as act as an authority in the purely spiritual domain within medieval Ireland.[6] The answer given by Tremayne, as we have intimated above, is that within medieval society no such strict separation may be perceived, since "they were incapable of isolating secular affairs from their supernatural context. To men who saw behind such natural events as storms, famines and eclipses the direct workings of divine providence, any attempt to do so would indeed have seemed the opposite of realistic."[7] The judge of a court case, as we would understand him or her today, would to medieval eyes not be ruling on a purely secular case; acting on behalf of the king (the chief arbiter of justice), their judicial authority as understood within medieval society was issued from the divine appointment of kingship itself. Throughout the chain, then, we find that (as witnessed by the importance of 1 Samuel 12:1, "I have set a king over you") the ultimate authority was religious, not secular, "for the Lord is our judge. The Lord is our Lawgiver. The Lord is our King."[8]

A similar problem to that of the priest comes when we try to recreate the medieval monk on screen. Speaking only of the situation in the United Kingdom, and England in particular, the sixteenth-century Dissolution creates a physical demonstration of Amy de la Bretèque's "coupure infranchissable" between then and now; that is, it reflects an unbridgeable gap between the medieval period and our own.[9] Medieval monasticism is thus fixed as a phenomenon of the medieval past which bears little obvious connection to the sporadic ruins of once great monasteries in existence today. This complex situation is compounded further in the United States, wherein the absence of even a medieval precedent (therefore no signified "monastery") means that any attempt to represent it risks being associated with any other available signified (including, most misleadingly, cults, sects and closed or maligned religious communities such as the Mormons, the Amish, and so on). Where, therefore, they have no *historical precedent*, this gap is compensated by a recourse to a literary model in several cases (such as Walter Scott or T.H. White's imagination of medieval monasticism), or — as we shall see — to a model inherited directly from other films, both paradigmatically and iconically. In order, then, to clarify the medieval referent to which these films are trying to establish a link, I will take three subsets of "those who pray" in turn, in order of their association and integration with society: first, the priest, followed by the monk, before finally giving an overview of medieval saints in film.

The Priest

> COURTOIS: *"There must be priests in Hell?"*
> ALBERTUS: *"Can't move for them."*[10]

We have seen above that the function of the priest in medieval society was fixed very much as the center of the village community, or in the case of towns — which certainly played no small part in the evolution of medieval society[11] — he would rank undoubtedly among the notaries and fulfill an official, as well as religious, purpose. Cantor observes that even as early as the tenth century:

> Churchmen were highly honoured and well-rewarded, but religious enthusiasm is only one explanation for the increase in their number during the late tenth and eleventh centuries. The demand for clerical services increased very rapidly because churchmen were still almost the only literate people in Europe and thus immensely useful in any task requiring writing.[12]

This is an idea which is echoed by A.R. Myers' assertion that:

> Earlier in the Middle Ages the clergy had gained authority not only because of their sacred calling, but because of their monopoly of literacy and learning, which naturally gave them immense influence in political and social life.[13]

In this sense, then, at least in the tenth to the twelfth centuries, he acts as something of a center of learning around which village life frequently rotated — a repository of information on a range of subjects, an independent adjudicator (especially prior to the implementation of the King's Court and sheriffs of Henry II, et al.) in cases of legal, marital or territorial dispute, as well as the minister of a spiritual salvation which was certainly no less important than the people's physical well-being.

Cinematically, though perhaps in many other ways as well, the priest can thus be conceived as a relic of the village elder, a connection not missed by Franklin Schaffner, in whose *The War Lord* the village elder is placed in direct parallel with the Christian priest as arbiter of justice and religion. Where the village elder rallies the besiegers as a spiritual, religious and military leader, in the Christian camp it takes two figures (the priest and the "War Lord" Chrysagon himself) to fulfill the same role, in which the priest is relegated to his modern function of tending to the purely spiritual needs of those inside the tower. However, even the reliance on this paradigm is not without problems, since the village elder was himself a difficult figure to understand historically. By constructing the Christian priest according to a largely modern understanding of him, Schaffner's film explores the tensions created by the wholesale restructuring of society by the "introduction" of Christianity and feudalism. Despite compressing centuries of historical events into one lifetime, the film stands as a metaphor for the incompatibility of two modes of life, and the necessity for compromise. As the film's Christian priest says of his new congregation:

> Well, now, fertility. Some say it's pagan. But who's not pagan in some matters? These young folks here think of nothing but frolic. "Desist!" I tell them, but they will go a-wantoning. So, lest the Devil take them, I preach them a text from holy writ. "Increase and multiply," I say. "Replenish the earth." And oh! how they obey me.

Thus we can see that the line between pagan elder and village priest is — in cinema at least — remarkably malleable, reflecting an uneasy amalgamation in the popular mindset of orthodox religion and an earlier belief system. As Power writes, historically Bodo the Peasant (one of her sample of "Medieval People") would be less likely to blindly accept the new tenets of the Church than to assimilate the new religion within his original schematic understanding of the world around him, and "the Church wisely did not interfere with these old rites. It taught Bodo to pray to the Ever-Lord instead of to Father Heaven, and to the Virgin Mary instead of to Mother Earth, and with these changes let the old spell he had learned from his ancestors serve him well."[14] This idea thus lends plausibility to the exasperated efforts of Schaffner's missionary here, in that it is not impossible to imagine the necessity to couch the tenets of the new religion within familiar terms of the old.[15]

When we turn away from Historical reconstruction of the medieval priest to look at his reflection in literature, however, a second problem begins to emerge. In addition to the mainstream image of a leader and pillar of society, we can clearly see a body of literature into which is instilled a current of anti-clericalism typified by the stock figure of the avaricious, licentious priest found in the fabliaux.[16] The figure of the priest is here linked to all types of consumption, such as an insatiable appetite, monetary greed, and unchecked concupiscence bordering on lechery, as he remorselessly "consumes" the poor man's goods — his wife included. The sheer popularity of such a subversive stereotype of the priest speaks volumes about the popular reception of the village priest, and — while certainly not a true depiction of the state of the priesthood during the period — indicates that there was some considerable support for such anti-clericalism. "Through negative stereotyping, conveyed through a series of memorable adventures, each of the characteristics purported to denote the priests' distinctiveness and superiority — sexual purity, financial purity, appearance, language, learning — is called into question or belittled through the power of humour."[17]

Such a prevalent, and indeed open, subversion of the sacred ministry thus provides a secondary iconic detail in the representation of medieval priesthood: that of riches and worldly consumption. Indeed, this secondary icon can risk overflowing into the paradigm of the priest/elder examined above, since too strong a focus on the priest's elevated status in society risks giving way to the era's rampant anti-clerical heritage. Consequently, instead of explicitly remarking that the priest was not the same as we know him to be today, the village elder must in turn be assimilated with a similar (yet secular) figure drawn from modern civilization, such as a mayor, councilor, or frontier-town sheriff to which modern audiences can relate and react.

It is perhaps as a consequence of the ambiguity of this paradigm, then, that films attempting to invoke the medieval priesthood have — as we shall see — often favored a critical position, drawing on the archetypal figure of the village priest as one too open to earthly temptation. The reasons for this, however, extend well beyond our purposes here, and are more likely to be sociologically rooted than to have any historiographic or semiotic explanation. Nevertheless, such a critical position even within the literary construct does suggest that the medieval referent was torn between the two extremes of seeking perfection while ultimately — if the literature is to be believed — falling foul of the most human shortcomings. When representing the priest, therefore, filmmakers have been forced to take a position about their own understanding of priesthood, in order to strike a balance between these two pervasive archetypes, which are formed by the combination of two or more features of iconic recreation. If riches on the one hand suggest leadership, they can also suggest caprice; if the power as village elder on the other can place them within a feudal hierarchy, then too strong an emphasis can suggest an abuse of this power. Thus, the two dominant *forms* of priesthood, high earthly status and "feudal" leadership, risk becoming two critical extremes of the same function when intended to continue this anti-clericalism, giving way to two symbols which the cinema has favored: the rich priest and the powerful priest, each of which comes replete with his own iconography.

RICHES AND LEADERSHIP OF THE CLERGY

"We have wealth and power. You, in your innocence, put us to shame...."[18]

The first "form of priesthood," then, is the wealthy priest, whose material wealth is frequently used as a symbol for his power within society, although it is just as often meant to be a slight on the perceived avarice of the medieval Catholic church. Nevertheless, in a society which equates money with power, we in the twentieth century have put in place a handy shortcut for filmmakers to portray their priests as powerful, simply by making them wealthy. Thus on the iconic level, in order to represent this twin function (religion + leader), cinema has perhaps had more recourse to the iconography of leadership than to that of religion. Where, for instance, Bretèque posits the ideogram of the crusader as:

CROSS + SWORD

We might here suggest that in order to communicate the two aspects of medieval priesthood, the corresponding ideogram should be:

CROSS + ELEVATION (where "elevation" uses the "kingly" cinematography of leadership); or, CROSS + RICHES (where "riches" signify high civic **and** religious status)

It is in this aspect, too, that the camera itself is able to make a contribution. This iconic construction can be effected in two ways; by emphasizing either the elevation/leadership, or by highlighting the priest's riches.

The riches of the Church are particularly highlighted nowhere else more than in films about the Franciscan order, since their narrative focus is necessarily on the humility and poverty of "Il Poverello," and the best way to do this is to juxtapose the riches of the Church with the poverty of Francis's own order, as Zeffirelli does in *Brother Sun, Sister Moon*. In order to emphasize the impiety of the clergy in contrast with Francesco's humility, he accentuates the riches of Bishop Guido of Assisi so completely that the clergyman can scarcely be seen beneath them, and to the point that they outweigh the overt signs of religion (i.e., the cross). An enormous cope encrusted with gold and jewels envelops him to the extent that it covers the lower half of his face, reducing him almost to caricature. The message from this imbalance therefore comes not through outright narrative criticism (which might be thought heretical within the context of the Middle Ages and thus seems incongruous in a modern film) but rather through iconic signification to demonstrate that the bishop is more worldly (riches) than spiritual (cross). The religious leader is further subverted when — in an attempt to cover Francesco's "shameful" nudity after he throws off his rich clothes in order to emulate Christ's poverty — he throws the heavy cope around the latter, creating something of a metaphor for the oppressiveness of Church dogma and at the same time a comical juxtaposition between the saint's nakedness, poverty and spiritual rebirth and the bishop's inability to escape the importance of vestments interpreted within a liturgical perspective.

The emphasis on vestments as an index of social status and function operates in the same way in *Francesco, Giullare di Dio*,[19] when we encounter Nicolaio, the tyrant of Viterbo, and again it is used in order to contrast him with the humility of the inchoate Franciscan order. Here the tyrant is shown engulfed in a suit of armor, so totally overwhelmed by its weight that it both conceals and inhibits him, requiring a gallows with chains to support it and allow any movement. The iconic message is the same; whether it be for war or for riches, when the outward signs are overloaded, their original purpose is lost. Where one is buried underneath his own armor, the other is submerged and spiritually buried beneath their zeal for worldly riches. Thus when the same motif is repeated in Zeffirelli's final scene in the papal palace, the pope's constriction by an enormous gilded cope (so heavy it must be attached to his throne), the film's central message becomes clear that — in contrast to Francesco's spiritual and physical nakedness — the church was excessively weighed down by material excess. It is, in fact, only by removing the gold and jewels (and thereby enacting his own spiritual rebirth, emerging in the white robe of the novice) that the pope is able to approach and understand Francesco's piety and humility. This separation is both anchored thematically (by his refusal, or perhaps inability, to speak to Francesco when fully robed, followed by his admission in the epigraph that "we have riches and power, and you [...] have put us to shame") and reinforced visually, by the divestiture of the jewel-encrusted robes, as well as a spatial separation when he comes down the steps to join Francesco with a low-angle shot picking up his acolytes rooted to their wealth in the background.

The second method by which this ideogram can be established is by emphasizing the symbols of leadership by the simple cinematographic convention of elevation, achieved through low-angle shots and high-level key lighting, or else on the iconic level, in which it can equally be communicated by the architecture and the mise-en-scène itself. As we saw in chapter 4, the authority of leadership can be established by centering the king within the frame and the architecture; usually this is done by placing him in a seated position at the end of a long, narrow hall, on a raised platform to signify his social elevation, flanked on each side by rows of attendants. It is no coincidence, of course, that within the spiritual domain, the architecture of the Church reflects exactly this same construction (or perhaps vice versa, which is a debate for another time), with the altar raised above the audience, at the focal point of the nave on the furthest point from the entrance to the church — and the cinema has often profited from this similarity by using the same sequence to establish the spiritual authority of the priest.

Brother Sun, Sister Moon is just one film to make use of this cinematographic device. Beginning with an establishing shot from the rear doors of the church, the lines of the architecture themselves are all seen to converge on the altar, or the minister of religion. Elsewhere, too, the Church's reliance on architectural symbolism has frequently been hijacked by cinema: the lectern as symbol of pedagogy establishes the priest as a scholar (*Alfred the Great*), the elevation of the altar relies on a sense of spectacle and authority (*Murder in the Cathedral, The Lion in Winter*, and *Ladyhawke*) and the raised pulpit as symbol of demagoguery allows the priest to be established as almost a political figure, and certainly a leader in films such as *The Reckoning*.[20]

In this last film one scene in particular shows how a cinematographic decision can have a number of effects on the way in which the audience will imagine the priest. The decision to shoot the village priest from the reverse-angle has as a consequent effect an interesting rapprochement between the various participants in the Sunday Mass: taken as a sign on its own, he could be said to represent any number of relationships with his congregation, from that of a schoolteacher (symbolized by the open book, the pedagogic attitude coupled with the upturned faces of the congregation), as well as a village official (indicated by the raised platform of the pulpit itself and the symbols of office which distinguish him from the drab grays and browns of Hollywood's peasant class), while at the same time the focus is deliberately deep enough to include him within them, rather than separating him from them by shot/counter-shot, by placing him in the same frame.[21] It is this last element which will prove to be crucial for a religious film which begins by the ceremonial resignation of its protagonist's religious vocation, for each camera movement during the opening sequence serves to paint him as a human and worldly figure who is subject to the same temptations as his flock. The raised pulpit, in fact, eventually comes to be a symbol of his hypocrisy in the first instance, for while he lectures on virtue his eye contact with a young wife (prominent thanks to her red hair, standing in the center of the crowd) in the audience hints at an affair which breaks the sacred vows of marriage (and that of celibacy which we tend to attribute to the period, even if it was not everywhere demanded).[22]

This latter concept of the pulpit is most clearly exploited in *The Reckoning* by the substitution of his lost congregation with a paying theatrical audience, when — thanks to a group of traveling players — he takes to the stage to deliver his metaphorical sermons. It is by a reliance on these same symbols of leadership, however, that the film is able to communicate its redemption quest theme — almost to the point of eclipsing the element of riches. In order to do so, they must first establish the character of Nicholas as a good priest, before moving on to undermine this, all the while ensuring that the audience is capable of distinguishing between the two. This is achieved by the use of flashback within the first scenes which anchors the priest within his appropriate milieu by a series of isolated images; preaching in the pulpit, followed by a reverseshot to his parishioners who are lit from the front and viewed from a high angle to reflect Nicholas's point of view, the priest speaking Latin (connoting scholarliness), dressed in surplice and vestments, but poorly, as befits a priest.

This iconography, however, is immediately reversed in order to show his disgrace, by juxtaposing these images with those of the same actor in a series of incongruent actions—adultery, breaking the "vow of chastity," running through the forests pursued by a low-angle tracking shot (thus subverting his former elevation), framing him as a renegade criminal. During the "deconstruction" phase of his priesthood the iconic signs of this station are removed one by one; the priest is shown shaving his head, removing his vestments and replacing them with the rough sack-cloth of the penitent, before finally "purifying" himself—washing away his sins—in a river, a clear reversal of the purification and absolution of the baptismal and ordination ceremony. Finally, from an overhead shot (for he has even turned his back on God) we see Nicholas throwing his clothes from a bridge into a river, indicating his cathartic final renunciation of the priesthood. All of this, crucially, takes place in a montage sequence without either dialogue or commentary, the director relying instead on the capacity of the iconic sign—and in particular on the symbolism of clothing—in order to express meaning.

Thus, the director has made use of the iconographic attributes of medieval priesthood (a concatenation of iconic signs) in order both to construct an "ideal priesthood," followed immediately by a disassociation of them in order to connote a "flawed priesthood." Yet as the film progresses there is a third process, in which the conceptual framework of the priesthood (i.e., those actions of the ideal priest) are retained and re-enacted by Nicholas on the stage—this time, however, they are re-enacted without the symbolic vestments of the priest. The message, then, becomes clear: Nicholas is a bad priest, but a good man, and even when he is divested of the outward signs of his faith, he is still a good Christian and effective "shepherd of lost souls."

THE FEUDAL HIERARCHY OF THE SECULAR PRIESTHOOD

"Monsignor Alvaro! As well as the ambassador, are you not also a bishop?"[23]

One of the major differences observable between the secular priesthood in medieval films and their monastic counterparts lies in the way that the "leadership model" of the churchmen is most often constructed using a feudal paradigm. This is, however, not altogether without historical precedent, since Heer observes that "the clergy were also at this date still firmly embedded in their own social class. The higher clergy, the bishops, the abbots and the cathedral dignitaries, shared to the full the lives of their secular cousins, in hunting, jousting, feasting and feuding."[24] So it is that, rather than being entirely distinct entities, there was an element of feudality in the Church, too, by which "the value assigned to each order [does] not depend on its utility, but its sanctity — that is to say, its proximity to the highest place."[25] Thus, "the Church was a spiritual hierarchy culminating in the pope, between clergy and laity there was a great gulf fixed."[26] As we have seen, this comes as a result of the process by which clerical positions increasingly involved duties that included the protection of the laity, causing the religious appointments to assume more political dimensions; "just as during the period at the end of Antiquity, so in the new political climate bishops were not solely charged with duties regarding the care of the souls, but in the rapidly changing conditions they also had to carry out numerous political functions."[27]

If the medieval clergy could therefore be understood as a kind of "spiritual hierarchy," then it follows that the pope must sit at its head — on earth at least — as a monarchic figure, who would consequently hold dominion over spiritual and terrestrial matters, since according to those who subscribed to a belief in ultimately religious power, "papal plenitude of power could permit no ultimate division of authority into separate spheres, spiritual and temporal."[28] Such a view of the papacy leads Brooke to term the whole as a "papal monarchy," since "the papacy claimed to be a spiritual monarchy; and it claimed to be the fount of justice in spiritual matters."[29] Throughout the Middle Ages, therefore, we can see that the rigid structure of the Church was *already* making use of a paradigmatic association of principles within "a framework of thought in which religious and political fields were not separated [and] which saw the work of priests and princes essentially as complementary means toward the same end...."[30]

As such, medieval opinion was sharply divided over the issue of whether these spiritual "kings" could legitimately lay claim to the same privileges as their terrestrial equivalents, on the basis that if "the King and the Priest are both, by grace, Gods and Christs of the Lord, whatever they do by virtue of this grace is not done by a man but by a God or Christ of the Lord."[31]

This argument is of course a radical simplification of what was in reality a complex debate of some longevity, since there are numerous arguments about which of the two powers held supremacy, such as Pope Boniface III's claim that if the two powers are two swords, then "both swords, the spiritual and the material, are in the power of the Church; the one, indeed to be wielded *for* the Church, the other *by* the Church ... one sword, moreover, ought to be under the other, and the temporal authority to be subjected to the spiritual."[32] It is a claim countered by John of Salisbury, for instance, who uses the same arguments to propose that "the prince is, then, as it were, a minister of the priestly power, and one who exercises that side of the sacred offices which seems unworthy of the hands of the priesthood."[33] The sheer volume of extant material devoted to this critical issue stands as a testament to its centrality to the period; what is most useful for our present purposes, however, is that there was indisputably, and for understandable reasons, a great deal of interplay between the two powers, with each freely borrowing and assuming some of their structures (paradigms) and appearances (icons) in the attempt to establish primacy and plenitude of power.

So the obvious question which arises next is whether and how this paradigm might work in film. If we are — as I have argued in chapters 3 and 4 — already finding difficulty in recreating the feudal hierarchy in film, how are we supposed to use it as a paradigm to support another field? The answer lies in the interplay of signs; given the impossibility of a wholesale transplantation, this hierarchy evolves from a construction of iconic signs which are then transported into a paradigm. We have seen above a tendency to rely on iconic indices of wealth (gold, jewels, ornate vestments, (etc.) in order to clothe bishops and higher clergy in appropriate symbols of their status, and this trend extends into a paradigm when it is transferred to the entire court. Modern audiences — accustomed to post–Barthesian status symbols which equate wealth with high status and power — are likely to interpret a hierarchy of riches as a hierarchy of authority. To give an example, we might refer back to Zeffirelli's *Brother Sun, Sister Moon*, in which he constructs the papal court of the closing sequence as a version of the palaces of the king in other films.[34] Claiming that he sought to film "a tremendously rich, dazzling place to make more clear the contrast between the poverty of Francis and the magnificence of the Papal court," he makes a clear use of the iconic symbols of wealth in his construction of the court, in order to juxtapose these worldly riches with Francis's disheveled, bare-footed troupe.[35]

However, in order to isolate the pope as the head of this spiritual monarchy, the director uses a mixture of two cinematographic ideas, both borrowed from pre-existent paradigms. First, he aligns the cardinals, archbishops and the papal court along a spectrum of riches, at the highest end of which he places the pope (Innocent III) himself, whose extraordinarily ornate cope recalls that of Bishop Guido of Assisi, in that its richness seems to overwhelm the human inside. In fact, it is shown to be so heavy that it is fixed to the chair, so that when the pope emerges from it to approach Francis's group, his frailty and comparative nakedness becomes an ironic echo of the nascent Franciscan Order, recalling perhaps an external influence at the iconic level, an intersemiotic transfer from Francis Bacon's notorious painting of Pope Innocent X.[36] In an environment in which there exists a dizzying complexity of ecclesiastical grades of superiority and authority, what better way is there to signal this hierarchy than by using a simplified range of outward signals to communicate this? Even if historically inaccurate, he arranges his body of colorful cardinals into a network of signs which is comprehensible at first glance and obviates the need for pages of explanatory dialogue. It is once again a case of sacrificing fidelity to form in order to preserve the underlying concept.

Second, Zeffirelli returns to the same use of architecture as we have discussed above, fixing Innocent III in the very center of the image and at the very end of the hall, whose reflected light resembles the sun itself. The long tracking shot follows Francis (shot from behind) along the length of the ornate court towards the pope, thereby using the Great Hall establishing shot to imply that the further one travels into the hall, the closer one gets to its spiritual zenith — it is both distant and on a higher plane.

Elsewhere this idea of a spiritual hierarchy is transplanted whole cloth from the paradigms of feudalism discussed above, yet it is taken much more for granted, to the extent that it ceases even to be questioned. It may come, therefore, as something of a surprise to see the "Bishop of Aquila" (John Wood) holding a very material and temporal power in Richard Donner's *Lady-hawke*,[37] though in the film, revealingly, there are no such awkward questions posed, let alone answers given. Rather than instantly to criticize what seems to be a giant leap of the imagination, it is certainly more fruitful to try to understand where this idea might have come from. Clearly, given the lack of icons functioning as signifiers here, we are working on the level of the paradigm, and one created by an amalgamation of the cloister on the one hand and the tenets of feudalism on the other. The concept of the monastic "cloister," then, is here taken to its etymologically logical conclusion, that its separation from the world is intended less to seek perfection (and its adepts segregated from the world) than to prevent any inhabitants from escaping, and to prevent the world itself from intruding. In this sense, its reconstruction as a fortress makes some sense at the conceptual level, offering as it does protection of a very real, and very concrete, nature.

Throughout this film the bishop is notably anchored within a position of power, established both within the narrative (characters showing deference) and cinematographically, through low-angle shots or frame composition (placing him on a raised dais, at the head of a procession, in close-up, (etc.). In one particular shot, dominating the right side of the frame, a tracking shot shows him leading a procession of his acolytes, who follow meekly (and lit using only the key light from the right, placing them in a relative darkness compared to the brightly lit bishop) in a visual signal of deference and subordination, a recognition of his terrestrial — rather than spiritual — power. Further, the composition of the shot itself picks up a visual echo, making the bishop seem like a mirror image of his subordinate (and therefore a holder of temporal power), while his official robes and brighter lighting, as well as his position at the head of the procession and turned away from his train, demonstrate his important status in the secular world as well as a higher dignitary of the spiritual one. This choice of constructing the bishop as a functionary betrays an interesting, and revealing, supposition on the part of the filmmakers that the functions of the bishop (as ward of a religious see based on geographical limits) and a lord (overseer of a manor *also* based on geographical boundaries) are by and large interchangeable.[38]

This same paradigm linking secular orders to the temptingly simple model of feudal hierarchies can be seen at work again in films coming from the European tradition (a tradition which we have noted so far is more prone to relying on iconic rather than paradigmatic signification). In *Krzyzacy*, a film based on the Crusades (and therefore operating in a gray area between military and religious spheres), we can find a substitution of the eponymous order of knights with that of a far more rigid feudal paradigm.[39] During the trial of a prisoner of war, we encounter a "court" of knights and monks deliberating on his release, and here we encounter once again a mixture of iconic signs with paradigmatic associations in order to connote a hierarchy at work with the *miles Christi*. The camera captures the scene from a high-angle establishing shot, but uses a static take with almost no cutting, and only a very slow zoom in order to represent the point of view of the spectator, as though viewing from the viewers' gallery usually placed at the opposite end of the hall to the High Table. Seated along the length of the far wall are a "panel of judges" (though such panels certainly did exist in the Middle Ages, given the place and date of the film's release, Poland in the 1960s, the cinematographic arrangement is more likely an ironic borrowing from parliamentary investigations, Supreme/High Courts, and, tellingly, McCarthy-era Senate sub-committees) at the center of which is seated the Head of the Order, identified indexically by his brightly colored robe, crown and ornate, throne-like seat. There are, furthermore, the same architectural icons discussed above in the scene, in the centering of the judge/lord/abbot within a vaulted arch, lit by key lighting coming from above, and he is seated on a raised throne and directly underneath a crucifix, intimating that he is subordinate only to God Himself. While the "historicons" here are working — for there is no doubt that we are back in the Middle Ages — we are witnessing a breakdown of the specific process of signification, for this scene mixes a number of confused and disparate elements from the Middle Ages — judicial, spiritual, ritualistic, military, regal and ecclesiastic in order to communicate a sense of the military court of the Order. The knights are *both monks and knights*, the king is *both leader and priest*, the crosses of the crusaders belong to the Knights Hospitalliers *as well as* to the Teutonic knights, and all are marked by a confused position with relation to their spiritual duties.

What this consequently indicates is that we are witnessing a general tendency to conflate (or confuse, which worryingly might be more or less the same thing) feudalism and priesthood, which begins to be insinuated within the tradition, to the extent that later films trying to evoke this Middle Ages of "those who pray" draw their influences not from the medieval "signifieds" (whatever these might be) but rather *they rely on other films*. Conflation thus does indeed become confusion, which goes some way to explaining *Ladyhawke*'s unquestioning acceptance of the two interlaced paradigms.

This confusion, however, is not restricted to the paradigms, as a closer reading of *Krzyzacy* reveals; the crosses of the knights on the right of the frame are visually echoed by the sword held by both the guard in the far right-hand corner and the official standing to the left of the throne. The guards on the extreme left of the frame further represent a confusion of religion and war, in that while one appears to stand behind the lectern, the slow zoom later reveals that he is in fact guarding the king, leaving the space behind the lectern empty. The whole mixture of knighthood and priesthood creates a scene which is almost exactly recreated in *Kingdom of Heaven*'s knighting ceremony, in which knights at the outer edges of the frame hold raised swords blade downwards so as to visually echo the crosses on the walls, just as the frame composition places the "panel" of knights in front of an altar.

This is not the only film to associate the icons of spirituality with those of the militia, for the striking resemblance between sword and cross is not only intentional, but also has been an effective symbol of the *miles Christi* throughout the medieval period and beyond; furthermore, there is no shortage of films in which this device can be seen.[40] Nevertheless, by confusing the individual *iconic* signs, or even ideograms (such as cross + sword = crusader; color + elevation = hierarchy; sword = power AND justice, and so on) in film we can see that the audience (no longer cognizant of the symbolic meaning of each icon) is being required to look beyond their individual iconic signification. Thus already by 1960, they are being required to interpret these conflicting codes and to *place them within an already familiar structure drawn from other genres* (such as a courtroom, a court martial, military films, (etc.).

Monasticism in Film

> "Outside of feudal society, there existed an even more important division: that between clergy and the laity."[41]

If this is the case with the priest who has an overt justification for fraternization within the secular domain, then when it comes to dealing with the priest's cloistered cousin (who ought to have very little to do with the mundane affairs of the world), the resort to a paradigmatic fusion with a "worldly" hierarchy seems no longer appropriate. If priests and knights are able to access the same paradigm based on their shared values in the secular domain, how then are we able to represent the medieval monk on film?

To answer this question, we must return to look at the evolution of the medieval monk and what it meant to contemporary society. Within the Middle Ages themselves, the path to religious and spiritual perfection led not to the church itself— since it too belonged to the mundane, secular world and was too susceptible to the temptations of daily life — but instead led directly to the gates of the monastery.

As Heer observes, "the 'heart' of the Church was in the cloister — not the Popes, theologians, universities or church,"[42] and it was here in the heart where monks were to shun the everyday world (the literal translation of *contemptus mundi* being "contempt for the world/mundane") in the quest to worship God in every aspect of life. Thus "monks must lead a *perfect* life. It was impossible to be perfect in the world, people knew, and therefore they expected perfection somewhere on Earth: the Cloister."[43] However, even this perception of the monastery was by no means a fixed concept throughout the entire medieval period, for over time this seclusion evolved into a less rigid barrier between the worlds.

In a sense, then, rather than offering a mere replication of the secular world in cloistered seclusion, the monastery grew to become itself an imaginary, constructed "ideal community," so that "those who set themselves a standard higher than the ordinary looked to the monasteries for their examples. It was from the monasteries that the countryside learnt its religion."[44] Thus, paradoxically precisely *because* the monks were expected to lead the way to perfection, the links between the secular and the monastic world became more and more frequent, in order that the monks could preach to and walk amongst the world. Instances of this intermingling between the formerly disparate spheres of life only served to diminish this distance between the ideal and the actual, since monks "were not town-dwellers like the friars who were appearing at the end of our period, but *they were seldom far from the centres of feudal government and social life.*"[45]

While the involvement of cloistered monks in some form of administration was not wholly condemned by the Church itself, it was certainly a cause for concern among the monastic authorities, who were anxious about the dilution of the perceived ideal. "There was nothing of which the church disapproved more than this habit, shared by monks and nuns, of wandering about outside their cloisters; moralists considered that intercourse with the world was the root of all the evil which crept into the monastic system."[46]

Consequently, over time, "as against the old ideal of retreat from the worlds, there emerged a new conception of the monastery, as a stronghold of prayer, of unceasing intercession on behalf of all Christian men,"[47] making of it a new form of monasticism, which Southern describes as "the expression of the corporate religious ideals and needs of a whole community."[48] Thus even in the medieval imagination of the cloistered monk, there arose a perception that there existed a marked divergence between the ideal and its practice, which was to be lampooned so memorably by Pasoloni's sexually frustrated nuns in *Il Decameron*, and eventually subverted wholly by the *Monty Python and the Holy Grail*'s Castle Anthrax, a semi-religious community of four score and ten nubile virgins who so memorably welcome Sir Galahad.

It is a perception, of course, not without foundation within the Middle Ages themselves, since many extant chronicles attest to the bad practices which were — to take them at face value — rife among the monasteries. This is, however, somewhat biased evidence, serving to demonstrate the old axiom that history is merely the surviving record, given that only those disobeying the order are committed to posterity;

> It is ... easy to stress too much the prevalence of unseemly behaviour among the monks. It was the business of Episcopal visitors to reveal and correct what was wrong, not to record success of sanctity, hence Episcopal registers have much to say about corruption, and very little [...] about satisfactory houses.[49]

There is further evidence of a more dangerous attack on the monasteries coming not from above but rather from "below," in the form of popular perception of these once perfect refuges. Coulton argues that the decline in strict adherence to monastic disciplines contributed to a general dissatisfaction among the populace who were often attached financially or bodily to the orders: "there is overwhelming evidence for a general feeling that the monastic Orders were no longer justifying their enormous endowments and their exceptional privileges."[50] This sense of injustice found its outlet frequently in the coarse jests of the fabliau tradition, for example, with its lusty priests and concupiscent friars, betraying a deep-rooted mistrust of those set above them to minister to their souls.[51] "The negative stereotyping of the priesthood in the Old French Fabliaux constitutes but one voice in a chorus of protest which sang loud against all ranks of the clergy, secular and regular, throughout western Europe during the Middle Ages."[52]

These tropes, however, also find their way into literature seemingly aimed at a more courtly audience, an indication perhaps of a more pervasive feeling throughout society that the religious houses were no longer living up their founding ideals,[53] as witnessed by a similar attack coming from Chaucer's notorious Friar Hubard.[54] At the crossroads between literature and reality, we are able to discover "visitational records [which] show that there was scarcely any attempt to appeal to the rule of strict claustration, and that Chaucer's *The Shipman's Tale*, where the monk of St. Denis comes out whenever he likes to visit his friends in Paris, is a perfectly natural picture of ordinary practice."[55] This tendency can be seen to continue well beyond the medieval period in the vitriolic writings of Erasmus and particularly in Rabelais, in whose *Gargantua* we find the character of Frère Jean, the "mâchemerde" (literally the "shit eater," given that they "eat" the sins of the world), which is intended to be a wholesale subversion of monastic austerity and asceticism. As Bakhtin writes, "in Rabelais' Friar John is the incarnation of the mighty realm of travesty of the low clergy. He is a connoisseur of 'all that concerns the breviary'; this means that he can reinterpret any sacred text in the sense of eating, drinking, and eroticism, and transpose it from the Lenten to the carnival 'obscene' level."[56]

Such a divergence between the ideal and its perception (if not actual reality) leads us in the twentieth century to a rather ambivalent — if not overtly contradictory — understanding of medieval monasticism. The symbols handed down to us by literature provide us with a rich mine of possible understanding, from a pious, sincere and ascetic example of devotion to the jolly, earthly friar ridiculed across the pages of their literary antecedents. These confused symbols, therefore, can be seen to evolve slowly within the popular cinema to provide us with two overriding archetypes of monasticism in all of its forms and despite its initial complexity: the studious, cloistered piety of William of Baskerville at one extreme, and the jolly, worldly merriment of Friar Tuck at the other.

THE MONK AS SCHOLAR: WILLIAM OF BASKERVILLE

"We must not allow ourselves to be influenced by irrational rumours of the Antichrist, hmm? Let us instead exercise our brains and try to solve this tantalizing conundrum."[57]

Umberto Eco's fictional monk William of Baskerville, taken from his novel *The Name of the Rose*, presents an interesting (and probably the most well-documented) case of a synthesis between iconic construction (perhaps rather unsurprisingly, given Eco's own synthesis of medievalism and semiotics), coupled with a demonstrable debt to paradigmatic reconstruction by genre transfer from the detective novel (although undoubtedly more noticeable in the film adaptation than the novel, even though the novel had its beginnings as a detective story set in the Middle Ages rather than a medieval novel in itself). Throughout the film, then, we can see how Annaud has relied on the construction of a series of both icons and paradigms in order to signify the medieval monk to a modern audience.

One of the most interesting aspects of the character of William of Baskerville is that it assumes a very different conception of the monk from the licentious glutton (which we will examine below)—for this monk, the "signified" referent is that of the scholarly, wise and pious monk who no doubt existed in abundance despite the hubris which the monasteries were later to suffer. By using this approach, the iconic construction of the character forces a filmmaker to emphasize his "unworldliness" (a result of the "contemptus mundi"). In the film version of *The Name of the Rose* (since we will be treating only the film version here) Annaud achieves this even within the first few scenes, by creating two "groups" of potential antagonists to his hero, William.

The first group, the monks of the Abbey, are emphasized by their uniformity: using hoods to symbolize their relative anonymity; gray, brown and black robes to signify their humility and lack of interest in the meretricious trappings of the secular world; their activity to symbolize the *ora et labora* credo. On the other "side," Annaud constructs the peasants as their secular "other"—though uncovered, a rapid series of jump cuts prevents the audience from distinguishing their features, making theirs an enforced anonymity; the same dark clothes are besmirched with mud and dirt to emphasize their squalor; their scurrying activity is relegated to the shadows and to the corners of the screen. The overall impression of the monastery, too, is represented in the introductory scenes as a closed, self-sufficient "state within the State,"[58] by the use of long establishing shots from outside of the walls, with Annaud using tracking shots and panning along the length of the walls to communicate an idea of a continued, contiguous space outside of the walls, as well as the solid, impenetrable mass of the monastery itself, raised like a fortress on embankments, a sense of dominance emphasized by low-angle shots and the darkness of its interior.

The second aspect of the characterization is in the attempt to emphasize his status as one of the "intellectuals" of the Middle Ages,[59] a category which does not fit easily into any of the traditional social strata of the medieval populace. This is, further, somewhat more difficult to communicate, since intellectualism is first and foremost an inward characteristic, and in any case, the modern cinematic codes to demonstrate scholarship rely on signs of its modern equivalent: glasses, rows of books, staid and drab suits, gray and disheveled hair—in short, more academic than monk. While some of these signals are included in the iconic construction of William of Baskerville, with spectacles and gray hair, there are patently problems with using the modern icons of dress and props. Nevertheless, by singling William out in the gray habit of the Franciscan order something interesting is taking place; while the signifier itself is unlikely to have any meaning to the average viewer, the process of isolating him from his fellow monks in the black habits of the Dominicans

or Benedictines and, more importantly, from the brown habit of the Capuch-
ins, separates him from both the morbid and sinister associations of black and
from any association with Friar Tuck and therefore with gluttony and lechery.

This iconic process is compounded, however, by a paradigmatic association. Instead of trying to use a paradigm of the "studious monk," a signified
which does not normally exist in popular cinematic vocabulary, William is
aligned to a more general archetype of the detective, the traditional repository
of seemingly supernatural knowledge achieved through honed skills of deduction and supposition.[60] The most obvious reference here is to Conan Doyle's
Sherlock Holmes, a character to which two overt allusions are made; first, the
name William of Baskerville itself recalls Conan Doyle's most famous Sherlock
mystery, *The Hound of the Baskervilles*, and second, in the initial investigations
of the monk's murder, the astounded Adso compliments William's perspicacity,
admirations which are dismissed by his response that his reasoning is "elementary." Other comparisons may equally be drawn here with obvious parallel
figures such as Peter Ellis's *Cadfael* and Trelayne's Sister Fidelma, both of
whom apply logical reasoning to seemingly mysterious medieval "whodun-
nits." "The popularity of *The Name of the Rose* and *The Return of Martin
Guerre*[61] has spawned a number of films centering on the precocious modernity
of detective clerics. These figures embody the contradictions inherent in the
modern wish to know the medieval past directly from a perspective that is at
once within and yet impervious to its radical alterity."[62]

To extend the paradigm, we can extrapolate that such curiosity and suspicion can be seen, in film and popular novels, to be afforded to closed societies
in general. Examples may be adduced from Shyamalan's *The Village*, which
has as its focus a Mormon community, as does Conan Doyle's novel *A Study
in Scarlet*, or *Eyes Wide Shut* which focuses on cults, not to mention the ultimate exploration (and parody) of conspiracy theories surrounding "closed
communities," *Foucault's Pendulum*, and its unfortunate progeny (oblivious
to its irony), *The Order* and *The Da Vinci Code*. The popularity of such an
"unmasking" of a secret/closed society can thus go some way to explaining
its continued assimilation with the Middle Ages — and especially with monasticism — for it comes in this way to represent a closed community *within* the
alterity of monasticism *within* the Other of the Middle Ages.

THE MONK AS REVELER: FRIAR TUCK

"What have we here? It's a girdled friar, and a fat one at that."[63]

Yet, of course, the monk as detective archetype is not alone in this process. Throughout numerous versions of medieval monastic films we can find

a similar process of iconic fusion producing what becomes the mirror image of William of Baskerville in the perennially popular paradigm of Friar Tuck. As mentioned above, the general perception of the monasteries was not always wholly positive and, although most recognized that this was by no means universally true, "the institution, as a whole, no longer deserved its exceptional place as a vast world-force in society."[64] As is common in the popular mindset, however, it is the most egregious exceptions which tend to form the rule, which opened the formerly austere and respected monk up to a satirical subtext. These satirical works (Chaucer, fabliaux, (etc.) transformed over time to become something of an accepted reality to audiences, even down to the present day, who are more accustomed to imagine a corpulent — and only too worldly — friar wandering at leisure around the secular world than they are to think of his cloistered descendent. The figure of fun thus becomes tainted with the twin accusations of gluttony and lechery, for "behind the comic device of the slothful cleric lies the stock-figure of the bombastic Vice of Gluttony personified in the medieval morality plays."[65] Thus:

> When the clean line between literature and history gets blurred, the mythopoeic process of the popular imagination transforms old archetypes into literary heroes, and historical and pseudo-historical persons often get caught up like stray fibers in the epical weaving process. Thus, the popular figures of the Dionysian Lord of Misrule, the French BonTemps, the English May Day trickster, and the medieval glutton are transformed and intertwined into the brown habit of the jolly friar.[66]

So it is that in film, too, we can witness this evolution even within the modern interpretation of Friar Tuck (the jolly friar to whom the quotation refers) from the Vice of Gluttony, Chaucer's Hubard and ultimately Rabelais' Frère Jean, bequeathing to the modern cinema a somewhat dubious, and certainly parodic, legacy. Beginning cinematic life as a straightforward caricature, in early Robin Hood films such as *The Adventures of Robin Hood*, we can see the prototype of Robin's friar from medieval tradition (which was, however, a later addition to the Robin Hood corpus), which frequently constructed him as a simple mirror of the equally portly Little John, played by the stock character actor Alan Hale. The main function of the friar in this early outing is as a comic foil to the epic, dashing — and certainly swashbuckling — Robin, and who initially represents the avarice and gluttony associated with this variety of monasticism. Even from his introduction, he is conceived as a natural target for Robin's gang. Shown sleeping under a tree with a fishing rod cast, his is both the antithesis of Robin's lithe, active and noble qualities, and the embodiment of the laziness and gluttony of the ruling elite which perpetuate social injustice according to the Robin Hood of legend, who traditionally "represents principled resistance to wrongful authority — of very different kinds and in many periods and contexts."[67]

Even when expressing caution, Robin's men reveal the duplicity and hypocrisy of the Church and its servants in their ironic warning; "careful Robin. That's the friar of Fountains Abbey. He's noted [winks] for his piety." He is also deemed to be "the most dangerous swordsman in the county," neither of which traits are engineered to give us faith in his religious devotion. However, to Robin, he also represents the requisite "moralism" necessary to legitimize his band of outlaws. On discovering him sleeping under a tree he exclaims, "He's just what we need, I'll enlist him," and later confides to the friar, "I live in the forest with a few score good fellows who have everything in life save spiritual guidance."

The character demolition continues by a repeated emphasis on his bodily size (an indexical reference to his lack of abstemiousness), so that while others are recruited to the band on promises of riches, vengeance or protection, Robin promises the friar only "the finest venison pastries ... and casks of ale." Rather than take offense, the friar's reply serves as a tacit acknowledgement of his preference for earthly pleasures; "you should have said that before, you would have saved us both a 'wetting' [from their fight in the river]." Further jokes about his stature only reinforce our impression of his hearty appetite ("it'll take half the deer in Sherwood forest to feed his belly"), so that by the time Will Scarlett arrives and is assured that "it's alright, he's one of us," his mockery is based on purely external impressions; "one of us? He looks like three of us."

From the outset, then, he becomes a comic figure, whose flustered helplessness is a mark of the indignation that peasants would rebel against their "place in society," a product of both the championing of the underdog and the confusion of modern and medieval ideas which is rife throughout medieval movies, as we will see in the next chapter. It is interesting to note that where once this mockery was a satirical jibe at the monastic lack of frugality, to a modern audience the satire is lost, and instead becomes merely something of a comic relief from the epic showdown between Robin and the sheriff. What began life as satire, "the most powerful weapon that the people have ever had in order to make clear to themselves, within their own culture, all the misdeeds and corruption of their rulers,"[68] loses that gleeful disrespect of authority figures and instead becomes simply the perpetuation of an archetypal irreverence, but poses no serious threat beyond the scope of the film.

Kaler traces a similar evolution of the character, in which the friar becomes less and less interested in saving his reputation (which initially helps to shield the gang, in both the 1938 film and in *Ivanhoe*, for example), and gradually becomes so insinuated within the Merrie Men that he becomes an outlaw by assimilation. It is only one more step, therefore, to see him reinvented as a defrocked monk in both *Robin Hood: Prince of Thieves*, and in *Robin Hood* of the same year.[69] By removing him from the monastery altogether, however, he is symbolically divested of the restrictions which his rule imposes on him, which loses the sense of protection, legitimacy and hypocrisy of active monks which was brought out initially in contemporary satires such as *The Shipman's Tale*. He thus comes to be constructed as something of a people's champion instead of a good apple in a bad crop, which in turn reinforces the anti-institutional feeling which twentieth-century Robin Hood films had so carefully crafted. What these two later films do offer, though, is a convincing depiction of the pervasive mistrust felt towards monasteries as a whole — though more likely to be drawing their ideas from a slew of recent films such as *Ladyhawke, Stealing Heaven*[70] (dir. Clive Donner, Amy International/Film Dallas/Jadran, 1988), and of course, *The Name of the Rose*.

In Reynolds' film, the figure of Friar Tuck is vaunted as a hero who uses his privileged status as a means of helping the poor and downtrodden peasants of Sherwood Forest.[71] Consequently, while in Curtiz's 1938 version he was engaged in a spiritual capacity and to tend to the babies "which need to be christened," his ecclesiastical credentials in Reynolds' film are minimized in an attempt to disassociate him from the shadows of the monastery, and his only religious function is to marry the protagonists at the end, though even this duty is interrupted and taken over by the newly returned King Richard. This distancing process is more marked in Irvin's film (also 1991), on which Jeff Nuttall's friar is demonstrably more tied to the pagan, nature-worship tradition than to the medieval church (something of a relief to Historians, perhaps, sparing them the sight of a friar wearing the Franciscan habit in a film set in the 1190s, some ten to twenty years before the foundation of the Franciscan order). Instead of the "sacred tradition of marriage" of *Prince of Thieves* which would require a priest, in a ceremony celebrating the couple's fertility, Marian agrees to the wedding because Robin "makes the May tree blossom and the bees buzz in my breast. I will take this man because he brings springtime to my heart." In the dénouement of the film, the friar is further removed from the Church as institution when he is dressed up as the Dionysian Lord of Misrule on the Mayday festivities, during which the cowled friar shouts to the gatekeeper "Welcome to Hell." By transposing the battle from heresy versus orthodoxy to one of a "principled resistance" to the corruption of the established church, and therefore resistance to corrupt institutions as a whole, we find that even after a substantial detour the wheel has turned full circle to the original cinematic tradition of Robin Hood, the "principled resistance to wrongful authority" mentioned above.[72] In this respect the friar fits

in with a general movement to transpose Robin from a noble to anti-estab-
lishment figure, which "developed by itself, with gradual, minor adjustments:
from the bandit to the gentleman outlaw, from this to the noble outlaw, and
finally into a political revolutionary [fighting] for a just cause."[73]

However, this movement away from monasticism sees its final phase, as
in so many cases, in the form of parody, in Mel Brooks' *Robin Hood: Men in
Tights*. In place of the usual Friar Tuck scene, the director himself cameos as
a maniacal "Rabbi Tuckman" who operates a mobile circumcision unit. Ignoring for one moment the bawdy and scatological humor, there is an interesting
criticism of Jewish invisibility within the Middle Ages, an undertone which
is perpetuated by running jokes about Judaism, such as the introduction to
the character Ahchoo (a jibe at *Prince of Thieves* Azeem), which is met with
the response "A Jew? Here?"[74] However, even within the realm of parody, the
association of Tuck and gluttony makes its appearance in the exchange between
Robin and the Rabbi. In a frame-by-frame recreation of the meeting between
Robin and Tuck in *Prince of Thieves*, the two characters' verbal sparring resembles the conversation in which the friar's initial reluctance to join the troupe
is overcome by his love of wine:

> ROBIN: Rabbi, you seem to be on the side of good. Will you come and share
> with us some of your wisdom, some of your council, and perhaps ... some of
> your wine?
>
> RABBI: Wisdom and council, that's easy. But this is sacramental wine! It's
> only used to bless things.
>
> [pauses]
>
> Wait a minute! There's things here! There's rocks, there's trees, there's
> birds, there's squirrels. Come on, we'll bless them all until we get vashnigy-
> ered.

When the BBC series of Robin Hood arrives some ten years later, therefore, it is scarcely a surprise to see that the complexity of the character of the
monk is excised in its entirety, and the entire band of Merry Men has been
scaled down to five who each embody the most perennially popular attributes
of their predecessors. The new band, comprising a powerful Little John, a
skilled craftsman Will Scarlet, a loyal Much the Miller's son, a crafty Alan A-
Dale, and the "Saracen" tomboy Djaq, adopt a noticeably twenty-first-century
moral code in their dealings with the sheriff, and in its production there are
clear signs that these difficult characterizations (aristocratic backgrounds, the
struggle between the establishment and the outlaws, the exact nature of Prince
John) have all been carefully removed to create a simple — and overtly laic —
approach to the legend.

There is, evidently, a great deal which could be said about the evolution
of this complex figure of Friar Tuck, for which there are a number of excel-

lent scholarly analyses.[75] But we can use another argument *ex silencio*—i.e., his gradual removal from the scene, or at least the trend of playing down his monasticism — in order to posit two explanations. The first is simply that the character of Friar Tuck, and the corpulent monk in general, has by its continued re-use and development become far too complex and far too stereotyped, so that it produces too many potential signifieds and no longer connects to the subversive image of the gluttonous monk. If this is the case, then it is easier to excise the character in its entirety (as has occurred with characters like Alan A-Dale in many cases) than to invoke the archetype while simultaneously trying to specify which idea of the medieval monk they are trying to invoke.

The second possibility is that filmmakers are willfully trying to move away from the stereotype by suppressing links with the Church, since not only does the prior existence of the paradigmatic "gluttonous monk" restrict freedom of character development, but also it would risk alienating modern audiences, who seek either a certain laicity in film or who might be offended by such a negative view of the Church — even the medieval church. Should the gang still require a spiritual element, we have seen that it can even (as in later Robin Hood films) be imported from other paradigms by genre transfer, so that Azeem of Reynolds' film — like Djaq of the BBC series — serves broadly the same function as a mystical healer and add a sense of exoticism, while at the same time avoiding any criticism of the modern Church and serving a general sense of postcolonial guilt.[76] It seems, for instance, scarcely a coincidence that these "Muslim Crusaders" who are treated kindly by the gang begin to appear in versions of Robin Hood taking place against a backdrop of armed invasions in the Middle East (1991, 2004–2005).[77]

Where I have argued above that there exists a polarization in film between the scholarly sagacity of the monk as detective and the gluttony and sloth of the revelling monk, we can find in some cases that there is a continuous thread running between them. This thread is, put in its simplest terms, their endearing popularity to cinematic audiences; namely their humanity. To err, as we know, is all too human, and so it is to their faults (in the latter case) and to their natural inquisitiveness (in the former) that most popular audiences can relate — even if they are certainly not able to relate to the initial signified of the "medieval monk." It is this underlying humanity which prevents them from eliding into the rather one-dimensional archetype of the serious monk or nun, who more often than not simply act as the unwitting "straight actor" to the protagonist's subversion. Nowhere, however, is this complex — and frequently delicate — balance between vilified and glorified medieval religion more visible than in the attempt to commit the lives of "superhumans" — saints — to celluloid posterity.

Saints' Lives in Film

A new problem thus arises, when we turn to this last category of "those who pray." If audiences can relate better to characters with human flaws, what does the cinema do to present a saint to a popular audience, a character whose sanctity, near-perfection and steadfast belief in their actions ought naturally to repel an audience more accustomed to the fallible — but endearing — characteristics of the underdog? Furthermore, when a saint withdraws from the world to attain a closer relationship with an (cinematically, at least) invisible God, how do films make anything exciting from the life of an ascetic who — by definition — repudiates any form of excitement and adventure?

This final problem comes once again at the level of signification and adaptation, in the transition from medieval hagiography to modern narrative. The former, being enormously popular throughout the medieval period (and experiencing a renewed popularity among medievalists),[78] were edifying accounts designed not to persuade nor to entertain, but rather to inspire the ordinary man with the deeds and works of an exceptionally pious human. The latter narratives, on the other hand, immediately come across those same problems outlined in chapter 1, which is that in any given "biopic," the necessity to interpret all of the acts of one person into a coherent, cohesive narrative structure inevitably involves the assumption of a certain ideological position and narrative "shaping," against which critics will almost inevitably levy accusations of distortion, inaccuracy and betrayal.

So how can this situation be resolved? To revert to our semiotic model, the problem of signification is as follows: we have a signified element (the saint him- or herself), whose signifier "saint" is necessarily only recognized as such *after having manifested those acts which bring about their canonization*, and therefore the future saint must, within their own lifetime, be constructed as an exceptional human being who is superior in degree but not kind. Given, however, that one of the most frequent attributes of these saints is their modesty, for "one is a saint only to and through other people,"[79] they must be also and at the same time a paragon of humility. We must, in order to create a signifier of this, therefore introduce this third-person ("other people") perspective in order to demonstrate to the audience that this is so. Thus our signifiers, both iconic and paradigmatic, must adopt this third-person perspective which serves to inform the audience of the sanctity of the film's protagonist, by either creating or relying on existing iconographical traditions as well as making use of a range of genre motifs (the most frequent of these, as we shall see below, being a paradigmatic association with Christ or His Apostles). Perhaps this complexity goes a long way to explain why Saint Cinema has so frequently favored St. Francis and Joan of Arc over any other medieval saint, making them the "two historical figures which have experienced the greatest popularity on the screen."[80] In these two cases, some of the work can already be done for them, as we shall see in the case of Saint Francis, when that saint already has a modern "signifier" in the legacy that he or she leaves behind. Furthermore, and tellingly, both saints find a ready-made popularity not by dint of their piety, but by a serendipitous alignment with contemporary concerns: Francis' love of nature chimes eloquently with the ecological green movement, and Joan's drive and determination are in tune with late–twentieth-century feminism. Such a timeliness thus both allows audiences to connect with and relate to these medieval saints, while at the same time ensuring their survival into the twenty-first century.

However, we are also able to draw a parallel here between the two intentions mentioned above, the medieval and modern narratives. Within the medieval hagiographic tradition there is — on a purely semiotic level — no need to construct the saint as such *iconically* (that is, by virtue of iconic or indexical signs), since this sanctity is *de facto* already accepted as such, for "a saint is a person whom others have seen as such and who has fulfilled this role for them."[81] The medieval saint's life was intended, therefore, not to prove his or her sanctity — nor even to communicate it — but rather to explain *why* and *how* he or she achieved this status, which is equally the intention of the twentieth-century narrative film. Neither serves to prove or even defend this canonization but to demonstrate the lessons which their lives have to offer; indeed, to continue the example of Zeffirelli above, with *Brother Sun, Sister Moon*, the director sought not to prove his sanctity, but to give his own interpretation of what the saint's life had to offer a modern viewer. In the wake of a number of "flower power" films, he observes that he wanted to "film the story of Saint Francis as a 'holy revolutionary.'"[82] The similarity between the two time periods shows us that although we may well be dealing with two distinctly different receptions and *personal motivations* for the films, the way in which that message is communicated remains at base the same: that Francesco had, in his time, effected what we would now understand as a revolution — even if it might not have been construed exactly in those terms then. Along the same lines as Zeffirelli, for example, Kozlovic proposes that "Francis, 'the thirteenth-century drop-out' made the Church uncomfortable by contrasting their spiritual posture with their actual temporal function,"[83] later referring to him as a "holy Rebel-with-a-Cause"[84] (providing evidence of a paradigmatic association, too).

It must be noted here that I am not asserting that Francis' movement *was* a revolution, for we are using loaded terms, and liable consequently to confuse the formal aspects of a modern revolution in so doing. Perhaps Six's more measured terms might be more appropriate, claiming rather that "respecting the historical facts means to acknowledge that Francis of Assisi did indeed, in his own period, effect a revolution, but not just any; not a revolution as we would conceive it today."[85] Nevertheless, in terms of the signifiers themselves, the iconic (and to some extent the iconographic) attributes of this "rebellion" or "protest" do present several parallels of which the twentieth-century cinema can make profitable use.

This protest and renunciation is most clearly seen in one of the most memorable scenes of Zeffirelli's film, when the young Francis renounces his earthly possessions in order to achieve the spiritual poverty on which his order was later based. While an incredibly difficult concept to communicate without dialogue, the film resolves this by translating this spiritual poverty into physical nakedness, which to a medieval audience as well as their modern descendants, lends itself to an exegetical process. His devotion to poverty was manifested — both then and here — by a temporal and material nakedness, which to a medieval audience had theological overtones.

According to medieval exegesis, Francis' nakedness reflects three aspects of wholesomeness, namely:

(a) nuditas naturalis (the natural state of being born into the world);
(b) nuditas temporalis (the lack of worldly goods and possessions);
(c) nuditas virtualis (the symbol of purity and innocence).[86]

He was moved to this in stages, in reality passing first to hermit's simple robe and sandals, and then, on hearing one preacher, was so moved that "he immediately put off his shoes from his feet, put aside the staff from his hands, was content with one tunic, and exchanged his leather girdle for a small cord. He designed for himself a tunic that bore a likeness to the cross."[87] The symbolism of his clothing therefore became of paramount importance both to his medieval followers — who as Pastoureau has argued were by no means immune to symbolism and iconography — and to modern audiences alike, accustomed from the silent era onwards to attribute meaning to the images placed on the screen before them. This gradual renunciation of earthly riches is achieved in Zeffirelli's film by passing through each of the above three stages in reverse, each with their own visual evocations.

The first stage of purity and innocence is demonstrated in the scene immediately following his convalescence; rising from his bed in a pure white tunic, he follows a tiny, chirruping bird across his balcony, then onto a rooftop where he walks to the end. When he finally captures the bird, the camera cuts between a series of shots which represent the viewpoints of the cynical towns-folk (from below in a static zoom, from the balcony in a medium-long shot), before a second medium shot shows his innocent smile. The whole frame resembles a religious painting of the Renaissance, in its very pure concept of line, the purity and simplicity of the colors and the emptiness of the frame, with the sole exception of the (messianic) subject, who is bathed in a strong (pure) fill light highlighting the brilliance of his long white tunic.

The second phase is less subtle; returning from the market, the camera follows Francis' father through the streets of Assisi as we see a flurry of rich clothes raining down upon the passers by. Tilting upwards from his father's point-of-view, we see Francis in the window throwing his worldly possessions to the waiting crowd in a very public demonstration of renunciation. The fact that the "possessions" which Francis is rejecting are items of clothing is itself telling, representing a literal interpretation of the *nuditas temporalis.*

This dramatic stage brings us directly to the third phase, the *nuditas naturalis.* Having been disowned by his father and the townsfolk, Francis walks naked through the square to the gates of the town, whereupon he passes through a long tunnel towards the sunlight of the countryside. The camera follows in a long zoom (and not a tracking shot, since we are too rooted in the riches and material wealth to be reborn), as we watch him emerge from the "birth canal" into the light in a clear symbol of rebirth. At this point, his spiritual rebirth complete, he raises his arms making of him a living crucifix seen from behind and silhouetted against the green of Nature and the yellow of the sunshine, before a cross-fade brings us into the next "act" of the film, which takes place almost entirely outdoors.

In order, however, to achieve this harmonization between medieval and modern sensibilities, the modern tradition is reliant on a process which reaches far more widely outside of the medieval iconographic tradition, instead making use of the synchronic trope of natural innocence (recalling the Edenic paradise of Genesis), and a diachronic appeal to the figure of the 1960s "flower child." This latter, evidently, is paradigmatic, for as we mentioned above "Zeffirelli had constructed the medieval St. Francis as a 1960s hippie and Christ-figure with a strong auto-biographical flavour,"[88] relying therefore on paradigmatic association to make his point. The former process is iconic, for in his mise-en-scène the director tries to demonstrate his harmony with nature, placing him among "lush seas of tall, green grass with red poppies and white daisies ruffled by gentle breezes against tangerine sunsets change into white, virginal snow, followed by yellow fields and more fields of green, red and purple." It is a doubly meaningful construction, however, for "these colours [also] have medieval allegorical meanings, namely: green for life; red for martyrdom, love and 'caritas'; white for purity and chastity."[89] While the medieval significance of these colors is almost completely lost on a modern audience, they do serendipitously relate to another iconic construction of the late 1960s, the flower-child, with one online reviewer commenting that "Francis [is used] as a metaphor to express the ideals of the Flower Power movement ... the patron saint of the Woodstock era."[90] There are other areas, too, in which medieval iconography is used, but which is still readily recognized by even non-religious audiences, such as the scene of the papal visit, in which — having received the papal blessing — "to visually tag Francis' holiness, Zeffirelli shows a fleeting shot of Francis' head surrounded by a yellowish halo, a saintly hallmark of Christian iconography that symbolises divinity, rank and sovereignty."[91] These same Messianic overtones are used elsewhere, too, in particular in the use of key lighting, an iconographic signifier of the divine presence, as witnessed in its use in the architecture of Abbé Suger's Notre Dame; according to Suger "light was the primary source of faith and divine inspiration."[92]

In Rossellini's *Francesco, Giullare di Dio* the young Francesco is lit in precisely the same way in order to identify him as a central, and almost divine, figure in the medieval religious context, most noticeable in an early scene when Rossellini places a cross in the center of the frame, behind which Francesco and a peasant farmer are seen praying. The vertical bar of the cross divides the monk from the peasant (the monastic from the secular), though the horizontal reunites the two on the earth (symbolizing the union of the two worlds in the missions of the mendicant friars), visually reinforced by the symmetry of the mise-en-scène. Most significantly though, Francesco's face is lit by a shaft of light coming from above and crossing his body diagonally, placing into prominence the future saint's holiness and innocence by comparison with the shadows which dominate the right side of the frame.

Again we see an uneasy mixture of both iconic and paradigmatic methods used in films about the other "superstar" of medieval sainthood: Joan of Arc.[93] Even when trying to avoid stereotypes, Besson's *The Messenger*, for example, tries to subvert the traditional paradigm of the physical frailty of the female body but thereby aligns itself to some extent with the "girl power" movement which frequently had as its focus the empowerment of teenage girls throughout the late 1990s.[94] Yet the most persistent recourse for these films is the iconic "visual tag," frequently achieved through key lighting, but which can also take place by a number of signifiers such as extreme close-ups, low-angle shots, color symbolism (in which white symbolises purity), tracking shots which retain the saint in the center, and so on.

In appealing to these two traditions, "saint cinema" thus communicates the sanctity of its heroes by a reliance on two planes of interpretation (iconic and paradigmatic), which attempt to please both camps at once: "it is astonishing that Francis fascinated both the fervently pious who sought to establish a community and the 'revolutionaries' who set themselves up against injustice."[95] Perhaps it is precisely this attempt to appeal to a mass audience against which critics often strongly react, because the symbols are reduced to a series of immediately striking elements which are not limited to the lines of plausibility and credibility to which other films are usually bound. Roger Ebert, for example, tells of *Brother Sun, Sister Moon* how he "hated, hated, hated this movie,"[96] bemoaning its ultra-modern significance which (in his eyes) betrayed the medieval meaning, and oversimplifying the Franciscan message, so that after an opening of "confusion and complexity [...] the movie levels off into one note, indefinitely held."[97] Just as Francis simply becomes a man at one with nature, the oversimplification of the Joan of Arc story equally leads to a very brief series of facts from which filmmakers tend not to deviate, reducing them to a simple checklist: a maid, visions, an army, a trial, a martyr.

Trying to film the ineffable, therefore, presents a number of problems, since they must first establish a generally accepted, codified series of icons in order to express this divinity, which more often than not resorts to the traditional association of light and religious iconography. If one of the problems is that there are no secular icons, Zeffirelli's film demonstrates — as does Besson's *The Messenger*— that there are no paradigms either, since the association of the divine and the mundane creates an uneasy mixture which borders on the iconoclastic. The final nail in the coffin here comes with Pasolini's jibe at medieval canonisation in *Il Decameron*, part of his subversive *trilogia della vita*.[98] Upon the death of Cepparello (played by Pasolini himself), he realizes that he need only confess to the most minor of sins in order that the confessor be so astounded by such "trifling sins" as to declare the manifestly wicked rogue Cepparello a saint; "once dead, Cepparello becomes Saint Chapelet, by means of the process which once again inverts sacred values: saints are opportunist rogues, and rogues are saints-to-be, if only they respect the rules of the game: a 'good' confession."[99] From his death scene onwards, Pasolini's frame composition uses precisely the "iconography" developed by the long Italian tradition of Saint Francis films (shafts of light, medium-long and low-angle camera shots, zooms in place of tracking shots) in order to visually construct him as a saint. The duality of the film, as a consequence, undermines the sanctity by a cruel dramatic irony, and at the same time sets up a conflict between the codes that we know and the codes that we see. It takes more than a halo, it seems, to make a saint.

Conclusions

To conclude this section, then, we may first restate the original propositions set out at the beginning of the chapter, that the characterization of this stratum of society is never neat, and rarely clear and unambiguous, owing to the continued existence of a modern equivalent of the priesthood whose outward signs differ radically from their medieval equivalents. Consequently, films seeking to recall through film the two most common figures among those who pray — that is, the priest and the monk — have had recourse to two overriding strategies of signification: iconic recreation and paradigmatic association, which we have seen work in slightly different ways to previous chapters.

Given that the priesthood must be separated from its modern equivalents, its material signs (the priestly clothing, riches of the Church) tend to be highlighted (instead of dog collars and black, we see monastic tonsures, albs, surplices and chains of office); in addition to this, the different *function* of the priest is frequently emphasized by the addition of iconic signs of pedagogy, mastery or paternity. The tendency of recent films to assume an a priori antagonistic position in relation to the medieval Church has also brought into being the recurrent archetype of the rich priest, emphasized in films like *Ladyhawke* or *Brother Sun, Sister Moon*, which uses highly prominent material wealth in order to criticize the religious offices and their avarice. This process is also supported by placing the priests into a feudal hierarchy which corresponds to the importance of their secular counterparts, so that audiences can more easily identify the specific role played by the priest within the feudal model with which we believe ourselves to be more familiar.

The second major figure in this field is the monk, a signified whose modern equivalent bears so little resemblance that we have produced a completely new signifier in the form of two recurrent archetypes, borrowed from other genres in a paradigmatic loan process, the scholarly monk and the jolly brown friar. The first is clearly drawn from the detective genre, and involves a simple equation of the studiousness of monks with the seeming omniscience of figures like Sherlock Holmes and Poirot, producing figures like William of Baskerville, Cadfael and even (to some extent) Nicholas in *The Reckoning*. The more common counterfoil to this is the monk as reveler, whose most prominent exemplar is of course Friar Tuck. Representing the worldly gluttony and avarice with which medieval monks were themselves accused, the archetype has continued into modern films initially to provide a comedic foil to the swashbuckling heroes. Over time, however, his overt religiosity has been increasingly played down, and we are beginning to see a new role of spiritual/moral adviser rather than ecclesiastical minister, culminating in his replacement by figures representing a more pagan, Merlin-style religion "of the people."

Finally, moving from the mundane to the sublime, we have seen that one of the most problematic of these figures has been the saint. In order to evoke both the humanity and the holiness and piety of these saintly figures, filmmakers have until recently tended to reject paradigms (given that it seems most unlikely that one might be available in any case) and focused on recreating those same iconic symbols as medieval iconographers have formerly favored: light, key lighting, elevation, isolation, innocence and symbolic meanings. However, the combination of these iconic symbols with elements intended to please mass audiences in recent years (such as Besson's *Joan of Arc*) have often ended up producing a series of spurious films which underplay the spiritual vocation and therefore tend rather to simplify their holy devotion.

A second notion which has dominated this has been the attempt to separate them from "the people," in an attempt to emphasize either their elevated societal status (in the case of the priest), or their *contemptus mundi*, and subsequent sequestration away from society (in the case of the monk). As a consequence, then, we can see that the people — those making up the major part of this "society" — become painted in such films as a vulgar, lowly and downtrodden stratum who bear very few individuating features, and therefore come to be treated as one homogeneous group. Over the course of my final chapter on medieval people, then, I will examine how cinema has attempted to represent "those who work."

6

Everybody *Not* Sitting on
a Cushion: Those Who Work

"France—fifteenth century—the Dark Ages ... the people were still gripped in ignorance and superstition."[1]

In this chapter we will turn to examine the social grouping[2] which has proved to be the most elusive, and the most difficult to establish within medieval film—the hordes of peasants, "serfs," freemen, laborers, and so on, the constituent parts of the "great unwashed," to use Edward Bulwer-Lytton's disparaging appellation (which Hollywood seems often to have taken literally as a stage direction rather than a metaphor). The question of *why* they are difficult to portray, however, is not quite as simple, being based on three complementary responses (examined in Part I), representing the three aspects of signification. These are, in short, that as an *object*, they are largely invisible within the pages of most history books; second, as a *concept* the social boundaries were not as rigid as filmmakers and popular opinion would have us believe; third, as *referents*, we are too influenced by modern ideas of class struggles, post–Marxist thought and oversimplification to connect with them in any meaningful way. There is also, as the epigraph suggests, a distinct problem of *period* when it comes to dealing with this class. While some filmmakers might recognize the subtle differences between twelfth- and thirteenth-century cavalrymen, tear off the Franciscan habit from their ninth-century monks, and are in most cases prepared to grudgingly remove the Vikings from their Hundred Years' War, to most filmmakers and audiences the medieval peasant is simply that: an unchanging and unnoticed background to society.

Despite this invisibility (or perhaps because of it), the peasant is nevertheless eminently recognizable, as I will propose in Part II, for in the popular imagination he lives on in more or less unadulterated form. He dresses in brown, he is covered in mud, he works in the fields and lives in a hovel, sleeping in straw with his wife and multitudinous children, along with a handful of farmyard animals to keep out the winter cold. Yet each element of this iconic (yet mostly erroneous) construction of the peasant, I will show, is in fact drawn from a particular understanding of their nature, status and function; reflected in their appearance, their spatial significance; and designed to reinforce the assumed weakness and helplessness of their social position, all of which are direct consequences of the problems of signification discussed in Part I. In the final section of this chapter, I will turn to examine the paradigms invoked to explicate the peasantry in film, which take an unusual form in that *precisely because* they are usually overlooked, their ubiquity and interchangeability make them into two paradigms themselves. The first is on the level of the individual, the stock figure of the peasant, while the second represents the unit as a whole, the homogeneous "mass" of "everybody not sitting on a cushion," as *A Knight's Tale*'s Chaucer has it.

The Medieval Referent

THE INVISIBILITY OF MEDIEVAL PEASANTRY

"Once upon a time, there was a peasant. He had a hard life, working all year 'round, little better off than a slave, and no say in what went on. He was diseased, he was downtrodden and he was dirty. Who on earth would have wanted to have been a medieval peasant?"[3]

One of the first things to understand about the medieval peasantry is the fallacy of our modern beliefs that the peasants were regarded as harshly treated, unwelcome blots on the landscape, who were looking for any opportunity to right the social wrongs and throw off the yoke of their oppression. When we examine the evidence in detail, we find a more interesting, and far more ambivalent, attitude to the social divisions, among which some evidence that they were regarded as an important, even indispensable element of what John of Salisbury, after Plutarch, describes as "the body social."[4] Writing about the anatomical arrangement of this 'body,' John of Salisbury writes that:

> Those are called the feet who discharge the humbler offices, and by whose services the members of the whole commonwealth walk upon solid earth ... all of which [occupations], while they do not pertain to the authority of the governing power, are yet in the highest degree useful and profitable to the corporate whole of the commonwealth.[5]

In a similar vein, Castellanus asserts that "God [...] created the common people to till the earth and to procure by trade *the commodities necessary for life*; he created the clergy for works of religion; the nobles that they should cultivate virtue and maintain justice, so that the deeds and the morals of these fine personages might be a pattern to others."[6] As such, and as so often is the case, those working in the background and providing those *essential* elements "necessary for life" are not looked down upon, but they are simply unrecognized and unacknowledged.

Looking from the other direction, too, we can see that it is those whose *individual* actions are sufficient to be attributed to a name who will enjoy the posterity denied to those who may have carried out the very actions for which the individual is recognized.[7] Thus Brooke's admission that

> The English upper classes fill the pages of this book, because they controlled the country's destinies, and because "those who worked" have left little memorial. But it is well to remember that the enormous majority of the million to a million and a half of eleventh- and twelfth-century Englishmen were peasants, farm labourers, or artisans.[8]

And all this despite the fact that, as Power argues, "History is largely made up of Bodos [the peasant]."[9] Such invisibility is in many respects based on a lack of physical records relating the contributions made by the lowest levels of society; when films try to recreate historical events, therefore, the absence of the peasants is almost by necessity transferred directly to the cinema, so that "the peasants are, with some notable exceptions, the great absents of historical cinema."[10]

There are, however, two further potential reasons for this invisibility in cinema, beyond the simple explanation that the historical records are scarce. Cinema (or at least historical cinema) is a medium of grand actions, of epic movements, and favors the leadership of committed visionaries. The dramatic tension of the individual who accepts the drudgery of his daily routine on the grounds that it is prescribed by God is somewhat less enthralling than the conflict engendered by a "hero" who challenges the status quo.

> Film insists on history as the story of individuals, men or women who are already renowned or who are made to seem important because they are singled out by the camera. Those who are not already famous are common people who have done heroic or admirable things.[11]

With few exceptions, the epic historical films are — like the pages of populist history books — full of larger-than-life characters whose behavior is both edifying and exemplary and whose actions have changed something, providing a direct link between *them* and *us*; whereas, from the little that we know about them — or perhaps precisely *because of* the lack of knowledge — there is little in the life of a medieval peasant to which most modern audiences can relate.

One second reason for their absence in film is their ubiquity (of which there is more in Part III), and consequently their lack of individual contribution to the narrative drive. A useful comparison may be drawn here between the medieval peasant and the foot soldier from military films. Both characters share the lot of obligation, danger, squalor, dirt and the necessity of unquestioning obedience to superiors, on whose orders their life often depends. Most crucially, in the cinema they often share a uniformity (quite literally in the sense of the military uniform) and dispensability, for if we do not see their faces, nor do we spend any significant screen time with them, it is difficult to establish any degree of audience empathy. They occupy a liminal space in the cinematic imaginary, since they are paradoxically both collectively indispensable (one of the prerequisites of a war film, after all, is almost always a large budget for extras) *and* individually dispensable at the same time (one has only to recall the opening scenes of the Normandy landing in *Saving Private Ryan* to consider how many soldiers are killed simply in order to communicate some of the horrors of war). Though the soldiers *as a group* are essential to the war effort, individually it is to the protagonist that we turn to learn their dreams and motivations.

So it is with the cinematic peasant, whose historical "significance" is often minimized on the level of the individual in order to celebrate the "great" heroes of our past. That is not to say, however, that we are not introduced to any interesting characters, nor that we are always indifferent to their individual motivations. In *Ladyhawke*, for example, we meet a misanthropic forester whose reclusive and eccentric wife communicates only in squeals. We, like the protagonist, might wonder whether they are perhaps being established for a greater prominence later in the film,[12] or whether they merely serve as an amusing interlude between the action. A similar iconic process is used in Bergman's *The Seventh Seal*, in which the group stumble across a village in turmoil as a young girl is burnt as a witch; rather than have any great importance to the plot itself, the episode seeks simply to establish the peasants as a group of simple minds made hysterical by the imminent death surrounding them. Their superstitious response functions in much the same way as modern disaster movies show panic-stricken families pointlessly stocking up on flashlights, batteries, tinned food and shotgun cartridges in response to an overwhelming natural — or supernatural — force beyond their control.[13]

These "invisible," simple peasants come therefore to embody those subsidiary characters which E.M. Forster describes as "flat characters,"[14] whose fate is by and large extraneous to the plot, and whom — from the narrative point of view — it is not worth individuating, given their relative inconsequentiality to the central story. In this sense, cinema defines the notion of the peasant by its function — who they *are* is far less important than what they *do*, which presents an interesting similarity to the medieval conception seen above in John of Salisbury's "body social." For the cinema, they embody a class of character who must simply "be there" to color in the background. The more visible they are, therefore, the more *in*visible they become.

MOBILITY OF SOCIAL BOUNDARIES

"Honestly, these country knights [...] some are no better than peasants."[15]

If the invisibility of the peasant fails to provide us with an "object," the second problem of signification comes at the level of the "concept," by which I mean the idea of the medieval peasant which modern cinema audiences are able to conceive. The problem with the conceptual idea is that — as we have seen in other chapters — this concept was by no means static throughout the medieval period, neither diachronically nor even synchronically. Within any given medieval period, it is misleading (though by no means uncommon) to consider the status of the peasantry to be little more than an institutionalized form of serfdom; the plain truth is that social boundaries were far from rigorous, and (as the epigraph above indicates) even between those strata which did exist there were sufficiently diverse variations to make classification a cumbersome, if not impossible, task.

The gradations between classes of freemen and unfree, villeins and laborers, reeves and elders, as well as their different meanings within any given area, were relative to a given zone, so that a reeve in one shire or manor might in practical terms be worse off than a villein of lower standing in another. Or even in the same shire, the cost of equipping and maintaining the trappings of a country knight might often prove to be so overwhelming that some knights might even be less well off than those holding lands from the same estate; some (admittedly exceptional) cases have even been found of knights who hold less land and are in practical terms "no better off than prosperous peasants."[16]

Even working at the level of the "basic feudal unit" of the peasantry, the manor, we find that individual variations are so multifarious that they ultimately render it "a term about as descriptive as 'the mammal.'"[17] Thus, although we have inherited the *concept* of a rigidly organized feudal model in the popular imagination, the historical reality is a great deal more subject to nuances. "The gradations of society were infinite and there was no close relation between status and wealth; it might not always be possible to say whether a man was a soleman or a sergeant, but at least he should know if he was free or unfree."[18] Thus, it falls to this central distinction of being "free" to provide us with a basic delineation of those who work, since it was undoubtedly an important division of medieval life.[19] Though we frequently re-imagine them as a wholly oppressed group, then, we must bear in mind that the unfree were not slaves, but rather "the unfreedom of the villeins lay mainly in their being tied to their plots of land; they were not free to move."[20]

It becomes clear, then, that far from being part of a straightforward hierarchical social structure, medieval peasanthood is by no means a fixed and stable concept. Not only are the material records of their existence scarce, but we are also faced with the problem of evoking a stratum of society which was blurred around the edges to say the least, and which does not permit us to propose broad generalizations without a great deal of qualification, something which we have seen that the cinema — unlike written History — is not able to do. In order, then, to try to connect to this medieval referent we are forced to look back through our own history, establishing links between "us" on the one side and "them" on the other. This, at least, is the aim in a number of recent films like *A Knight's Tale* or *The Advocate* when they use paradigms to compare "those who work" to a sports crowd, suppressing their individuality by reducing them to caricatures, so as to provide a distinction with the "freedom" of its protagonists. Conversely, when the peasant is isolated on screen — as we see in *Ladyhawke*, or the Robin Hood tradition — the caricature uses traditional, iconic Hollywood imagery of the unfree "slave," an archetype born of the Hollywood epic. These two approaches, however, bring into play the third problem of signification, the recognition of our own ideas about the period.

MODERN APPROACHES TO THE PERIOD

"Oh, king, eh? Very nice. And how'd you get that, eh? By exploiting the workers. By hanging on to outdated imperialist dogma which perpetuates the economic and social differences in our society."[21]

This final problem involved in understanding the medieval peasant is inherent in the third part of the process of signification: the referent. Even after having defined the concept (or rather, as I have done above, having eroded the fixed sense we hold of it), we must also recognize that we are unwittingly using a distinct frame of reference which is constructed not from Historical enquiry but from "the universe of signs" which surrounds us today.[22] By the persistent interruption of inappropriate conceptual models (which are essentially paradigms in embryo), any attempts by a modern audience to understand the feudal model are bound to be frustrated, since modern history's focus on the series of revolutions taking place from the eighteenth century through to the modern day perhaps inevitably causes us to perceive the feudal model as an oppressive regime, reframing the peasants' plight in terms of a Marxist class struggle. Huizinga, recognizing this phenomenon, cautions that "nothing could be falser than to picture the third estate in the Middle Ages as animated by class hatred, or scorning chivalry. On the contrary, the splendour of the life of the nobility dazzles and seduces them."[23]

Cinema, however, likes to depict — and thrives on depicting — the medieval "underclass" as perpetually in a state of dissatisfaction with the ruling class, since there is something indisputably appealing about rewriting their story as one of a class-based struggle. After all, as Aumont argues, "to film history is to film popular struggles, *class struggles*."[24] This is often achieved by reversing the symbols of Hollywood chivalry, so that the honorable nobility of the knights becomes depicted instead as a ruthless exploitation of a servile underclass, working on the premise that, "in the cinema, on the level of representation, feudalism can be represented as the antithesis of chivalry."[25] This representation is supported by unnecessarily lavish costumes which separate nobles from peasants, gestures to designate allegiance to one side or another, and language, which functions to separate out layers of nobility.[26] They become, in a sense, the "external signs of 'historical' films."[27] In doing so, however, the liberties taken are frequently achieved by a distortion of the historical records to fit them into such a modern mindset, rather than inspired by a sincere attempt to return to "the facts" themselves.

This process is demonstrated particularly clearly in *Braveheart*, a film which prompted criticism from numerous historians over its "rewriting of history" based on pre-conceived ideological notions.[28] The problem — whatever historians and critics might believe — is not *really* one of historical inaccuracy, for it is a difficult story to retell, admittedly. We have very few reliable sources, and (like his English counterpart Robin Hood) much of Wallace's legacy has been appended posthumously, meaning that to excise it would be to eschew a dubious modern construction in order to return to a dubious historical construction. The problem is rather that the whole issue has been reframed according to modern ideologies, which makes it *feel* like an anachronism. Part of this, then, is already in operation long before cameras even started rolling, because "Wallace lives in the popular imagination as a champion sprung from the common people, although he was the son of a knight," meaning it is "difficult to assess the 'historical' nature of these films [since they] deal with figures who are as much legends as historical individuals."[29]

Given that legends and the "popular imagination" are difficult to commit to film, Gibson has tried to expand this popular struggle by transposing it onto a class struggle, thereby inevitably (though probably unintentionally) inviting comparison with modern class "warfare." In order to polarize the division between the Scottish and the English, for example, Gibson has tried to take this concept of a racial antagonism — which in any case did not exist in those terms — one stage further by transposing it into a vertical arrangement, making the Scots into poor *and therefore oppressed* vassals of a rich *and therefore cruel* English tyranny. In the first instance, the two "therefores" in italics are by no means verifiable logical deductions, making his polarization a little too hasty and oversimplified. In the second instance, by transposing the national conflict into a hierarchical "feudalism," he has also had to alter (or ignore) some of the facts in order to fit them into this ideology. Wallace thus becomes a poor orphaned child instead of the son of a gentleman; rather than suffer the pillaging of his country, in Gibson's version it is his wife who is the victim of the *ius primae noctis* (presented here almost as institutionally sanctioned rape), a topos which is only later extended to "occupied" Scotland as a whole. This vertical contrast is further emphasized by dressing the English troops in armor while leaving the Scots scarcely clothed and equipped with sticks, pikes and farming equipment, as well as transforming Wallace's chief advisers into men drawn from his childhood village. Finally, the determination to present Wallace's story from the point of view of a social revolution has meant that the film "suffer[s] from the weakness of asserting the moral superiority and importance of the poor but then relegating most of them to the status of victim."[30]

Yet this is only to consider one perspective of the ideological referent. While Huizinga et al. argue that the class struggle did not exist during the Middle Ages, that is not to say that the peasants lived in an harmonious, contented idyll, at peace with indulgent, benevolent masters; rather, it means that *the notion of a class struggle did not exist in the same terms as we would define it in modern terms*. The relationship, first, cannot be construed as exclusively one-way, for "it is misleading to picture the relation of the lord and tenant in the post–Carolingian age simply as those of the exploiter and exploited. One must remember what the domain was: a self-sufficient social unit."[31] It could, for instance, be mutually beneficial in certain cases, born of necessity in periods such as the early medieval period, for "in the state of perpetual wars ... in which Europe henceforth lived [after the collapse of the Carolingian state] man more than ever looked for chiefs, and chiefs for vassals."[32] Thus, even a repugnant phenomenon such as serfdom could potentially be reciprocal, and was certainly an enduring relationship; "there was nothing abhorrent about the idea of servitude — everything depended on its object."[33]

Finally, the possibility for a "class consciousness" in the form which we know it today is simply not conceivable in medieval terms; without the means of mass-communication, media, movement and political theorization, little faith can be held in the idea that the peasant "class" could have seen themselves as a "united front" of opposition against the exploiters. The "violence inherent in the system" which Monty Python's Dennis so famously decries, was simply not a model of society to which medieval man of any social stratum would have had recourse, for "on the whole, peasant life, bound to the soil, allowed little room for class solidarity to develop."[34] The neo–Marxist worldview, in short, has little place in a society in which social status and social utility were inextricably intertwined, and whose overall structure was decreed by the absolute authority of God Himself.

Thus we have seen that on the level of signification — using once again Peirce's triadic model — we can find problems on all three sides in trying to approach the medieval peasant. As a signified *object*, a dearth of historical records prevents us from establishing an accurate picture of him, while at the same time, the instability of the *concept* prohibits its assimilation within a more general conceptual framework (regional variations mean that we cannot, for example, write a general history of the European peasant). Finally, we have seen that the application of modern political paradigms (viewing it as a bipolar social structure) inevitably colors our view of the period, and forestalls any attempt to understand the Middle Ages in their own terms, denying us a concrete *referent*. Cognizant of these limitations in even approaching — not to mention reconstructing — the medieval peasant, therefore, we are able to see more clearly that the methods of signifying "those who work" are orientated so as to emphasize one *particular* aspect or another, resorting to iconic or paradigmatic associations to fill the gaps left by our failure to understand them. It is to these two processes, then, that we will now turn.

Iconic Recreations

First, in terms of the iconic process of recreating the medieval peasant, we can recognize that we are rarely beginning *ab initio*; more often than not these portrayals are — in many ways like their literary precedents — constructed as an antithesis of the courtly model of literature. For every knight we see onscreen serving his lady in accordance with the dazzling virtues of chivalry, his opposite reflection is found in the self-serving peasant's coarse and ribald subversion of those same tenets, for "courtly literature and the fabliau are merely reverse images of each other."[35]

This notion can be seen clearly in Paul Verhoeven's *Flesh & Blood* (aka *The Rose and the Sword*),[36] a rather confused concatenation of heterogeneous medieval elements composed together in what might have become a competent pastiche, had it not taken itself so very seriously. Throughout the film the actions of the peasant band led by Martin (Rutger Hauer) are constantly intended to caricature the effects of those from one social stratum trying to ape those of another — here the nobility. There seems little doubt, of course, that the real butt of the joke was neither the coarseness of the peasantry, nor their incapacity to grasp social niceties, but rather the emerging nouveau riche of the twentieth century, which the early '80s economic boom had spawned — another demonstration of the intertext with the present which films about the past inevitably contain.

Nevertheless, or perhaps precisely because of this, it is a useful film to study when looking for signs of cinema's peasantry, since there is still a good deal of screen time spent ridiculing the common man's bemusement when faced with such baffling trappings of etiquette as cutlery, clothes, servants and money, most egregiously demonstrated during a "feast" held to commemorate the capture of a castle. Throughout the scene the vulgarity of the peasant (working on the perception of the Middle Ages as a barbaric, dirty period) is counterpoised by a jump cut between them and their captive, the noble Agnes. Agnes, the daughter of a feudal lord, serves as an embodiment of the "ancien régime" in her composure and refinement throughout the scene; cutting her food quietly with a knife and fork, delicately placing tiny morsels into her mouth and chewing noiselessly, an attempt to juxtapose the quiet dignity of "old money" with the brash coarseness of the aspirational, would-be aristocrats who are unable — or unwilling — to emulate her manners. The scene, reminiscent of Pasolini's visually shocking conclusion to *I Racconti di Canterbury*, quickly descends to a lurid series of rapid cuts between the diners, each engaged in an unacknowledged contest over who can demonstrate the most inappropriate table manners. The attempts by Martin to emulate Agnes may, perhaps, be intended to evoke sympathy and mild amusement, but the extreme close-ups and unsteady camera work construct the feast as a carnivalesque spectacle encouraging us instead to laugh at the others' obliviousness to polite society.

The joke at work here, as I have hinted above, is based on what Eco has posited to be the "Middle Ages as a barbaric age, a land of elementary and outlaw feelings,"[37] and what Williams has subsequently rephrased as simply the "dark, dirty and violent" Middle Ages.[38] It does, however, simultaneously subvert the cinematic "rags to riches" motif, too, making its target both medieval society and our own, playing on the rising trend in films to portray social classes solely as a barrier to be overcome, a trend termed memorably by Aronstein and Coiner as "the Middle Ages of Democratic Possibility":

> In these versions of the Middle Ages, the heroic fantasy is enacted in a "time" figured as American pre-history, and it follows that the narrative outline provided by the American Dream of the local boy who, through his gumption, imagination, and hard work, achieves financial and familial success.[39]

The real punch line to the joke, therefore, works on a use of traditional iconography which is then juxtaposed with the plot and narrative circumstances. Though they may wear the clothes of the aristocrats, eat their food, sit at their table and drink their wine, amid the fraught details of social niceties (in the world according to Verhoeven), a peasant is a peasant is a peasant. Even in Hollywood's version of the Middle Ages, it seems, the clothes maketh not the man.

This trope, however, is by no means restricted to Verhoeven's *Flesh &*

Blood. There seems to be a pervasive idea that the peasant as "savage" was either unwilling or simply incapable of obeying the rules of "civilized" society. In a film like Poiré's *Les Visiteurs,* for example, it is precisely this unchallenged assumption of the peasant's inherent primitiveness which forms the basis of the film's joke — though this film, too, reaches beyond the Middle Ages to poke fun at the "bon chic bon gout" ethos of the early 1990s. What is especially interesting about this film is that by the introduction of a time-traveling theme, the filmmaker has been forced to add a new layer of "barbarity." Put simply, Godefroy de Papincourt is an aristocrat, but is also a product of the "dirty" Middle Ages. Consequently, despite his aristocratic status, he must be shown to be uncouth, dirty, violent and uncivilized in order to create a contrast with his twentieth-century descendents. However, given that he travels with his squire, Jacquouille,[40] the social gap between the two medieval protagonists must equally be demonstrated, requiring that his squire be seen to be *even less sophisticated* than Godefroy himself. In these purportedly "medieval" films, predicated on an ideological belief of the inherent superiority of the twentieth century, such interplay between the courtly nobility (even when subverted, as with *Les Visiteurs* or Twain's *Connecticut Yankee* films) and the peasantry is common, so that the latter very often *is constructed with reference to the former.* Most crudely, then, they are simply the opposite side of the coin; for everything that the nobility are, the peasant must necessarily be the reverse.

Throughout this next section, therefore, we will look at how this mirror image is constructed, using three specific features of iconic construction: where "those who fight" were represented iconically as clean, free and strong, we shall see that the peasant's lowly status is signified by a reverse process of appearance, spatial signification, and weakness.

COSTUMES AND APPEARANCE

"The peasants are revolting."
"They've always been revolting, but now they're rebelling."[41]

Nowhere is this iconic reversal more noticeable than in the purely external appearance of the peasant. Where, as we saw in chapter 3, the ranks of chivalry are visually underscored by the dazzling array of colors, raiments, trailing sleeves, armor and so on, the cinematic peasant is almost always iconically constructed by a negation of the these. The costumes are designed to separate the nobles from the peasants, which support the gestures and language as indices of social status,[42] acting as indexical aspect within a larger class of "external signs" mentioned above.[43] We might therefore propose that the typical cinematic peasant became codified during the MGM epics of the 1950s which mark the inauguration of a codified, and mutually influential, series of signs.

Even as early as *The Black Rose* and *Ivanhoe*,[44] the peasant is almost always decked in the drab browns and grays of the soil with which he works, clad in simple, homespun (and undyed) clothes cut from rough cloth, tied loosely around the waist with a loose belt; the whole is frequently topped by an arming cap of simple cloth or a hood.[45] This is, we must observe, not entirely without foundation, for both History and the artistic depictions of the period bear out Pastoureau's argument that clothing was "the most conspicuous chromatic support in day-to-day life," though he does add that "contrarily to popular opinion, in the Middle Ages all clothing was dyed, including that of the poorest"; it was in fact the solidity, density, and quality of dye which distinguished them one from the other.[46] So while our image of the undyed cloth of the peasant is not necessarily supported by extant historical records, it conveys the same idea which Pastoureau was trying to make, that the outward appearance of clothing served as a signifier of social status, a semiotic distinction which is consequently transferred intact to the cinema.

As well as being an index of wealth (or its absence), clothing undoubtedly served as a functional signifier, too, for these are the clothes of the field, not the court, much more suited for manual labor in harsh conditions than the fine silks and delicately tinted fabrics of those who rule. They consequently serve a dual iconographic purpose as a visual connotation both of poverty and of métier. A further iconographic device adopted by the cinema has been to extend the symbolic nature of the clothing to their appearance in general, through which the narrative cinema likes to reflect the "earthy" nature of the peasant by covering their clothes and faces in dirt and mud. So powerful, in fact, are these signs and expectations, that within the medieval world of *Timeline*,[47] a series of sackcloth rags are all that is needed for the twentieth-century archaeologists to pass themselves off as medieval peasants.

The dirtiness of the peasantry in a film like *Le Retour de Martin Guerre*, for example, serves to establish both an indexical sign of their status as "field laborer" as well as to allow the spectator to differentiate between those of the town and those of the fields; as Monty Python so famously put it, we know that Arthur "must be a king ... [because] he hasn't got shit all over him like the rest of us." The second advantage of this iconography is that a range of secondary connotations are evoked in our minds without the necessity of explicit commentary. Their dirt and squalor not only suggest bad personal hygiene, but also a lack of emphasis on physical appearance, bad physical living conditions and ultimately serve to associate these with disease (most frequently the Plague) which to a modern mind is often part and parcel of medieval peasants (of any period throughout the epoch).

This final proposition reveals a second assumption on the part of the spectator, offering support to the proposition asserted above, that the peasantry of the cinema do *not* evolve throughout the Middle Ages in the same way as the knights, ladies and kings do, but rather that the peasant always belongs to the fourteenth century of the Black Death (given that, for some reason, films having peasants as their main focus seem overwhelmingly to be set in the period 1300–1380). So it is, then, that after a slew of films featuring four-teenth- and fifteenth-century peasants — such as *Le Retour de Martin Guerre, Flesh & Blood, The Navigator: A Mediaeval Odyssey*[48] — Reynolds' *Robin Hood: Prince of Thieves* unthinkingly uses the same costumes for his peasants. The problem here, of course, is that Robin's initial escape from Jerusalem in the service of King Richard I places him indisputably in another period (that of the beginnings of the Third Crusade in 1184), making his peasants some 300 years ahead of the "fashion."

The final attribute of the cinematic peasant is the tendency to emphasize their lack of individuality (and consequently reflecting their "invisibility") by favoring crowd scenes and medium-long to long shots rather than close-ups, as well as showing group scenes rather than individual protagonists. It ought perhaps to be no surprise when group shots are favored over close-ups in blockbuster epics like *Ivanhoe* or *A Knight's Tale*, since the very nature of the historical epics in both the 1950s and the early years of the twenty-first century both favor the spectacular visual effects of fast-paced action sequences such as battles and tournaments, as well as hordes of extras and mass signification (in overhead crane and, later, helicopter shots, for example). This is also not to mention the technological factor that both periods saw the development of comparatively high-definition/resolution shooting and the advantages of widescreen (first seen with CinemaScope, and in the 2000s by the market-wide introduction of 16:9 aspect ratio home theatre), since the main disad-vantage of widescreen images is that they tend to "abhor the vacuum" left at the sides of medium shots with only two figures in them, hence the preference for crowd scenes.[49]

However, such group scenes cannot be destined exclusively for "epic" films if this same preference for crowd scenes is demonstrable in other films of significantly lower budget and those using 4:3 aspect ratio. One such film is Pupi Avati's excellent *Magnificat*, in which the protagonists of the opening sequence are shot by an alternating sequence of close-ups and long shots, and the work of makeup and wardrobe departments has (one must assume delib-erately) provided the viewer with a group of villagers who are almost indis-tinguishable (a trope further encouraged by the deliberate rejection of famous actors). As the camera pans along one assembled crowd of peasants, for exam-ple, the depth-of-field coupled with the tan-colored clothing and tightly grouped figures precludes any ability for a spectator to identify, let alone sympathize with, the villagers, rendering any attempt to establish individuality virtually — if not actually — impossible.

Yet each of these iconic attributes has a further indexical value, which acts as a testament to a prevalent trend among modern films trying to evoke the Middle Ages. Rather than serve as an iconic value attempting to connect the modern viewer with a specific historical "reality," if we read the signs in reverse we can see that they are appealing for their interpretation to a specific image held by the viewer (and created by the cinema), which corresponds to a belief about how people "back then" might have lived. Within the iconic range of values established by Avati's *Magnificat*, in addition to the value of the historicon (that this rough cloth is the rough cloth worn by peasants "in the Middle Ages in general," and therefore intended to signify that "this represents a medieval peasant and I am watching a medieval film"), we have the further values of connotation. This connotative value is drawn not from the icon itself but by interpreting it within the context of the ideas we have, by what we "know" about the period. In this instance, then, we can see that it is not only a peasant's robe, but we also assume that it is his *only* robe; where we see numerous costume changes among the other characters of the film, we only see the peasant wearing this same robe throughout. We also assume this from the denoted image. The robe is dirty, and we are attuned to a society in which dirty clothes should immediately be substituted for clean ones; ergo he has no clean one to change into. We also assume this because we have seen numerous peasant "hovels," but never a wardrobe. We "know" that he is poor and must therefore make or barter his own clothes because we have seen images of medieval characters sleeping in their own/only cloak (*Robin Hood: Prince of Thieves, The 13th Warrior, The Seventh Seal*).[50] We know something of the noble class, so attuned to the importance of clothes as a material object of more than functional value, and we therefore assume that such luxuries are beyond the reach of the humble peasant. In fact, in *A Knight's Tale*, William's attempt to pass as a member of the aristocracy seems to be successful in all aspects bar the clothing, and in one scene he is asked to describe what clothes he will wear to the ball ("so that my lady may dress to match"), whereupon his "squire" simply stares off screen to describe the tent cloth which will become the disguise of "Sir Ulrich."

These assumptions based on what we think we know about the period are also constructed upon the unchallenged acceptance of a series of either mythical, exaggerated or wholly fallacious beliefs, some of which have been enumerated in an interesting — though non-academic — site hosted, curiously enough, by a math department at the University of New South Wales.[51] The peasant is dirty because, "as we all know," he lives in one room with his whole family, sleeps in straw with his animals inside — sleeping with the pigs for warmth during winter — and is therefore almost certainly flea-ridden, probably diseased and certainly a prime candidate for the plague which we "know" is around the corner. He is toothless because there was no dentistry, and because there is no toothpaste we can only imagine his halitosis. One article proposes that if you "think of medieval England [...] you are likely to conjure up an image of a wizened hag with black stumps for teeth," for without twentieth-century dental hygiene it is certain that teeth will rot and fall out.[52]

It is possible, given the lack of any conclusive evidence at our fingertips, that such suppositions may one day transpire to be true, but what is important is that in the cinema, their representation is rather less historically orientated than a series of assumptions about peasants drawn from what we think we know about them, and are assumptions which largely go unchallenged. Consequently, once an iconic identity for the medieval peasant has been sketched out — drawn from the need for a preconceived function — this iconic value moves from film to film, its essential quiddity being fixed more and more rigidly (and questioned less and less frequently) the more it is used.

SPATIAL SIGNIFICATION

"I am Ergo the Magnificent. Short in stature, tall in power, narrow of purpose and wide of vision. And I do not travel with peasants and beggars. Goodbye!"[53]

In addition to these "signes exterieures," there is also in film — just as in art — a strongly controlled sense of spatial signification, which generally works to assign relative or comparative importance to subjects by an apportioning of space. This is an extremely significant device used (often unconsciously) in order to allow other characters to develop or to be developed, while using the peasants as a yardstick by which we can measure that character's place in society. To give an example, in *The Black Shield of Falworth*, we are presented with, initially, the protagonist Myles as a humble farm hand, dressed in the drab monotone of the peasant. The camera, placed at the same height as the character, frames him in a series of neutral medium- to medium-long shots, and follows him with tracking or panning shots, so as to create a rapprochement between him and the spectator. During the first stages of his training, however, as the plot unfolds and moves towards his recognition as a noble, the camera begins to frame him in close-ups, speeds up his movements by a rapid montage, and we begin to see him dressed in brighter colors so as to align him more closely with the "nobles" of the court. Most importantly, however, we begin to see him framed in low-angle shots, while also distancing him from his peers, which serves as a visual identification of his social ascent.

The crucial detail required to chart his rise, however, is not to make the peasants disappear altogether but rather to emphasize the distance between them (while keeping them on-screen). This distance, therefore, comes to be measured spatially as well as indexically.

A similar use of space can be seen by the use of horses, a "standard" prop for medieval-themed films. In *The Return of Martin Guerre*, for example, the opening scenes separate out the *parliamentaires* from the crowds of peasants by a simple device of mounting them on horseback. In doing so, the cinematography noticeably supports this narrative distinction; the long shot raises them above the level of the crowd (which merges into one homogeneous entity), thus indexically connoting their superiority, while obviating the need for supporting explanation. Furthermore, even in a close-up on the mounted dignitaries, in order to recreate a natural perspective the camera is obliged to tilt upwards, thereby framing them from a low-angle shot against the sky (and back-lighting them in this case), both of which serve as cinematic shortcuts to establish superiority (by its rapprochement with statues on pedestals). So it is that in *A Knight's Tale*, as we shall see below, William/Ulrich's rise to fame is accompanied by an increasing number of shots placing him on horseback and shooting from a medium- to medium-long shot. This framing device works especially well in the film's widescreen format (the film was shot using anamorphic, 2.35:1 aspect ratio) to separate him from the crowd by his elevation above them, while simultaneously suggesting thematically that he is losing touch with his "peasant" origins.

While none of these films tries to produce a valid historical hypothesis about medieval peasantry, their combined focus on spatial representation has indeed, somewhat serendipitously, stumbled upon a correlation with medieval imagery. As Alexander argues:

> In the earlier [medieval] period, class differences are made clear in the images, but most peasants are presented in most examples relatively neutrally. [However] ... by the end of the period, as the social structure was increasingly strained and open revolt occurred in both England and France, [negative peasant imagery] received support in overtly negative images.[54]

This negative peasant imagery began to use space as a means of characterization, hence "a purely descriptive presentation of labor and leisure is transformed into an antithetical characterization of divergent milieus."[55] It comes, therefore, as no surprise that the peasants come to be associated logically with the soil both iconically (in their soiled clothing, etc.) and spatially (seen working in fields), embodying a literal interpretation of Asser's division of society into those who "work the soil"—and which interestingly also contains hints of Adam's post–Lapsarian condemnation to till the soil.[56]

This somewhat oversimplified spatial allocation has readily been seized and exploited in cinema, since it offers a guide to the infinite social gradations[57] examined in the first section of this chapter. It finds, in fact, its bathetic nadir in one famous scene from *Monty Python and the Holy Grail*, in which Dennis the peasant is first introduced with his wife foraging not for buried foodstuffs but for nothing more precious than the mud itself. The joke — as with many other parodies of the Middle Ages — is not at the expense of the Middle Ages themselves but of other films made about the period, and in this particular instance the target is Hollywood's ubiquitous peasantry who seem purposefully to seek out dirt. The discovery of "some lovely mud over here" is also good news for the viewer, since without dirt to signify their attachment to the soil (and therefore their station in the "rigid hierarchy") one wonders whether we would still be able to recognize them as peasants.

The very fact of being bound to the soil, then, has become cinematic shorthand for modern filmmakers to signify a number of frequently paradoxical qualities which we have inherited regarding the medieval peasant: poverty, oppression, opprobrium, labor, idleness, small-mindedness, superstition and dirt. This "shorthand" can even continue when this is not entirely true, for "during the Middle Ages men and women, even of the most modest means, were often on the road, either to change their 'seigneur' or town (thinking that they would find advantages there, live better, (etc.), or to attend a fair, or to visit a site of pilgrimage," which means that their spatial captivity is by no means universally tenable.[58] Yet film persists in ignoring these movements, just as it ignores the social gradations, presumably because it is, in many ways, easier to believe in their immobility; the lack of movement away from the manor to which we — somewhat erroneously — believe they were tied fuels our belief that they belonged to a world whose horizons formed the literal edge of their consciousness. In film then, the limitations which we place around their freedom also serve to limit their power, which leads us to the next aspect of their iconic construction: their portrayal as weak and helpless members of society.

WEAKNESS AND HELPLESSNESS

"Help! I'm being repressed!"[59]

The third and final iconic construction of the medieval peasant which I will examine here transcends both their appearance and their spatial signification, concerning instead their construction as weak and helpless members of society. The imagination of the peasant as such has at its roots a fundamentally modern conception of empowerment, one based on the notion of a human being as an agent of change put forward by post–Enlightenment thought. Belief in the modern construct of the self-made man transforms the argument into a retrospectively applied one: if man is born free (as Rousseau would have it), then one who is born into "captivity" is denied humanity. From the moment that one is no longer free to move or to lead, then according to our definition of freedom one instantly becomes a weak and downtrodden underclass. This notion, though by and large not applicable to medieval society for reasons outlined in the first section above, is translated iconically in three ways: a physical incapacity, an absence of sophistication, and a societal passivity.

Physical Incapacity

The first way of communicating helplessness is by emphasizing the physical incapacity for retaliation, which is most frequently implied by absence; what we do not see is here just as important as what we do. In *Magnificat*'s line of peasants, for example, the foreground is dominated by strong-limbed, healthy fighting men sent by the duke to procure men from the peasants of his estate. Among the assembled line of potential "volunteers," the camera tracks slowly from right to left along the line, revealing a series of physical (and therefore visible) defects in each one — toothlessness, warts, swellings, probosces, etc. — with only one exception: the boy who will be selected. Already, then, the same distancing effect is at work which we saw above, since by separating him from the visually tagged "weak and helpless," Avati simultaneously explains the villagers' incapacity to fight back against the regime: there are no men (save the one who is to be led away) who would be hardy enough to fight in the first place. Consequently, if the strong, tall, young man becomes the iconic sign of /a man capable of doing battle/, then the *absence* of this iconic sign within a village translates to the incapacity of a given village to defend themselves; this would, in fact, explain why in crowd scenes of villagers and peasants the majority are so often women, children, the elderly, the ill or the infirm.

It is not only in battle, either, that fortunes may change. We can see in any number of "youth movements," from the Children's Crusade through to the 1960s, that the capacity for a spirited idealism often associated with youth can often be a useful antidote to an oppressive regime. Here films about the Middle Ages make no exception, and in films made during the 1960s and '70s "one notices above all the characteristic 'youthism' of other medieval films of the same era," seen in both of Zeffirelli's major works, *Brother Sun, Sister Moon* and *Romeo and Juliet*, as well as Huston's *A Walk with Love and Death*, and Donner's *Alfred the Great* and, though made much later, *Stealing Heaven*. Throughout these films, the idealism of Woodstock and youth movements makes youthfulness become itself a symbol of idealistic rebellion.[60]

By such a focus on young people and their importance to the medieval period (for we have remarked elsewhere that "it was a world governed by young men"),[61] we can see that their absence symbolically weakens their capacity for retaliation against those who fight. This trope is notably used in Kurosawa's *The Seven Samurai*[62] in which the villagers' capacity to fight against the raiders is visually reinforced by the absence of "fighting men"; during the scenes in which the samurai first enter the village, the camera continually pans over the faces of a number of women, old men and children, before cutting back to the faces of the samurai themselves, serving to visually underscore the imbalance between the two (an imbalance explicitly recognized by one villager's earlier observation that "we're farmers, not soldiers"). Repeatedly throughout the film, the mise-en-scène places the samurai in opposition to the villagers, contributing to a spatial division; where two samurai fight in the foreground, in the background the villagers form a crowd of passive spectators behind a broken wall, emphasized by the depth of field which is unable to individualize their features, making of them a homogeneous whole. Elsewhere, Kurosawa uses the frame itself to emphasize this difference, by directly contrasting the infirmity of the villagers with the fighters; in one scene an old man with a stooped back stands hunched behind the tall, strong lines of the samurai, both looking forward in profile and shot from a low-angle representing the villagers' awe at the powerful samurai. This same trope is used elsewhere in medieval film, to the point that it becomes an accepted characteristic of medieval villagers that they either cannot fight themselves (as in *The Seven Samurai* or *Dragonheart*) and must consequently place all their hope in a "protector," or that they have the means but not the skill, and must rely therefore on the leadership of an outsider (*First Knight, Black Knight, Braveheart, Alfred the Great* or *King Arthur*).

Absence of Sophistication

The second way of signifying their helplessness is by casting doubt on their intellectual ability and emphasizing their lack of sophistication, intimating that "those who work" do so in a blissful state of primitivism. One common trait which David Salo discusses is the use of regional accents within the UK,[63] so that a West Country accent is assigned to the backward farmer, a Northern accent to a worker, a Gaelic accent to the remote peasant, or — as with Vincent Ward's *The Navigator*— by a total confusion of these accents. Such a device is prominently used in Peter Jackson's *Lord of the Rings*, in which the Hobbits of the Shire use either a West Country (Samwise Gamgee) or Scots accent (Peregrin Took), which jars alarmingly with the Received Pronunciation of both Gandalf and Saruman, just as the peasant's misuse of English distinguishes — and disbars — him from the educated and sophisticated echelons of the aristocracy.

This primitivism is also demonstrated by the absence of sophistication, which hints that they do not seek to improve their station. Ward's *The Navigator: A Mediaeval Odyssey* is rather unique in its ability to use this primitivism as the starting point for a very interesting film which explores the role of spirituality and a quest motif against the background of the Great Plague. Nevertheless, in order to construct the medieval village, he resorts to an iconic construction of a primitive state of such bleakness that even had it not been filmed in monochrome, it would certainly seem in any case to be dominated by black and white. The harsh existence of the villagers, dressed in dark, thick clothes, is set starkly against the driving snow and the absence of sunlight, "to provide an almost documentary-like feel of what must have been a harsh and colourless existence."[64] Everything in the mise-en-scène reflects a sparse minimalism, from the mechanical pulleys and ratchets, to the exposed, craggy peaks of the village which corresponds to our belief in the absence of luxuries in the world of the medieval peasant; the cold harshness of existence is reflected by every object half-buried in the winter snows.

This "colourless existence" is an iconic reversal of other strata of society, for just as we have seen in chapters 3 and 5 that light has been used for both pageantry and divinity, its absence here plunges the medieval village into a primitive, primal state.[65] This darkness works on a number of significations and interpretations, each based on the various re-appropriations of light as an iconographic symbol; where light has a number of iconic meanings, darkness can be seen to work as a contrast and subversion of each[66]:

Light	*Darkness*
- learning, Enlightenment	- ignorance
- Christianity, Divinity	- Diabolic practices, paganism
- Inspiration	- Primitivism
- Honesty	- Duplicity

And, of course, most of all, by extension we come to the term "the Dark Ages," whose very label comes to hint at an absence of sophistication. So it is that even though "the medieval period represents itself in ringing tones ... [and] identified beauty with light and colour," when we wish to construct the ignorant, primitive underside of that same society, we find a proliferation of the iconic symbols of darkness to denote an absence of sophistication.[67]

Another, more general attack on the primitivism of the medieval peasant is, while still indexical in one sense, a good deal less sophisticated, and takes place on the scatological level. In order to represent a given character as primitive, unsophisticated and crass, then there seems to be a very popular trend to take shortcuts by insulting *our* morals and sensibilities rather than trying to elaborate what would be considered rude to a medieval audience. In Terry

Gilliam's *Jabberwocky*,[68] his second and considerably less capable "medieval film," the primitive nature of the hero Dennis' fellow villagers is underscored by a perpetual resort to lavatory humor.[69] We meet the father of his lover Griselda as he leans over a pier in order to defecate into the river below, an introduction which is immediately followed by the use of flatulence to undermine the gentillesse of Dennis' one true love. The same process is used to pour scorn upon the unsophisticated medieval world in *Les Visiteurs*, and even more so in its remake *Just Visiting*,[70] which reduces the sophistication of the first film's linguistic jokes (in the French version, a good deal of humor derives from the word-play and puns made using a pseudo–Old French) to rather less witty toilet humor. Jacquouille's character in particular falls victim to this crassness; where in the original his absence of sophistication was indicated by his inability to grasp linguistic niceties (using, for example, the wrong verb endings), in the English-language remake his baseness is communicated by farting and burping in inappropriate locations. While we moderns balk at such behavior, when such crudeness is tolerated by the other characters within the medieval period it becomes a way of suggesting their unsophisticated "barbarity" to a modern audience.

Passivity

One final way of demonstrating the peasants' general weakness is by their representation as inert and passive in the face of their perceived oppression, and by answering violence with silence. Whereas those who fight, we have seen, are elevated to heroism by their bravery and mastery of weapons, those who work are frequently represented by cowardice in their refusal to fight even in the face of cruelty and repression. This is a much broader condemnation of the populace than it might initially seem, since it works on our tendency to portray them as a group; to retaliate, we have seen, raises the individual to heroic status (which is in fact the premise of the "reluctant hero" who emerges from the crowd to fight against aggressors); conversely, then, the lack of retaliation condemns the peasant to conformity within the group. Such is the case with *Braveheart*, one of several films to evoke the postmedieval myth of the *ius primae noctis*, in order to emphasize the oppression and exploitation to which the peasants are subjected.[71] It is a myth which embodies the sort of "durable representation of medieval aristocratic power [which] ... is still featured in popular images of the medieval period," becoming "an emblem of arbitrary lordship, of resentment over clerical control over marriage, as something both comical and intolerable."[72] In order to demonstrate the strictly one-way permission of violence, the villagers stand passively by in recognition of their impotence in the face of a force capable of, and prepared to use, violence as a means to subdue the populace. The reason for the power of the *ius primae noctis* is based on Hollywood's taboos, since rape in particular presents an unambiguous and indefensible abuse of power, which continues to provoke a powerful reaction among audiences. While it has been delicately and powerfully treated in a number of films like *La Passion Béatrice* and *Alfred the Great*, it is seemingly far more frequently used in films about the medieval past than the present, being used to symbolize extreme human cruelty in *Braveheart, Flesh & Blood, The Messenger, A Walk with Love and Death, The Virgin Spring*,[73] and *The Reckoning*, as though to intimate that violation was simply the norm in such a primitive, barbaric time period. In each of these films, the actual or attempted rape of the loved one (wife, daughter, sister, lover, daughter and a series of young boys, respectively) is used to connote three aspects simultaneously — the cowardice of the perpetrator, the impotence of the hero and the barbarity of the period as a whole — all the while providing a plot motivation by appealing to the patriarchal values and legitimizing any subsequent aggression in the vicarious gaze of a male viewer. By broaching such a fundamental societal taboo, these films force even the most liberal viewer "onto the ropes" and to assume an unambiguous moral position not only with respect to the perpetrators but about the period as a whole. The society which does not retaliate thus becomes by extension guilty of the same crime by their silence and passivity, and the hero becomes an agent of vengeance, allowing the spectator to avenge him- or herself vicariously and to reassert his or her own power in the face of his or her former social impotence. Most importantly, however, is that the demons of our "barbarous past" are exorcized by the twentieth century's own brand of vigilante justice.

Yet by employing passivity to condemn the peasants to a collective abdication of individuality, here we begin to move away from the direct iconic signifiers which are designed to convey the objects, and are working on a far more conceptual level. In an era in which, increasingly, cinematic heroism consists of standing out from the crowd (as we saw with the "reluctant hero" in chapter 3), the combination of passivity, ignorance and weakness serves to undermine any sense of individuality or individual personality among those who work in the medieval period.

By treating the social grouping as a unit, we must recognize that we are here moving away from the iconic signifiers with which we have been engaged until now, and instead we are beginning to create a "concept" of the generic peasant. The abandonment of iconic signifiers of appearance, function and récit-cadre makes recourse to a wider, more general "unit of signification" which emphasizes their homogeneity and, crucially, their rapprochement with modern audiences, a mass-signification which has of course more in common with the concept of the paradigm which I have been developing here. It is therefore to the level of these paradigms that I will now turn, for when it comes to paradigmatic reconstruction, as I will show, the invisibility and passivity of the peasant becomes so prevalent that we can begin to treat not the individual icons of the villager, but the concept of the village itself.

Paradigms and Mass Signification

In terms of paradigmatic representation, the interesting case with the majority of these characters is their consistently flat nature in film, since throughout all of the films studied in this book, only a very few peasant characters seem to function as anything more than an "extra." Further, something of a paradox comes into play here, for the more cinema concentrates on one of these characters, the more they tend to be revealed as peasants who are able to embrace the values of the aristocracy (and thus demonstrating the democratisation of the Middle Ages), or else "nobles" in the guise of peasants, using precisely this anonymity as their protective veil: in *The Black Knight*,[74] it falls to the blacksmith John to rise up and save the kingdom by proving himself as a knight, as it does for Myles as disinherited noble in *The Black Shield of Falworth*. Elsewhere, displaced Saxon nobles are forced to prove their mettle in both *The Black Rose* and *Ivanhoe*, Sir Knolte of Marlborough must recover from his fall from grace in *Black Knight*, not forgetting of course the use of the same topos in the Bel Inconnu motif.[75]

Given this frequently "flat" nature of "non-noble peasants," we find that in the cinema their distinguishing characteristics are all but ignored, and so rather than spending valuable screen time in carefully constructing the nuances of character, that is in understanding *the object*, cinema frequently makes use of simply *the concept* of a downtrodden proletariat. The paradigm is therefore an assimilation of the people taken from any time period, in any place, "the people" whose individuality history, like the cinema, frequently either ignores or lumps together.[76] This grouping together of the people, in fact, gives us two seemingly contradictory paradigms which we will examine below: the generic peasant *qua* peasant and the village as a mass unit of signification.

THE CINEMATIC PEASANT

Before providing a full definition of the paradigmatic "cinematic peasant," it is first necessary to distinguish it from the iconic process of signification mentioned above. Where this latter relies on specific formal signals designed to connote his or her specific station and role in the feudal hierarchy (by emphasizing dirt, lowliness and weakness, for example), the paradigmatic symbols of the peasant are a result of a sort of accidental signification which results precisely from their similarity to other cinematic peasants. Put simply, the peasants of Hollywood — to a much greater extent than in auteur films — are drawn from *other films about the medieval period*. To develop this point, we can look at an example from a diachronic perspective, by looking at the peasant as constructed iconically in *The Return of Martin Guerre*, then paradigmatically in *Robin Hood: Prince of Thieves*, and again in *A Knight's Tale*. In the first film, the debut by Daniel Vigne, we first encounter the peasant working in the fields around the village. While it would be perhaps naïve to imagine that the filmmakers had intensely studied the image of the peasant in early–fifteenth-century France, the presence of Zemon Davis is not without influence, and there is some visual evidence that in terms of the cinematography the filmmakers had at least a passing familiarity with the *Très Riches Heures* of the Limbourg brothers. Both in the busy scenes of peasant activity in the foreground, as well as the pastoral scenes in the background, there seem to be sufficiently strong visual similarities to support the argument that the film has been informed — though to what degree we might be hard-pressed to say — by visual evocations of peasantry from the late Middle Ages themselves. Thus, to condense a long argument, it seems safe to say that the process is iconic; it refers back to a communal image drawn from cultural memory, if not directly from contemporary sources, and in doing so tries to reconstruct the object and its relevance to a contemporary referent.

Moving through a decade, however, we come across Reynolds' *Robin Hood: Prince of Thieves* and find that the focus is once again on a man entering the peasant community as an unknown, but this time the director has a clear agenda (dictated to some extent by the requirements of the legend), that the peasants must not be vilified, but represented as hard-working, upright members of an oppressed level of society. The peasants here are consequently drawn from a stock repertoire of Hollywood's "simple folk," elaborated over the twentieth century by formerly iconic representations.[77] By a close reading of the sequence in which Robin first returns to Nottingham Castle, we can see that many of the same formal elements are present in this film, too: in the literal shadow of the castle in the background, the peasants form simply a uniform, nameless crowd of drab grays, browns and dark colors, which the depth of field reduces to a blur. Occupying less than half of the frame, the line of peasants serves little more purpose than set dressing, and in themselves become a form of historicon and, by drawing on their uniformity, become in a sense their own paradigm. In this case, there is no iconic attempt to re-establish the object, but they represent a simple link to the concept of "a peasant class," essentially iterable throughout films of this nature. Speaking of the necessity of such "invented elements of character," Rosenstone proposes that:

> The very use of an actor to "be" someone will always be a kind of fiction.... If the individual has been created to exemplify a group of historical people (a worker during a strike, a shopkeeper during a revolution, a common soldier on the battlefield) a double fiction is involved: this is how this sort of person (whom we have created) looked, moved, and sounded. [These] can obviously be no more than approximations of particular historical individuals, approximations that carry out some sense that we already have about how such people acted, moved, sounded and behaved.[78]

The secondary problem which this borrowing poses is that Reynolds' film is putatively set some 300 years earlier, yet makes no attempt to adjust their images of peasants accordingly. The only ostensible "authority" voiced by the film is by the filming of the Bayeux Tapestry during the opening credits; even if we ignore the fact that the film's peasants bear absolutely no resemblance to those of the Norman conquest, we are again faced with a problem of chronology (since the tapestry relates to events taking place over a century earlier). Furthermore, where *Martin Guerre* draws from contemporary artistry geared towards a rich elite, there is a concomitant sense of what has been termed negative peasant imagery[79]; it is somewhat ironic, then, if Reynolds borrows from Vigne's film, when *Robin Hood* is to be constructed as a heroic defender of the peasantry. When the paradigm as a concept is copied, therefore, its reference to the object is lost and the whole risks coming to mean something quite different — albeit unwittingly — from its original purpose.

When we move forward another decade to 2001, we can find yet another instance of the same paradigmatic cinematic peasant being used again for a film with a different conception, in *A Knight's Tale*, reflecting the ambivalent relationship which cinema has with the medieval peasantry. At one level, of course, the rags-to-riches tale of William Thatcher is intended to be a mirror image of the descent of Count Adhemar, furthering Hollywood's favorite dictum that true nobility is found in the man and not his social status. This message is supported visually, by the use of armor as disguise at each end of the social spectrum, so that both William the peasant and Edward the Black Prince must both falsify their identity and fight in disguise in order to get their fair trial on the great arena of the tournament.[80] However, at the same time as this message is being offered, we can see that it is simultaneously being undermined by the film's reliance on the paradigm examined above, since the crowds of peasants are directly compared to the noisy rabble at a contemporary sports match, holsteins are clashed together by corpulent, bare-chested men, who stamp, chant and boo with the rest of them. This bawdiness, of course, is so much more familiar to the everyday viewer that we cannot help but side with them against the repressed silence of the nobles. That the film is addressed to the everyman and not the nobles can be seen from Chaucer's introduction which forms the title of this chapter; the distinction is not between the vulgar crowd and their social superiors, but instead he addresses "Lords, Ladies, and everybody *not* sitting on a cushion." Thus we encounter here the fusion of two paradigms elaborated over the course of a decade; though the film is clearly indebted to a traditional Hollywood paradigm which highlights the grubbiness of the peasant class (tying them, we remember, to the soil) and the spatial separation mentioned above, the director Helgeland has also incorporated a sporting paradigm by appealing to the understanding of the twenty-first-century referent.

Nevertheless, the reliance on such a paradigm designed to re-evaluate our modern notions of the medieval peasant falls down when we consider the narrative development of the film. Where at the beginning of the film he and his followers explicitly court the common crowd and pay no heed to any offense which his populist behavior might cause among the nobility, as his success in the lists increases, he begins to enact the same spatial separation from the masses as his ostensible enemy, Count Adhemar. Just like the modern notion of "celebrity," William's rise to fame throughout the film is achieved not by emphasizing his affinity with the peasantry (whence he came), but by highlighting his *individuality*, a concept which once again becomes the hallmark of the non-peasant. If the peasantry comprise a homogeneous mass-unit, then by rejecting his association with the peasant class, and by slowly adopting the mannerisms and customs of the aristocracy (attending balls, dressing to match, designing bespoke armor, writing love poems, courting a lady), William becomes more of a rounded character, and is afforded more of an individual persona — which means that he breaks free of the paradigm of the "ordinary" cinematic peasant. This rejection of the paradigm is visually supported by a slow evolution from dirtiness to suavity, from rusticity to urbanity in his clothing, and by my earlier arguments about his increasing distance from the crowd, so that in two separate instances he rides on horseback through the crowds to symbolize superiority within a social hierarchy.

To this end, then, we can see that William's social ascent is marked not by an inversion of the paradigm as the filmmakers would perhaps like to have believed, but in fact by a damning consolidation of them. One secondary result, here, is that as William and his followers effect a spatial separation from the peasants, so too does the camera adopt more distance shots of the peasantry in general and far fewer close-ups, which has as a result the amalgamation of the individual paradigmatic peasant into a single, one-dimensional unit.

MASS SIGNIFICATION

So it is, therefore, that paradigms of mass peasant signification function in part as a distancing technique, serving in one sense (i.e., on the individual level) as a means of distancing the viewer by constructing them as sufficiently foreign to preclude any direct viewer sympathy, while simultaneously recreating the concept of a mass movement, whose fate is of prime significance to modern society.

To demonstrate this, we can look at a modern form of mass signification in the crowd scene in the classic "Odessa steps" sequence of Eisenstein's *Battleship Potemkin*. Throughout the film, Eisenstein has carefully established an iconographic dialectic between the mundane uniformity of the sailors — both literally in the sense that they all wear identical uniforms, and on the level of the mise-en-scène, in that the wide frames, long shots and high overhead camera angles recreate the sense of looking in on history "from above," to use Ferro's terminology.[81] So it is then that we arrive at the filmmaker's central theme — in the "peasant" uprising at Odessa, the same series of shots treat the peasants as one single unit, rather than singling out any individual characters. The only exception to this uniformity is found in the series of shots (much beloved by film theorists) which depict the stampeding of the old woman with the pram. Nevertheless, even in this shot, once we put aside our natural empathic instincts, we realise that this shot is intended not to arouse our sympathy for the individual, but is used as a disposable characterization (cinematic metonymy) to highlight the cruelty and callousness of the soldiers (regime) towards the individual (the people). The mass movement of the people becomes the thread which links them to us, and ensures the relevance of past concerns to those of the present.

So it is with the model of mass signification in the Middle Ages; we frequently care little for the individual peasant (and, arguably, neither do the filmmakers who rarely include them in their credits), but more for the mass movement which they represent, or in certain cases perhaps more for their relationship to the protagonist in the realization of their cinematic goal. William/Ulrich's ultimate measure of success is when (like Maximus in *Gladiator*) he "wins the crowd," which means simultaneously that a) he is no longer part of it and b) that they have elided into one mass, inseparableunit.

The cinema, like History itself, is often primarily concerned with the great deeds of notable individuals, and leaders of movements such as Moses/ Israel, Washington/USA, Napoleon/France, and so on; "both dramatic feature films and documentaries put individuals in the forefront of the historical process."[82] This indeed is the central message of a film such as *Alfred the Great* with its overtly liberal agenda (more pertinent to the late 1960s than to its putative ninth-century setting), whose crisis comes when the heroic king loses touch with his people. This notion is represented literally by the same long shots, high angles and uniformity seen above with Eisenstein, and it is only when he approaches his most lowly followers and becomes an "outlaw" himself (playing, of course, on a Robin Hood motif) that he is able to acquire the necessary skills to lead his people to victory. He must, in short, learn to view history "from below," a history lesson not without resonance in the era of the *Annales* School of historiography.[83] This rapprochement of king and people, however, is still looking at history from the top downwards, and in no way individuates the peasant class, nor does it develop their characters (they rarely have a "back story," or motivation, for example), but instead it establishes an iconic rapprochement between the king and his subjects (to the extent that Alfred begins to adopt their external characteristics of peasants outlined above). Becoming first dirty and disheveled, the camera gradually places him both within the same frame and on the same level as his peasant followers/subjects, even showing him in positions of physical submission (pinned down by the peasant leader, or by high-angle shots and rapid shot/counter-shot editing which accords him the same importance as — and no more than — his interlocutors).

This scheme of a leader of the people is used elsewhere, too, in *Braveheart* and *A Knight's Tale*, in which the leader is drawn from his people and has learned his skills of governance and leadership purely by the application of common sense achieved by keeping in touch with their subjects/followers. The same cinematographic devices are used, too, in the closed frames which place the leader firmly within his people, and there is nowhere the same use of raised daises and architectural iconography used for kingship and power (see chapter 4). The consequent effect of this, however, is in fact that the people themselves become a mass unit with little or no individuation.

This, then, becomes the unit of mass signification itself; the peasants become equated with the people in the modern sense of popular revolutions, and are ultimately a homogeneous body who are dispensable to the cause which is marked by the protagonist's goals. Revolutions, struggles and revolts are rarely without bloodshed, yet one of cinema's most crucial rules is that the protagonist as leader must embody the plight, and must therefore survive to see its fruition. Immediate objections will of course be raised here, yet it must be borne in mind that the exceptions to this, such as *El Cid*, *Braveheart*, etc., frequently play on a pseudo–Messianic motif which conversely *requires* the sacrifice of the hero for the cause. The poignancy and power of such films become then the exceptions which prove the rule, celebrating the fact that in this case the movement (i.e., the mass signification) is greater than the individual. Without being accustomed to the survival of the hero we would miss the point of such an altruistic self-sacrifice altogether.

Conclusions

The representation of the medieval peasant thus stems in most cases from an initial problem of *understanding* the peasant in the first place. I have demonstrated that this problem of understanding came from three interconnected hurdles: their Historical invisibility, the continual variation within the concept of the peasantry, and the tendency for modern audiences to view the peasants as an oppressed underclass engaged in a political class struggle. These three issues represent the three problems of signification in the cinema, since the *object* is invisible, the *concept* is elusive and continually subject to evolution and the *referent* is distorted by the prism of post–Marxist thought; all of which issues create an essential instability in the sign itself.

I identified some of the more prominent iconic aspects which are used as shorthand in medieval films. The costume and appearance, for instance, serve as indexical reminders of the function and nature of the peasantry during the Middle Ages; mud and soil remind us of their labor, dirt serves as an index of their poor hygiene (as we perceive it), drab, ill-fitting and well-worn clothes indicate their poverty. Similarly, the use of spatial signification in order to anchor "those who work" within their habitual milieu enables filmmakers to create a division between social groupings. The final iconic form of signification is the helplessness and weakness of the peasantry, communicated in the cinema by the absence of "fighting men," and of the sort of sophistication which allows us to establish connections more readily between the nobility and our own era, as well as a general passivity which explains their invisibility in the pages of history, reducing them to passive bystanders on the margins of cinematic history.

Finally, I showed that the concept of the medieval peasant was governed by two major paradigms. First, their invisibility establishes a connection with a whole series of oppressed and downtrodden underclasses such as Mexicans, Native Americans, African Americans, Jews, women and so on, coming to form the great Other to our cinematic imagination, which in turn plays down their individuality to form a one-size-fits-all paradigm of the cinematic peasant. The second effect has been that it facilitates the use of a second paradigm of mass signification, meaning that, far more than the individual peasant, it is the general, collective group of peasants which has been used in Hollywood films in particular. This is permitted in part by the habitual lack of any "rounded" peasant characters with whom we can identify, demoting the peasants to a general, homogeneous rabble, or a "rent-a-crowd" for filmmakers, which most often serves simply as either support for the hero's cause or as an obstacle to thwart their goals.

PART III

WORLDS

7

Constructing Medieval Worlds: Conventions, Inventions and Images

"We need to ask just what we expect of a screen version of an ancient poem, or a representation of the past, and to make sure that what we look for is reasonable or even possible. It is less a question of asking 'is it authentic?' than 'what does my Middle Ages look like?'"[1]

Over the first two parts of this book, I have so far tried to show that the representation of the Middle Ages in film is first and foremost a semiotic process, based on a twofold negotiation of historiography on the one hand and cinematography on the other. In Part I, I demonstrated that historiographic criticism has served to undermine the traditional authority attributed to the written, Historical record, which has in turn weakened the assumed dialectic between History and film posited by early theoreticians working on film and History such as Smith, Rollins and even Carnes (as well as challenging — as we shall see in Part III — the dialectic between accuracy and inaccuracy). Instead of Historically absolute values, I have used the arguments of historiography proposed by Veyne, Rosenstone and above all White to suggest that even before its reconstruction in film the period lives on in our cultural capital as an a priori imaginary referent, a vague idea which we hold about both the past and our present (given that we recognize our role as descendants of that same past).

In Part II, consequently, I turned to cinematography to evaluate how the cinema went about reconstructing this medieval referent using signifiers which were identifiable to modern audiences as "signs of the past," or as models (paradigms) of a comparable modern relationship. As such, my focus in this second section was necessarily on the people who make up these imaginary past worlds, from the king to the peasant, showing that various characteristics of medieval people were often incarnated as a visual icon (a historicon) or a structural model (a paradigm) to help the spectator understand the central semiotic message that "this is a medieval peasant," and that *therefore* "this film is set in the Middle Ages." Nevertheless, with the exception of a very few avant-garde films, it is obvious that these characters, in short these medieval people, do not occupy an empty stage, but that the stage is assumed from the "therefore," by a process of logical deduction. This being the case, it becomes clear that this "stage," which I will here call the medieval world, is equally a part of this semiotic process: we only know it is a medieval world by reading the signs of the medieval and filling in the mental gaps. In fact, so critical is this world in which the medieval characters are placed that we can safely pro-pose that *the world itself forms the second part of this semiotic process*: it is just as constructed as the medieval knight, king, monk or peasant, and it is based just as much on the medieval imaginary held in common among a given audi-ence. It is, therefore, to this world as stage that this final part of my book will be addressed. In the first instance, in this chapter, I broach the problematic question of how we *know* this is a medieval world, by looking at conventions in constructing a medieval world, and how we can assert its authenticity, before moving on in chapter 8 to look at how guides are used to signal this world to us in a more overt capacity.

Part of this argument, then, will focus on the first proposition that there exists *a medieval world*, as a singular, unchanging entity. This proposition, however, presupposes that there exists a fixed, Historical identity of the medieval world; that the knight, as we have asserted above, had a fixed mean-ing throughout the medieval period in its entirety. This, naturally, is a mark-edly erroneous — and potentially deleterious — presupposition, since even in a signifier as seemingly "stable" as the medieval knight, it is possible to identify enormous changes in the appearance, function and understanding of such a concept.[2] Not only has chapter 3 highlighted that much of what we "know" about the medieval knight is, in fact, a post-medieval construct, but we must now equally recognize that there was never really a single instance of an "orig-inal" in the first place. A tenth-century warrior, for example, has very little in common with a fourteenth-century knight, though they might both bear the same appellation.

It has, then, become a symbol in itself, which has as a consequence that when we try to recreate it "accurately," we are trying to create *a mediated symbol of an already mediated symbol* (the same might, incidentally, be true of the Middle Ages as a whole). To assume that images from the era (or indeed the era itself) can be presented or imagined as a contiguous whole is therefore to betray their significant complexities in the original, as well as their subse-quent reconstructions.

These two propositions, taken together, do present a certain contradiction: we have two symbols in our cinematic "vocabulary," say the tenth-century warriors of *The War Lord*, and the fourteenth-century soldier of *The Messenger*, both of which we have learned to identify as a cinematic symbol for the knight. Equally, within cinematic evocations of the same period — say the shimmering knights of *The Black Shield of Falworth* and the dark barbarity of *The Advocate's* medieval world — we are presented with two very different symbols of knighthood which are almost wholly contradictiory. Both are, in a strictly semiotic sense, "accurate," in that they serve to convey the information to us that "this is a knight," but each difference in its manifestation makes it *inaccurate* in another sense.

One way around this problem is to posit the existence of medieval "worlds," rather than a single, definitive version of them. In this case, we can accept that there might be two co-existent signs meaning the same thing but having a vastly different appearance (just as, for example, "car" might refer to anything from a Mini to a Lamborghini). A secondary result is that we can begin to identify the source of a further "distortion," in the possibility that, prior to the incarnation of a particular Middle Ages on film, the filmmaker has been somehow forced to choose the prism through which he or she conceives the period. In this respect, William D. Paden proposes three broad types of medieval movies, which we may loosely divide into "historical," "literary" and "allegorical" respectively:

1. Films which act "as though the camera was taken back to the Middle Ages themselves,
2. [ones which] try to reflect the literary inventions of the Middle Ages,
3. films which can be compared interestingly to some medieval work."[3]

It is a threefold separation which sounds initially tempting, yet one which I cannot help but feel is markedly more difficult to implement practically than to accept theoretically. It most certainly betrays a (perhaps unintentional) historical bias in its approach, for it masks the underlying assumption that there exists a sharp delineation between historical works and literary works, as though we were able to argue that "x" is the way in which their literary tradition sees them, while "y" is its actual implementation. This is a delineation which is hard to defend, for of course as we saw above, "the distinction between history and fiction cannot, in its modern clarity, be applied to medieval books or to the spirit in which they were read."[4] Second, the use of the wide-ranging term "the Middle Ages" in the context of the reception of an era which straddles a thousand years is one which requires the utmost caution, for otherwise it risks the assumption that somehow there exists (or indeed existed) some Otherworld, unconnected to our own, which the films in Paden's first category are going out (and not back) to revisit. In this sense the period becomes foreign and inaccessible, and not what it was — an antecedent. The second corollary of this is that they come to constitute the pre-packaged, "oven-ready" Middle Age which overlooks difference in its conception of the period as a contiguous whole. This generic grouping of the period thus becomes opposed to history and set apart, reflecting their "ahistoricism," according to which "where films of the more recent past habitually reconstruct their subjects as existing in linear and causational relationship to the present, films of the medieval period present their matière in an analogical relation."[5]

Conventions

Paden's model, however, can be useful in that it at least introduces the fundamental notion that not all medieval films begin from the same premise. Just as over time we have witnessed a proliferation of the types of medieval worlds imaginable, what I am proposing here is that each "medieval" film discussed in this survey begins with a particular conception of the Middle Ages (which may be compared with a journalist's "angle" on a story, or to use a more medieval analogy, the narratorial "stance" of a given poet, often explicitly clarified at the beginning of a poem). Since this is precisely the aspect which interests historians working on film and has been explored relatively extensively elsewhere, I will avoid any in-depth discussion of it here, but what I hope to highlight instead is that while each may begin with a different conception governed by its personal "angle" on the period, in its implementation there exist a number of conventions which govern its construction in film.

These "conventions," of course, are by no means stringent demands or rigid formulae acting like assembly instructions or dressmaking patterns. Rather, they reflect trends in the implementation (if not conception) of the Middle Ages by each individual filmmaker, and seek to regulate the "type" of Middle Ages produced as a result. In this way,

> the medieval has been reduced to a recognizable, Technicolor paradigm by a semi-filmic distant past that swiftly encodes a visual grammar of adventure, wooing, jousting and rebelling. We "read" medieval-themed films not only through the filter of what we know of the past but also via what we have seen on the screen already, generating a sort of double-fictionalizing process along the way.[6]

What emerges from this, then, is that where the "people" discussed in Part II may be formed by an attempt to semiotically reconstruct figures from the period, when it comes to our ideas about the worlds they inhabit, we are frequently influenced by other details gleaned from a range of sources. Most notable among this range of sources are, understandably, other films (which is why we require this dual reading), for "all [medieval] films made after the 1950s require in effect a dual reading: their constructions are self-referential, an effect of citation and an intertextual recapitulation of that decade's corpus of chivalric films."[7] The reason for this, it seems, is that where information can be relatively easy to access about specific details regarding the people (a historical consultant, for example, would most probably be able to confirm whether there were stirrups, or plate armor in a given period), when it comes to the "world" as a whole, this is most often the ideological prism through which the medieval is refracted — and is thus significantly more difficult to be categorically refuted or confirmed.[8] If this were true, then it would certainly go some way to explaining why so many medieval films begin to resemble each other, giving rise to these conventions, since together they come to form a convincing — even if erroneous — picture of the period which is palatable to the audience. In general, providing there are no rogue medievalists in the auditorium, many of these medieval worlds are likely to pass unchecked by even the most cynical spectator.

Before condemning out of hand the reliance on such conventions drawn from other works of art, however, we must observe that conventions of one sort or another are scarcely anything new. Looking at the medieval works themselves, we can see that they exist throughout medieval literary tradition as a "set of cultural forms" which Zumthor defines as being characteristic of medieval poetics.[9] The often overt references to pre-existent conventions crop up as a recurring topos throughout medieval literature, such as in Marie de France's claim to be rhyming pre-existent lais,[10] in Renaud de Beaujeu's claim to form a romance from a familiar "aventure,"[11] and we meet them again in Chrétien de Troyes' *conjointure*. These overt references to pre-existent structural forms and modes of expression establish — in the minds of their medieval audiences — an already familiar set of conventions governing the form (fabliau, forme fixe, romance, rondeau, (etc.), and the means of expression ("as the book says," or "these deeds were handed down joyfully in oral tradition"[12]) which, by the late Middle Ages, begin to function as a way of codifying specific behavioral patterns and norms, by the original variations of which the story-teller achieves his aim. Thus the arguments of Jauss come to the fore in his theory of the "horizon of expectations," by which each reading of the text conditions and moderates subsequent readings. Interestingly, then, we see a convergence between medieval romances and their cinematic avatars since in both, "representations of heroes and their noble ladies were *governed by conventions*."[13] In terms of genre expectations, in most cases "the fifteenth-century author and reader knew already what will happen — what they want to know is how the situation is to be worked out on the basis of these known quantities, and the criterion of success is the degree of unexpectedness in the answer supplied by the author."[14] While for the fifteenth-century poet the subject of the poem is to a greater or lesser extent the art of the poet, the means by which he arrives "is tied down by tradition," the conventions of the poetic form acting something like the tracks of a train, guiding without controlling.

In precisely the same way, modern audiences are perhaps less concerned about accuracy to the dusty and remote Middle Ages of traditional scholarship, but are already conditioned by previous medieval-themed films to know what to expect from a cinematic Middle Ages, thanks to conventions established by other films making up the genre. Most appropriate to film are visual conventions which each aim to evoke to the spectator an element of "medievality": those icons which I have termed "historicons" — a mediated form of the Barthesian "empty signifiers" which serve to connote a recognizable element of our medieval past, elements which for us "stand for" the Middle Ages as a whole.[15] We might roughly — though not exactly — equate them with what Amy de la Bretèque has called "iconogrammes," which he describes as "those iconic elements which are sufficient to summon up the Middle Ages."[16]

For us to consider a historicon as a convention, we must first recognize that it does not necessarily have to be an object, but can in certain cases take human form — the king adorned with crown, for example, a knight in armor, a tonsured priest, corpulent monk or a peasant in sack-cloth — or they can (by extension) be pursuits in which we find our characters engaged — tilling the soil, for example, or searching for mud like Monty Python's Dennis the peasant; they are the trains of knights riding out from a forest, or the passing flagellants of Bergman's millenarian *The Seventh Seal*.[17] More than this, they can also embrace the landscape itself; *La Passion Béatrice*'s barren wasteland ("what branches grow / Out of this stony rubbish?"[18]) is indebted more to T.S. Eliot's re-use of a medieval topos than to a directly medieval precedent, or the dank marshlands of *Alfred the Great* and *The War Lord*, embodying a perception of Dark Age Europe as an era of desolation, isolation and transience, threatened on all sides by man's inability to conquer nature (yet...). They may also include their antithesis in the frequently lush, verdant forests of Hollywood's "High Middle Ages," which depict their synthetic medievalism as a nostalgic return to a halcyon age of innocence and harmony with nature, in *Ivanhoe* and the Robin Hood legend, for example, in which the forest plays host to England's protectors, or in *First Knight* or *Excalibur*, in which it shelters the lovers' trysts whose relationships are insupportable within the stony confines of civilization. Furthermore, as metonyms in themselves, the pathetic fallacy of these natural historicons can combine powerfully with the themes of the film, as with Bresson's *Lancelot du Lac*, in which the juxtaposition of the castle and the forest play their parts in the cosmic, Jungian battle between the universal feminine and the pervasiveness of male destruction. Consequently, by negotiating these signs which "stand for" the Middle Ages (and more specifically by their repetition), the individual historicons can come to form conventions in and of themselves.

To demonstrate the far-reaching influence of these conventions, we need look no further than parody, for "the familiarity of conventions allow for parody, which becomes possible only when conventions are known to audiences."[19] It is precisely by the subversion of these "known quantities" that, for example, *Don Quixote* retains its comic force from the seventeenth century down to a twentieth-century audience, its comedy drawing on his adherence to already outdated romantic conventions: his application of the fashions of speech, manner of dress and quest for adventures in the name of his Dulcinea. It is a parodic and iconoclastic tradition which is upheld into the modern day by Jean-Marie Poiré's *Les Visiteurs* (with which McMorran posits a direct link to Don Quixote),[20] the Python troupe, Monicelli or Dino Risi — all of whose humor is *predicated in the first instance on the successful invocation of these conventions* in order to subsequently subvert them, "to evoke a whole series of religious and social aspects of the Middle Ages, only to demolish these taboos and traditional (cultural) values by the corrosive power of laughter."[21]

When we move towards the field of reception theory, we find that these conventions are similarly at work governing subsequent readings of other works, "to orient the reader's (public's) understanding and to enable a qualifying reception,"[22] so that in time "the experience of the first reading becomes the horizon of the second one."[23] By priming the reader/viewer/audience to the "category" of the work which is being proposed, the formal aspects of the work recall exactly those preliminary formalities of medieval texts mentioned above. At the other end of the spectrum, when it comes to film, we can see that genre theory asserts a similar process taking place in the mind of the spectator, both the star system and the genre of the film to some extent sketching out the cadre and therefore ultimately the mode of reception expected of the film. More concretely, we can assert that the genre of the film, along with the concomitant publicity surrounding the film, will most certainly influence the reading of it. "The repetition of certain visual patterns in genre movies allows audiences to know immediately what to expect of them by their physical attributes, their dress and deportment,"[24] so that the mainstream Hollywood blockbuster will clearly have in mind already the kind of audience expected, and the level of the film may be adjusted accordingly.[25]

Necessary Invention

It is nothing new, then, to assert that audience expectations can have as much influence in the construction of the Middle Ages as the historical period itself. Neither, however, is it any longer an outrageous effrontery to suggest that films trying to depict this period are prone to committing any number of errors, from minor technical errors — the wrong, or least plausible, type of helmet here,[26] or a rather inexplicable hand-held crossbow there[27] — to major ideological (and, one suspects, deliberate) changes. This latter group include changes which have direct import on the interpretation of the material or the audience's reading of the character and perhaps understanding of history — downgrading William Wallace from noble to peasant[28] or repackaging Robin Hood as a noble outlaw.[29]

In fact, given the prevalence and relative tolerance of these errors, as well as taking into account the distortions which the conventions discussed above introduce, there arises the possibility that — in order to overcome the interpretative "abyss" ("coupure") mentioned above — there does from time to time occur an element of "necessary invention."[30] "Necessary" in that in the transition from page to screen, from past to present, or most probably as a result of both, something is happening which foregrounds the process of making the period seem less alien over and above the notion of fidelity to the period. As one critic observes, "Film is a medium that has its own conventions and genres, and that *necessarily* invents and departs from the historical record."[31] As Keith Kelly remarks in his insightful essay on precisely this subject, "Film as a form of art that seeks to express meaning while at the same time offering dramatic entertainment, is in essence not well suited to historical accuracy (aside, perhaps, from the documentary). The creation of a complete narrative requires conjecture and fabrication."[32]

Perhaps, then, we are looking at it from the wrong direction. Returning to historiography, Veyne argues that "in history, as with theatre, to show everything is impossible. Not because it requires too many pages, but because there is no such thing as an elementary historical fact, an atomic unit within the history of happenings."[33] Bearing this in mind, we might then better understand if a dogmatic subordination to historical "accuracy" might cede to the fantasy "of imaginative reconstruction, and the necessity to make the past communicate with the present audience."[34] To pursue this logic further to its *reductio ad absurdum*, we would be forced to observe the fundamental impossibility of any form of exact replication, since everything is constructed, leading Paden to conclude that "by definition *the entire film is an anachronism*."[35]

In fact, if historiography has demonstrated that historians still debate the finer details of a given era, event or character, then it seems somewhat unjust to criticize a filmmaker's synopsis of the agreed facts, or even his own hypothesis drawn from them. "There is no single correct vision," Airlie reminds us, with the additional caveat that "there are, of course, ways of getting it wrong."[36] There is also something fundamentally naïve about criticizing the historicity of most popular films, since even within the ranks of historians, discrepancies emerge. "Demanding that filmmakers [...] shape up and 'get their facts straight' is disingenuous, insofar as it suggests that medievalists and [...] historians are all on the same page. These latter groups are not, and their discrepancies are sometimes mirrored in popular representations of their craft."[37] As Rosenstone astutely observes:

> Without the enormous amount of invention, condensation, and compression undertaken by even the most "accurate" attempt at film, the historical would not be dramatic, but a loose, sprawling form far less able to make the past interesting, comprehensible and meaningful. In one sense, of course, such films are entirely an invention.... This convention for telling the past on screen is certainly artificial but, if one stops to think about it, no less so than our current, accepted convention — words on the page. We must remember that such words also are not the past but only a way of evoking, pointing at, talking about, and analyzing the past — and by so doing, turning its traces into what we call history.[38]

This contention is reiterated, with specific attention paid to dramatic invention, in his later claim:

> Of all the elements that make up a historical film, fiction, or invention, has to be the most problematic (for historians). To accept invention is, of course, to change significantly the way we think about history. It is to alter one of history's basic elements: its documentary or empirical aspect. To take history on film seriously is to accept the notion that the empirical is but one way of thinking about the meaning of the past.[39]

In fact, there can often be some value gleaned from looking at *where* and *why* filmmakers "get things wrong." Just as historiography has helped us to elucidate the extent to which a viewpoint of history influences the history told within that school, so too can discrepancies in "popular representations" give us valuable insight into the conceptions about the medieval era from which the filmmaker is working, since "departures from history ... or the text ... are fault lines through which we may be able to glimpse the inner rationale of the film, to gain an understanding of how it is trying to connect the medieval spectacle to the modern spectator."[40] If Prince Valiant bounds around energetically, leaping gracefully and fighting villains without a scrap of armor, we gain more insight by recognizing Hathaway's debt to the Hollywood swashbuckler than haughtily disparaging his lack of Historical training. When we try to understand specific characterizations of social groupings, the gaps filled in by necessary invention are frequently the cracks through which ideologies are prone to slip.

Finally, however, a note of caution to those who approach historical films in general — and most especially medieval films — only seeking to enumerate the inaccuracies in the translation from History — even those generously termed "necessary inventions." The tendency to return to legend, or transmute the Middle Ages to a remote and alien otherworld often has a consequent effect of extirpating the action from any real, dateable history, and devolves into dreamtime, and therefore what Eco calls (albeit somewhat light-heartedly) "dreaming of the Middle Ages."[41] To criticize a dream for its failure to adhere to "reality" seems a rather futile exercise, especially since "the temporally abstract Middle Ages, unconnected to any period before or after, is the preferred one. Far more medieval films ... are based on folklore and romance ... than on history."[42] I am reminded of one spectator, on leaving the cinema after Peter Jackson's *Lord of the Rings: The Fellowship of the Ring*, whom I overheard authoritatively commenting that the "armor was wrong for the period"; his claim does rather beg the question about which period exactly the film was alleged to be recreating. This same caveat particularly applies to the wide range of Arthurian films, for as Helmut Nickel observes, "given the legendary nature of the Matter of Britain, any flight of fancy concerning costume and setting could be equally well justified."[43] While there is by no means a shortage of fodder for our criticism on the level of accuracy, we must always be careful not to get carried away in our rejection of anything which does not conform to what is, after all, most often simply our own idea of the Middle Ages. It is for this reason that I prefer to work from the tacit acceptance of this sometimes "necessary invention" in order to further probe the more logical (and, in my view, more interesting) questions about what effect these inaccuracies have on — or even what they tell us about — a given perception of the era.

Creating a Medieval Image

In fact it is only when we begin to look at the problem from the reverse angle that we can better understand the construction of the Middle Ages in film. If the construction of a world is achieved by negotiating conventions as well as by necessary invention to fill the gaps, we can see that the process of creating a medieval image is by no means a case of simply telling it like it was. Rather than deprecating the cinema with the claim that no film can "do history" (thereby demanding that the cinema effectuate the same exacting process of Historical reconstruction as historians are expected to produce), we might more usefully ask "how might we go about evoking the most faithful transition from then to now on the screen?" One answer, favored by Rohmer (as we have seen), and by Zeffirelli in his *Hamlet*, as well as Bergman in his *Seventh Seal*, has been to return to the medieval artistic imagination in illuminations of manuscripts of the period, in which case "the illumination of medieval texts becomes the model for the film's cinematography and mise-en-scène."[44] This may seem a reasonable supposition, that by returning to the contemporary views of artists and essentially animating twelfth-century miniatures, we would at least succeed in recreating their world as they themselves perceived it. Yet this is to apply a logic which we would not accept if applied to our own society, and to misunderstand the medieval image on three counts: *the form, the function and the interpretation.*

In *form*, if we were to imagine future societies earnestly and meticulously animating a Picasso or Kandinsky painting so as to evoke the "reality" of twentieth-century everyday life, we can at once see the limitations of assuming that art is a direct and infallible representation of nature. Where a visual reference to a painting might help to set the tones for a scene, "the current habit of quotation from painting [...] goes well beyond this: colors, light, and composition drawn from paintings now represent the 'realities' of their time."[45] The problem with this is that it makes no contribution to historical "accuracy," since "the painter is a privileged witness, yet his or her vision is but one cultural artefact among many. Authenticity can be obtained only when it is derived from such an understanding."[46]

Just as the notion of representation in modern art would require several book length studies to introduce, we must bear in mind equally that "the medieval image never 'photographed' reality. It was certainly not made for this purpose, neither in its forms nor in its colours."[47] Thus "the maxim of truth to nature does not apply as this was not the artist's intention. It is a highly sophisticated style that sacrifices optical veracity to narrative clarity."[48] A red dress, for example, was by no means necessarily red in reality (the accompanying text might even describe it as blue, or green) but may only exist to oppose it to other colors, both inside that image and by opposition, by visual "echoes." What is absent is often just as pertinent as what is present. What is true of images, then, is also true of texts: if we are told that someone wears a blue gown, it by no means indicates to us that this robe was actually blue, but rather that we are to think of her as regal (Capetian/royal blue), pure (the Virgin), or whatever other significance the color had at the time of writing.[49] The matter is further complicated by the fact that by the thirteenth century, with the prominence of lay workshops, the conventions of each workshop come to be applied to both religious and secular texts, creating a rift between text and image.[50] Therefore, a medievalized image — even one based on an "authentic" medieval image — risks taking too literally the inherent fictionalization.

In cinema, we can find the same process taking place in the creation of a medieval image, in which the form is moderated not to reflect the reality, but to conform to *moduli* within cinematographic conventions. In Robin Hood films, the wandering Friar Tuck might appear (as he often does) in a brown habit, which belongs to the Franciscan order and is thus — for those films which place Robin Hood in the Crusades — an anachronism, since the Order was born only in the thirteenth century. However, the black habits of the Benedictines have been assimilated in the popular imagination with evil monk motifs, from Rasputin (such as in the 1917 film *Rasputin, The Black Monk*) to *The Name of the Rose*, and the white robes of the Cistercians are so rare in iconographic representations that audiences might risk missing the allusion. Thus it is to gray and brown that filmmakers turn, forsaking historical probability for the sake of comprehension.

Second, the assumption that the medieval image reflects reality is to fail to take into account the *function* of medieval images. Within the period, the creation of a work of art played an essential part of the worship of God, since the act of work was itself an attempt to imitate the beauty of a transcendental deity.[51] Honorius of Autun, for instance, cites three purposes of painting: first "that the House of God should be thus beautified; [second] that it should recall to mind the lives of the Saints; (third that) painting ... is the literature of the laity (*pictura est laicorum litteratura*),"[52] to which Georges Duby adds a fourth purpose, that "the work of art was an affirmation of power."[53] Therefore we can see already that — aside from the first function — the function of art in the medieval mentality transcends the purely decorative function which we attribute to it in the twentieth and twenty-first centuries; "medieval thought, like classical thought, did not consider that art necessarily had to do with the production of beautiful things or the stimulation of aesthetic pleasure."[54] Although we are still able to admire the remnants of our ancestors' artistic output, the same artworks have lost for us their transcendental function, and "we do not understand these forms in the same way as our predecessors saw them."[55] In the words of Curtius, "modern man immeasurably overvalues art because he has lost the sense of intelligible beauty that Neo-Platonism and the Middle Ages possessed.... Here a beauty is meant of which aesthetics knows nothing."[56] A modern eye sees here a problematic dialectic between form and function, between art and usefulness. For us they are frequently *either* works of art *or* they are functional; for our medieval forefathers they were both. As such, the stylization of forms, the strict control of space, and gesture all serve a distinct purpose beyond basic prettification. Film, falling within the remit of Art, is thus seen as a part of the aesthetic function, and not necessarily part of the instructive aspects of everyday life. To return to the medieval image in film, then, is to reconstruct a meaningful work of art without its transcendental function.

Third, on the level of *interpretation*, the order of reading medieval images was the reverse of our modern cinematic priorities, reading from the background to the closest object, whereas the camera operates from the reverse principle. Our eyes, trained by the evolution of photography and a century of the cinema, now operate by our learned habit of picking out a static point of focus and subordinating the background, so that the arrière-plan proceeds as a complement of the central object, in turn drawing the eye away from the focal point to the point-de-fuite.[57] Such an order of reading the image, then, operates in the opposite way to the reverse perspective of medieval art for whom size and proportion were used predominantly to accentuate importance, rather than to produce an accurate recreation of the exact perspectival proportions of the eye.

In medieval art, it was not, in fact, until the late fourteenth century when the reintroduction of perspective had the effect that "instead of the constriction imposed by architectural frames, flat-patterned backgrounds and the frontal images needed for action, there [was] now the opening out of a composed landscape."[58] Prior to this movement towards modern sensibilities of perspective and composition, the tendency to eschew perspective regulates (and stylizes) the sense of space, ascribing importance to the subjects via a complex system of codes, conventions and symbols. Given also the functional aspect of the image, and the sacred subjects they were often required to mediate, the attempt to render representations of religious themes in three dimensions would have seemed wholly unnecessary; on this theme we find Bernard d'Angers observing the absurdity of trying to render the ineffable in stone. There should only be "painting, rigorous but discreet. But never, in any case, in relief."[59]

The space is highly regulated, too, so that a closed frame delineates an enclosed space, drawing the eye inward, or the frame can be formed by a character, forcing the depicted subject to fold itself inside an initial letter C, for example. In cinema, this aesthetic limitation of the frame is by no means as strictly observed, certainly in the latter half of the twentieth century, with open frames, close-ups and fractured images mediating and traversing the diegetic film-space, or with the imaginary continuation of the image outside of the frame serving to structure our sense of space in the narrative cinema. One striking similarity does occur, however, with the advent of the anamorphic lens, whose extended frame began to assert a noticeable influence over the types of films which were being produced; the CinemaScope epic favoring large casts and dynamic mass movement over psychological intrigue, for "a very wide horizontal screen emphasises scenic display, but can be of little use in suggesting ideas or the course of human relationships."[60] Despite this exception, however, we must observe that neither the interpretation nor the function of the two arts are by any means comparable on a wider scale.

Given these fundamental differences in aesthetic perspective between the two periods (medieval to modern), even in terms of the construction of the basic image, we can see that even the most sensitive translation from image to screen would betray the original sense of the artwork in terms of the form, function and interpretation of the image. When it comes to populating this image, too, we find a certain paradox in that the minimization of what we might call "translation loss" can best be achieved rather by a process of approximation than by a hyperfaithul adherence to any sense of an "original." Trying to represent a society of individuals for whom almost any item could possess its own symbolism over and above its functionality, from an axe to a nut tree, from hair color to a character's métier,[61] would inevitably result in a loss of original meaning. On the other hand, by equating one object with another — even its antithesis — on the semiotic level we are (somewhat paradoxically) better able to approach its original significance. This essentially semiological relationship is summarized as "this essential theme: Image-Audience-History," that is, for our purposes, an essential conflict between the "fact," its representation, and the observer decoding the visual symbols. It is an "analytical filter to move from the signifier to the signified, and eventually to the referent."[62]

To give an example, we might use the minor character operating on the fringes of a great number of romances: the passerby. In his attempt to find Arthur's castle, the "naïf" Perceval encounters "un charbonnier" whom he asks for directions to Carduel.[63] Pastoureau contends that a "coal-burner" — who works with fire and is therefore the natural enemy of the forest — becomes a figure of horror for those within established society. If a lost knight (albeit one who has not yet fulfilled his potential as the Grail knight) must ask them for directions, we are presented with two extremes: the future hero of chivalry, champion of the castle and civilization, juxtaposed with the baseness of the charbonnier, nemesis of the forest.[64] For Perceval, consequently, it marks a twofold separation from society; he is now outside both chivalry and his native forest, consorting with the "enemies" of both, a symbolism with important ramifications as a symbolic point on his journey. When we come to make a film of this, however, destined for a society for whom all this symbolism has disappeared, how do we represent that same meaning? Rohmer (in the only direct adaptation of Chrétien) tries to evade this by having one of his chorus enact the part, thus symbolically representing Perceval's status outside society (just as the chorus, by enacting bit parts, operate both within and outside of the action, diegetically and non-diegetically simultaneously). Bresson had also attempted the same device a few years earlier, placing his interlocutors in the center of a forest, isolated from "civilization." Nevertheless, since a great deal of this symbolism is irrecoverably lost, we must settle for a compromise and an inevitable degree of translation loss.

A similar paradox occurs with the basic choice — essentially a cinematic choice rather than a historical one — between set design and on-location shooting; here again fidelity to the content over the form conceals a striking paradox. Opting for the "real" medieval location — the castle, the cathedral, the monastery and so on — is in fact to work on the premise of a false, mediated past, as transformed by the centuries since its original completion. In a film like Bresson's *Lancelot du Lac*, filming in the milieu of a now-ruined castle complex shows us the past as it is now, and not the past as it once was. Conversely, the artificiality and, ultimately, falsity of a constructed set design or sound stage can (in its purest form) be construed as an attempt at least to rebuild the past as it really was, or rather, as we believe it to have been; for "is not the reproduction of an illusion in a certain sense also its correction?"[65] One thinks of Jorvic's "medieval village" in Yorkshire, for example, to see a false past "brought to life" yet animated in such a way as to be more immanent than the abandoned sites of real historical locations such as Sutton Hoo. This paradox is brought to light when we think of the Universal Studios' medieval castle, "which must have been the most familiar standing set in Hollywood to swash-fans."[66] The idea that one of the most recognizable emblems of the era is not Castle Doonan (despite its popularity as "real" film location) but rather a papier-mâché simulacrum thrown together in the Universal Studio's parking lot in Los Angeles calls to mind Baudrillard's contention that the reconstruction of a false history becomes a "pure simulacrum," more real than its "original," and like the replica of the Lascaux caves, "the duplication is sufficient to render both artificial."[67] Where for Guy Debord, all that "was once lived directly has moved away into representation,"[68] when it comes to the Middle Ages, and the compression of a thousand years of retransmission and re-use, we seem to be, as Marcus Bull contends, "both witnessing, and to some extent enacting, a pastiche of a pastiche of a pastiche."[69]

8

Guides to the Medieval Worlds

"I must leave at once.... Please, who would guide me? I will pay money to anybody who would guide me."[1]

Having outlined the semiotic problems inherent in the construction of a medieval world, we will here progress to look at the ways in which these worlds are more overtly communicated to modern audiences. In the cinematic Middle Ages, even supposing that the inevitable inaccuracies involved in the theoretical evocation of the past have been overcome, we are immediately confronted by the problems we have already encountered of communicating this past to a contemporary audience for whom the period is remote, distant or at least unfamiliar. These audiences are, in the main, the popular audiences for whom "history is what you can remember. The Middle Ages is what you can remember mainly from films and television documentaries."[2]

Thus over and above the reconstruction of medieval people, we are faced with the reconstruction of the medieval worlds which they inhabit, communicated predominantly by the conventions outlined in the previous chapter. In this chapter, therefore, I will look in more depth at the means by which these worlds are directly explained to the viewer, often by the use of "guides." These guides, I will propose, form two main groups, which I have labeled "internal" and "external," though it must be stressed that the use of these "guides" is by no means restricted nor prescribed in any sense, making alternate use of both the two modes of recreating the signified Middle Ages in the cinema. Thus a film can make use of the internal guides which often function by recreating the iconic objects from within the picture, while at the same time using the physical/external guides which work in the opposite direction, by making explicit references to the concepts, thereby reproducing the paradigmatic structure from outside the picture.

The Internal "Signs of Medieval-ness"

Though diverse in their form and appearance, the uniting factor among these "guides" is that their purpose (like the "insistent fringes" of Barthes' *Romans*) is that they become, to paraphrase Barthes, "quite simply the label of medieval-ness."[3] These guides, then, might be

1. guided images which evoke a particular era (knights, castles, princesses, etc.— that which I have referred to above as "historicons");
2. the use of symbolic tropes, images or sequences of events (feasting scenes, kings in state, peasants at work, etc., which have been identified above);
3. manners of speech (such as "mock-medieval," "a convention developed in the nineteenth-century ... that becomes a means of indicating that the speakers are not using English at all")[4];
4. conventions and systems of representation (tournaments, duels, dubbing ceremonies, rescues and so on — those recurrent modal stages of the film which Amy de la Bretèque has dubbed "figures obligées"[5] or "passages obligés").[6] These often function to send us back to the past by purely evocative — and not explicative — means, for "our conclusions that an advertised film is set in the past are more likely to come from visual and aural information such as costumes, sets, soundtrack and perhaps even an archaic mode of speaking."[7];
5. allusion to an intertextual model (which in essence amounts to more or less the same thing as the "passage obligé," since the references are developed precisely by the repetition of the "passages" which ultimately become "obligés"). This last element calls most strongly upon Jauss's theories of reception which we encountered above.

Of course, these guides are by no means mutually exclusive, for any number of films drawn at random from our corpus would be very likely to include one, two or more simultaneously — particularly if the film is dealing with a subject which is not immediately familiar to all modern audiences, in which case some form of guide is indispensable. By their recurrence throughout films, and their continued re-use, these codified symbols begin to transcend the nature of simple conventions and elide into something more like an archetype, moving from film to film and serving to conjure up a number of secondary characters and consequences. However, this is to anticipate the argument at hand, which is needed to explain in more detail how these guides can be seen in operation.

In order to relate the theory to the practice, I will offer below some examples of these types of guides which will be explored in their relations to specific films in later chapters. The most straightforward way to demonstrate how these guides can be in operation simultaneously is to select a film which makes constant use of all five in its evocation of the generic, "oven-ready" Middle Ages I have posited above. One strong candidate for this is undoubtedly Jerry Zucker's *First Knight*, which attempts to make reference to a culturally shared idea of the Hollywood tradition. In other words, it is using these internal guides explicitly, in order to make a link to other films in the Arthurian tradition and beyond, thus using iconic links within a paradigmatic framework. In doing so, therefore, the film inevitably makes obvious these internal guides.

We might assume, along with the filmmakers, that the spectator in 1995 had no particular expertise in the medieval field, other than that gleaned from vague recollections of high-school history and extratextual references. We were initially returned to the Middle Ages then by the title itself, playing on the cultural familiarity with idealized knighthood, as well as making a knowing reference to that other mythical medieval device which exists in Hollywood's Middle Ages (if not in its historical predecessor): the *ius primae noctis*, as evoked in no higher authority than *Braveheart* (also 1995).[8] The concept of the "right of the first night," it seems, appeals to our deepest fears and — perhaps — our most prominent post-colonial guilt, that the feudal hierarchy was rife with instances of abuses of power, the most egregious of which can be seen in the institutionally sanctioned rape of a virgin bride. It is invoked here, if only by nuances, in the seeming unnaturalness of the match between paternal Arthur and his young queen: attuned to a slew of romantic comedies and melodramas (dating back to no less than Chaucer's *Merchant's Tale*, and later Moliere's *École des Femmes*) in which the old man is cuckolded as revenge for his vanity and — the subtext reads — his inability to satisfy the bodily needs of his younger wife.[9] As Dagonet jokingly observes, in *Lancelot and Guinevere*, "Good King Arthur, late in life, took himself a youthful wife."[10]

The first type of guide, the guided image, is therefore conceived and connoted by the combination of the title and the publicity poster itself, which makes a play on that same cultural familiarity with the Arthurian saga. We are presented with a silver-haired Connery (still fresh from his portrayal of King Richard in *Robin Hood: Prince of Thieves*, and the veteran of numerous medieval films) separated from Gere's armor-clad (and noticeably padded) Lancelot by Excalibur, in which is reflected Guinevere (Julia Ormond), who stares, forlorn, down and to her left at Lancelot.[11] All of the requisite "medievalisms" are present in sufficient form to enable a viewer to understand what kind of Middle Ages is about to be invoked: a king, a sword, a princess, a knight and — on close inspection — a "Disney-esque," round-turreted Camelot shimmering on the breast plate of Connery's Arthur. In fact, were we to pursue the reading further, we can see that the entire Arthurian saga is contained in this one image, narrated by the layout of these icons in themselves; Arthur stares out from the center of the image, with his dream of Camelot reflected over his heart ("Camelot is a belief which we hold in our hearts"); he is divided from his queen and his first knight by Excalibur (echoes of the Tristan and Iseult love triangle).[12] Excalibur thus becomes at once a divisive object and the sign of the king's power, as well as symbol par excellence of the innate violence of the period called forth on occasion to ensure peace (as Arthur observes, "There's a peace only to be found on the other side of war. If that war should come I will fight it"). The remaining half of the poster contains Lancelot, his back turned to Arthur but similarly staring out at the viewer, matching Arthur's challenge and reflecting his Oedipal struggle for supremacy and for Guinevere, who stares down at Lancelot as a proleptic sign of her future adultery. By combining the image of the sword and of Guinevere, and dividing the poster in half, we are reminded of the duality of knighthood as an agent of both love and death, and the importance of honor and the protection (patriarchal repression?) of women (Guinevere's soft flesh and pastel dress juxtaposing sharply with her two armored paramours).

Moving on from the poster itself, the film opens with a high-angle wide shot of troops moving over a serene, natural landscape, a classic opposition of the dialectic between Man and Nature; tellingly, the shot recalls the opening scenes of Ford's *The Searchers*, and the cinematography is an almost exact recreation of that of Leone's *The Good, the Bad, and the Ugly*. Within the first few scenes, however, Zucker brings us back to our familiar view of the Middle Ages as a time of barbarism and bellicosity with a close-up shot of Lancelot fighting off a stocky warrior in a circle formed by the bloodthirsty villagers of Hollywood's Merrie Olde England.[13] Here is, then, our second guide in the image-motif or "iconogram," which plays a minor role in the clumsy arrangement of disparate, vaguely medieval scenes constructed over the course of the film, from Arthur's public trial (more bloodthirsty villagers), to attacks on the village (bloodthirsty villains) or attacks on children and women (cruel, bloodthirsty villains).

These image-motifs become embedded within locales themselves to create a Manichean dialectic; in so doing, they become drawn out into our fourth type of guide, the figures obligées. A colorful, crenellated Camelot becomes the seat of all things good, bathed in luminescence, home to the bravest knights, symbolically becoming the bastion of safety against the threat of external forces, playing on intertextual paradigms from sources as diverse as the police headquarters of the detective movie, or the bridge of the U.S.S. *Enterprise* (as indeed their one-piece suits suggest). At the other extreme, Malagant's underground lair becomes the logical culmination of decades of

Bond villains and malevolent masterminds (only here taking the idea of a criminal "underworld" to its literal, and bathetic, conclusion). Outside of these two polarities, the world is filtered into two "cadres": the archetypal village, in which existence itself is precarious, and the verdant forests, which play host to the lovers' first encounter and subsequent tryst (Tristan and Iseult's pre–Raphaelite re-invention). The ensemble intimates that the successful resolution of the fraught medieval society is by a just and even application of the law, which demands no divine intervention but rather in the use of military might for good — betraying perhaps a hint of T.H. White in the process.[14] The godless rule of Camelot finds its conclusion by borrowing another figure obligée in the rather incongruous Viking burial which, to Jerry Zucker at least, demonstrates that the Hollywood Middle Ages seemed to last for only a few days, and that "the 'spirit' at the centre of the film is derived not from Malory per se but from the trans-historical, trans-national ideal of Camelot (quondam civitas et civitas futura) that is an essential part of the cinematic inheritance."[15] In this sense, the film can be read in one way as no more than a museum piece, or indeed pastiche, wherein we are privy to a rapid pageant of all of the figures obligées which Hollywood has ever dreamt up about the European Middle Ages — and certainly the Middle Ages as they would have preferred it to be.

By carefully placing typical symbols of the Middle Ages into a procession of tableaux-vivants drawn from a jumbled mix of medieval bricolage based, in turn, on other modern instances of the Middle Ages, we can see that *First Knight* operates on both a paradigmatic and iconic capacity, using the icons not to return to the medieval itself, but drawing on the cinematic imaginary of the period, since "the target audiences for such films [as *First Knight* and *A Knight's Tale*] will know the Middle Ages chiefly through its representation in earlier films and popular culture."[16] It is, in short, a hypertextual medievalism, which is of course why it is such an indispensable tool to measure the popular reception of the period.

In addition to being *hyper*textual (and indeed self-referential), the film works on an *inter*textual level, making great use of these borrowed image-motifs, our fifth type of guide, to the extent that it becomes, rather than an update of the Arthurian legend for the 1990s, something of a palimpsest of other formulaic action films which just happens to be set in the Middle Ages. Overall, the film resembles nothing so much as the Navy Flight School of one of Gere's previous blockbusters, *An Officer and a Gentleman*, in which a maverick young warrior is recruited to a military school to learn how to use his innate, Perceval-esque martial skills to uphold the "forces of good." The school is in turn presided over by a paternal "establishment" figure, and Lancelot/ Mayo must learn to obey the hierarchical structure of his new environment and win the girl by recognizing the values of love and the place of violence within the establishment. Sean Connery, too, becomes once again the figure of "benign paternalism overseeing a young man's transition into manhood,"[17] reflecting in this respect the role of *An Officer and a Gentleman*'s Gunner Sergeant Foley ("your momma and your daddy for the next thirteen weeks"), and drawing on an off-the-peg medievalism elaborated in roles such as the Green Knight to the young Gawain, Richard I to Robin Hood, Ramírez to McCleod, William of Baskerville to the novice Adso, which all reflect an identical pairing of the avuncular and the naive.[18]

The internal guides, therefore, can be seen to work on different levels of the film, seeking either — like the image-motifs, and guided images — to refer the viewer back to a widely held imagination of the medieval period, or — like the intersemiotic references and genre conventions — to refer the viewer out of the picture to another mode of representation. The uniting feature of these two, however, is that both make reference to a previously established signification to reconnect the signified reality of the Middle Ages with the modern observer.

Physical Guides

Outside of the narrative sphere of a given film, however, we can also observe a few more direct ways in which filmmakers might go about using a metatext to communicate these medieval worlds to their audiences. Time-traveling films prove to be particularly useful here as their attempts to differentiate between the two worlds almost inevitably foreground the ontological construction of their medieval "stages." The evocation of two distinct (and usually incompatible) worlds inevitably invites a comparison between the two, even in those cases wherein the milieu from which the traveler has come is not shown: like any fish-out-of-water yarns, the narrative impetus comes from the unsuitability of the character's actions to the new environment in which he finds himself. Thus because the past (or indeed future) world is a new universe, the time traveler is placed outside of the world and can thus serve as a physical guide for us, the audience. Among the numerous variations among time-traveling films featuring the medieval era, there are three major groups, which each serve to elucidate a different kind of comparison:

1. A guide from the modern era is sent back to the Middle Ages (retrospective comparison).
2. A guide from the Middle Ages is sent forward into the twentieth century (prospective comparison).

3. A guide (in this case almost always Merlin or his equivalent) familiar
with both periods is allowed to overtly compare the two (interstitial
comparison).

While all three inevitably invite some form of comparison between the two
periods, the ways in which they do so, as well as the conclusions they reach,
produce an enormous difference in the spectator's judgment of that world.

In the first instance, retrospective comparison, we can use the example
of Jamaal in Gil Junger's *Black Knight*. After falling into the moat of the
medieval-themed amusement park for which he works, Jamaal (Martin Lawrence) finds himself transported back to the (vague) Middle Ages, nominally
the fourteenth century, where he (despite his rather incongruous American
football shirt) is mistaken for a messenger from Normandy. "Although the
film's primary raison d'être is to provide Martin with a vehicle for comic antics
in an alien environment," Jamaal, as a self-concerned "pragmatist," is evidently supposed to be a rather thinly veiled version of the modern spectator,
his odyssey intended to highlight the difference between time periods.[19] The
comparison initially works by a process which we might call "interrupted
expectation," by which the traveler arrives and interprets the attributes of this
unfamiliar world as simply foreign elements within their own world: here
Hank Morgan's description of armor as "that iron union suit"[20] is reflected in
Jamaal's continued belief that he has simply arrived at a rival medieval-themed
amusement park, and his compliments that everything is so realistic. The
protagonist's gradual realization that his once familiar world is actually a foreign parallel, serves initially to perpetuate our modern insistence on the alterity
and backwardness of the Middle Ages. Almost the entire canon of time-traveling films included here seem to risk, if not give way entirely to, a spirit of
colonialism which charts the progress of our civilized explorer penetrating the
Dark Continents of our past and — once there — discovering some sentimental,
Robinson Crusoe–style lessons taught to them by these noble savages. In *Black
Knight*, for example, after teaching the "primitives" the finer details of modern
culture (such as break dancing and creating fire with a cigarette lighter), he
begins to learn from them the concepts of honor, nobility and the selfless service of a greater cause, all of which eventually cedes to the rather sanctimonious
sermonizing of the film which was in any case obvious from the outset — that
the initial criticism of the primitive state of their world is in fact a criticism
of the lack of honor, concern and what we might call "community spirit" of
our own. In both processes (the criticism of our world by the invocation of
theirs — interrupted expectation) the same fundamental confusion is taking
place: the time traveler is confusing the form with the content.

To give another example, in *A Knight in Camelot*, the Hank Morgan character is this time a female scientist sent back to the "Dark Ages" (though no specific chronology is offered)[21]; once there she immediately sets about industrializing these "primitives" and creates a steam-powered engine to turn the grindstones of the flour mill. What the film fails to recognize, however, is that these attempts at industrial progression simply create a suitably "medieval" simulacrum of the machine, but its significance to their society is bound to differ to an inestimable degree. Industrialization of the labor force was of course by no means brought about by Stephenson's "Rocket" alone, but rather the inverse is true: the Rocket was a product of the revolution in technological and scientific thought. Therefore, by simply creating the "form" of modernity within the medieval worlds, Goldberg's character has no more modernized the medieval world than she has improved it. The consequence of this process is that the uncivilized nature of our era is brought to light by our attempts to "civilize" theirs: those elements which we hold as hallmarks of civilization, we are supposed to realize, are in fact diabolic to a community for whose use these mechanized tools are wholly inappropriate.

Given that the second category (time travel from medieval to modern) works in the opposite way, we might originally suspect that the reverse process is taking place. Nevertheless, the audience is still looking at the world from the point of view of the twentieth or twenty-first century, and consequently the criticism of the Middle Ages is yet again a way of highlighting the shortcomings of our own. To criticize the past that we have ourselves constructed, it seems, is to critique the means of construction, and the same is true of these films. In criticizing their fictitious worlds, these films are elaborating the shortcomings of our own era: they are not the target; we are. Thus the primitive Middle Ages of a film like *Les Visiteurs*, which follows the knight Godefroi de Papincourt as he is magically transported forward into France in the late 1980s along with his squire, seems to descend into a laundry list of complaints levied against our medieval forebears. It is a world of poor personal hygiene, of barbaric feudal subjugation, and of mysticism and superstition; in short, it is Eco's "shaggy medievalism"[22] fringed by a hint of Huizinga's view of the period as one of cultural extremes.[23] Yet there is a point about halfway through the film, when we see the reactions of the modern sophisticates to the exaggeratedly grotesque manners of the medievals, which in a short time passes through prudishness to a final moment in which we find the medieval vision of ourselves more agreeable than that of our contemporaries. The "dirty" Middle Ages of *Les Visiteurs* is thus working at subverting more than the Middle Ages themselves: "they gradually show up the shallowness of the bon chic, bon genre world of the present and we can thus see how this sort of juxtaposition of past and present can be used not simply as a stick to beat the past but as an effective way of satirizing the present."[24]

Thirdly, the transition from medieval to modern might be effectuated by a time-traveling Merlin, practically a prevalent enough motif to warrant a category to itself. A guide familiar with both worlds, medieval and modern, offers the advantage of a conscious comparison between the two periods, brought particularly noticeably to the foreground with the use of Merlin himself as narrator in both *Excalibur* and Steve Barron's *Merlin* (the latter can in many ways be seen as a continuation of many of the themes and precepts addressed in Boorman's film).[25]

This latter category can also make use of a second form of interstitial guide, one which is anchored temporally within the period, but is spatially far enough removed to allow them to act as rather like a museum curator as we tour our cinematic medieval worlds. By ostracizing these characters from their milieux, they become closer to us as "tourists" than to them as "natives." In *The Advocate*, for example, the Parisian lawyer (tellingly named Richard Courtois to continually remind us of his "courtly" roots) is continually torn between a number of tertiary guides whose credibility is continually called into question: the ex-lawyer, the priest, the suspect, the victim's family and the lord of the manor, thereby objectifying the truth and immersing the viewer in the same confusion in which our hero is enmeshed.[26]

The temporal or spatial dislocation of the guides, more than anything else, allows the filmmaker to recreate the historical footnote, providing an intra-diegetic need for the spurious lines of dialogue which are clearly intended more to clarify the proceedings to us than to the intra-diegetic characters who would, we assume, be familiar with the "rules" of their worlds. These include Prince John asking how a medieval trial should be conducted, Count Adhemar explaining the rules of the tournament to Jocelyn, Godefroi de Ibelin reminding Balian of the duties of a knight, or a messenger explaining the rules of succession to a group of villagers to whom they would undoubtedly already be known.[27] The purpose, we must therefore conclude, of an interstitial guide within both time travel and other medieval films is not to explain the inconsistencies of the two worlds to the protagonists, but to help us, the audience, to recover from our own version of this "interrupted expectation." After all, we must not forget that as twentieth-century audiences thrown back in time into these medieval worlds, we are in many ways the time-travel protagonists ourselves, and consequently have frequent recourse to the (often simplified) explanations of the guides precisely in order to understand the meaning of the signs, symbols and objects which are unfamiliar to us.

While, then, the incarnation of a guide for us as viewers can be used in order to guide us through the individually foreign elements of these past worlds, they cannot reach outside of the film itself to introduce us to the filmic world as a whole; in this case we have recourse to one last type of guide who exists outside of the diegesis, but can authoritatively introduce us to that world. Thus we come onto one last form of guide: the extra-diegetic narrator.

Prologue as Guide

> *Now this here story I'm about to unfold took place in the early '90s — just about the time of our conflict with Sad'm and the I-raqis. I only mention it because sometimes there's a man.... I won't say a hero, 'cause, what's a hero? Sometimes, there's a man.... Sometimes, there's a man, well, he's the man for his time and place. He fits right in there. Sometimes there's a man, sometimes, there's a man. Well, I lost my train of thought here. But ... aw, hell. I've done introduced it enough.*[28]

For a period which is remote or foreign to a modern audience, one of the most frequently used devices is the extra-diegetic prologue, which acts as a bridge between the two worlds by using something familiar (historical narrative) to explain something foreign (the history itself). This process works in broadly the same way that, in a time-travel film, the modern world serves as a point of transition between the two temporal planes, since "only after this confrontation can we be taken through that barrier into the 'real' life of the old."[29] One of the major disadvantages, however, of the reliance on a prologue to furnish the viewer with the requisite knowledge of the period is the same problem which we have encountered in chapter 1; namely, that in trying to condense eons of history to a narrative sequence with beginning and finite ending, there is a necessity to simplify and in some cases to mislead. Consider, for example, Orson Welles' booming introduction to Richard Fleischer's *The Vikings*:

> Cramped by the confines of their barren icebound northlands, they exploited their skill as shipbuilders to spread a reign of terror then unequalled in violence and brutality in all the records of history.... Their abiding aim was to conquer England, then a series of petty kingdoms, each one the jealous rival of the next.... It was no accident that the English Book of Prayer contained this sentence: "protect us, O Lord, from the wrath of the Northmen."[30]

The summary seems to propose the theory that the Vikings' sporadic looting and pillaging was the result simply of a lack of space, which may be by and large dismissed along with most of the film's pretensions to "historical veracity" as pure quasi-historical hokum.[31] It ignores the fact that most of the attacks came from Denmark and not the "barren icebound northlands" and fails to fully appreciate the colonizing and integrating (and not necessarily diasporic) nature of their expansion from the North.[32] A similar process takes place in

Alfred the Great's gloomy titles which simply read, "In the ninth century England was divided into independent kingdoms of which the richest was Wessex," or *The 13th Warrior*'s opening lament, "things were not always thus.... [Once] life was easy and I lived without care." The epic-sized introductions which either extol the virtues of chivalry or opine the gloom of plague, war, famine and death[33] each set up an opposition of darkness and light reflective of a general acceptance in the popular imagination of Huizinga's cultural extremes more than any earnest historical gesture towards verisimilitude. The omniscience of the narrator can thus lead to a misleading (at best) or deleterious (at worst) undermining of historical investigation in the popular imagination.[34]

By situating the action of a film in a separately defined space, the film runs a second risk of uprooting its subject matter from its historical context and therefore removing any ideas of causality or consequentiality outside of the film, placing the film alongside us in a hermetically sealed, mythical "no-time," transporting the subject to folklore or fantasy. The early medieval "Dark Age" period (precisely because of the lack of a universally accepted timescale implied by this appellation)[35] is particularly susceptible to a hijack by the "sword and sorcery" influences taken from heroic fantasy, in heroic film cycles such as *Conan the Barbarian* and its post-modern avatars.[36] This can further erode the traces of causality among films treating this period by a misrepresentation of what Historical "facts" are known in an effort to streamline the events treated within the film and to present them as part of an enclosed, completed sequence of events, extemporalized and extirpated from its sequential and chronological context. As Burt writes,

> The prologues and title sequences perform a crucial role in creating a history effect by framing and thereby heightening analogies not only between film and earlier media but also between that earlier medium, seen in the film, and the historical medium it simulates.[37]

By insinuating itself into a paratext — and courting an association with the assumed reality of the medieval "originals," the resultant effect of the film's prologue is that it actually places the whole film *outside* of the ongoing debates about History and historiography, instead placing their films in an unassailable, closed medieval world.

The consequent compartmentalization of the Middle Ages, then, can often lack a general overview, or any sense of chronology. Few spectators, for example, would immediately recognize in the drunken Prince Hal of *The Black Shield of Falworth* the future King Henry V (better known as Laurence Olivier or Kenneth Branagh to a contemporary audience). The only clue to this identity is given in the opening credits, which announce that the film takes place "in the Reign of King Henry IV." While of course it is not entirely surprising that the son of Henry IV ought logically to be Henry V, such a supposition nevertheless requires a certain familiarity with History (Henry III, for example, was not the son of Henry II, and neither was Richard I succeeded by Richard II). Furthermore, the fact that this early title card remains the sole instance of an attempt to cement the period in any datable period speaks volumes about the importance of "real" historical events to the plot. It is here, then, that the prologue is revealed to be most important, as it provides the requisite narrative stability for a series of isolated, ahistorical medieval films. To rely on historical events occurring outside of the film's narrative would equally be to rely on a given audience's familiarity with the Historical record, which in an international film market geared towards the much-maligned "average viewer," is understandably a risky strategy. A prologue, on the other hand, provides a capsule history of the film's context, providing just enough data to understand the film — even at the expense of the complexities of the past.

A great number of other medieval films, too, work on the same lines; the film acts as one narrow window onto the past without any attempt to place it within the whole corridor of history,[38] so that we are presented with a rather heterogeneous series of "historical" characters instead of an earnest historical attempt to recreate a character situated within a real historical context. How else, for example, could we fail to recognize in *The Lion in Winter*'s Henry II the same Henry of the Thomas Becket assassination — even when the same actor, Peter O'Toole, played Henry in the earlier *Becket*? More shocking to modern audiences raised with so many Robin Hoods is failing to spot the future Prince John and King Richard as the beleaguered king's offspring. Conversely, of course, no serious objections seem to be raised to what I have elsewhere termed the peripatetic Arthur syndrome,[39] in which the desperate attempts for new Arthurian material have caused him to encounter Vikings, Robin Hood, and Kurosawan samurai,[40] which seems to lend support to the claim that "a temporally abstract middle ages, unconnected to any period before or after, is the preferred one."[41] One historical period comes to be a surrogate for any other moment in the same period, so that within the tentatively reconstructed Middle Ages, it matters little to modern audiences if the protagonists first fight off the Vikings before leaving (with Robin Hood, and Ivanhoe) for the Crusades, battle against the Plague and finish up choosing sides in the War of the Roses. Provided that we are given a vague temporal period (via a prologue, for example) to conjure up the relevant medieval imaginary, we are rarely disturbed by such achronicity.

While, of course, we can scarcely expect to do justice to tomes of historical investigation in two or three sentences, if we look at it from the reverse angle, we can see an obvious advantage that it fills in background information which would otherwise take pages of dialogue to convey, and sets up — in the narrator — the insinuation of an implied omniscient narrative stance and a clearly defined historical space within which the narrative is allowed to unfold. These guides, by being anchored within the historical worlds being created, escape unscathed from even the most egregious divergences from history, allowing the filmmaker — via the narrator — to invent, omit, conflate or insinuate entire tracts of history which would be denied to films dealing with a more familiar or recognizable period. To begin a World War II film, for example, with the words "in the middle of the twentieth century, Europe was ravaged by belligerent forces" would be a vaguely tenable yet ridiculously simplistic proposition; however, we do not encounter nearly the same reaction when we read that "in the fourteenth century, England and France were engaged in a war that would last a hundred years."[42]

This process of invention within a prologue thus remythologizes the Middle Ages, constructing a cinematic version of the period within "a region in which the action is myth, and where the medieval appears not as subject, or even setting, but rather in the form of signals that lend a certain required air of reality."[43] The prologue, along with the guides outlined elsewhere in this chapter, function not by transporting modern audiences *back to the past*, but by creating a *parallel* medieval world in which to situate their narrative events. The differences in agenda and implementation aside, each of these guides serve to color in the background and carefully to delineate the boundaries of each newly constructed Middle Ages, which are jettisoned once they have served their narrative functions.

My argument here, in its simplest form, is that films made in the true Hollywood classical epic tradition have often come to develop a single-use, "disposable Middle Ages," which are not intended to serve any Historical purpose, but most often become the backdrop for yet another Technicolor romp through Merrie England. They are created from a series of signs which operate by evoking accepted historicons, "iconogrammes" and "passages obligés" only inasmuch as they serve the narrative impetus, highlighting one of the essential problems outlined in chapter 1, for "films, particularly Hollywood films, try to show through linear narrative driving towards closure, concentration on individuals and 'invisible' technique that the world can be rendered unproblematically on screen."[44]

Nevertheless, one complication of placing audiences and "experts" at polar opposites does arise with a new direction of criticism in a recent article by Richard Burt, in which he examines the prologues, title sequences and "making of" sections of historical film releases.[45] Over the course of his fascinating article, he gradually makes a strong case that popular filmmakers were increasingly going to great lengths to use these marginalia (what he calls the "paratext") to impart historical credibility to their films. Such credibility, however, is revealed to be a double-edged sword, since it might induce the non-expert viewer to accept its authority, but this also brings upon the film-maker the responsibility to "get the details right" and rescinds the freedom previously afforded to them as pure entertainment.[46] If future filmmakers want their Middle Ages to be taken seriously as historical efforts, then they must accept that in doing so they are no longer immune (if ever they were) from criticism and debate over those painstaking details which rage among History and Literature departments throughout academia. As Shippey writes in a recent article on the claims to veracity by the makers of *King Arthur*, "there is something incipiently pedantic about professional medievalists quibbling over the accuracy or otherwise of commercially produced movies, but the strident claims of historical truth made by the producers of this one perhaps license one to say, in reply, that its history is at best dubious, and its geography frankly ludicrous."[47]

While such marginalia are scarcely new — promotion material has lauded the "scholarship" of filmmakers at least as far back as de Mille — it does bring to light one of the more contested sites of credibility within the use of a prologue (and DVD "bonus features") as a guide to the period, since the device of placing an omniscient narrator outside the sphere of action imparts — however unwittingly — a sense of objectivity to the representation of the past, an impartiality which we have seen is denied to the historian *in stricto sensu*. To proceed from here, then, there arises a clear need for further research into how, when and why the marginalia/paratext has been used and what effect this has on filmmakers' attempts to reproduce history. To be effective, such a study would also need to bring to bear a more sociological angle which takes into account the reactions of audiences to such strident claims to authenticity and/or accuracy, since it seems likely that theories of reception must by necessity play a part in creating this sense of authenticity in the first place.

9

Authenticity and Accuracy in Medieval Worlds

In this final chapter, we arrive at the point at which we must fuse together the theoretical and analytical discussions broached so far. In the first section of this book, I proposed (along with Haydock and Amy de la Bretèque) the existence of a medieval imaginary, in which many of the popular ideas we hold about the medieval period come to form a recognizable set of signs and ideas, coming eventually to form a reflection of the period which—though imaginary—was paradoxically perhaps more "real" to modern cinema audiences than the Historical equivalent. In the second, more analytical, section I used these arguments to show that modern filmmakers were suffering from a semiotic "rupture" (which reflected the "coupure infranchissable" between the past and the present), which meant that we were no longer able to connect to the referent to its cinematic signifier. These two arguments, then, serve to demonstrate that when we are talking about medieval films in terms of accuracy, we are sometimes asking less about the accuracy *in stricto sensu* than about their authenticity. If—as we saw in chapter 7—a plurality of verisimilar medieval worlds can exist, then we can see that a film need not necessarily replicate verbatim the medieval worlds created by historians and academics, but rather need only generate a medieval world which has the right "feel" to it and which alows a spectator to make a connection to the medieval imaginary. Such accuracy, then, is based less on facts known in the scholarly domain, but must conform to the medieval imaginary, which is often at several removes from this domain.

Consequently, we must first of all outline exactly what is meant by the terms "accuracy" and "authenticity." Studies of history on film have sometimes treated these two terms as synonymous, working on the (understandable) assumption that sufficient accuracy within the text (footnotes, credibility, plausibility, (etc.) will inevitably provide the requisite authenticity in the histories they retell. However, this is to rely on the demands and conventions of

written History, which I have shown in chapter 1 are by no means indiscriminately applicable to its filmic counterpart. Furthermore, it is to assume that
filmmakers dealing with historical subjects are necessarily engaged on a quest
to recreate the period in the same way as written history; the reality, for both
economic and social reasons, is that "not all medieval films have as their goal
historical accuracy."[1]

If, therefore, they are all aiming to do different things, and they are not
all aiming for a hyper-fidelity to the period, we consequently find ourselves
in need of a tool in order to analyse them accordingly. It seems unfair to criticize their inaccuracy, for this would be to criticize them for failing to do
something which they never proposed to do in the first place. To demonstrate
this point, we might use two films which both seek to recreate "the Middle
Ages" in its various forms: Ingmar Bergman's *The Seventh Seal* and Richard
Thorpe's *Ivanhoe*.

Now, if we were to approach these two films from the standpoint of film
criticism alone, there would be plenty to say about them. We might criticize
Ivanhoe's melodramatic acting, for instance, or identify in the epic mise-en-
scène relics of the swashbuckling genre, as we see in Derek Elley's reading of
the film;[2] we might, like Amy de la Bretèque, make deep insights into the use
of space in the tournament scenes.[3] We might even choose to pursue this film
by drawing comparisons between it and medieval symbology, as Pastoureau
has done, eventually coming to the conclusion that while it betrays the spirit
of the Middle Ages, it simultaneously and paradoxically updates it.[4] We might,
however, do none of these, and look at the films from the point of view of
each filmmaker, focusing for example on whether *The Seventh Seal* accords
with the auteurism of Bergman's oeuvre, or trace trends across the studio productions of the era, or the size of the frame, and the use of sound or costume.
Whatever approach would be taken from a cinematographic point of view,
however, it would be difficult to conclude that they were simply "bad" or
"inaccurate" films, without a good deal of support.

If we approach them from an historical standpoint, however, we may
again have some words to say about them. There will almost certainly be the
odd anachronism, the occasional misunderstanding of a specific detail; the
knight's return from the Crusade may be unlikely at this time, the armor
might date to a different period, and so on. But we are still not able to dismiss
it solely on these criteria as a "bad film," since we are only criticizing the historical details, and we must also remember that these are intended for an
audience who would not be thinking necessarily along those same lines: provided there are no wristwatches and aeroplanes, modern audiences are remarkably forgiving. When it comes to authenticity, "what is interesting is not how
seldom Hollywood makes such a mistake [...] but how unusual it is that a

lapse of authenticity tears the fabric of the viewer's sense of the authentic. As an audience, we are extraordinarily tolerant of inconsistencies."[5]

So, having proposed a way of analysing the *production* of these films (using semiotics, icons and paradigms to expose the means of their construction), we now come to the point at which we must come up with a new way of analyzing their *reception*. One very common historical criticism levied at such films — albeit encountered anecdotally rather than critically — amounts to the rather vague complaint that they just don't have the right "feel" to them. Such a dismissal is of course inadequate not only from the two perspectives outlined above, but also because to make the claim that they do not "feel" right presupposes that there is a "right feel" in the first place — that there is somehow a kind of "truth" about the Middle Ages which filmmakers can find, but historians cannot.

A Standard Form of Criticism?

Thus even in the event that two films deal with the same subject (let's say, for argument's sake, the Crusades of the late twelfth century), we might well find ourselves confused by what will almost certainly be two very different portrayals of roughly the same period. We thus begin to see that criticisms based on rigidly historical criteria of accuracy or inaccuracy are not likely to get us very far, for we are trying to compare films and history according to two very different critical standards. Thus accuracy versus inaccuracy — one of the most dominant modes of criticism of historical film up to this point — is no longer the only, nor even the most useful, way of measuring and analyzing these films, for two main reasons:

1. There is, as we saw above, no definite "single" version of events from which we can accuse them of deviating — this is the historiographic approach.
2. They are not necessarily intended to be accurate "historical" reconstructions in the first place — this is the cinematographic approach.

A cautionary note is required, however, for this second point. It is perhaps too easy to excuse a "betrayal" of history as pure entertainment, on the basis that films in this tradition are merely harmless foibles. The reason for this is that, over the past few years, a number of the most prominent critics of historical film — including Hayden White, Marc Ferro, Peter Rollins and Robert Rosenstone — have all devoted many pages to showing that films with historical themes can be important as historical works in themselves, and can, in certain circumstances, function as history in their own right, albeit differently to the written historical text.[6] Such a conclusion is most explicitly reached by Marnie Hughes-Warrington, in assertion that "films are not a form of history but *are* history."[7] To dismiss them or to explicate them as simply a non-serious distraction is thus to exonerate them from the duty of what Rosenstone terms "responsible historical recreation."[8] It is clear, then, that historical filmmakers cannot have their cake and eat it; if they are to be granted the freedom to write history through film, then they must also assume the concomitant responsibility of serious historical reconstruction, or else divest themselves of the "filmic history" mantle altogether.

So we come to something of an impasse: these films are not historical in the same sense as we would apply that word to a written History of the medieval period, for example, but they are not wholly entertainment either, for they should make some attempt at least to stay as close to the facts as they can. We are also — and more importantly — dealing with a problem of how to *approach* these historical films in terms of authenticity, given that they work on a variety of levels. If historical accuracy is, for reasons explored above, an elusive quality, then how do films go about creating a sense of authenticity? Where does this authenticity come from? Zemon Davis does employ one revealing phrase of relevance to my argument below, when she comments that, in the film *Day of Wrath*, "historical authenticity comes first and foremost from the film's credible connection with 'the spirit of the period' — *in its large forms and sometimes in its small details.*"[9]

The answer to the problem of authenticity, then, might lie in these small details. On this basis, this final chapter will put forward the proposition that we are working with two levels in our filmed medieval worlds — one of accuracy and another, quite different, of authenticity. These levels can be identified with two levels on which the film is based: the level of objects (the material worlds), and the level of the worlds themselves.

Material Worlds and the Historicon

On the basic level, the level of the set, soundstage, location, props, etc., we have the material worlds, the world of objects, or "the world of things."[10] Put simply, the inclusion of a sufficient number of these "things" can serve to create a sense of historical accuracy, on the basis that "the truth of an historical phenomenon can be realised through the sheer accumulation of contemporary signs of the real."[11] We can see how this functions in the opening scene of Bergman's *The Seventh Seal*, for the mise-en-scène is based on the accumulation of a number of identifiable medieval objects, framed by a static, medium-long shot, recreating the gaze of an impartial — and distinctly non-medieval —

observer. These include things like the dagger, the white cross of the crusader (even if this belongs to the Hospitaliers, whose heyday lay further back in the twelfth-century Crusades), the sword belt and chain mail. The clothing thus becomes a sequence of signs which adhere sufficiently to received iconology (whether from film, art or elsewhere is a study for another time) for us to be able to identify the roles without prompting: armor and cross belong to the knight; the snood, dagger and more dishevelled clothes force us to assume that his companion is a squire. Finally, since we are by now no strangers to combinations of signs which Eisenstein has identified as ideograms (and which François Amy de la Bretèque calls an iconogram), our knowledge of the knight + cross image together points to a crusade, and their appearance on a beach + absence of ship = victims of a shipwreck.[12] The proliferation of material objects is sufficient to pinpoint a specific period to us. Without recourse to subtitles or title cards, we already "know" that we are watching a film which will be about the Middle Ages. We have also, by the combination of a few basic signs and motifs, been able to piece together a rough background to the story—a (possibly shipwrecked) knight and his squire have returned from the Crusades. Furthermore, as a result of Bergman's mastery of cinematic minimalism, a few simple gestures from the knight suffice to connote a sense of the existentialist despondency which plagues the film throughout.

Thus, we have seen so far that there can exist a certain series of "signs," which I have referred to in this book as "historicons," and which are sufficient in most cases for us to summon up an entire time period with a surprising degree of accuracy and specificity. Celebrity culture has, after all, bequeathed to us a series of iconic signs which recall heroes of yesteryear (a blonde with flying skirts for Marilyn Monroe, a narrow moustache and a cane recall Chaplin, and Bogart can be recreated by a simple curled lip by Jean-Paul Belmondo in *A Bout de Souffle*), and which have taught us to identify certain visual symbols with certain cinematographic or cultural phenomena. In the same vein, then, we can see what are otherwise very modern takes on historical subjects can use a simple accumulation of these objects in order to signal to us, the audience, that this takes place in the past. In the recent series *The Tudors*, for example, we are presented with a very modern take on Henry VIII; despite this, the overall feel of the period is communicated to us by the period details, such as the use of those large headpieces which we now call, conveniently, Tudor hats. Similarly, Sofia Coppola's *Marie Antoinette* attracted a great deal of criticism for her take on the period, yet none of these disputed the essential premise that the film was supposed to be set in the late eighteenth century, a premise supported by the consistent use of appropriate details and things. A "historicon," therefore, functions on this level simply as an indicator of a historical period, and can take the form of almost any object, item, character, gesture or historical reference, provided only that these objects conform to what we think they might have looked like at the time. These objects can nowadays even include CGI–created actors for crowd scenes, christened with the wonderfully self-explanatory neologism "synthespians."

The next logical question which arises is how we can use these signs to build up a "world." We have seen already that in the opening scenes of his *The Seventh Seal* Bergman is able to provide us with a number of these signs on the first level which we can combine to produce a second level, a level on which we begin to assign "meaning" backwards to produce a "back-story" (remember that we have not, at this point, had any intradiegetic dialogue before making our judgment). We read the medieval historicons and extrapolate a "back-story" (of a knight returning from the Crusades, in this instance). Therefore, these primary signs on the level of the material world form, by their accumulation, a sense of an entire world of the past.

It is this accumulation of signs which we might describe as "ambientalism," and which is frequently the area which the historical advisor is called in to supervise; it is therefore the area to which many filmmakers pay their closest attention. Both Zemon Davis and Guneratre after her observe that the "usual marks of historical authenticity in films ... [consist of] period props, paintings, locations and local people" though, admittedly, "they add to the credibility and genuine historicity of the film only insofar as they are used with some discernment about their truth status."[13] Those films which rely on a proliferation of these signs often have very little to do with the evocation of a world, either, for it is these films which bring in the historical consultant to lend credibility to their projects, but their advice is often sought only for this lower level of historicons. Robert Brent Toplin, for one, laments that "many historians who have worked behind the scenes as consultants to film projects are not happy with their experiences. They complain that filmmakers often assign them to advisory roles only to advertise that the films received a scholarly stamp of approval."[14] Yet in this case it does seem as though the filmmakers are right; outside of scholarship, it seems that the period look is a frequently evoked measure of authenticity, since "when viewers argue the authenticity of a film or the lack of it, they usually mean realism based on decorum or fittingness."[15] A lack of attention to such details, on the other hand, creates flaws which "destroy the consistency of the illusion, eroding our emotional investment in the film ... the sense of historical depth disappears, and we are left looking at a movie set."[16]

In the realm of the material world, however, historical films very often seem to go too far in their attempts at verisimilitude on this level, eventually achieving a paradoxical "false hyper-reality," by the revealing tendency to focus on the details at the expense of the overall "feel" for the period. Such films become "increasingly obsessed with what might be called 'accuracy in antiques'— having no anachronistic objects appear in the frames of pictures about the past."[17] The food for Ridley Scott's *Gladiator*, for example, was flown in from a food art specialist in London since according to the chef "there's nothing worse in a historical film [...] than having fruit straight from the supermarket."[18] Now, anybody who has ever spent a lot of time studying historical films will know that there is, in fact, a great deal that is worse than the wrong type of fruit in a historical film.

The advent of digital technologies such as CGI, bluescreen and post-production editing has particularly marked a renewed focus on the details over the specific world, so that in *Kingdom of Heaven*, for instance, just as in *Gladiator*, one piece can be made in fantastic detail, and subsequently digitally grafted onto the scene. The capabilities of digital technologies have thus given modern filmmakers incredible scope for developing the details of the worlds, the historicons, to the extent that even the weather itself can be changed to match the mood of the film.[19] The films, to paraphrase Baudrillard, might risk becoming "their own pure simulacrum," by dint of the absence of material relation to the basic historical reality.[20]

The World as Forum

However, where the theoretical model proposed in this book differs from existing writing on the subject is that my theory of icons and paradigms means that something else is happening beyond this. If the details are verified by historical consultants as respected as Zemon Davis, Le Goff and Rosenstone, then how is it that the films made as a result are so often criticized? One way to explain it, therefore, is by proposing that this attention to the material details of the past world represents only the first level of the recreation of the worlds. This world may be correct, and beyond the criticism of all but the most pedantic critic, but the film may be accused of betraying history on the grounds of what they do with it on another level. This second level becomes, then, the world which is constructed from these material objects; in a sense, it becomes the "world" itself.

This world, needless to say, is from the outset a more complicated notion and one which is more elusive, precisely because it is the most difficult detail to spot. In many ways it is like the (probably apocryphal) ramblers failing to find the Uffington white horse from the ground, while of course from the air it is unmistakeable, or like those getting lost in a maze, when from a distance the solution is often immediately clear. If the details of the material world may be termed "historicons," the corresponding term for the world itself, I have argued, might perhaps be the "forum." In its simplest manifestation, this forum is the background of the world itself, or even the prism through which we see the period. "Necessarily, what is constructed ... is a communal fantasy. This agreed-upon fantasy is the core truth of every medieval film. A world that lives in the imaginations of writers and directors is brought to the screen in such a way that it breaches the walls of our disbelief."[21]

Here I want to refer back to the some of the films mentioned above to explain more clearly. We saw that both the "serious" films (let's say, for argument's sake, those which employ historical advisers, such as *Martin Guerre* or *The Seventh Seal*) as well as the more "populist" works (like *Ivanhoe* and *A Knight's Tale*, clearly aimed at a less scrupulous audience) had made some efforts — however successfully — to populate their material worlds with appropriate objects for the relevant period. Nevertheless, we can see instantly that the two films were operating from entirely different *conceptions*: that is to say that they approached the period from two very different starting points. Even by the time of its production, a film like *Ivanhoe* has already been filtered through a number of difficult and conflicting forums (Walter Scott's romanticism, nineteenth-century medievalism, twentieth-century nostalgia; text-to-film adaptation, film-to-film adaptation, and so on, not to mention the 1950s climate of Cold War paranoia). Thorpe's 1952 version has consequently taken a somewhat idealized, pre–Raphaelite approach to the medieval period in which humans are ultimately good and the unjust are punished, and where simple values prevail. As David Williams puts it, in the world of *Ivanhoe*, "battles are vigorously fought, people are wounded and die, but they shed little visible blood; the sun shines as on a May morning, and the colourful costumes seem to be of a stuff that repels dirt."[22]

On the other side of the coin, we have Bergman creating his medieval world using the same material signs, and roughly during the same period (only five years separate the two films), but viewed from the opposite perspective. In this case, the filmmaker finds parallels between the apocalyptic millennialism of the Cold War in Europe and the threat of the Black Death in the mid–fourteenth century. He was also highly influenced by his upbringing as the son of a preacher, who was continually exposed to religious artworks, and consequently his vision of the medieval period is also drawn from the logic of medieval religion, from wall paintings and "the strangest vegetation of medieval paintings and carved figures on ceiling and walls," most prominent among which is the Totentanz — Dance of Death — a visual topos which he obviously imports directly into his work — and which served to color his view of the period as a dark scourge of religious mania.[23]

Criticism of these two films is thus often directed not at the material details, but to the ways in which the pasts have been imagined — through their forum. When we are rejecting a medieval film on the basis of its "feel," then, we must recognize that it is to this latter world — the forum — that we are often objecting most vehemently, and to which more serious objections can be made. Where entire websites can be created to outline "goofs," anachronisms, and historical inaccuracies on the level of the details and objects, when we come to examining the forum — the framework into which we are placing our medieval films — it is here that we are in more difficult territory. How, for example, do we prove that Gil Junger's *Black Knight* of 2002 is a "bad medieval film"? Is it perhaps just a bad film which happens to be set in the Middle Ages (which, I would argue, on one level it is), or is it that it somehow betrays the Middle Ages (which it may also be doing, but this is much more difficult to prove)? Thus it is most often when the forum of the medieval world does not align with our own image of the period that we are most likely to take exception, not to its *accuracy* per se, but its *authenticity*. It is at the level of ideology and authenticity that we are prone to dismiss a film with the claim that it just doesn't "feel" right.

Accuracy vs. Authenticity

It is also on this level, the creation of a medieval world, at which we find the most difficult arguments about accuracy and inaccuracy. In fact, such is the disproportionate emphasis which critics often place on these terms that it seems likely that we are looking in the wrong places. Perhaps, instead of a dialectic between accuracy and inaccuracy, for example, there might exist *degrees* of inaccuracy? Acceptable inaccuracy, for instance, might occur when a tournament setup from the fourteenth century replaces the appropriate twelfth-century version as in *Ivanhoe*, since this can be explained as a purely cinematographic "necessary invention or anachronism." Unacceptable inaccuracy, on the other hand, might be when the knights are equipped with the kind of hand-held crossbow seen in *First Knight*, since we are dealing here not with an historical misplacement or oversight, but wanton (and perhaps irresponsible) invention which seeks to reinvent Camelot as a Western-inspired space opera more akin to *Star Trek* than to the legend of King Arthur. These issues are coupled with a more complicated one of authenticity, since the example given above of the wrong kind of tournament comes from *Ivanhoe*, a film which the noted medievalist Michel Pastoureau, for one, considers to be "one of the best films ever made about the medieval period.... By its very fidelity, it plunges the spectator into a universe at one familiar and fabulous."[24] If such a film receives the stamp of approval by such respected medievalists as Le Goff, Pastoureau and Cantor, then it seems churlish and unnecessarily pedantic for others to hold the film to account for minor misdemeanors.

One way through such a potential labyrinth of authenticity can be provided by the field of Reception Theory. The basic tenets of this theory argue that any notion of authenticity within a given form of representation (novel, film, TV series) is created in part by the audience's horizon of expectations, which govern and define the expected form of the narrative.[25] As a consequence, these are not necessarily historically inclined, but linked to genre and are, put simply, "what the members of the audience are used to," meaning that to be considered authentic, the representation needs only to conform to those expectations. This does not, of course, preclude inaccuracies, but explains them as elements which are alien to audiences' expectations of the period — which is a very different thing altogether. In short, to be authentic a film need not conform to the historical reality (whatever this might have been), but only to what audiences *think* the period looked like. As we mentioned above, medieval dentistry may well have been more advanced than we once thought, making depictions such as *Les Visiteurs* somewhat inaccurate. Nevertheless, we are so conditioned to bad teeth in medieval films that a hero with perfect, pearly-white teeth (such as Miles O'Keeffe in *Sword of the Valiant*) would seem inaccurate — and so the bad teeth remain. Thus, it seems a logical corollary that audiences and filmmakers both come to play a role in the construction of the authentic medieval past — perhaps far more than historians and medievalists ever can.

The same can also be said for the details, too. If audiences reject films like *Robin Hood: Prince of Thieves* or *First Knight*, we can see that it is not because they are historically inaccurate (since few audience members would be qualified to make such choices), but because it *seems* to be so. We thereby recognize that antipathy towards *First Knight* is not because of its inaccuracy in the details, but its forum or ideology is so inaccurate and unusual that it breaks the suspension of disbelief, and consequently ruptures our belief in its authenticity. Such a proposition finds a great deal of support in the general reception of a film like *Kingdom of Heaven* or *A Knight's Tale*, both big-budget films with sizeable box-office returns, but neither of which could genuinely be held up as a shining example of accuracy.

Ivanhoe, on the other hand, clearly falls into a different category. Given the "stamp of approval" often afforded to it, perhaps we can argue that it fits into a degree of inaccuracy which ranks within authenticity, the sort of error which is used to preserve our belief in its authenticity, like those inaccuracies in the historical novel which Georg Lukács terms "necessary anachronism" and which Rosenstone calls "necessary invention."[26] These are deviations from the historical record wherever there is either a narrative necessity to do so (for Ivanhoe, he must fight five opponents in a masked tournament, and we must never lose our ability to recognize which knight is our hero), or in those more frequent occasions in which there simply is no historical record (we simply do not know how some characters might have spoken, for example). In any modern evocation of the period,

> There are notably many gaping holes in the evidence but also, and more insidiously, half-gaps which create as many problems of interpretation as they appear to resolve. In these circumstances, we are regularly required to draw on our imaginative resources — which is not, it must be stressed, the same as "making things up" — in order to compensate for the grey areas in our understanding.[27]

The authentic in such instances is consequently a creation, a necessary invention, which must only conform to custom and audience expectations (though informed by accuracy, it is not necessarily required to respect it), which explains many of the semiotic paradoxes encountered above. In fact, many of those paradoxes are predicated precisely on the eschewal of accuracy in order to be authentic; we now *expect* Robin Hood to meet King Richard, since the reiteration and repetition of this form of the legend has led the myth away from its literary origins. Such a proposition also goes some way to explaining why initial misunderstandings (such as the *ius primae noctis*) are frequently perpetuated throughout other films so often that they have begun to pass unchallenged, accepted by the cinema as a genuine phenomenon of the period. By repetition, the audience comes to expect it; through a process of accretion, ironically *the inaccurate thus becomes authentic*.

A similar case occurs — though this time in the classical world — in *The Epic That Never Was*, telling of the aborted filming of *I, Claudius*, in which the authentically costumed six Vestal Virgins are rejected by the director, von Sternberg, on the grounds that this accurate reality is not sufficiently spectacular for the screen. "I want sixty," he is alleged to have said, "and I want them naked."[28] The accuracy was replaced by inaccuracy, the filming continued and the end result looked sumptuous, since the excess was precisely the sort of "feel" which we associate with Rome, even if, as Fraser concedes, "it had nothing to do with Roman religion." Thus, we can see here a curious case in which accuracy (the cold, unforgiving bedfellow of the academic historian) is sacrificed in order to retain authenticity (a slippery and ultimately subjective notion, and therefore one which is ideally suited to an art form like the cinema). The decisions taken here, I am arguing, are questions which directly affect the creation of the world, rather than those errors of ambientalism, which are simply setting the scene.

The introduction of reception theory thus serves to reiterate many of the claims made above in Part I, that we are working in the first place from an imaginary Middle Ages, which means that filmmakers are often trying to recreate the "feel" of the period, rather than the facts. The decisions taken about what kind of medieval world to evoke are therefore subject to a very personal view of the Middle Ages. Just as the medieval world on screen is evoked from an "accumulation of the objects and signs," so too is the image of the medieval world evoked from the facts available to the filmmaker (who is not, we must remember, working within an academic milieu). In this way, we might argue that these thought worlds are created from popular ideas about the Middle Ages, and not a willful misrepresentation of the period, because the popular cinema is frequently working on a general consensus about the Middle Ages which has filtered down from the academics.

This is, in part, the reason for which I feel we need a theory of separate worlds when analyzing these films, because it is the only way that we can objectively begin to go about deconstructing what is wrong or right with a given medieval-themed film. Such notions also go some way to answering why we find it hard to establish a standard form of criticism with regards to historical films. But all of this means that instead of one level of accuracy, that of the material props, locations, characters and even events, we have these several degrees of accuracy within the inception of the "forum." The degree to which a film adheres to a faithful depiction of the medieval period is thus dictated by the way in which we imagine it as much as, if not far more than, the demands of historical accuracy. The medieval world, therefore, comes to have been evoked not in an attempt to faithfully recreate the period in the same way as the historian or literary critic would try to achieve, but instead they are seen through an ideological prism in order to serve a pretext. This pretext is the way in which the medieval world is used; it is simply *what the filmmaker wants the Middle Ages to be* for the purposes of his or her story.

Pretextual Medieval Worlds

In this last section, then, I want to examine the use, and frequently the abuse, of the Middle Ages as a pretext. This represents a third level of interpretation through which medieval films must be filtered, since not only must careful attention be paid to the level of the objects (the historicon) and the world constructed from them (the forum), but we must also recognize that these worlds are being viewed through the eyes of the present and not the past.

To return to our example of *The Seventh Seal*, using the theory of levels we can see that the objects represent this first level, in that they are being used as appropriate images drawn from the Middle Ages in order to satisfy the accuracy of the material world. The second level is thus the creation of the world, which is arguably what Eco calls the "barbaric, harsh medieval period" in which life was, to use Hobbes' famous dictum, "brutal, nasty and short."

This is the brutal but beautiful image of the medieval world which Bergman has deduced from the paintings and mystery plays to which he was exposed at an early age, as well as the religious zeal which he associated with the era (as seen in the witch-burning scene). Consequently, his film views the plague as a scourge of God, which in turn created a belief in the imminent demise of the world. Yet the third level, the pretext or use of the Middle Ages, is constructed by his understanding of the medieval world within his own context. When he sees the world living in the knowledge that a deadly force is everywhere, threatening entire communities with frightening randomness, a deadliness which makes no distinction between social class, which has no pity, an indiscriminate and wholly real threat of death, he understandably makes links between this feeling of helplessness and anxiety and his own fears in the late 1950s. The nuclear threat and the shadow of the three-minute warning thus underpin and overshadow his very conception of the medieval period, and infuses his work with a sense of very real concern for the apocalyptic millenarianism of his own era. In this way (as we saw in chapter 1) the present is fused with the past so that while the film is unquestionably about the Middle Ages, it is also and at the same time about the 1950s. The conflation of temporary planes means that the film time is in fact neither past nor present, but instead the "Nevernever-but-always-land of twentieth-century European high modernism. If we are in any historical period, it is less the 1340s of the plot premise than the sub-atomic early 1950s, with universal death looming out of the northern sky."[29]

A more disturbing turn of events can be seen in other films from the same period, such as *Ivanhoe*, *Knights of the Round Table* or *The Black Knight*. While retaining events from Scott's original novel, the filming of *Ivanhoe* in 1952 reveals some of the same formal elements as other epics from the MGM stable, such as *Knights of the Round Table*, which reads retrospectively as a product of the nascent Red Scare operating in the background of the public consciousness during the era.[30] Thus in the same way as *The Seventh Seal* later reflected the paranoia of nuclear crises, making a medieval film in the context of Hollywood in the 1950s when Cold War propaganda was nearing its height can lead to honest, patriotic, Christian knights fighting for freedom against the dark forces of pagan spies infiltrating and challenging their way of life. Thus in *Knights of the Round Table*, *The Black Shield of Falworth*, *The Vikings* and most notably in *The Black Knight*, the material world is completely ignored, and the American accents — elsewhere conceived as an inaccuracy — are in fact heightened to emphasize its patriotic American values. We come face to face with the courts of kings which are all representative institutions of distinctly American dreams — and by extension they are fighting against "un–American activities."[31]

Lest we become too enthusiastic about condemning the past for its inability to separate history from the present, and that we would no longer dream of such brazen propaganda, we must remember that a similar process is happening today, too, the only difference being that perhaps it is too early to see it. We can already see hints of this manipulation of the past when we examine Ridley Scott's 2005 *Kingdom of Heaven*, in which cultural attitudes to the ongoing Middle Eastern crisis, not to mention the influence of post-colonial theories on representations of the Crusades, cause the film to take a distinctly, and noticeably, modern take on the attack on Jerusalem. The attribution of blame to a few determined men acts in some sense as an expiation of contemporary cultural guilt and causes the film to attack on two levels simultaneously, relating as much to the past as it does to the present.[32]

Once again, and still more recently, this "pretextual" third level is revealed in the current BBC series of *Robin Hood* (beginning 2005), where we find a consciously updated Robin legend in the throes of dealing both with his mythical past (and hence the liberties taken with the "source material") and with contemporary concerns. This finds its manifestation again in a general disapproval of war in the Middle East, together with a multicultural grouping which champions the oppressed underdog with diplomatic aplomb. To remove any doubt on the ideology through which this troubling period of our medieval past is being re-addressed, when Keith Allen's Sheriff of Nottingham introduces stricter security measures in Nottingham, they are justified by the rationale that the Crusades are, and I quote, "a War on Terror."[33]

Thus this third level, the use and pretext of a medieval world, works on the persistent link seen above between the present and the past, and indeed the conflation of the temporal planes which is ineluctable when talking about our past, a conflation which Vivian Sobchack attributes to the "Persistence of History."[34] This is not, however, necessarily a criticism of the process, but is in some ways unintentional — and perhaps even inevitable. For a film like *Ivanhoe* especially, the epic film is not intended to appeal to a medieval specialist, but to popular audiences, who are looking for very different things from a film. These audiences, while shrewd and for these reasons not to be patronized, are in the main willing to accept both the material world and the general inception of the medieval world on the condition that the diegesis is not shattered by an unbelievable event. "Despite their mythic overtones and romance coloring, films with medieval themes, like medieval histories, are required by their audiences to deliver a convincing picture of life."[35] To make this world a convincing picture, then, it must be continuously authentic, and to be authentic it is less important that it adheres to the material objects at the level of the historicon, but demands rather that people behave in a logical way. What is more, we must remember that this logic is the logic of the present time and not of the past, which does seem to suggest that, technically speaking, "by definition the entire film is an anachronism."[36]

Conclusions

And so we return to the point raised above, about degrees of accuracy, and authenticity. If we accept the propositions I have put forward, then we are able to tentatively propose a way of accessing medieval films — or, more importantly, a means to go about evaluating them — by first double-checking that we are sure about exactly what we are criticizing. In this way, we can take a film like *Kingdom of Heaven*, and rather than dismiss it as a "bad" or "good" medieval film, we are able to first ask whether there are any inaccuracies on the first level, in the material world, before accepting or rejecting the medieval forum proposed to us by Ridley Scott. Our concern, we may discover, might be simply that they are misusing the medieval world of the Crusades to make a point about the present-day invasion of Iraq, in which case we realise that we are not, in fact, criticizing the historical impulse (to use Marc Ferro's terminology), but rather the use made of the historical details.[37] This is very different: *it is not inaccurate, but inauthentic*.

Similarly, when we see two different historical worlds existing alongside one another — as we did with *Ivanhoe* and *The Seventh Seal*— we can therefore avoiding asking the impossible question of which interpretation is correct, or accurate, or authentic, but rather begin to question why the filmmaker has imagined their world *in this way* rather than according to an alternative interpretation. Given that both forum and pretext are, in the last analysis, imaginary, perhaps we as critics should be a little less hasty to condemn the inaccuracies as the work of an amateur historian, and instead begin to ask *why* they have been changed. Just as a historian is an expert in interpretations, we must bear in mind that a filmmaker is an expert in stories, too, and is a great deal more sensitive to the nuance of a visual sign. We might also, perhaps, begin to ask whether such betrayals in the name of authenticity, or semiotic paradoxes, might actually help to understand the medieval period for those who would not necessarily be likely to conduct any academic research on it. It seems to me to be broadly comparable to the use of metaphor when explaining difficult concepts to students, in which the assimilation of a heterogeneous modern paradigm is sometimes necessary in order to explain the realities of medieval life as we understand them. It would be a very strict historian indeed who would object to the inaccuracies of the metaphor as a means to understand the period.

In this respect, we might profitably turn to the assertion by David

Williams that, in examining a representation of the medieval period, "it is less a question of asking 'is it authentic?' than 'what does my Middle Ages look like?'"[38] There are, we saw, a variety of factors which risked producing a dissatisfactory Middle Ages, beginning with the sheer volume of details which need to be accurately represented and ranging to its polar opposite, in those areas which must be "filled in" by the imagination of the filmmakers. The enormity of information carried by a historical film set — from the minutiae of dress, furniture, tools, objects, hairstyles and even posture, all the way through to the landscapes and the film space itself— itself constitutes a momentous possibility for factual error, not to mention that even if a film *did* "get the details right," it would still risk being derailed by an inauthentic plot. Furthermore, in the unlikely event that there were no historical inaccuracies, the filmmaker *still* cannot win, since too strong a focus on the minutiae symptomatic of "ambentialism" can actually have the opposite effect from its intention, serving to undermine accuracy. One archetypal flogged horse in this respect is the tent of Marcus Aurelius in Ridley Scott's *Gladiator*, which is often argued to be *too* full of objects to be a faithful representation of the era, whose artifacts would be unlikely to be coeval. A person, even one of History's "Great Men," is likely to fill a room with objects which are imbued with meaning and drawn from a range of past periods.[39] As Rosen puts it, "temporal hybridity [...] underlies modern historicity and must therefore be a component of any historicization."[40] Small wonder, then, that even the most imaginative scholars working on historical films have rarely dared to go further than Ferro in wondering aloud whether film could *ever* "do history"?

The inquiry into, and interpretation of, medieval literature and history yields such highly contradictory, intriguing and mysterious results that even amongst academics, there is wide scope for scholarly debate. As I have consistently suggested throughout this study, I genuinely believe that it is a debate to which the cinematic incarnations of the Middle Ages have much to contribute, but we must be clear about what exactly those contributions are to be. In order to avoid lapsing in the sort of circular criticism which I identified in chapter 1, it is essential that this debate must not be allowed to descend to a squabble over the inaccuracies on the level of the material world. Although I am by no means denying that this degree of accuracy is important, what is more useful is to separate out the details of the world which surrounds the medieval film, and to criticize this forum in which the filmmaker has situated a hypothetical Middle Ages. We must also recognize the link between the histories being retold and the climate of its retelling, for the use of a medieval world has potentially much to reveal about the status of neo-medievalism in the modern world. When, for instance, *The Advocate* opens with the claim that the medieval world was mired in "ignorance and superstition," we are able to recognize that the power of this statement comes not from an denigration of the Middle Ages themselves, but an attempt to recognize that we ourselves are mired in our own postmodern confusion about what the medieval world really was.

Whatever the case, looking at the reasons behind narrative decisions, rather than enumerating accuracies, has at least revealed one certainty; that critiques of films on the basis of accuracy, authenticity, fidelity or credibility are no longer the same thing. More crucially, nor are they any longer a useful standard, since I have shown that any such criticisms must first be anchored within a degree of factual certainty, a certainty which is no longer available to History in the same way as it might once have been. I began, before embarking on this study, by taking up a challenge laid down by Rosenstone, to

> apply these [historiographic] sorts of standards to historical film. Rather than focus on how film gets the past wrong (as do many historians), or theorize about what film should do to or for the past (which is the burden of many ideological critiques), or how it *should* construct history, we had better first study the way in which historical filmmakers have actually been working for the last century.... Studying the work of filmmakers over time can suggest just what are the rules of engagement with the past for history rendered on the screen.[41]

What I hope to have offered over the course of this book is a set of theoretical means which might allow us to do so, to separate out the various processes of signification and to get some ideas about where films might be drawing their ideas from, what problems they might encounter, and how they have gone about resolving them. What is needed in the future, therefore, is a means by which we can analyze not only *when and where* these films deviate from the accepted version (versions?) of the Middle Ages (though not necessarily the "True" version), but *whether* they have deviated from them, and *why*. Perhaps such insight might only be obtained by a greater dialogue with filmmakers themselves, in an attempt to move beyond the typically dichotomous expert/creative relationships seen until now (though, I confess, I do share Rosenstone's view that "adding historians to production teams or turning them into directors will certainly not [...] remove the problematics from the dramatic historical film").[42]

Maybe such a partnership might finally give us some answers about which "facts" (if any) are seen to be the most important in a filmic depiction of the medieval period, for it is only after we have established whether they were even trying to "stick to the facts" or, as Rosenstone would say, "get the details right"),[43] that we might we stand a chance of evaluating whether film can ever really "do history." And, in my view, it is only *then* that we might begin to find out exactly what kind of history that might prove to be.

Glossary

Authenticity and Accuracy: Rather than adhere to a traditional elision of these two terms, one of the main outcomes of my study here has been to identify a semiotic paradox, which occurs when accuracy is lost for the sake of authenticity. Most forcefully outlined in chapter 4, I have shown how, for example, in order to successfully convey the concept of a wise king, filmmakers have betrayed the historical record by making their kings older than they are known to have been. It might also, however, be argued that the paradigmatic approach is, by definition, reliant on such a paradox, since the medieval referent is assimilated within an "inaccurate" signified, purely to retain authenticity within the film's diegesis. See also my forthcoming "Historical Spaces, *Gladiator* and Marcus Aurelius' Tent," in which I elaborate this paradox in more detail.

Concept/Signified: In many respects this is the other side of the coin to the object. Here, the concept (kingship) is used to summon up the object (a king) in the viewer's mind, which in turn will produce a sign (medieval kingship). Throughout this book I have argued that it is on the basis of these concepts that filmmakers often recreate the social relationships to form a paradigm (see "Object/Signified").

Empty Signifiers: Originally found in Barthes, to mean a signifier with no signified, that is, a (predominantly) visual essence which has either a floating, highly vague, or else non-existent "meaning."[1] In practical use, this becomes a sign that only means that it means, like the inclusion of a particular historical artifact in a medieval film, which has no purpose other than to represent the sort of thing that they might have had in the period being represented. A proliferation of these empty signifiers, I have argued, therefore risks eliding into ambientalism, a term coined by Zemon Davis, given that they serve no signifying function other than to play a part in the ambiental "sign" of the past.[2]

***Figure obligée*:** Where the *passage obligé* is essentially an element of the narrative which serves to establish the genre of the film, I have used Amy de la Bretèque's term, the *figure obligée*, to refer to an entirely visual sequence such as the tournament, whose external signs are recognizable. In this sense, they are made up of "image-motifs," which are, as far as I understand, individual signifiers which have a particularly recognizable meaning.

Griot: The griot is a West African poet/bard, who represents a source of history transmitted through oral tradition, and this can be seen as a contemporary source of mythopoeic and/or historical (decidedly with a lowercase "h") narration. The first reference in which I have encountered its connection with the historical filmmaker comes in Robert Rosenstone, "Oliver Stone as Historian," in Robert Brent Toplin (ed.), *Oliver Stone's USA* (Lawrence: University Press of Kansas, 2000), 26–39, in which Rosenstone suggests "perhaps Oliver Stone is a kind of griot for a new visual age" (38–9).

Guided Image *see* **historicon**

Historical film: In the 1920s, when the possibilities of film were only just beginning to emerge, the International Iconographical Commission restricted the term "historical film" to include only "those films which record a period or a person from a time after the invention of cinematography and without dramaturgical or 'artistic' purposes," and "expressed its strong disapproval of all attempts to include the so-called historical film [...] in this context."[3] Such narrow confines would thus rule out all of the films studied herein, and restrict the historical film to a very constricted corpus of documents.

This, however, is to fall foul of a naïve belief in the objectivity of photographic documents, and one which I have demonstrated in chapter two to be untenable and ultimately fallacious. A better definition, in my view, is offered by Schultz, who argues,

> "Historical films" — sometimes called historical dramas, historical fiction films, period films, or costume dramas — might simply be described as those feature films that depict events, people, and societies of the past.... Such films enjoy the freedom to employ a mix of fact and fiction in their desire to reconstruct the past and tell a good story.[4]

A similar definition is offered by Leger Grindon (and quoted in turn by Schultz), which classifies them as "fiction films that have a meaningful relationship to historical events,"[5] which is supported by Sorlin's view that it offers "a reconstruction of the social relationship which, using the pretext of the past, reorganizes the present."[6] An amalgamation of these, then, gives us my definition that a historical film is any feature film which sets its action in the past, and seeks to recreate historical events and reconstruct social relationships, basing their past worlds on models offered to us by present Historical and popular re-conceptualizations of them.

Historicon: This is a term which I have coined in order to convey a signifying aspect which is iconically linked to a historical period, person or event. In this respect, they are the reverse of the empty signifier, in that their iconic, direct correlation with the historical signified means that they are imbued with historical meaning (and indeed, the diegesis might even depend on this iconic relation in order to function). Pared down to their most basic element, these can be seen as props, say, in a theatrical evocation of the past, in which a musket might suffice to conjure up for an audience the whole Napoleonic era. A cinematic example comes from Stephen Weeks' *Sword of the Valiant*, in which O'Keeffe's Gawain is dressed in such an incongruous mixture of period clothing (a musketeer's billowing shirt, modern jodhpurs and nineteenth-century boots), that we are reliant on the iconic association of the sword and armor with the medieval period to be sure that the film is intended to be set in the Middle Ages at all. As Amy de la Bretèque terms it, "what permits us to situate the action in the Middle Ages are the decorative forms."[7]

Historiophoty (chapter 1): Historiophoty is a term which was coined by Hayden White in his study "Historiography and Historiophoty," in which he describes it as "the representation of history and our thought about it in visual images and filmic discourse."[8] The notion was subsequently taken up and discussed by Rosenstone (in *History on Film/Film on History*), but for me the best definition remains that of Satish Bajaj, which compares it directly to historiography; "History ... has begun to be represented and thought about in visual images and filmic discourse. As distinguished from historiography which is a representation of the past in verbal and written discourse, the former is described as historiophoty."[9] The term "historiophoty" thus comes to represent the possibility of "telling about the past in a meaningful and accurate way,"[10] by placing it in alignment not with History, but with historiography, making of it a representation of our thoughts and ideas about history as well as an attempt to directly recount them.

History/history: The separation of History and history, elaborated in chapter one, section one: "History on Film" and in Rosenstone's *Visions of the Past*, has been used to distinguish between the academic construction and the existence of "things past." Amy de la Bretèque, in fact, goes one step further, offering us useful distinctions between "l'histoire" (fiction), "l'Histoire" (historiographical discourse) and "l'HISTOIRE" (the totality of past events as they have been 'objectively' collated).[11] For the sake of clarity of expression, I will be following Rosenstone in using the word "History" in the sense of the written, scholarly variety of historical enquiry; in those instances where I mean history as an abstract consciousness of things past, or one which is disputed by two or more extant sources, I will use the lower case "history" (see particularly Paul Veyne, *Comment on écrit l'histoire*). In those instances where both meanings could be inferred — i.e., a given notion is both constructed/agreed on by historians *and* belongs to an abstract consciousness of past events — I have used the more inclusive, non-capitalized, term "history" and its derivatives.

Icon/Paradigm: See chapter 1 and chapter 2. The principal definitions which I offer for the purposes of the films studied here are that they are two ways of trying to communicate the medieval referent.

The first, **the icon**, is based on an emphasis on the visual network of meanings (iconography) which are elements of the Middle Ages familiar to modern viewers (which includes, somewhat circuitously, films themselves: see Chapter 9). My ideas about such an iconography are drawn from a fusion of Panofsky's masterful work on the subject and Eco's complex but definitive study of the sign.[12]

The **paradigm**, on the other hand, seeks to recreate modern relationships and transfer them to the Middle Ages posited in the film. To this end, what they are doing is using modern concepts (social structures) and applying them to the various guides outlined in chapter two, section three. My understanding of the "paradigm" in the first place has been drawn from the hard sciences, most notably in Kuhn's *The Structure of Scientific Revolutions*, in which he proposes that "in [its] standard application, the paradigm functions by permitting the replication of examples, any one of which could in principle serve to replace it."[13]

Ideogram: Drawn originally from Eisenstein, in which he defines it as the combination (for him: montage) of two objects corresponding to a concept (based on his arguments about hieroglyphs).[14] Amy de la Bretèque reprises and re-uses the notion of an "idéogram," placing it within a motif/theme schema in which each "unité" relates to a specific "size" of the film's signification, as follows:

1. the "**récit-cadre**," which corresponds to the narration (le scénario);
2. the "**passage obligé**" or topos (a siege, a battle, etc.), a passage which establishes the genre. For a list of these, see *L'Imaginaire medieval*, 1053–69;
3. the "**idéologème**," which is the totality of the visual signs which refer back to a historical reality (Crusades, knights, etc.);
4. finally, the "**iconogramme**," which is made up of "pure" icons (in the Peircean sense) and ideograms (in the Eisensteinian sense), which each correspond to a modern notion about the Middle Ages (even if such a notion may not have existed in reality).[15] Amy de la Bretèque defines them as "those iconic elements which are enough to signify the Middle Ages."[16]

Ideology / Mode of Approach (chapter 1): As stated in my comments no other sense of ideology is intended other than the way in which filmmakers approach past events — or the prism through which they view it. The use of the term "ideology" in this way comes from Ferro, in *Cinema et histoire*, in which he gives the example of Eisenstein and Tarkovskii's visions of medieval Russia, "two films with opposite meanings." "In each case, and without having to justify or legitimise his choice, the filmmaker chooses those historical facts and elements that provide fodder for his demonstration, leaving out the others. This makes him happy, as well as those who share his faith and constitute 'his public.'"[17] This is elaborated by his theory of the "modes of approach" as explained in chapter 1, and in Ferro, p. 163.

Image-motif: literally, "image repeated as a motif," by which I mean certain key, identifiable "scenes" from the Middle Ages. Though, at base, it functions in more or less the same way as the historicon, I have retained its use here to talk of entire scenes, at the level of the cinematography, instead of the props and artifacts within the film.

Medieval Film: A temptingly simple definition comes from David Williams, who begins by specifying "not films from the Middle Ages, of course," but rather seeks to examine those which "have contributed to, and continue to reflect, widespread ideas and feelings about the Middle Ages in our time."[18] Throughout my study, I have classified as "medieval films" all those narrative, fictional films who place their diegesis within a medieval setting, broadly understood. These include films which are based on factual events or characters within the period (such as *Becket*), or on those films which make use of a prologue including a date within those generally believed to be medieval (that is, between the end of the classical and the beginning of the Renaissance periods), or those films based on texts which were themselves written in the period and which seek to depict their contemporary worlds (so including *Perceval le Gallois*, say, but not *Tristana* or *La Femme d'à côté*, which have been argued to update the Tristan theme to the modern day). However, I have in general tried to avoid working with any films belonging to the "sword and sorcery" genre, since those tend, in the main, to take place in rather loosely defined, putatively medieval periods, and have a general tendency to draw on mythical archetypes, eliding their world into the Fantastic (*Dragonslayer*), prehistoric Waste Lands (*Conan*) or even futuristic, neo-medieval dystopias (such as, perhaps, *Mad Max*).

Medieval Imaginary: In defining the "medieval imaginary," I willingly align myself with both Haydock and Amy de la Bretèque, whose studies both ably discuss the concept of a "medieval imaginary," a concept which contains something of Sorlin's (by way of Bourdieu) concept of "historical capital."[19] The idea here, which coincides neatly with a semiotic study, is that throughout its imagination, recreation and retransmission, there comes to exist a sort of "repository" in which all of our beliefs, dreams and phobias about the period come to be discarded, and from which modern versions of the Middle Ages often draw freely — and in some cases indiscriminately.

Montage (esp. chapter 1)**:** Interpretations within the field of film studies differ wildly when it comes to defining precisely its effects and purpose, but at its most basic meaning, cinematic montage is the effect which comes as a result of two images being placed next to each other to "create" a narrative meaning. How this is achieved (i.e. whether by contrast, continuation or Hegelian dialectic), however, is something of a hot topic in film theory even today, and one which I have tried, in the main, to avoid.

Narrative (chapter 1)**:** While the everyday meaning of the term "narrative" is obvious, given the current volume of critical material on classical film narrative in cinema and rhetorical modes of discourse elsewhere, it is perhaps worthwhile specifying my understanding of narrative here. Throughout my arguments, I have understood narrative to mean the recounting of a story, with the subtext that there is necessarily a central consciousness which arranges and recounts the story. Such a modernist definition, I concede, does not take into account arguments of theorists of post-modernity who contest the possibility of such a narrative, an omission which I feel is justified when we consider that for most filmmakers and popular audiences alike such issues of representation are rarely a barrier to their viewing.

Object/Signifier: My use of the terms object and signifier (largely interchangeable) has been influenced by Metz and Lotman's work on the semiotics of cinema. Cinematographically speaking, to try to communicate a notion there must be some kind of image placed on the screen (say, a man with a crown), which becomes an object intended to summon up a corresponding concept (kingship) in the viewer's mind. Therefore, I have argued, the object becomes a signifier to connect not to the referent (the complex intricacies of medieval kingship) but to a signified concept (a medieval king). I have argued throughout that these objects are not necessarily medieval, but are simply understood as such (and are consequently icons; see "Referent/Medieval Referent").

Periodization: My use of the term refers to "an act or instance of dividing a subject into historical eras for purposes of analysis and study." The arguments which I raise against it in chapter 1 are that it presupposes — or else forces — a homogeneity on the past, ignoring vital difference in order to maintain neat classifications.

Récit: I have taken my understanding of "récit" originally from Ricoeur's work on the subject, *Temps et récit*, in which the meaning goes beyond its traditional definition of "narrative" (and which is why I have left the term in the original French). My use of the term here is something like the act of speaking or retelling a narrative event — the whole process of retelling a narrative, in a way. The reason for such specific distinction is that historiographic criticism of the term "narrative" has undermined its credibility and efficiency, leaving a need to describe the film's "récit" as a way of retelling the past as a whole, and not an individual contribution to (and understanding of) historical events.

Referent/Medieval Referent: Once again, I have freely adapted Peirce's schema to suit my present needs. My use of the term "referent" has been to refer to the medieval meaning (or imagined meaning) of the given sign. In this, my arguments about historiography notwithstanding, I have simply tried to understand what such-and-such a notion might have meant to a medieval audience, and what it is that filmmakers are trying to incorporate into their corresponding signs.

Sign: The sign is simply the combination of all three elements: signifier, signified and referent. It can be said to have functioned when the filmmaker successfully conveys the idea of the medieval king (for example) to the audience via the cinematography.

Triadic Unity: Given that C.S. Peirce's semiotic units are renowned for their complexity, I have here reduced them to three principle constituent parts, each of which make up a sign: Referent, Object/Signifier, and Concept/Signified. Clearly much could be made of the chain of signification (Firstness, Secondness, Thirdness, etc.) in this area, since I have argued that the medieval referent was itself a construct, and so we are faced with a chain of meaning which is continually constructed and reformulated by subsequent generations. Nevertheless, such a study would take me away from the focus here on the recreation of the Middle Ages on film — which is why I have filtered down the semiotic units to these three.

Notes

Preface

1. Stuart Airlie, "Strange Eventful Histories: The Middle Ages in Cinema," in *The Medieval World*, edited by Peter Linehan (London: Routledge, 2001), 165.

2. Nickolas Haydock, *Movie Medievalism: The Imaginary Middle Ages* (Jefferson, NC: McFarland, 2008).

3. François Amy de la Bretèque, *L'Imaginaire médiéval dans le cinéma occidental* (Paris: Champion, 2004).

4. William D. Paden, "I Learned It at the Movies: Teaching Medieval Film," in *Studies in Medievalism XIII: Postmodern Medievalisms*, edited by Richard Utz and Jesse G. Swan (Cambridge: D. S. Brewer, 2004): 79–98; David Williams, "Medieval Movies," *The Yearbook of English Studies* 20 (1990): 1–32; Airlie, "Strange Eventful Histories," 163–183; Umberto Eco, *Travels in Hyperreality: Essays*, translated by William Weaver (London: Picador, 1987).

Chapter 1

1. W. G. Sebald, *Young Austerlitz* (Harmondsworth: Penguin, 2005), 31 (emphasis added).

2. Umberto Eco, *Travels in Hyperreality: Essays*, translated by William Weaver (London: Picador, 1987), 61.

3. David Williams, "Medieval Movies," *The Yearbook of English Studies* 20 (1990): 2.

4. Stuart Airlie, "Strange Eventful Histories: The Middle Ages in Cinema," in *The Medieval World*, edited by Peter Linehan (London: Routledge, 2001), 163.

5. Mark C. Carnes, Ted Mico, David Rubel, and John Miller-Monzon, *Past Imperfect: History According to the Movies* (London: Cassell, 1996), 9.

6. Pierre Sorlin, *The Film in History: Restaging the Past* (Oxford: Blackwell, 1980), 20.

7. Paul Smith (ed.), *The Historian and Film* (Cambridge: Cambridge University Press, 1976), 4.

8. Robert A. Rosenstone, *History on Film/Film on History* (Harlow: Longman/Pearson, 2006), 2.

9. George MacDonald Fraser, *The Hollywood History of the World: From One Million Years B.C. to Apocalypse Now* (Columbine: Columbine Trade, 1989), 10 (emphasis added).

10. John Aberth, *A Knight at the Movies: Medieval History on Film* (New York and London: Routledge, 2003), 299.

11. Review of *The Adventures of Robin Hood*, directed by Michael Curtiz (Warner Bros. Pictures, 1938), by the National Board of Review of Motion Pictures. Quoted in *From Quasimodo to Scarlett O'Hara*, edited by Stanley Hochman (New York: Frederick Ungar, 1982), 285.

12. See Michael T. Isenberg, "A Relationship of Constrained Anxiety: Historians and Film," *The History Teacher* 6, no. 4 (Aug 1973): 553–568.

13. William Hughes, "The Evaluation of Film as Evidence," in Smith, *The Historian and Film*, 54.

14. Peter C. Rollins, *Hollywood as Historian: American Film in a Cultural Context* (Lexington, KY: University Press of Kentucky, 1983), xi.

15. Marc Ferro, *Cinéma Et Histoire* (Paris: Denoël, 1977), 163. For quotations in English I have used Naomi Greene's translation *Cinema and History* (Detroit: Wayne State University Press, 1988).

16. See Glossary: History/history.

17. Nickolas Haydock, "Arthurian Melodrama, Chaucerian Spectacle, and the Waywardness of Cinematic Pastiche in *First Knight* and *A Knight's Tale*," in *Studies in Medievalism XII: Film and Fiction: Reviewing the Middle Ages*, ed-

ited by Tom Shippey and Martin Arnold (Cambridge: D. S. Brewer, 2003), 7.

18. Robert A. Rosenstone, "The Reel Joan of Arc: Reflections on the Theory and Practice of the Historical Film," *The Public Historian* 25, no. 3 (Summer 2003), 63.

19. Rebecca A. Umland and Samuel J. Umland, *The Use of Arthurian Legend in Hollywood Film: From Connecticut Yankees to Fisher Kings* (Westport, CT: Greenwood Press, 1996), xii.

20. Rosenstone, *History on Film/Film on History*, 35.

21. "Una lettura del film rivolta solo all'aspetto storico (cioè alle fonti e ai retaggi culturali) o solo all'aspetto cinematografico (tecniche di regia, scenografia, musica, costumi, ecc.) è parziale e quindi incompleta." Antonio Pileggi, *Medioevo e commedia all'italiana: Indagine storico-critico sul film l'Armata Brancaleone* (Cosenza: Le Nuvole, 2001), Premessa, 7 (my translation).

22. Paul Halsall, *Internet Medieval Sourcebook*, June 8, 2002, http://www.fordham.edu/halsall/medfilms.html.

23. Ferro, *Cinema and History*, especially chapter 16.

24. Peter Burkholder, "Popular [Mis]conceptions of Medieval Warfare," *History Compass* 5 (2007): 510.

25. Rosenstone, "The Reel Joan of Arc," 73.

26. Introduction to *American Beauty*, directed by Sam Mendes (DreamWorks SKG, 1999).

27. Hayden V. White, *The Content of the Form: Narrative Discourse and Historical Representation* (Baltimore & London: Johns Hopkins University Press, 1990); Paul Ricoeur, *Temps et récit* (Paris: Seuil, 1991).

28. See Geoffrey Chaucer, "The Franklin's Prologue," *The Canterbury Tales*, lines 1–7.

29. C. S. Lewis, *The Discarded Image: An Introduction to Medieval and Renaissance Literature* (Cambridge: Cambridge University Press, 1964), 179. An interesting — and related — discussion of such attempts to divide "forms" of literature can be found in Terry Eagleton's essay "What Is Literature?" *Literary Theory: An Introduction*, 3rd ed., edited by Terry Eagleton (Minneapolis, University of Minnesota Press, 2008), 1–14.

30. David Herlihy, "Am I a Camera? Other Reflections on Films and History," *The American Historical Review* 93, no. 5 (1988): 1187. There is, however, a possible and valuable argument to be made about whether or not artistic films can be said to have a true ending, or whether there might be a playfulness or open ending which precludes the kind of narrative "rounding off" under discussion here. While certainly such a discussion would be valid and pertinent, the thrust of my argument is that the events must be shaped, and the end of the film — notwithstanding those with an open or playful ending — must signal the closure of the "retelling" of the sjuzhet, even if not the fabula.

31. Rosenstone describes this "just the facts, ma'am" approach as "Dragnet History," which he argues is in fact a fallacy of the historian, rather than a viable methodological approach in itself. For more on this, see Robert A. Rosenstone, *Visions of the Past: The Challenge of Film to Our Idea of History* (Cambridge, Mass: Harvard University Press, 1995), 7, though his thoughts on film history are more profoundly elaborated in his later *History on Film/Film on History*.

32. White, *The Content of the Form*, 2.

33. "La représentation sous son aspect narratif, comme sous d'autres aspects que l'on dira, ne s'ajoute pas du dehors à la phase documentaire et à la phase explicative, mais les accompagne et les porte" (my translation). Paul Ricoeur, *La Mémoire, L'histoire, L'oubli* (Paris: Seuil, 2000), 307.

34. Quoted in White, *The Content of the Form*, 36; cf also "The Discourse of History" in Roland Barthes, *The Rustle of Language* (Berkeley: University of California Press, 1989), 127–140.

35. "Rendering the past usually means telling stories — and the meaning of stories is usually shaped by the medium of the telling." Robert A. Rosenstone, *Revisioning History: Film and the Construction of a New Past*, edited by Robert A. Rosenstone (Princeton: Princeton University Press, 1994), 3–14.

36. Aristotle, *Treatise on Poetry* (London: Cadell & Davies, 1812), partially reprinted as *Poetics* (Mineola, New York: Dover Publications, 1997), 17.

37. There is, however, an argument to be made here about what specifically is meant by "accuracy" and "inaccuracy," since there is a great deal of difference between giving a medieval soldier the wrong kind of helmet and giving him a machine gun. For a clarification of this, see A. Keith Kelly, "Beyond Historical Accuracy: A Postmodern View of Movies and Medievalism," *Perspicuitas* (February 2004), accessible online at http://www.uni-due.de/perspicuitas/articles.shtml, or else my discussion on accuracy and authenticity in chapter 9.

38. Cf Jean Mitry, *Semiotics and the Analysis of Film* (London: Athlone, 2000), especially Chapter XII, "Narrative Structures," pp. 170–184.

39. Quoted in White, *The Content of the Form*, 51.

40. Carnes et al., *Past Imperfect: History According to the Movies*, 9.

41. Rosenstone, *Visions of the Past*, 227.

42. "Making of" feature for *Marie Antoinette*, directed by Sofia Coppola (Columbia Pictures, 2006).

43. In comparing, say, his *Secret Histories* with his *History of Justinian's Wars*.

44. Thucydides, *The Peloponnesian War*, translated by Rex Warner (London: Cassell and Company Ltd., 1962), pp. 24–25.

45. White, *The Content of the Form*, 20.

46. Harper Lee, *To Kill a Mockingbird*, Part 1, Ch. 7.

47. See Thomas Burger, "Droysen's Defense of Historiography: A Note," *History and Theory* 16, no. 2 (May 1977), 168–173.

48. Jean-Paul Sartre, *La Nausée* (Paris: Gallimard, 1962), 56 and 79 (translated by Lloyd Alexander).

49. Jeffrey Kluger, "Michael Moore's New Diagnosis," *Time Magazine*, 2007, http://www.time.com/time/health/article/0,8599,1622178-2,00.html (accessed 13 November 2007).

50. Sartre, *La Nausée*, 56.

51. See also Umberto Eco's description of this event as an example of the historical "ablative absolute" and cosmological linearity, in Umberto Eco, *Interpretation and Overinterpretation* (Cambridge: Cambridge University Press, 1992), 28.

52. The standard translation of Bazin's principle of "montage-roi."

53. See David Bordwell, "The Use of Montage in Soviet Art and Film," *Cinema Journal* 11, no. 2 (Spring 1972): 9–17; or Stephen Prince and Wayne E. Hensley, "The Kuleshov Effect: Recreating the Classic Experiment," *Cinema Journal* 31, no. 2 (Winter 1992): 59–75.

54. Louis D. Giannetti and Scott Eyman, *Flashback: A Brief History of Film* (Englewood Cliffs, N.J.: Prentice Hall, 1986), 90. See also Ernest Lindgren, *The Art of the Film* (London: Allen & Unwin, 1963), esp. chapters 4 and 5.

55. André Bazin, *Qu'est-ce que le cinéma?* (Paris: Du Cerf, 1994). The quotation is from Hugh Gray's translation: André Bazin, *What Is Cinema?* (Berkeley: University of California Press, 1967).

56. Bazin's "myth of a total cinema" (as advanced in his *What Is Cinema?*) is a somewhat contentious element of film theory, in which he advances his belief that montage is unrealistic, on the grounds that it distorts "reality," thereby denying the viewer the "total" image. Here I am not expressing my agreement with Bazin's rejection of montage, but only insofar as this applies to my theory of historical montage outlined above.

57. This anti-Catholic sentiment has been reinforced recently by films such as *The Da Vinci Code*, *The Order* and the sub-genre of question-able "historical" works on Opus Dei, the Templars, and Masonic Orders which conspiracy theorists have spawned.

58. This same suggestion of cruelty and lack of compassion can be seen in the pain juxtaposed with pleasure in Pudovkin's *Mother* (1926); see chapter 4 of Lindgren, *The Art of the Film*, for further discussion.

59. It is also interesting to note that F. Murray Abraham later went on to play Stalin in *Children of the Revolution* (1996).

60. Bazin, *What Is Cinema?*, 35.

61. *The Name of the Rose*, directed by Jean-Jacques Annaud (Neue Constantin Film / ZDF, 1986).

62. For a full analysis of this idea from the point of view of gestalt psychology and the mechanism of perception, see Jacques Aumont, *L'Image* (Paris: Nathan 1990)/*The Image* (London: BFI, 1997), especially chapter 1.

63. Bryan Haworth, "Film in the Classroom," in Smith, *The Historian and Film*, 157.

64. Sorlin, *The Film in History*, 16.

65. *Ibid.*, ix.

66. Norman Cantor, *Inventing the Middle Ages: The Lives, Works, and Ideas of the Great Medievalists of the Twentieth Century* (New York: William Morrow & Company, 1991), 37.

67. Jeffrey Richards, *Swordsmen of the Screen, from Douglas Fairbanks to Michael York* (London: Routledge and Kegan Paul, 1977), 109.

68. Ferro, *Cinéma Et Histoire*, chapter 16.

69. *Ibid.*, 163.

70. Cantor, *Inventing the Middle Ages*, 45.

71. "Puisque tout est historique, l'histoire sera ce que nous choisirons" (my translation). Veyne, *Comment on écrit l'histoire* (Paris: Éditions du Seuil, 1971), 42.

72. Jeremy Black, *Using History* (London: Hodder Arnold, 2005), 9. See also Marcus Bull's *Getting Medieval* to see how the Middle Ages has come to be viewed as "public property." Marcus Bull, *Thinking Medieval: An Introduction to the Study of the Middle Ages* (Basingstoke: Palgrave Macmillan, 2005).

73. Marnie Hughes-Warrington, *History Goes to the Movies: Studying History on Film* (New York & London: Routledge, 2007), 165–186.

74. Frank Sanello, *Reel v. Real: How Hollywood Turns Fact into Fiction* (Lanham, MD: Taylor Trade Publishing, 2003), pp. xi–xii.

75. Exchange between Monk/Historian Brother Gilbert of Glockenspur and Bowen, Knight of the Old Code, in *Dragonheart*, directed by Rob Cohen (Universal Pictures, 1996).

76. Sorlin, *The Film in History*, viii.

77. Dr. Jones, in *Indiana Jones and the Last Crusade*, directed by Steven Spielberg (Lucasfilm/Paramount Pictures, 1989).

78. Ranke's dictum appears in the preface of his *History of the Latin and Teutonic Nations, 1494–1535*. My version quoted here is taken from E. H. Carr, *What Is History?* (Harmondsworth: Penguin, 1964; 1990), 8.

79. Johann Gustav Droysen, *Outline of the Principles of History (Grundriss der Historik)* (New York: H. Fertig, 1967), 219.

80. Black, *Using History*, 179.

81. To see the explanation behind — and defense for — this term, see Georg Lukács, *The Historical Novel* (London: Merlin, 1962), 61. Lukács is in turn drawing on Hegel's concept of a past "distance." Georg Hegel, *Aesthetics: Lectures on Fine Art* (Oxford: Clarendon Press, 1975) 1: 272–277.

82. Marc Bloch, *The Historian's Craft* (Manchester: Manchester University Press, 1954). My summary of this text is paraphrased from that of Cantor, *Inventing the Middle Ages*, 141.

83. Carr, *What Is History?*, 9.

84. See note 70, above.

85. "un livre d'histoire apparaît sous un aspect très different de ce qu'il semble être; il ne traite pas de l'Empire romain, mais de ce que nous pouvons savoir encore de cet Empire" (my translation). Veyne, *Comment on écrit l'histoire*, 22.

86. Carr, *What Is History?*, 16. See also Barraclough: "The history we read, though based on facts, is, strictly speaking, not factual at all, but a series of accepted judgements." Geoffrey Barraclough, *History in a Changing World* (Oxford: Blackwell, 1955), 14.

87. Black, *Using History*, 184.

88. *What Is History?*, 94. See also chapter 4, "Causation in History," 87–108.

89. "Décrire … et à ne rien présupposer d'autre; à ne pas présupposer qu'il existe une cible, un objet, une cause matérielle…" (my translation). Veyne, *Comment on écrit l'histoire*, 211.

90. *Gawain and the Green Knight*, directed by Stephen Weeks (Sancrest, 1973), later remade as *Sword of the Valiant*, directed by Stephen Weeks (Golan-Globus Productions, 1983).

91. Martha W. Driver and Sid Ray (eds.), *The Medieval Hero on Screen: From Beowulf to Buffy* (Jefferson, NC: McFarland, 2004), 5–6.

92. Such as, Cawley suggests, the Duke of Suffolk. See A. C. Cawley, *Everyman and Medieval Miracle Plays* (London: Phoenix, 1993), 105–123.

93. "The Wakefield Pageant of Herod the Great," in *Ibid.*, 121.

94. Greta Austin, "Were the Peasants Really So Clean? The Middle Ages in Film," *Film History* 14, no. 2 (2002): 137.

95. Tison Pugh, "Review of *Hollywood Knights: Arthurian Cinema and the Politics of Nostalgia*," *Arthuriana* 16, no. 2 (Summer 2006): 97–98.

96. Cantor, *Inventing the Middle Ages*, 79–117.

97. White, *The Content of the Form*, 36; discussed also in Robert A. Rosenstone, *History on Film/Film on History* (Harlow: Longman/Pearson, 2006): 91. See also Section 1.1 above.

98. See White, *The Content of the Form*, especially chapter 3, "The Politics of Historical Interpretation," 58–82.

99. Pam Cook, *Screening the Past: Memory and Nostalgia in Cinema* (London: Routledge, 2005), 11.

100. Paul Willemen, *Pier Paulo Pasolini* (London: British Film Institute, 1976), 34–35.

101. Vivian Sobchack, *The Persistence of History: Cinema, Television, and the Modern Event* (London: Routledge, 1996).

102. Ricoeur, *Temps et récit*, especially vol. 3, section 4, "Temps Raconté." For a useful overview of Ricoeur's oeuvre, see chapter 7 of White, *The Content of the Form*, "The Metaphysics of Narrativity: Time and Symbol in Ricoeur's Philosophy of History," 169–184.

103. *Alexander Nevskii*, directed by S. M. Eisenstein (Mosfilm, 1937).

104. *Andrei Rublev*, directed by Andrei Tarkovsky (Mosfilm, 1966).

105. Hayden White, "The Modernist Event," in Sobchack, *Persistence of History*, 17–38, here 17.

106. Bill Nichols, "Historical Consciousness and the Viewer: *Who Killed Vincent Chin?*," in Sobchack, *The Persistence of History*, 56.

107. Christian Metz, *Film Language: A Semiotics of the Cinema* (Oxford: Oxford University Press, 1974), 18.

Chapter 2

1. Norman Cantor, *Inventing the Middle Ages: The Lives, Works, and Ideas of the Great Medievalists of the Twentieth Century* (New York: William Morrow & Company, 1991), 38.

2. *Ibid.*, 413.

3. Laurie A. Finke and Martin B. Shichtman, *Medieval Texts & Contemporary Readers* (Ithaca, NY: Cornell University Press, 1987), 1.

4. Cantor, *Inventing the Middle Ages*, 30.

5. Carr, *What Is History?* 2nd ed. (Harmondsworth: Penguin, 1990), 13 (emphasis added).

6. Greta Austin, "Were the Peasants Really So Clean?" *Film History* 14 (2002): 139.

7. Marcus Bull, *Thinking Medieval: An Introduction to the Study of the Middle Ages* (Basingstoke: Palgrave Macmillan, 2005), 94.

8. Neither, for that matter, did the Renaissance immediately following it, nor Antiquity,

Classical or otherwise, at the height of Rome's power. Like all men at all times, rather, they conceived of themselves as living in the present day, existing at the end of that long sequence of events which we call history.

9. In fact if anything, a significant topos running throughout the medieval era seems to have been a feeling of Armageddon, Apocalyptic millenarianism, conjoined with a sense of the impending Day of Judgment, if we are to judge by the Dance of Death frescoes, the recurrent theme of the Harrowing of Hell in *Piers the Plowman*, or the *Everyman* morality plays. We even find a sense of Götterdämmerung in sources as early as the alleged appeals of Viking-ravaged England, such as the eighth-century prayer containing the lines "A furore normannorum libera nos domine": "free us, O Lord, from the fury of the Northmen."

10. See Morris Bishop, *Middle Ages* (London: Cassell, 1969), 11.

11. Barbara H. Rosenwein and Lester K. Little, *Debating the Middle Ages: Issues and Readings* (Oxford: Blackwell, 1998), 1.

12. Paul Zumthor, *Toward a Medieval Poetics* (Minneapolis: University of Minnesota Press, 1992), xvii–xviii, originally published as Paul Zumthor, *Essai De Poétique Médiévale* (Paris: Seuil, 1972), my emphasis.

13. Zumthor, *Toward a Medieval Poetics*, xvii.

14. "Le moyen âge," François Amy de la Bretèque, *L'Imaginaire médiéval dans le cinéma occidental* (Paris: Champion, 2004), 30. In fact, in this respect, English is one of the least ambiguous languages, when we consider that while we pluralize the term, it is reduced even further to "le moyen âge" in French, "das mittelalter" in German, "il medioevo" in Italian and "la Edad Media" in Spanish. See Jacques le Goff and Jean-Maurice de Montrémy, *À la recherche du Moyen Âge* (Paris: Éditions Louis Audibert, 2003), 41; Cantor, *Inventing the Middle Ages*, 17. See also Rosenwein and Little, *Debating the Middle Ages*, 1–2. For what is in my opinion the most in-depth and authoritative critique of this position, however, see Fred C. Robinson, "Medieval, The Middle Ages," *Speculum* 59 (1984): 747–749.

15. "La 'culture médiévale,' quoique plus homogène que la nôtre, ne fut pas monolithique," Paul Zumthor, *Parler Du Moyen Âge* (Paris: Les Éditions de Minuit, 1980), 86 (my translation).

16. Carr, *What Is History?*, 60.

17. Johan H. Huizinga, *The Waning of the Middle Ages* (Harmondsworth: Penguin Books Ltd., 2001), 262.

18. Bull, *Thinking Medieval*, 43.

19. *Ibid.*, 60.

20. Maurice Keen, *A History of Medieval Europe* (London: Routledge and Kegan Paul, 1967), 11.

21. Cantor, *Inventing the Middle Ages*, 28; Goff and Montrémy, *À la recherche du Moyen Âge*, 43; Umberto Eco, *Travels in Hyperreality: Essays*, translated by William Weaver (London: Picador, 1987), 66.

22. Bull, *Thinking Medieval*, 15.

23. "Deux images se superposaient: un Moyen Âge "noir" et un Moyen Âge idéalisé." Goff and Montrémy, *À la recherche du Moyen Âge*, 15 (my translation).

24. Literally, "else*where* replaces else*when*," which might be paraphrased as "'In a land far, far away' replaces 'once upon a time,'" Amy de la Bretèque, *Imaginaire médiéval*, 9. Cf. Eco's oft-quoted "Ten little Middle Ages," Eco, *Travels in Hyperreality*, 68–72.

25. Cantor, *Inventing the Middle Ages*, 63.

26. Eco, *Travels in Hyperreality*, 72 (emphasis added).

27. "Il cinema — non solo il cinema — non ha il compito di riprodurre né l'intento di spiegare il Medioevo: al contrario, esso lo "reinventa," lo ricrea ricostruendolo senza vincoli filologici e con una potenza immaginifica senza pari" (translation my own and emphasis added). Raffaele Licinio, *Cinema e Medioevo: Tutti i film sul Medioevo o di 'atmosfera' medievale*, www.cinemedioevo.net/index.htm.

28. Eco, *Travels in Hyperreality*, 74.

29. This is particularly true of the genre of films which have variously been called "Heroic Fantasy" (Philippe Bordes, "Moyen Âge or Heroic Fantasy?" *Cahiers de la Cinémathèque* 42/43 (1985): 171–182), fantasy films and "sword and sorcery." While films of this type have by common consensus been placed in a putative Dark Age period, there is absolutely no evidence that directors intended such a temporal identification.

30. Bull, *Thinking Medieval*, 9.

31. Stuart Airlie, "Strange Eventful Histories: The Middle Ages in Cinema," in *The Medieval World*, edited by Peter Linehan (London: Routledge, 2001), 170.

32. "Le Moyen Âge de tous côtés nous assiège et nous provoque." Zumthor, *Parler Du Moyen Âge*, 120 (my translation).

33. Roland Barthes, *Mythologies* (London: Vintage, 2000), 128; see also "The Photographic Message," in *Image, Music, Text*, translated by Stephen Heath (London: Fontana, 1977), 15–31. (See Glossary: empty signifier.)

34. "Coupure infranchissable," Amy de la Bretèque, *Imaginaire médiéval*, 94. Zumthor also speaks of this as a "cassure" which creates the Middle Ages as an "Other," separating the object of alterity from the person studying it (*Parler du Moyen Âge*, 35).

35. "L'éloignement du moyen âge, la distance irrécuperable qui nous en sépare." Zumthor, *Essai De Poétique Médiévale*, 31 (my translation).

36. See, for example, Amy de la Bretèque: "Comment acquiert-il [the normal spectator] la conviction que ce qu'on lui represente, c'est "du Moyen Âge"? Pour parvenir à cet accord minimal, énonciateur et destinataire doivent être d'accord sur un certain nombre de traits définitionnels simples."" "Le regard du cinéma sur le Moyen Âge," in *Le Moyen Âge Aujourd'hui: Trois Regards Contemporains sur le Moyen Âge: Histoire, Théologie, Cinéma*, edited by Jacques le Goff and Guy Lobrichon (Paris: Cahiers du Léopard d'Or, 1997), 292 (my translation).

37. This "belief contract" is termed a "pacte de créance." *Ibid.*, 293.

38. "S'insère dans les "blancs" de l'Histoire: ... a pour fonction de *combler les interstices du réel.*" Amy de la Bretèque, *Le Moyen Âge Aujourd'hui*, 292 (my translation and paraphrase).

39. I am here using the basic triadic unit as outlined in Peirce's semiotic model. While I am conscious of omitting a great deal of Peirce's secondary and tertiary units, for the purposes of our investigation here it seems far more appropriate to retain historiographic clarity even at the expense of semiotic theory. See also Glossary of Terms.

40. I am conscious that objections might be raised at this juncture along the lines that in the United Kingdom there still *does* exist the concept of a knight (as in OBEs, KBE, and so on) and of a distinct class of knighthood (aristocracy, celebrity, etc.). However, such objections only bolster my assertion that these "types" of knighthood have lost their initial significance: one has only to imagine those same "knights" leading the charge at Agincourt to realize how misplaced and transformed these concepts have become. In this sense, then, /knight/ has become *both* an empty signifier vis-à-vis the medieval referent, *and* a signifier of a totally different referent ("celebrity," "KBE") in our society.

41. Claude Lévi-Strauss, *Myth and Meaning* (London: Taylor & Francis Group, 2003), 7.

42. David Williams, "Medieval Movies," *The Yearbook of English Studies* 20 (1990): 1.

43. *Perceval le gallois*, directed by Eric Rohmer (Les Films du Losange/France 3, 1978). I have written elsewhere ("The Place of Arthurian Literature in French Cinema," unpublished MA thesis) about the noticeably divergent directions often taken by French filmmakers in particular when dealing with their medieval pasts, but here only that the connection is based on a literary — and not mediated — fidelity, which has several effects on the French "vision" of the past.

44. Airlie, "Strange Eventful Histories," 170.

45. Here I am consciously paraphrasing Rohmer's defense of his film in an interview with Nadja Tesich-Savage, "Rehearsing the Middle Ages," *Film Comment*, 14 (Sept-Oct 1978): 51.

46. See Sorlin, *The Film in History*; Rosenstone, *History on Film/Film on History*; and especially Ferro, *Cinéma et histoire*. A very impressive discussion on this can also be found in Laurie A. Finke and Martin B. Shichtman, *Cinematic Illuminations: The Middle Ages on Film* (Baltimore: Johns Hopkins Press, 2009), 3–67 ("Part One: Theory and Methods of Cinematic Medievalism").

47. F. W. Ankersmit, *Historical Representation* (Stanford, CA: Stanford University Press, 2001), 12.

48. Julian Barnes, *Love, Etc.* (London: Picador, 2001), 85–86.

49. *Ivanhoe*, directed by Richard Thorpe (MGM, 1952).

50. Williams, "Medieval Movies," 10, paraphrasing Marcel Oms, "Les Yankees à la cour du roi Arthur," *Cahiers de la Cinémathèque* 42/43, Special edition, *Le Moyen Âge au Cinéma* (1985): 62.

51. I am here using the standard Western codes as laid out in John G. Cawelti, *The Six-Gun Mystique* (Bowling Green, OH: Bowling Green University Popular Press, 1975).

52. Jonathan Harker, "Review: [The Hidden Fortress]," *Film Quarterly* 13, no. 3 (1960): 59.

53. Austin, "Were the Peasants Really So Clean?" 137.

54. Robert A. Rosenstone, "The Reel Joan of Arc: Reflections on the Theory and Practice of the Historical Film." *The Public Historian* 25 (Summer 2003): 69.

55. "Avec quelle habilité un très bon film commercial sait utiliser une sorte de syncrétisme, mythologie où se retrouvent à la fois les archétypes d'un imaginaire collectif alimenté par des siècles de contes populaires, de légendes, de mythes, d'hagiographies simplifiées, de superstitions et de figures emblématiques remodelées pour le circonstance. [C'est] ... une idée que se fait les américains d'un Moyen Âge alibi, merveilleux, fantaisiste et intemporel dans lequel peuvent reprendre vie et retrouver forme les contes de fées." Oms, "Les Yankees à la cour du roi Arthur," 68 (my translation).

56. See Veronica Ortenberg, *In Search of the Holy Grail* (London & New York: Hambledon Continuum, 2006), 193–223 (chapter 9, "Camelot Goes Celluloid").

Chapter 3

1. "Such is the paradox of the two most readily recognizable features of medieval warfare: the heavily armoured knight on his horse and the mighty castle or wall." Peter Burkholder, "Popular [Mis]conceptions of Medieval Warfare," *History Compass* 5 (2007): 508.

2. David D. Day, "Monty Python and the Holy Grail: Madness with a Definite Method," *Cinema Arthuriana: Twenty Essays* (Jefferson, NC: McFarland, 2002), 131.

3. Cf T. H. White's "might *for* right" and not "might *is* right," in *The Once and Future King*, "The Queen of Air and Darkness," 244–245.

4. Johan H. Huizinga, *The Waning of the Middle Ages* (Harmondsworth: Penguin Books, Ltd., 2001), 45.

5. C. S. Lewis, *The Discarded Image: An Introduction to Medieval and Renaissance Literature* (Cambridge: Cambridge University Press, 1964), 10.

6. Martha W. Driver and Sid Ray, *The Medieval Hero on Screen: Representations from Beowulf to Buffy* (Jefferson, NC: McFarland, 2004), 6.

7. Geoffrey Chaucer, *The Canterbury Tales* (New York: D. Appleton, 1855), lines 43–79.

8. The militia Christi were, according to Richard Barber, *The Knight and Chivalry* (Woodbridge, Suffolk: Boydell Press, 1995), an attempt by the Church to modify their original anti-war stance, perhaps to use the military forces to serve their own ends (see Chapter 11: "The Church, Warfare and Crusades," 249–265). While these ends may have initially been religious in intention, it soon became apparent, already by the late eighth century, that there arose missions like "the Carolingian wars against the Saxons [which] had a definite political objective, but were presented as religious exercises" (249). In time, "the idea of the 'soldiers of Christ' led by St. Michael is brought in to replace the old warrior paganism with Wotan as its deity, and the *militia Christi* of St. Paul are no longer the meek and spiritual martyrs, but the all too earthly soldiers of Charlemagne's armies" (250).

9. Barber, *The Knight and Chivalry*, 28.

10. *Ibid.*, 250.

11. Northrop Frye, *Anatomy of Criticism: Four Essays* (Princeton & Oxford: Princeton University Press, 1957; 2000), 33.

12. *La Chanson de Roland* (Paris: Livre de Poche, 1990), verse 170, lines 2284–2291; the English version comes from Howard S. Robinson's translation, *The Song of Roland* (London: J.M. Dent, 1972), CLXX, 67.

13. "Par rapport au héros moyenâgeux, qui est le plus souvent (toujours?) un noble, un puissant de naissance, nos héros sont des gens du peuple…. Made in USA." Philippe Bordes, "Moyen Âge or Heroic Fantasy?" *Cahiers de la Cinémathèque* 42/43 (1985): 172 (my translation). I am thinking here of Dark Age warriors witnessed in *Conan the Barbarian*, *Dragonslayer* and *Eragon* and — in a parodic context — *Willow*.

14. See Barber, *The Knight and Chivalry*, 27.

15. T. A. Prendergast, *Medieval Heroes and Legendary Nations* (Ann Arbor, MI: UMI, 1995), 6. However, while this terminological distinction might be useful when examining the emergence of knighthood and chivalry in literature, I am not adopting its use here for the primary reason that cinema — as I will argue below — has not retained such as subtle difference in either appellation or conceptualization. Hereafter, I will therefore continue to use the term "knight" to mean those who fight, and "chivalry" to refer to the (predominantly literary) codes governing their conduct. Should we wish to specifically discuss the bellicose, early medieval, warrior-knight mentioned above, it is perhaps easiest to retain the term "warrior" for simplicity's sake, since — as I have mentioned — the figure of the warrior has generally been reworked by the heroic fantasy/sword and sorcery genre, which has frequently been transported outside of the medieval era and therefore reaches well beyond the scope of this thesis. For an excellent discussion of these themes see Bordes, "Moyen Âge ou Heroic Fantasy?"

16. Frye, *Anatomy of Criticism*, 34.

17. These examples are drawn from, respectively, Chrétien de Troyes, *Le Chevalier de la charrette* (Paris: Livre de Poche, 1992), lines 4651–4679; *Ibid.*, lines 3021–3150; Chrétien de Troyes, *Le Chevalier au lion* (Paris: Livre de Poche, 1994), lines 4230–4248.

18. *Le Chevalier de la charrette*, lines 2734–2766.

19. *Le Chevalier au lion*, lines 5620–5675.

20. Barber, *The Knight and Chivalry*, 29.

21. Frye, *Anatomy of Criticism*, 34.

22. *Ibid.*, 34. The "list" to which Frye refers here is an inventory in which he enumerates the various modes of literary heroes. At the summit lies the "mythic" mode, at which the hero is a divine being, and the list continues through the Romance, High-Mimetic, Low-Mimetic (in which the hero is "one of us," concluding with the Ironic mode, in which the hero is demonstrably inferior. See Frye, *Anatomy of Criticism*, 33–34.

23. Barber, *The Knight and Chivalry*, 210.

24. Huizinga, *The Waning of the Middle Ages*, 71.

25. See chapter 22, "Critics of Chivalry and Advocates of Reform," in Barber, *The Knight and Chivalry*, 326–335, especially page 333.

26. R. Howard Block, *Medieval French Literature and Law* (Berkeley: University of California Press, 1977), quoted in Emma Cayley, *Debate and Dialogue: Alain Chartier in His Cultural Context* (Oxford: Clarendon, 2006), 20.

27. *Ibid.*

28. "Entre la lumière éclatante du rêve et la

banale grisaille de l'existence quotidienne." Michel Pastoureau, *La vie quotidienne en France et en Angleterre au temps des chevaliers de la table ronde* (Paris: Hachette Littérature, 1991), 106 (my translation).

29. Huizinga, *The Waning of the Middle Ages*, 75.

30. Such as Chartier's *Le Bréviaire des Nobles*, or Llull's *Le Libre del Orde de Cavelleria*. For more on this, an excellent overview can be found in Richard W. Kaeuper, *Chivalry and Violence in Medieval Europe* (Oxford: Oxford University Press, 1999), especially Part One: Issues and Approaches, 5–39, and once again Barber's *The Knight and Chivalry* provides a fascinating summary; see chapter 9, "Chivalric Biographies and Handbooks," 144–155.

31. Derek Elley, *The Epic Film: Myth and History* (London: Routledge & Kegan Paul, 1984), 136.

32. "Le Chevalier, c'est l'homme qui possède un cheval." Jacques Le Goff and Jean-Louis Schlegel, *Le Moyen Âge expliqué aux enfants* (Paris: Seuil, 2006), 23.

33. For an explanation of "passages obligés," see Glossary, and Marcel Oms, "Les Yankees à la cour du roi Arthur," *Cahiers de la Cinémathèque* 42/43 (1985): 61–69.

34. Díaz de Gámez, "The Chivalric Ideal," in *The Portable Medieval Reader*, edited by James Bruce Ross and Mary Martin McLaughlin (Harmondsworth: Penguin, 1949; repr 1977), 91.

35. Richard Harris as Arthur in *Camelot*, directed by Joshua Logan (Warner Bros. Pictures, 1967).

36. Barber, *The Knight and Chivalry*, 326.

37. Sean Connery as King Arthur in *First Knight*, directed by Jerry Zucker (Columbia Pictures, 1995).

38. Caroline Jewers, "Hard Day's Knights: *First Knight, A Knight's Tale*, and *Black Knight*," in Martha W. Driver and Sid Ray, *The Medieval Hero on Screen: Representations from Beowulf to Buffy* (Jefferson, NC: McFarland, 2004), 197.

39. *Ibid.*, 194.

40. In *The Messenger, Tristan and Isolde* (directed by Kevin Reynolds, Scott Free Productions, 2006), *Beowulf and Grendel* and *The Princess Bride* respectively. See also Haydock, *Movie Medievalism: The Imaginary Middle Ages* (Jefferson, NC: McFarland, 2008), especially chapter 1.

41. See Helmut Nickel, "Arms and Armor in Arthurian Films," in Kevin J. Harty, *Cinema Arthuriana: Twenty Essays* (Jefferson, NC: McFarland, 2002), 236.

42. John G. Cawelti, *The Six-Gun Mystique* (Bowling Green, OH: Bowling Green University Popular Press, 1975), 60.

43. See Richard Burt, "Getting Schmedieval:

Of Manuscript and Film Prologues, Paratexts and Parodies," *Exemplaria* 19, no. 2 (Summer 2007): 217.

44. David Williams, "Medieval Movies," *The Yearbook of English Studies* 20 (1990): 7–8.

45. *Excalibur*, directed by John Boorman (Orion Pictures, 1981).

46. Robert the Bruce (Angus Macfadyen) in *Braveheart*.

47. "Le schéma d'intégration": "C'est la version démocratique et liberale du mythe de la chevalerie," *L'imaginaire médiéval*, 1044.

48. Oliver J. Thatcher and Edgar Holmes McNeal, *A Source Book for Medieval History* (New York: Scribners, 1905), 516–517.

49. For more on this use of the Crusades as a metaphor, see *Hollywood and the Holy Land: Essays on Film Depictions of the Crusades and Christian-Muslim Clashes*, edited by Nickolas Haydock and E. L. Risden (Jefferson, NC: McFarland, 2009).

50. Oath spoken by Godefroi de Ibelin in the dubbing ceremony of *Kingdom of Heaven*.

51. Susan Aronstein and Nancy Coiner, "Twice Knightly: Democratizing the Middle Ages for Middle-Class America," *Studies in Medievalism*, 6, Medievalism in North America (1994): 212.

52. My use of the term "reluctant hero" is drawn in part from the Campbell mold of the same name — Joseph Campbell, *The Hero with a Thousand Faces* (Princeton: Princeton University Press, 1968) — in which the hero of the people is faced with a "Call to Adventure" (49–58) and is initially inclined toward the "Refusal of the Call" (59–68). The refusal, which constitutes the "reluctance" comes about when "the subject loses the power of significant affirmative action and becomes a victim to be saved" (59), which fixes the subject firmly among "the people." The "Call to Adventure," when eventually answered, thus propels the subject to the fore, confirming his or her hitherto latent state of heroicism. Alongside this, we might also place the Proppian motif of the leader's conflict, which is eventually overcome by lack/need. The first stage of overcoming this refusal of the call is when the conflict is heightened, such as when "the villain causes harm or injury to a member of a family" (Vladimir Propp, *Morphology of the Folktale* [Austin: University of Texas Press, 1968], 30–35), an injury which "is exceptionally important, since by means of it the actual movement of the tale is created" (30–31). The Reluctant Hero thus responds (either positively or negatively) to this need (see "The Hero's Reaction," 42). These two morphologies can both be neatly applied to Balian in our example, since he initially refuses his calling, only responding when his living "family" comes under threat; a

similar reading can be found in *Braveheart*, in which the *ius primae noctis* causes a devastating blow to the "family" (in this case his wife), and prompts his rebellion.

53. Roger Lancelyn Green, *King Arthur and His Knights of the Round Table* (Harmondsworth: Penguin Books, 1980), 63.

54. Nickel, "Arms and Armor in Arthurian Films," 236.

55. As is, of course, the motif of the Black Knight, perhaps most explicitly in *Perlesvaus*, in which the knights clad in black armor come from the castle of the Black Hermit, "which signifies Hell ... and the Black Hermit is Lucifer." Nigel Bryant's introduction to *Perlesvaus* in *The High Book of the Grail*, edited by Nigel Bryant (Cambridge, D. S. Brewer, 2007), xiv.

56. See, for example, "The Aristocratic Practice of Signs," in R. Howard Bloch, *Etymologies and Genealogies* (Chicago, IL: University of Chicago Press, 1986), 75–91, especially 78.

57. Barber, *The Knight and Chivalry*, 23.

58. Friedrich Heer, *The Medieval World: Europe 1100–1350*, translated by Janet Sondheimer (New York: George Weidenfeld and Nicolson, 1962), 127.

59. Kaeuper, *Chivalry and Violence*, 22 (emphasis added).

60. *Lancelot du lac*, directed by Robert Bresson (Mara Films/O.R.T.F., 1974).

61. Bresson famously refused to use the term "actors," preferring instead to use non-professional actors whom he called "modèles."

62. *The Court Jester*, directed by Melvin Frank and Norman Panama (Paramount Pictures, 1956).

63. Jeffrey Richards, *Swordsmen of the Screen, from Douglas Fairbanks to Michael York* (London: Routledge and Kegan Paul, 1977), 93.

64. *Ibid.*, 4.

65. "Un type héroïque bondissant, chevaler-esque et sportif qui doit plus au dynamisme à l'américaine qu'aux traditions européenes proprement dites...." Oms, "Les Yankees à la cour du roi Arthur," 61 (my translation).

66. *Indiana Jones and the Last Crusade*.

67. *Knight for a Day*, directed by Jack Hannah/Bill Peet (Walt Disney Productions, 1946).

68. *Robin Hood: Men in Tights*, directed by Mel Brooks (Warner Brothers Pictures, 1993).

69. I am thinking here of the hero of the eponymous romance *Le Bel Inconnu* (Paris: Champion, 2003), which has been used by, for example, Boorman, to demonstrate an "everyman" topos which we will see in more depth in section 3.3 on The All-Action Hero.

70. Stuart Airlie, "Strange Eventful Histories: The Middle Ages in Cinema," in *The Medieval World*, edited by Peter Linehan (London: Routledge, 2001), 177.

71. *Ibid.*, 177–178.

72. "Perpétuant la convention d'un chevalier à fine moustache proche en même temps de la figure de Robin de Bois ... et ses descendants romantiques plus ou moins conditionés par la relecture des thèmes du cycle breton à travers la sensibilité du XIX siècle anglo-saxon." Oms, "Les Yankees à la cour du roi Arthur," 66 (my translation).

73. Richards, *Swordsmen of the Screen*, 10 (quoting Henry Beers).

74. *Ibid.*, 72.

75. Williams, "Medieval Movies," 7–8.

76. For a history of the epic film and its treatment of history, see Elley, *The Epic Film*; for the Middle Ages in particular, see chapter 11, 136–159.

77. Richards, *Swordsmen of the Screen*, 84.

78. "Le cinéma 'moyenâgeux' s'est épanoui surtout dans les années '50." Amy de la Bretèque, *Imaginaire médiéval*, 20 (my translation).

79. *Shane*, directed by George Stevens (Paramount Pictures, 1953).

80. *The Magnificent Seven*, directed by John Sturges (Mirisch Corporation/Alpha Productions, 1960).

81. Cawelti, *The Six-Gun Mystique*, 55.

82. "Il medioevo cinematografico è invece evocazione di uno spazio ben definibile, come il Western." S. Pittaluga and M. Salotti, "Premessa," *Cinema e Medioevo* (Genova: Università di Genova, 2000), 6 (my translation).

83. Bob McCabe, *Dark Knights and Holy Fools* (London: Orion Press, 1999), 69 (emphasis added).

84. *Knights of the Round Table*, directed by Richard Thorpe (MGM British Studios, 1953).

85. "Dans sa lettre, ce serment semble répéter ce que les textes romanesques médiévaux disent de la mission de la chevalerie céleste. Mais il s'est coloré, en fait, de l'idéologie démocratique, laïque et moralisante, qui est celle de l'Amérique." François Amy de la Bretèque, "La figure du chevalier errant dans l'imaginaire cinématographique," *Cahiers de l'association internationale des études françaises*, 47 (May 1995): 57 (my translation).

86. Jennifer Moskowitz, "The Cultural Myth of the Cowboy, or, How the West Was Won," *Americana* 5, no. 1 (Spring 2006), unpaginated.

87. See, for example, J. Zimmerman, *Chivalry is Not Dead, It Simply Rode West: The Medieval Knight and the Nineteenth Century American Cowboy as Archetypes of Nation* (Vermillion, SD: University of South Dakota, 2002); M. W. Fishwick, "The Cowboy: America's Contribution to the World's Mythology," *Western Folklore* 11, no. 2 (1952), 77–92. For an interesting article tracing the link between the two, see Moskowitz, "The Cultural Myth of the Cowboy," unpaginated.

88. Cawelti, *The Six-Gun Mystique*, 1–3, introduction.

89. A fall from grace which is generally attributed to the box office flop of, appropriately, Anthony Mann's *The Fall of the Roman Empire*, with the last medieval offering of this standard Hollywood fare being *El Cid* in 1963, also directed by Mann.

90. Robert A. Segal, *Hero Myths: A Reader* (Oxford: Blackwell, 2000), 9.

91. Nickolas Haydock, "Arthurian Melodrama, Chaucerian Spectacle, and the Waywardness of Cinematic Pastiche in *First Knight* and *A Knight's Tale*," in *Studies in Medievalism XII: Film and Fiction: Reviewing the Middle Ages*, edited by Tom Shippey and Martin Arnold (Cambridge: D. S. Brewer, 2003), 17.

92. I am excluding from this category any of the sword and sorcery/fantasy genre films which saw a brief explosion of popularity in the early 1980s, since these films make no pretence at situating their medieval worlds in anything real or datable, and perhaps might more profitably be termed as sci-fi which simply happen to be situated in the "Dark Age" period. "It is a Middle Ages which functions as a myth ... which takes place simply "a long time ago" and [which is] obscure enough to allow us to freely project our current fantasies" (my translation). Bordes, "Moyen Âge ou Heroic Fantasy?" 171; see also Glossary under "Medieval Film."

93. *King Arthur*, directed by Antoine Fuqua (Touchstone Pictures, 2004).

94. *Robin Hood: Prince of Thieves*, directed by Kevin Reynolds (20th Century–Fox, 1991).

95. I will explain this scene, along with the concept of the sub-king, in much more depth below, in chapter 4, section 3.2.

96. And which, of course, spoke to the recent experience of World War II, as well as the then nascent Red Scare.

97. *The Lord of the Rings: The Fellowship of the Ring*, directed by Peter Jackson (Newline Cinema / Wingnut Films, 2001). It also bears a strong resemblance to guerrilla tactics of a great deal of late-twentieth-century conflicts, in which a minority group fight back against an oppressive regime.

98. See section 2.2, above.

99. It ought, then, to be scarcely a surprise to discover that Ridley and Tony Scott are listed as executive producers on *Tristan and Isolde*, which was made by their production company, Scottfree Productions.

100. Barber, *The Knight and Chivalry*, 210.

101. See Marcus Bull, *Thinking Medieval: An Introduction to the Study of the Middle Ages* (Basingstoke: Palgrave Macmillan, 2005), 7–41 (chapter 1).

Chapter 4

1. King Philippe in *The Lion in Winter*, directed by Anthony Harvey (AVCO/Haworth, 1968).

2. See especially Peggy McCracken, *The Romance of Adultery: Queenship and Sexual Transgression in Old French Literature* (Philadelphia, PA: University of Pennsylvania Press, 1998). For more on English queenship in the medieval period, see J. L. Laynesmith, *The Last Medieval Queens: English Queenship 1445–1503* (Oxford: Oxford University Press, 2005), or *Medieval Queenship*, edited by J. C. Parsons (New York: Palgrave Macmillan, 1997), especially Pauline Stafford's essay in the latter collection which examines the representation of queenship within the medieval period itself: "The Portrayal of Royal Women in England, Mid-Tenth to Mid-Twelfth Centuries," 143–168. Finally, for a wider study of queenship in its European context, see *Queens and Queenship in Medieval Europe*, edited by Anne J. Duggan (Woodbridge: Boydell Press, 1997).

3. One possible exception which springs to mind might have been Gabriel Axel's *Prince of Jutland*, which is a loose retelling of Saxo Grammaticus's precursor to *Hamlet*. However, after an initially interesting characterization of a strong queen, the focus rapidly shifts to the insane prince, flattening out the character of the queen almost to a stereotype. A similar case might be made for films depicting Medieval Scandinavia in general, since the Eddas' legacy of powerful, "enabled" female heroes is often felt more strongly in film. Nevertheless, given the multifarious and markedly diverse societal arrangement in this region, their inclusion can contribute little to the present study. For more on Northern European cinematic representation, see the forthcoming Kevin J. Harty (ed.), *Reel Vikings: Medieval Scandinavia in the Cinema* (Jefferson, NC: McFarland, 2011).

4. "A eccezione di alcuni recentissimi svolgimenti ... le protagoniste dei film e dei romanzi ambientati nell'Età di Mezzo sono viste come oggetti da prendere o da usare oppure come tesori da rubare o da contendere." Matteo Sanfilippo, *Il Medioevo secondo Walt Disney* (Roma: Castelvecchi, 1993), 165.

5. François Villon experienced a brief cinematic explosion of popularity in the first half of the twentieth century, notably in *The Beloved Rogue* (1927), but also in two film shorts which seem to be essentially the same film, *The Higher Law* (1914) and *The Oubliette* (also 1914), starring the future hunchback of Notre Dame, Lon Chaney. Better known films made about the poet, however, remain versions of Justin McCarthy's play, first released as *If I Were King*

(1921) and remade with sound by Frank Lloyd in 1938 with swashbuckler Ronald Colman and stock villain Basil Rathbone in the main roles. The play was also rewritten and remade as *The Vagabond King* in 1930 and again in 1956, whereupon Villon has — to the extent of my knowledge — fallen equally as suddenly out of favor.

6. Dagobert I appears in *Le Bon Roi Dagobert*, directed by Dino Risi (France 3/Gaumont, 1984); the Dauphin plays a distinct second fiddle to Joan of Arc; Louis VI briefly appears in *Les Visiteurs*, directed by Jean-Marie Poire (Canal+/ France 3, 1993), though it is Jean Reno as Godefroi who is the real hero; and Philippe I (a young Timothy Dalton) is overshadowed by Peter O'-Toole's Henry II in *The Lion in Winter*, directed by Anthony Harvey (AVCO/Haworth, 1968).

7. "Les rois par excellence, dans le cinéma moyenâgeux, sont les rois anglais." François Amy de la Bretèque, *L'Imaginaire médiéval dans le cinéma occidental* (Paris: Champion, 2004), 547 (my translation). In translating "cinéma moyenâgeux," I have continued to use the more literal "medieval film" rather than follow Haydock in using the term "movie medievalism"; although he makes a good case for the term, it seems to me unlikely that any confusion might arise from its use. See my Glossary, and the preface to Nickolas Haydock, *Movie Medievalism: The Imaginary Middle Ages* (Jefferson, NC: McFarland, 2008), 1.

8. "Le cinéma, quand il veut mettre en scène les aspects politiques d'un moment d'histoire, s'adresse volontiers au moule théâtral" Amy de la Bretèque, *Imaginaire médiéval*, 617.

9. Boethius, *Consolatio Philosphiae* (London: J.M. Dent and Co., 1902), Book 1, Metrum 10.

10. Ernst H. Kantorowicz, *The King's Two Bodies: A Study in Mediaeval Political Theology* (Princeton: Princeton University Press, 1957); John Figgis, *The Divine Right of Kings* (Cambridge: Cambridge University Press, 1922); Christopher Brooke, *The Saxon and Norman Kings* (New York: Macmillan 1963). For an interesting viewpoint on the outward symbols pertaining to kingship (of particular relevance to the cinematic king), see also Percy Ernst Schramm, *A History of the English Coronation* (Oxford: Clarendon Press, 1937).

11. Brooke, *The Saxon and Norman Kings*, 194.

12. See Figgis, *The Divine Right of Kings*, 7.

13. For more discussion of this, see Schramm, *A History of the English Coronation*, 6–8, and Kantorowicz, *The King's Two Bodies*.

14. H. Sawyer and I. N. Wood, *Early Medieval Kingship* (Leeds: University of Leeds, 1977), 1–2.

15. "S'organise fortement autour de deux principes d'ordre: le roi et la pyramide féodale." Michel Pastoureau, *La vie quotidienne en France et en Angleterre au temps des chevaliers de la table ronde* (Paris: Hachette Littérature, 1991), 30 (my translation).

16. Henri Pirenne, *Mohammed and Charlemagne* (London: George Allen and Unwin, 1939; 1965), 266.

17. Kantorowicz, *The King's Two Bodies*, 363.

18. Macrobius, *Commentary on the "Dream of Scipio"* (Columbia: Columbia University Press, 1952), 12.

19. The young King Arthur in *The Sword in the Stone* (1963).

20. Although, of course, it is seemingly impossible to classify a "Stoic temperance" as a uniquely external sign, we can observe that as far as indexical signs are concerned, the slow movements and long pauses are often used to connote the meditation of the wise sage. Consider, for example, the representation of the *sensei* in Japanese martial arts films, in which questions are met with long pauses for reflection to counterpoise the impulsive actions of the "adepts."

21. Though, in many ways, by relying on the star-system and the repetition of these "stock characters," they are using these signifiers of wisdom in their paradigmatic capacity rather than their indexical capacity.

22. *The Black Rose*, directed by Henry Hathaway (20th Century–Fox, 1950).

23. Though according to this film, *Becket*, and the novel by Thomas B. Costain, *The Black Rose* (New York: Bantam, 1950), this rivalry lasted for two centuries, such a fissure is not upheld by historical investigation.

24. In fact, Currie and Aylmer were to be paired in nine separate cinematic encounters, of which two — *Ivanhoe* and *Saint Joan* — take place in the Middle Ages, and a further two — *Glamorous Night* and *The Improper Duchess* — have been set in the fictional Ruritania, providing a further link with Thorpe, whose 1952 *Prisoner of Zenda* deals with monarchical succession in Ruritania.

25. Nickolas Haydock, "Arthurian Melodrama, Chaucerian Spectacle, and the Waywardness of Cinematic Pastiche in *First Knight* and *A Knight's Tale*," in *Studies in Medievalism XII: Film and Fiction: Reviewing the Middle Ages*, edited by Tom Shippey and Martin Arnold (Cambridge: D. S. Brewer, 2003), 18.

26. Connery famously played Arthur in *First Knight* and Richard I in *Robin Hood: Prince of Thieves*. Other medieval characters played by Connery include William of Baskerville in *The Name of the Rose*, Robin Hood in *Robin and Marian*, the Green Knight in *Sword of the*

Valiant: The Legend of Sir Gawain and the Green Knight, Draco in *Dragonslayer*, Ramírez in *Highlander*. His establishment as a symbol of "benign paternalism" is further consolidated by film roles such as King Agamemnon in *Time Bandits*, Jimmy Malone in *The Untouchables* and Professor Henry Jones in *Indiana Jones and the Last Crusade*.

27. *King Richard and the Crusaders*, directed by David Butler (Warner Bros. Pictures, 1954).

28. It will come as no surprise to learn that this film is based on Walter Scott's *The Talisman*, and consequently reflects Scott's, rather than history's, memory of the crusading king. This idea of the crusading, rampaging king calls to mind a similar exchange of blows between Richard and Friar Tuck in *Ivanhoe*, a sequence sadly omitted from the film version two years earlier.

29. "l'attribut obligé de tout détenteur de pouvoir." Michel Pastoureau, *Une Histoire Symbolique du Moyen Âge Occidental* (Paris: Seuil, 2004), 50 (my translation).

30. Marc Bloch, *Feudal Society*, translated by L. A. Manyon (London: Routledge & Kegan Paul, 1962), 73.

31. *Ibid.*, 73.

32. I am here conscious of seeming to fall into a common trap, which is to place a potentially "mythical" Robin into a "factual" twelfth-century (for an excellent discussion of this, see Matteo Sanfilippo, *Robin Hood: La Vera Storia* (Firenze: Giunti, 1997), especially "E gli storici?" 54–57, and "Il Mito è la realtà," 58–60). However, given that the films under discussion tend to depict Robin as a Crusading hero, any "King Richard" would have to be Richard I, whose absence on the third crusade occurred around 1190–92, thereby making him 32–35.

33. In *Kingdom of Heaven*, *Robin and Marian*, directed by Richard Lester (Columbia Pictures, 1976); *King Richard and the Crusaders*, *Robin Hood*, directed by Wolfgang Reitherman (Walt Disney Pictures, 1973; voice-over only); *Robin Hood: Men in Tights* and *Robin Hood: Prince of Thieves* respectively. Even Anthony Hopkins, at the age of 30 when filming *The Lion in Winter*, was still four years older than Richard would have been in 1183. It is interesting to note that within the corpus studied, *Ivanhoe's* Norman Woolland at the age of 41 during production is the only actor to be of roughly the right age.

34. Thomas à Becket (Burton) and King Henry II (O'Toole) in *Becket*, directed by Peter Glenville, Paramount Pictures, 1964).

35. *Black Knight*, directed by Gil Junger (20th Century–Fox, 2001).

36. Here I am re-using Jauss's term "the horizon of expectations." I will discuss this, and

generic assumptions and audience expectations in chapter 7, below; for more on this see also Hans Robert Jauss, *Toward an Aesthetic of Reception* (Brighton: Harvester, 1982).

37. Edward Norton as King Baldwin IV of Jerusalem, *Kingdom of Heaven*.

38. *Alfred the Great*, directed by Clive Donner (MGM British Studios, 1969); *The War Lord*, directed by Franklin J. Schaffner (Universal Pictures, 1965).

39. Peter O'Toole as Henry II, *The Lion in Winter* (1968).

40. While, of course, I recognize that there is a difficulty in placing King Arthur into a twelfth-century context, my arguments are based on both the convention of filmmakers to adopt the temporal setting of the Arthurian romanciers, and Goimard's assertion below that the Middle Ages, "to Hollywood at least, means the fifteenth century." Jacques Goimard, "Le film historique," *La Cinématographie française*, 2042 (December 1963): 12.

41. Arthur Lindley, "The Ahistoricism of Medieval Film," *Screening the Past* 3 (May 1988).

42. *A Walk with Love and Death*, directed by John Huston (20th Century–Fox, 1969).

43. Boorman's quotation comes from *Excalibur*. For more on this Fisher King connection, the standard authorities are Jessie L. Weston, *From Ritual to Romance* (Gloucester, MA: Peter Smith, 1983); Joseph Campbell, *Hero with a Thousand Faces* (New York: Princeton University Press, 1949); and James Frazer's landmark *The Golden Bough: A Study in Comparative Religion* (Macmillan, 1890).

44. As Brooke writes of Alfred's later writings, his penetrating mind would later realize that "a king must have men who pray and men who work *as well as* soldiers...." Brooke, *The Saxon and Norman Kings*, 60.

45. The use of a democratic paradigm is not entirely unfaithful to the medieval precursor, however. In the paradigm of king as knight, there is a sense that he must be nominated, deemed worthy and elected, which is not wholly contradictory to Brooke's claim that "inheritance, election and designation, in some way or another each ... entered into most acts of king-making in western Europe in the Middle Ages." *Ibid.*, 24.

46. Roger Lancelyn Green, *King Arthur and His Knights of the Round Table* (Harmondsworth: Penguin Books, 1980), 31.

47. "Perpétuant la convention d'un chevalier à fine moustache proche en même temps de la figure de Robin de Bois ... et ses descendants romantiques plus ou moins conditionnés par la relecture des thèmes du cycle breton à travers la sensibilité du XIX siècle anglo-saxon." Marcel Oms, "Les Yankees à la cour du roi Arthur,"

Cahiers de la Cinémathèque 42/43 (1985): 66 (my translation).

48. In *Knights of the Round Table*, *Ivanhoe* and *Quentin Durward* respectively, although it must be noted that nowhere does Thorpe ever try to anchor his Malorian Arthur in any historically definable period, setting it rather in something of an Ivanhoe-esque oneiric Middle Ages instead.

49. Goimard, "Le film historique," 12.

50. "Le cinéma aime montrer les rituels et les codes chevaleresques tels qu'ils avaient été fixés à la fin du Moyen Âge, car ils sont plus spectaculaires." Amy de la Bretèque, *L'Imaginaire*, 72.

51. "Il Medioevo del Novecento si trova ... nel cinema che tratta non il Medioevo, ma l'idea di Medioevo che il Novecento si è costruita." S. Pittaluga and M. Salotti, "Premessa," in S. Pittaluga and M. Salotti (eds.), *Cinema e Medioevo* (Genova: Università di Genova, 2000), 6 (my translation).

52. This emphasis on the knights even leads to the rather audacious move of renaming Malory's *Morte Darthur* to, tellingly, *Knights of the Round Table*. Interestingly, though, history later took revenge in Bruckheimer's 2004 medieval project, abandoning the working title *Knights of the Round Table* in favor of *King Arthur*.

53. There is an interesting trend — though this is a study for another time — for the 1950s historicals to reconcile the divine right of kingship to an essentially democratic audience by a rapprochement with the concept of Manifest Destiny. Seen from this perspective, it becomes an ideological prism through which the divinely appointed king is transformed into essentially a self-made man whom Providence has favored along the way.

54. Though, again, there is some suggestion here of a continuity with medieval society; Cantor claims that "kingship as a vague idea was popular. But there was almost universal hostility to the actual intervention of the royal government in private, family and communal existence." Norman Cantor, *Inventing the Middle Ages: The Lives, Works, and Ideas of the Great Medievalists of the Twentieth Century* (New York: William Morrow & Company, 1991), 282.

55. Bruckheimer/Fuqua's film, like *First Knight*, can profitably be compared in this respect to the Cinemascope epics. See Robert J. Blanch and Julian N. Wasserman, "Fear of Flyting: The Absence of Internal Tension in 'Sword of the Valiant' and 'First Knight,'" *Arthuriana* 10 (2000): 15–32.

56. See Tom Shippey, "Fuqua's *King Arthur*: More Mythmaking in America," *Exemplaria* 19, no. 2 (Summer 2007): 310–326.

57. See chapter 3, section 2.3. This is particularly interesting as it uses icons of knighthood within a paradigm of kingship in order to conflate the hitherto rather disparate notions of kingship and knighthood. Thus, in terms of semiotics, the king is *both king and knight*.

58. Perhaps, in fairness, a great deal of this "flair" in Boorman's film is indebted to a reading of it as a pastiche of earlier Arthurian epics, given that *Excalibur*, at least, seems to recognize its own burlesque.

59. The subject of Lancelot and Guinevere's seemingly chaste adultery is a somewhat contentious debate in the field of Arthurian film. See Haydock, "Arthurian Melodrama"; Kevin J. Harty, *Cinema Arthuriana: Essays on Arthurian Film* (London: Taylor & Francis, 1991); Rebecca A. Umland and Samuel J. Umland, *The Use of Arthurian Legend in Hollywood Film: From Connecticut Yankees to Fisher Kings* (Westport, CT: Greenwood Press, 1996). Whether originally a product of the restrictive framework of the Hays Code more than a symptom of prudishness on the part of the filmmaker, the chaste love affair somewhat dampens the physical threat of Lancelot and renders the adultery more of a treasonable matter than a tragic love story in the tradition of Tristan and Iseult, Diarmaid and Ygraine, or Helen and Paris.

60. An intergeneric borrowing which reflects another of the growing trends in the 1950s film, the equation of the knight with the cowboy (see chapter 3). The quotation is from Albert Johnson, "The Tenth Muse in San Francisco," *Sight and Sound* 24, no. 3 (1955): 155.

61. Ironically, this aspect of the paradigm renders them more accurate than their iconic counterparts. Bloch, *Feudal Society*, 73.

62. For example, in the recent Stephen Frears film, *The Queen* (2006), debates about constitutional limitations of government, it is implied, still cause divisions between Buckingham Palace and Downing Street. See also Jean de Paris, *On Royal and Papal Power* (Toronto: Pontifical Inst. of Mediaeval Studies, 1971), John of Salisbury, *The Statesman's Book of John of Salisbury: Being the Fourth, Fifth, and Sixth Books, and Selections from the Seventh and Eighth Books, of the Policraticus* (New York: Russell & Russell, 1963), Marsilius of Padua, *Writings on the Empire: Defensor Minor and De Translations Imperii* (Cambridge: Cambridge University Press, 1993) and the great body of scholarship which continues to analyze this issue, particularly Figgis, *The Divine Right of Kings*.

63. Furthermore, it is worth mentioning that the Church as supreme authority is an abstracted notion of the Church by metonymy, and not represented by human agents. It is this abstract, faceless aspect of the Church as Institution which facilitates its elision (and eventual replacement) by the chivalric code in film.

64. As we saw in chapter 3, in which the violence of the knight is tempered by its insinuation into a "Higher Power."

65. This distinction between idealized "Olde England" and England becomes crucial when we come to consider anti–English (or at least anti–Imperialist, which to Mel Gibson et al. seems to be much the same thing) sentiments in *Braveheart*, *The Patriot* and *The Messenger: The Story of Joan of Arc*, all of which rage against the English state as it is today, and not the temporally fractured state of England during the Middle Ages.

66. While of course Zucker's *First Knight* dates from 1995, my inclusion of this film with those of the 50s and 60s is based on my reading of it as a nostalgic return to the style of these films. Nickolas Haydock also claims that "*First Knight* marks a sentimental, nostalgic return to the classic Hollywood style...." Haydock, "Arthurian Melodrama," 24.

67. Although, I suspect there would scarcely be any difficulty in producing a study comparing these roles to a number of other similar structures in film: Ivanhoe and Isaac or Cedric; Walter of Gurney and Balan/Alfgar/Roger Bacon (in *The Black Rose*); Balian, King Baldwin and Godefroi in *Kingdom of Heaven*.

68. As hinted above, this triumvirate could be argued to exist as a paradigmatic borrowing from the Western genre, since they appear to fit neatly with the traditional sheriff, town elder, and drifter archetypes respectively.

69. Cf. John 18:36, "My kingship is not of this world."

70. It is here, reduced to its structural components, that many scholars tend to read Cold War propaganda into the big budget historical films of this era. See, for example, Kevin J. Harty, "Agenda Layered on Agenda," in *Hollywood and the Holy Land: Essays on Film Depictions of the Crusades and Christian-Muslim Clashes*, edited by Nickolas Haydock and E. L. Risden (Jefferson, NC: McFarland, 2009), 161–68, and Alan Lupack, "An Enemy in Our Midst: *The Black Knight* and the American Dream" in *Cinema Arthuriana: Twenty Essays* (Jefferson, NC: McFarland, 2002), 64–70.

71. Walter Scott, *Ivanhoe* (Harmondsworth: Penguin, 1994), 348.

72. "[A]u Moyen Âge, l'opposition entre le haut et le bas est 'projetée dans l'espace': on construit des tours et des murailles très hautes, bien visibles, pour montrer qu'on veut échapper au bas." Le Goff and Schlegel, *Le Moyen Âge expliqué aux enfants*, 42 (my translation).

73. "Le couleur dynastique de la famille capétienne." Pastoureau, *Une Histoire Symbolique*, 156, and also 129.

74. Though not in *Robin Hood: Prince of*

Thieves, directed by Kevin Reynolds (Warner Brothers Pictures, also 1991), which attempts to broach the racial "otherness" theme by an introduction of the Muslim Azeem.

75. Exclamation by Lancelot in John Boorman's *Excalibur*.

76. Brooke, *The Saxon and Norman Kings*, 24.

77. *Edward II*, directed by Derek Jarman (BBC/Working Title, 1991); *Siege of the Saxons*, directed by Nathan Juran (Columbia Pictures, 1963).

78. Cary Elwes as Robin Hood, in *Robin Hood: Men in Tights*.

79. For more on this dehumanization, see also chapter 3, "Knighthood as Institution."

80. This notion that a foreign ruler cannot accede to the throne seems to be a predominantly filmic device. From historical evidence, we know that foreign accession was by no means rare (in the case of England alone). It is — for reasons which seem obvious — during wartime or periods of national crisis that such a rejection of foreign leaders is at its most vehement in the cinema. Compare, for example, the two versions of *Prince Valiant*, in which the nationalistic element is significantly stronger in Hathaway's version, made during the Cold War and McCarthy era, than the 1997 version, whose agenda was more feminist than nationalist.

81. Here we might also note the representation of John in both *Ivanhoe* and *Prince of Thieves* as a somewhat slippery and sneering coward.

82. Prince Geoffrey to (future King) John in *The Lion in Winter*.

83. *The Princess Bride*, directed by Rob Reiner (Buttercup Films Ltd., 1987).

84. In fact, an argument might convincingly be made that in this respect he adheres to the same interfilmic character development as Currie and Aylmer (see section 2.1, above), in that he had previously played not only the role of an outlaw in the Richard Green TV series *The Adventures of Robin Hood*, but would also be known to the world as evil genius/Bond villain Hans Glaubin *A View to a Kill* in 1985, two years before *The Princess Bride*, thus disbarring him from an ideal and appropriate kingship in the public mentality.

85. A trope also used to great effect with King Théoden in *The Lord of the Rings*.

86. *The Black Shield of Falworth*, directed by Rudolph Maté (Universal International Pictures, 1954).

87. Elizabeth I in *The Virgin Queen*, directed by Coky Giedroyc (BBC Pictures, 2005).

88. A contention confirmed by director himself on the special features of the DVD, in which he observes that having first seen Thewlis as

Naked's Johnny, he considered his on-screen persona to be ideally suited to the role.

89. *Merlin: The Return*, directed by Paul Matthews (Peakviewing Productions, 2000); *Berserker: Hell's Warrior*, also directed by Matthews (PeakViewing Transatlantic, 2001).

90. In fact, this medieval typecasting was to continue from there. Robert Addie was later to play Brother Arris in *Crossbow* (a William Tell teleseries made by Cinecom and RHI), a later version of the Sherwood saga in *The New Adventures of Robin Hood*, before ultimately returning to feature-length TV productions in Steve Barron's *Merlin* and *A Knight in Camelot* (both 1998).

91. Here I am using, for brevity's sake, narrative terminology derived from the Three Act Structure model taken from Syd Field, *Screenplay: The Foundations of Screenwriting* (New York: Dell Publishing, 1984).

92. *Ibid.*, 31.

93. *The Messenger: The Story of Joan of Arc*, directed by Luc Besson (Gaumont, 1999).

94. Which again draws on classical mythology for validation, Rufus Sewell reusing the same persona as his portrayal of a cruel, despotic Agamemnon in John Kent Harrison's 2003 *Helen of Troy*.

95. Though Propp's concept of the lack/shortage is classified as that which arises as a direct result from villainy, I am here using it in its secondary sense, as an essential "shortage which promulgates the quest." See Vladimir Propp, *Morphology of the Folktale* (Austin: University of Texas Press, 1968), 35–36.

96. A name borrowed perhaps from Henry V, or the Grimm Brothers' fairy tale *The Magic Fountain*, adapted for the cinema in 1961, two years before the release of *Siege of the Saxons*.

97. The remaining two films are—as we shall see below—*A Kid in King Arthur's Court*, directed by Michael Gottlieb (Walt Disney Pictures, 1995) and the two cinematic versions of *Prince Valiant* (1954 and 1998), which I have counted as one given that both are clearly adaptations of the same text.

98. The character of Robert Marshall is here dragged somewhat inexplicably into the Arthuriad, either totally invented or feasibly a garbled memory of William Marshal, given that both were landless in origin, and gained power and status by martial prowess.

99. Though it must be noted that this was, in fact, an important factor in the recognition of women's contribution to government. As the dynastic importance of monarchical succession grows, so does the importance of the royal woman as progenitor; Duggan writes that "the key role of royal women in the area of dynastic continuity ... extended far beyond the purely biological acts of conception and birth." Duggan, *Queens and Queenship in Medieval Europe*, xviii.

100. In films such as *Tank Girl* (1995), *GI Jane* (1997), *Girlfight* (2000), *Lara Croft: Tomb Raider* (2001), and *Resident Evil* (2002).

101. See Duggan, *Queens and Queenship in Medieval Europe.*

Chapter 5

1. *The Lion in Winter*, directed by Anthony Harvey (1968).

2. Anton K. Kozlovic, "Saint Cinema: The Construction of St. Francis of Assisi in Franco Zeffirelli's *Brother Sun, Sister Moon*," *Journal of Religion and Popular Culture* 2 (Fall 2002): 1–21.

3. Johan H. Huizinga, *The Waning of the Middle Ages* (Harmondsworth: Penguin Books Ltd., 2001), 65.

4. "Eurent alors le sentiment d'appartenir à un même ensemble d'institutions, de croyances et d'habitudes: la chrétienté." Jacques Le Goff and Jean-Louis Schlegel, *Le Moyen Âge expliqué aux enfants* (Paris: Seuil, 2006), 89 (my translation).

5. G. G. Coulton, *The Medieval Scene: An Informal Introduction to the Middle Ages* (Cambridge: Cambridge University Press, 1960).

6. Peter Tremayne, *Our Lady of Darkness: A Celtic Mystery* (London: Headline, 2000), vii–xiv.

7. Maurice Keen, *A History of Medieval Europe* (London: Routledge and Kegan Paul, 1967), 61.

8. Isaiah 22:33. This duality of the kingship, along with the secular and spiritual powers, is, as we saw in the previous chapter, a far more complicated argument than I have intimated here, as the long dispute throughout the late twelfth and early thirteenth century attests. Nevertheless, let it be said that for our purposes the ferocity of the argumentation itself (and the extent of the debate) is sufficient to indicate that there was a profound entanglement of spiritual and secular matters, meaning that we cannot pretend that the place of the medieval priest in society was limited only to the spiritual realm.

9. François Amy de la Bretèque, *L'Imaginaire médiéval dans le cinéma occidental* (Paris: Champion, 2004), 94.

10. Exchange between lawyer Richard Courtois and Priest Albertius in *The Advocate.*

11. See Henri Pirenne, *Medieval Cities: Their Origins and the Revival of Trade* (Princeton: Princeton University Press, 1925).

12. Norman Cantor, *Inventing the Middle Ages: The Lives, Works, and Ideas of the Great Me-*

dievalists of the Twentieth Century (New York: William Morrow & Company, 1991), 23.

13. A. R. Myers, England in the Late Middle Ages (Harmondsworth: Penguin Books, 1952; repr. 1965), 68.

14. Eileen Power, Medieval People (Harmondsworth: Penguin, 1924; 1937; 1951), 24.

15. As, of course, happens with the physical construction of the Christian churches on the original footprint of pagan or non–Christian worshipping sites as both a visual and metaphorical reminder of the mutual exclusivity of the two religions. Perhaps the clearest example of this can be seen in the conversion of Rome from pagan epicenter to home of the Vatican, as described in John R. Curran, Pagan City and Christian Capital (Oxford: Clarendon, 2000). This process, however, seems to have already happened in the Romano-Celtic temples built on already sacred sites, according to Ken Dowden, European Paganism: The Realities of Cult from Antiquity to the Middle Ages (London: Routledge, 1999), 143, which may well have been the case in the European Middle Ages. Nevertheless, in either case, the conflation of the two — as opposed to their confrontation — is more likely to have been the model followed.

16. For more on this fascinating character, see Daron Burrows, The Stereotype of the Priest in the Old French Fabliaux: Anti-clerical Satire and Lay Identity (Bern, Oxford: Peter Lang, 2005).

17. Ibid., 205.

18. Alec Guinness as Pope Innocent III in Brother Sun, Sister Moon (Fratello Sole, Sorella Luna), directed by Franco Zeffirelli (Euro International Film, 1972).

19. Francesco, Giullare di Dio, directed by Roberto Rossellini (Rizzoli, 1950).

20. The Reckoning, directed by Paul Mc-Guigan (Renaissance Films, 2004).

21. For a full explanation of this iconic construction of the peasantry, see chapter 6, "Those Who Work," especially section 2.1.

22. "There had been for centuries laws forbidding the clergy to marry, but they had never been strictly enforced over most of Europe." Christopher Brooke, From Alfred to Henry III: 871–1272 (London: Sphere Books, 1969), 144.

23. Lord Robert to Monsignor Alvaro in Elizabeth, directed by Shekhar Kapur (Polygram/Working Title, 1998).

24. Friedrich Heer, The Medieval World: Europe 1100–1350, translated by Janet Sondheimer (New York: George Weidenfeld and Nicolson, 1962), 59.

25. Huizinga, The Waning of the Middle Ages, 56.

26. R. W. Southern, Making of the Middle Ages (London: Hutchinson, 1967), 127.

27. Karl August Fink, Papsttum und Kirche im abendländishen Mittelalter (München, Dt. Taschenbuch Verlag, 1994), my translation from Chiesa e Papato nel Medioevo (Bologna: Il Mulino, 1987), 95.

28. Keen, A History of Medieval Europe, 135.

29. Brooke, From Alfred to Henry III, 146.

30. Keen, A History of Medieval Europe, 317.

31. Writings of the Anonymous of York, quoted in Southern, Making of the Middle Ages, 91.

32. "Unam Sanctam," in Select Historical Documents, edited by E. Henderson (London: Bohn, 1892).

33. John of Salisbury, The Statesman's Book of John of Salisbury: Being the Fourth, Fifth, and Sixth Books, and Selections from the Seventh and Eighth Books, of the Policraticus (New York: Russell & Russell, 1963), quoted in James Bruce Ross and Mary Martin McLaughlin (eds.), The Portable Medieval Reader (Harmondsworth: Penguin, 1949; repr 1977), 255; see also Frederick Barbarossa's assertion of "the Independence of the Temporal Authority" in Frederick Barbarossa, "The Independence of the Temporal Authority," in Ross and McLaughlin, The Portable Medieval Reader, 259.

34. Most notably epic films of the Cinemascope era, dealing with Biblical tales or classical antiquity, which became famous for the sumptuous lavishness of their sets. Though there is yet to appear a study of this theory, I have proposed elsewhere that the frames of the screens, too, might well have influenced these decisions, since the horizontal elongation of the screen removes the possibility of creating vertical hierarchies, and therefore a new set of signs to indicate elevation must have become necessary.

35. Quoted in Betty Demby, "An Interview with Franco Zeffirelli," Filmmakers Newsletter 6, no. 11 (1973): 33.

36. There is also a suggestion here of the separation of the pope as king and the pope as human being, that the status exists even when Innocent leaves the throne. This would therefore be an extension and visual evocation of the king's two bodies mentioned above and in chapter 4.

37. Ladyhawke, directed by Richard Donner (20th Century–Fox/Warner Bros., 1985).

38. See Heer, The Medieval World, and Power, Medieval People, in which this concept of lordship is explained in more depth.

39. Krzyzacy / The Knights of the Teutonic Order, directed by Aleksander Ford (Zespol Filmowy, 1960).

40. As in, for example, Ladyhawke, in which Navarre (Rutger Hauer) kneels before a makeshift cross formed by simply driving his sword into the ground. See also Monty Python and the Holy Grail, directed by Terry Jones and

Terry Gilliam (Python Pictures/Michael White Productions, 1975); *Kingdom of Heaven,* directed by Ridley Scott (20th Century–Fox, 2005); and *Les Visiteurs,* directed by Jean-Marie Poire (Canal+/France 3, 1993), in all three of which victory in battle is followed by a prayer using the sword (blade downwards) as a makeshift cross.

41. "À part de la société féodale, il existait une division plus importante: celle des 'clercs' et des 'laïcs.'" Goff and Schlegel, *Le Moyen Âge expliqué aux enfants,* 60 (my translation).

42. Heer, *The Medieval World,* 61.

43. *Ibid.,* 62.

44. Southern, *Making of the Middle Ages,* 152.

45. *Ibid.,* 149 (emphasis added).

46. Power, *Medieval People,* 92.

47. Keen, *A History of Medieval Europe,* 62.

48. Southern, *Making of the Middle Ages,* 154.

49. Myers, *England in the Late Middle Ages,* 60.

50. Coulton, *The Medieval Scene,* 82.

51. See, for instance, *Le Bouchier d'Abevile,* among others.

52. Burrows, *The Stereotype of the Priest in the Old French Fabliaux,* 201.

53. However, an over-reliance on this argument would necessitate a comprehensive study of the audiences of both fabliaux and courtly tales, which clearly reaches beyond our present concerns here. Consequently, I am following Schenck's arguments that "courtly literature and the fabliau are merely reverse images of each other," in Mary Jane Stearns Schenck, *The Fabliaux: Tales of Wit and Deception* (Amsterdam, Philadelphia: John Benjamins, 1987), 11, which would mean that if both traditions are constructing the same image of the monk, then it seems reasonably safe to assert that this image was held at different levels of society.

54. Geoffrey Chaucer, "General Prologue," line 269, in *The Riverside Chaucer,* edited by Larry D. Benson (Oxford: Oxford University, 1988).

55. Coulton, *The Medieval Scene,* 81.

56. Mikhail Bakhtin, *Rabelais and His World,* translated by Helene Iswolsky (Bloomington: Indiana University Press, 1984), 86.

57. William of Baskerville, *The Name of the Rose,* directed by Jean-Jacques Annaud (Neue Constantin Film / ZDF, 1986).

58. Coulton, *The Medieval Scene,* 82.

59. Jacques Le Goff, *Intellectuals in the Middle Ages* (Cambridge, MA; Oxford: Blackwell, 1993).

60. For a full evaluation of the figure of the detective and his semiotic process of deduction, see Umberto Eco and Thomas A. Sebeok, *The Sign of Three: Dupin, Holmes, Peirce* (Bloomington: Indiana University Press, 1983). For an ex-

position of the reverse argument — that a modern detective can function like a medieval monk — see my own article, "Mr. Monk and the Medieval Monks," in *Mr. Monk and Philosophy,* edited by Dylan E. Wittkower (Chicago, IL: Open Court Publishing, 2009): 159–60.

61. *The Return of Martin Guerre,* directed by Daniel Vigne (Dussault/France 3, 1982).

62. Nickolas Haydock, *Movie Medievalism: The Imaginary Middle Ages* (Jefferson, NC: McFarland, 2008), 32.

63. *The Adventures of Robin Hood,* directed by Michael Curtiz (Warner Bros. Pictures, 1938).

64. Coulton, *The Medieval Scene,* 84.

65. Anne K. Kaler, "Who is That Monk in the Hood?: Friar Tuck, Francis of Assisi, and Robin Hood," *Journal of Popular Culture* 30, no. 4 (Spring 1997): 59.

66. *Ibid.,* 51.

67. Stephen Knight, *Robin Hood: A Mythic Biography* (Ithaca, New York: Cornell University Press, 2003), xi.

68. Dario Fo, *Mistero Buffo: Comic Mysteries* (London: Methuen, 1969; 1988), 8.

69. Played by Michael McShane in *Robin Hood: Prince of Thieves,* and by Jeff Nuttall in *Robin Hood,* directed by John Irvin (20th Century–Fox, 1991).

70. *Stealing Heaven,* directed by Clive Donner (Amy International/Film Dallas/Jadran, 1988).

71. This approach, rather ironically, aligns him with the titular Prince of Thieves, since both come to be icons of the privileged helping the poor, rather than symbols of a real "grassroots" revolution. The undertone, consequently, comes to be rather the reverse of what the popular legend of Robin was about, that of the "nobility" of the outlaws rather than the rather condescending necessity for the rich to stoop to help the poor.

72. Knight, *Robin Hood,* xi.

73. "Si sviluppa su se stesso, con piccoli slittamenti progressivi: dal bandito al fuorilegge gentiluomo, da questo al nobile fuorilegge e infine al ribelle politico per una giusta causa." Matteo Sanfilippo, *Robin Hood: La Vera Storia* (Firenze: Giunti, 1997), 58 (my translation).

74. I am not necessarily arguing here that Brooks is furthering a scholarly in-joke, but rather that the joke only works because of its seeming incongruity within the Middle Ages, which does suggest a proportional invisibility of Jews in artistic (if not historical) representations of the period. See also Norman F. Cantor, *The Sacred Chain: A History of the Jews* (London: HarperCollins, 1994).

75. Notably Thomas Hahn, *Robin Hood in Popular Culture: Violence, Transgression, and Jus-*

tice (Cambridge: D. S. Brewer, 2000); Kaler, "Who is that Monk in the Hood?"; Knight, *Robin Hood*; and Sanfilippo, *Robin Hood*, to name only a few.

76. At the time of writing, this series has entered its third season, and tellingly the BBC version has finally resolved this contentious issue by including a black medicine man who is designed to assume the "spiritual" role of the sub-king paradigm which we saw in chapter 4 (section 3.2), with Little John assuming the physical counterpart to Robin's kingship. The whole topic of religion in the sense of an institution is still, however, entirely avoided.

77. See also Andrew Fiala, "Crusades, Just Wars and the Bush Doctrine," *Peace Review* 19, no. 2 (April 2007), 165–172. For an insightful overview of parallels made between the two phenomena, see Nickolas Haydock and E. L. Risden (eds.), *Hollywood in the Holy Land: Essays on Film Depictions of the Crusades and Christian-Muslim Clashes* (Jefferson, NC: McFarland, 2009), especially Haydock's introduction, "The Unseen Cross upon the Breast: Medievalism, Orientalism, and Discontent," 1–30.

78. See, for instance, Emma Campbell's recent *Medieval Saints' Lives: The Gift, Kinship and Community in Old French Hagiography* (Woodbridge: Boydell and Brewer, 2008), something of a call to arms for a modern re-evaluation of the hagiographic tradition to reach a greater understanding not only of the chronicled saints, but of the "kinship" communities in which they were located.

79. André Vauchez, *Sainthood in the Later Middle Ages* (Cambridge: Cambridge University Press, 1997), 141.

80. "Deux personnages de l'histoire qui ont connu la plus grande popularité à l'écran...." François Amy de la Bretèque, "Au 'temps des Cathédrales': En hommage à Georges Duby, historien, biographe, et ... scénariste de film." *Cahiers de la Cinémathèque* 42/43 (1985): 27 (my translation).

81. Vauchez, *Sainthood in the Later Middle Ages*, 87.

82. Franco Zeffirelli, *Franco Zeffirelli: The Autobiography* (London: Arena, 1987), 239–240. Quoted in Kozlovic, "Saint Cinema," 2.

83. Kozlovic, "Saint Cinema," 8.

84. *Ibid.*, 9.

85. "Respecter les données de l'histoire c'est apercevoir que François d'Assise a, dans son temps, opéré une révolution, mais pas n'importe laquelle, pas une révolution telle qu'on la voit aujourd'hui." Jean-François Six, "François d'Assise," *Cahiers de la Cinémathèque*, 42/43 (1985): 34 (my translation).

86. Mario Aste, "Zeffirelli's Personal Encounter with St. Francis: Brother Sun, Sister Moon," *Romance Languages Annual* III (1991): 1–17. Quoted in Kozlovic, "Saint Cinema," 7.

87. Marion A. Habig, *St. Francis of Assisi: Writings and Early Biographies: English Omnibus of the Sources for the Life of St. Francis* (Chicago, IL: Franciscan Herald Press, 1983), 247. Quoted in Kaler, "Who is that Monk in the Hood?" 68.

88. Kozlovic, "Saint Cinema," 1.

89. *Ibid.*, 9. For more on color symbolism, see also Michel Pastoureau, *Une Histoire Symbolique Du Moyen Âge Occidental* (Paris: Seuil, 2004), especially "Voir les couleurs du Moyen Âge," 113–209.

90. Viewer comments on the Internet Movie Database, accessed at http://us.imdb.com/title/tt0069824/usercomments-3.

91. Kozlovic, "Saint Cinema," 12.

92. Norman F. Cantor, *The Encyclopedia of the Middle Ages* (New York: Viking, 1999), 398.

93. Given the volume of existing material on Joan in the cinema, it seems unnecessarily repetitious to conduct an in-depth study here. For a full review of films relating to the life of Joan of Arc, see Kevin J. Harty, "Jeanne au cinéma," in *Fresh Verdicts on Joan of Arc*, edited by Bonnie Wheeler and Charles T. Wood (New York: Garland, 1996); Sylvie F. Richards, "Keeping Up with the Joans: The Maid of Orleans in Literature and Film," *West Virginia University Philological Papers*, 2000; chapter 6 of John Aberth, *A Knight at the Movies: Medieval History on Film* (New York and London: Routledge, 2003), 257–298; and Gelda Lerner, "Joan of Arc: Three Films," in *Past Imperfect: History According to the Movies* (London: Cassell, 1996), 54–59. Bibliographic information can further be found in Kevin J. Harty, *The Reel Middle Ages: American, Western and Eastern European, Middle Eastern, and Asian Films About Medieval Europe* (Jefferson, NC: McFarland, 1999), and Nadia Margolis, *Joan of Arc in History, Literature, and Film* (New York: Garland, 1990). Although I have been unable to obtain a copy, it seems that a more in-depth study can be found in Margaret J. Maddox, *Portrayals of Joan of Arc in Film: From Historical Joan to Her Mythological Daughters* (New York: Edwin Mellen, 2008).

94. See in particular Martha W. Driver and Sid Ray (eds.), *The Medieval Hero on Screen: Representations from Beowulf to Buffy* (Jefferson, NC: McFarland, 2004).

95. "Que François fascine tout ensemble les pieux fervents qui cherchent une communauté fusionelle et les révoltés qui se dressent contre les injustices à quelque chose d'étonnant." Six, "François d'Assise," 30.

96. Roger Ebert, *I Hated, Hated, Hated This Movie* (Kansas City: Andrews McMeel Publishing, 2000), 59–61.

97. *Ibid.*, 60.

98. *Il Decameron*, directed by Pier Paulo Pasolini (Produzioni Europee Associati/Artemis Film, 1971). The "trilogia" also includes *I Racconti di Canterbury (The Canterbury Tales)* (Produzioni Europee Associati, 1972) and *Il Fiore delle mille e una notte (Arabian Nights)* (Produzioni Europee Associati, 1974).

99. "Une fois mort, Cepparello devient Saint Chapelet, au terme du processus qui, une nouvelle fois, inverse les valeurs 'sacrées': les saints sont des gredins arrivés, et les gredins sont des saints en devenir, si toutefois ils respectent la règle du jeu: une 'bonne' confession." Guy Freixe, "Approche du Décameron de Pier Paulo Pasolini," *Cahiers de la Cinémathèque* 42/43 (1985): 149 (my translation).

Chapter 6

1. Opening titles to *The Advocate*.

2. A qualification is, however, here necessary, in my use of the term "those who work." Given the growing ranks of what we might nowadays call "professionals" in the form of notaries, lawyers, and so on, it is clear that by the late medieval period there were substantial numbers of "workers" who fall outside of the present study. In this chapter, therefore, I am focusing on those involved in manual labor whom thinkers most probably had in mind when they originally divided society into *oratores*, *bellatores*, *laborares*, the semantic field of the latter term not quite matching up to our modern understanding of "work."

3. Terry Jones's opening narration to his series, *Medieval Lives*, series 1, episode 8 (BBC television, first aired January 24, 2004).

4. John of Salisbury, "The Body Social": "a Commonwealth, according to Plutarch, is a certain body which is endowed with life." Quoted in James Bruce Ross and Mary Martin McLaughlin (eds.), *The Portable Medieval Reader* (Harmondsworth: Penguin, 1949; repr. 1977), 47–48. I have also used the term "the body politic" elsewhere to describe the same phenomenon, since I believe it more accurately depicts the political (rather than directly social) arrangement of feudal society.

5. John of Salisbury, *The Statesman's Book*, quoted in Norman F. Cantor (ed.), *The Medieval Reader* (New York: HarperCollins, 1994), 129.

6. Quoted in Johan H. Huizinga, *The Waning of the Middle Ages* (Harmondsworth: Penguin Books Ltd., 2001), 56 (added emphasis).

7. Here I am thinking of the grand histories which tell us that Nelson won the battle of Trafalgar by attacking enemy ships from close quarters, which becomes a form of historical metonymy since it was, naturally Nelson's forces which were deployed in this way — or perhaps even more significantly if the supposed agent did not actually take part in the battle, then the "forgotten" nature of the militants is even more extreme.

8. Christopher Brooke, *From Alfred to Henry III: 871–1272* (London: Sphere Books, 1969), 123.

9. Eileen Power, *Medieval People* (Harmondsworth: Penguin, 1924; 1937; 1951), 33.

10. "Les paysans sont, à quelques exceptions notables près, les grands absents du cinéma historique." François Amy de la Bretèque, *L'Imaginaire médiéval dans le cinéma occidental* (Paris: Champion, 2004), 1046.

11. Robert A. Rosenstone, *History on Film/Film on History* (Harlow: Longman/Pearson, 2006), 47.

12. Though in this case, rather disappointingly, she is not.

13. See, for example, *The War of the Worlds*, *Armageddon*, *The Day After Tomorrow*, and *Signs*, for example, in which the "average Joe" protagonist reacts to national catastrophes by thoroughly — and endearingly — mundane responses.

14. E. M. Forster, *Aspects of the Novel: and Related Writings* (Harmondsworth: Penguin, 1988), 73–81.

15. Count Adhemar (Rufus Sewell) in *A Knight's Tale*.

16. Sally Harvey, "The Knight and the Knight's Fee in England," *Past and Present*, 49 (November 1970): 4.

17. Brooke, *From Alfred to Henry III*, 125, quoting a remark alleged to have been made by Eileen Power.

18. R. W. Southern, *Making of the Middle Ages* (London: Hutchinson, 1967), 98.

19. *Ibid.*, 96.

20. Brooke, *From Alfred to Henry III*, 128.

21. Dennis the Peasant's opinions on feudal society in *Monty Python and the Holy Grail*.

22. I am here consciously paraphrasing Eco's celebrated dictum "un mondo di segni," taken from Umberto Eco, *Il segno* (Milano: Mondadori, 1980), 13.

23. Huizinga, *The Waning of the Middle Ages*, 124, though such a statement does cause us to question how he could know this to be the case. Could Huizinga, too, be interpreting the peasant class through his own ideological perspective?

24. "Filmer l'histoire, c'est filmer les luttes populaires, la lutte des classes." Jacques Aumont, "L'histoire au Cinéma: Comment on écrit l'histoire," *Cahiers du Cinéma* (May-June 1972): 71 (my translation and emphasis).

25. "Dans le cinéma, au niveau des représentatives, féodalité peut être présentée comme l'an-

tithèse de chevalerie." Amy de la Bretèque, *L'imaginaire médiéval*, 1046 (my translation).

26. Aumont, "L'histoire au Cinéma," 65–66. For a discussion of iconography, see also Jonathan Alexander, "Labeur and Paresse: Ideological Representations of Medieval Peasant Labor," *The Art Bulletin* 72, no. 3 (1990): 436–452.

27. "Signes extérieures du film 'historique.'" Aumont, "L'histoire au Cinéma," 66 (my translation).

28. See A. E. Christa Canitz, "'Historians ... Will Say I Am a Liar': The Ideology of False Truth Claims in Mel Gibson's 'Braveheart' and Luc Besson's 'The Messenger,'" in *Studies in Medievalism XIII: Postmodern Medievalisms*, edited by Richard Utz and Jesse G. Swan, 127–142 (Cambridge and Rochester: D. S. Brewer, 2004); T. Edensor, "Reading Braveheart: Representing and Contesting Scottish Identity," *Scottish Affairs* (1997): 135–158; Michael D. Sharp, "Remaking Medieval Heroism: Nationalism and Sexuality in Braveheart," *Florilegium* 15, no. 1 (1998): 251–266. Another interesting perspective comes from another Scottish medievalist, Sharon Krossa, who provides a shot-by-shot breakdown of factual and conceptual errors in the opening 2.5 minutes of the film (see http://medievalscotland.org/scotbiblio/bravehearterrors.shtml).

29. Elizabeth Ewan, "Review: [Braveheart, Rob Roy]," *The American Historical Review*, 100, 4 (1995): 1219.

30. *Ibid.*, 1220.

31. Maurice Keen, *A History of Medieval Europe* (London: Routledge and Kegan Paul, 1967), 49.

32. Marc Bloch, *Feudal Society*, translated by L. A. Manyon (London: Routledge & Kegan Paul, 1962), 160.

33. Southern, *Making of the Middle Ages*, 101.

34. Keen, *A History of Medieval Europe*, 236.

35. Quoted in Mary Jane Stearns Schenck, *The Fabliaux: Tales of Wit and Deception* (Amsterdam, Philadelphia: John Benjamins, 1987), xiii. This binary opposition can, in fact, be used as the basis of entire films, such as Poiré's *Les Visiteurs* and — to a greater extent — in its very poor remake, *Just Visiting*.

36. *Flesh & Blood* (aka *The Rose and the Sword*), directed by Paul Verhoeven (Impala/Riverside Pictures, 1985).

37. Umberto Eco, *Travels in Hyperreality: Essays*, translated by William Weaver (London: Picador, 1987), 69.

38. David Williams, "Medieval Movies," *The Yearbook of English Studies* 20 (1990): 10.

39. Susan Aronstein and Nancy Coiner. "Twice Knightly: Democratizing the Middle Ages for Middle-Class America," *Studies in Medievalism* 6 (1994): 213.

40. The squire's name, Jacquouille, is itself a crass joke which plays on the name Jacques and "couille" (testicle). The pun was successfully retained in the English translation by calling him "Jacquasse" (which would be pronounced "Jackass").

41. Exchange between Prince Einon (David Thewlis) and his henchman, Brok, in *Dragonheart*.

42. Aumont, "L'histoire au Cinéma," 65–66. See also Alexander, "Labeur and Paresse."

43. Aumont, "L'histoire au Cinéma," 66.

44. Though even this may have been influenced by, for example, Rossellini's *Francesco, Giullare di Dio*, in turn preceded by Eisenstein's *Alexander Nevsky*. The most important detail here (and the reason why I cite the MGM historicals) is not that it represents necessarily the *first* instance but the most widespread instances. These latter therefore emerged as the moment at which they became *codified* as symbols of peasantry.

45. It is interesting to suggest that the modern world has perhaps come to re-imagine its own medieval past through the cinematographic images discussed here, rather than by any other route, a suggestion supported by sites like Medieval Collectibles (http://www.medievalcollectibles.com/). The site offers a range of medieval and Renaissance clothing based seemingly not in historical accuracy but on "figures obligées" drawn — one can only assume — from the cinema, which act as indices of popular memory, such as "Robin Hood hats," "Henry VIII" or "Rembrandt" hats, or even the seemingly oxymoronic "Deluxe Medieval Hood" for the peasant.

46. "Le support chromatique le plus présent dans la vie quotidienne"; "contrairement à l'idée reçue, au Moyen Âge tous les vêtements sont teints, y compris ceux des classes les plus pauvres." Michel Pastoureau, *Une Histoire Symbolique Du Moyen Âge Occidental* (Paris: Seuil, 2004), 129 (both translations my own).

47. *Timeline*, directed by Richard Donner (Paramount Pictures, 2003).

48. *The Navigator: A Mediaeval Odyssey*, directed by Vincent Ward (Arenafilm/NZ Film Commission, 1988).

49. I have conducted a more in-depth discussion of this relationship in my unpublished research paper, "Reframing the Past: The Effects of Technology on Historical Films."

50. *The 13th Warrior*, directed by John McTiernan (Touchstone Pictures, 1999).

51. Accessible online at http://jeriwesterson.typepad.com/my_weblog/2008/05/top-ten-myths-a.html. The list has been written and compiled by modern writer of medieval fiction Jeri Westerson. See also James Franklin's inter-

esting site at http://web.maths.unsw.edu.au/~jim/medmyths.html.

52. Though, on this latter point, the BBC article narrates an interesting (if counter-intuitive) argument put forward by the British Dental Association that medieval teeth were considerably better cared for than we imagine. Jane Elliott's article, "Medieval Teeth — Better than Baldrick's," remains accessible on the BBC archive, at http://news.bbc.co.uk/1/hi/health/3722598.stm (last accessed 23 November 2009).

53. Ergo the Magnificent, *Krull*, directed by Peter Yates (Columbia Pictures, 1983).

54. Alexander, "Labeur and Paresse," 436.

55. Erwin Panofsky, *Early Netherlandish Painting: Its Origins and Character* (Princeton, NJ: Princeton University Press, 1953), 66 (quoted in Alexander, "Labeur and Paresse," 438).

56. "Cursed is the ground because of you; through painful toil you will eat of it all the days of your life. It will produce thorns and thistles for you, and you will eat the plants of the field. By the sweat of your brow you will eat your food until you return to the ground, since from it you were taken; for dust you are and to dust you will return" (Genesis 3:17–19).

57. Southern, *Making of the Middle Ages*, 98.

58. "Au Moyen Âge les hommes et les femmes, même modestes, étaient souvent en chemin soit pour changer de seignerie ou de ville (parce qu'ils pensaient y trouver des avantages, vivre mieux, etc.), soit pour aller dans une foire, soit pour se rendre sur un lieu de pélerinage" Jacques Le Goff and Jean-Louis Schlegel, *Le Moyen Âge expliqué aux enfants* (Paris: Seuil, 2006), 72 (my translation).

59. Dennis the Peasant in *Monty Python and the Holy Grail*.

60. "On remarque surtout le 'jeunisme' caractéristique d'autres films moyenâgeux de la même époque"; "Woodstock n'est pas loin." Amy de la Bretèque, *Imaginaire médiéval*, 211 (my translation).

61. See chapter 4: "Those Who Rule." The quotation here is from Bloch, *Feudal Society*, 73.

62. *The Seven Samurai*, directed by Akira Kurosawa (Toho Company, 1954).

63. David Salo, "Heroism and Alienation through Language in *The Lord of the Rings*," in *The Medieval Hero on Screen: Representations from Beowulf to Buffy*, edited by Martha W. Driver and Sid Ray (Jefferson, NC: McFarland, 2004), 23–37.

64. Michelle Nayman, "The Navigator: Vincent Ward's Past Dreams of the Future," *Cinema Papers* 69 (May 1988): 30.

65. This concept will be discussed in more detail later. While I recognize that I am here risking a conflation of villager with village, I will explain in section 3.2 why such a conflation can often be appropriate.

66. See also Michel Pastoureau, "Lumière ou matière?," *Une Histoire Symbolique*, 136–139.

67. Umberto Eco, *On Literature* (London: Vintage, 2006), 18.

68. *Jabberwocky*, directed by Terry Gilliam (Python Films/Umbrella Films, 1977).

69. Though it is never explicitly stated, it seems possible that this Dennis might well be an extended characterization of the Python's Marxist peasant, given the humor of the incongruous name and the fact that both roles are played by Michael Palin.

70. *Just Visiting*, directed by Jean-Marie Poiré (Gaumont, 2001).

71. Other films to make use of this notion include *The War Lord* and *Dragonheart*, with very different degrees of success. For more on this, see Alain Boureau, *Le Droit de Cuissage: La Fabrication d'un Mythe* (Paris: Albin Michel, 1995).

72. Paul Freedman, "Review: [Le Droit de Cuissage: La Fabrication d'un Mythe (XIIIe–XXe Siècle)]," *Speculum* 71, no. 3 (1996): 696–697.

73. *Jungfrukällan (The Virgin Spring)*, directed by Ingmar Bergman (Svensk Filmindustri, 1960).

74. *The Black Knight*, directed by Tay Garnett (Warwick Film Productions, 1954).

75. One might note here that the prevalence of the word "black" in the titles of such films is perhaps an indication of this notion of disguise, especially so, considering the use of the black or white knight in medieval literary precedents, who were often used as a means of disguising the hero's identity.

76. These, as we will see below, include cinematic "hoi polloi" like the foot soldier, the revolutionary crowd, the Victorian "poor," the street urchin; when in Hollywood, however, this hierarchical structure is frequently translated into a racial distinction, producing the classic Others of the Mexican or the Native American, as well as the alterity outlined in the series of blaxploitation films appearing during the 1970s, which assumed a racial polarity broadly comparable to the feudal divisions here, in that the structural/hierarchical arrangement of society is deemed to be inflexible and pre-ordained from birth.

77. It is interesting to note that in this film, perhaps more than any other, Reynolds is playing on the star-system in order to show that his "simple folk" are in fact noble souls. His Merrie Men, for example, include Christian Slater (from *The Name of the Rose*), Nick Brimble (as Little John), who had previously appeared in two William Tell productions and *Robin of Sherwood*, in

which latter production he appeared alongside Daniel Peacock, who also played an outlaw in *Prince of Thieves*, as well as household names like Morgan Freeman and Kevin Costner.

78. Robert A. Rosenstone, "The Historical Film: Looking at the Past in a Postliterate Age," in *The Historical Film: History and Memory in Media*, edited by Marcia Landy (New Brunswick, NJ: Rutgers University Press, 2001), 60–61.

79. Alexander, "Labeur and Paresse," 436.

80. Here we encounter well-worn territory reprised almost wholesale from the tales of persecution and triumph over adversity which have been played out most famously in that other "sporting" arena: the Coliseum. The narrative structure of *Knight's Tale* thus bears a striking resemblance with *Ben Hur*, *Spartacus*, and *Gladiator*, which all represent their "peasantry" as enslaved nobles rebelling against a corrupt regime.

81. Marc Ferro, *Cinéma et histoire* (Paris: Denoël, 1977), 163.

82. Rosenstone, "Looking at the Past in a Postliterate Age," 55.

83. Of which, of course, both Ferro and le Goff were prominent figures.

Chapter 7

1. David Williams, "Medieval Movies," *The Yearbook of English Studies* 20 (1990): 3.

2. See, for example, Richard Barber, *The Knight and Chivalry* (Woodbridge, Suffolk: Boydell Press, 1995), which requires no fewer than 415 pages merely to elaborate the varying status of the knight both diachronically and, given that the knight had various duties within different societies, even synchronically.

3. William D. Paden, "I Learned It at the Movies: Teaching Medieval Film," in *Studies in Medievalism XIII: Postmodern Medievalisms*, edited by Richard Utz and Jesse G. Swan (Cambridge and Rochester: D. S. Brewer, 2004) 79.

4. C. S. Lewis, *The Discarded Image: An Introduction to Medieval and Renaissance Literature* (Cambridge: Cambridge University Press, 1964), 179.

5. Arthur Lindley, "The Ahistoricism of Medieval Film," *Screening the Past* 3 (May 1988): unpaginated.

6. Caroline Jewers, "Hard Day's Knights: *First Knight*, *A Knight's Tale*, and *Black Knight*," in *The Medieval Hero on Screen: Representations from Beowulf to Buffy*, edited by Martha Driver and Sid Ray (Jefferson, NC: McFarland, 2004), 193.

7. "Tous les films postérieurs aux années 50 nécessitent en effet une double lecture: ils se construisent en autoréference, par effets de citation et de réélaboration intertextuelle du corpus des films de chevalerie de ces années là." François Amy de la Bretèque, *L'Imaginaire médiéval dans le cinéma occidental* (Paris: Champion, 2004), 302 (my translation).

8. For more on this, see William F. Woods, "Authenticating Realism in Medieval Film," in Driver and Ray, *The Medieval Hero on Screen*, 38–51. For more on the separation of the worlds, see A. Keith Kelly. "Beyond Historical Accuracy: A Postmodern View of Movies and Medievalism." *Perspicuitas* (February 2004); and my discussion of authenticity and accuracy below, in Chapter 9.

9. Paul Zumthor, *Toward a Medieval Poetics* (Minneapolis: University of Minnesota Press, 1992), xvii.

10. "Puis que des lais ai comencé, / Ja n'iert par mun travail laissé : / Les aventures que j'en sai / Tut par rime je les cunterai." ("Now that I have undertaken these lais / I will not stop leaving any of them untold. / All of the adventures I know, / I will recount them in rhyme to you.") "Yonec," lines 1–4, in Marie de France, *Lais* (Paris: Gallimard, 2000), 222 (my translation).

11. "Por li veul un roumant estraire / D'un molt biel conte d'aventure." ("For her I want to concoct a romance out of a very fine tale of adventure.") Renaut, *Le Bel Inconnu* (Paris: Champion, 2003), lines 4–5 (my translation).

12. Geoffrey of Monmouth, *The History of the Kings of Britain* (Harmondsworth: Penguin, 1966), 51.

13. Stuart Airlie, "Strange Eventful Histories: The Middle Ages in Cinema," in *The Medieval World*, edited by Peter Linehan (London: Routledge, 2001), 177 (emphasis added).

14. Janet M. Ferrier, *Forerunners of the French Novel: An Essay on the Development of the Nouvelle in the Late Middle Ages* (Manchester: Manchester University Press, 1954), 4 (emphasis added).

15. Or more specifically, to those with a particularly ardent semiotic bent, they form a sign of medievality. They do so by signifying a referent which no longer has the same signification to a modern (i.e., twentieth-century) observer, but whose meaning is understood by a consciousness of the archaism of the signified. For example, a conical helmet with nosepiece belongs today in a museum and is a current signifier of the signified /antique object/. However, in film, it signifies that the character is a soldier, that he is drawn from eleventh- or twelfth-century Western Europe, and so on. Therefore, the combination of signifier "helmet" and signified/ twelfth-century soldier/ in cinema functions as a sign which we are to interpret as "this film takes place in twelfth-century Europe."

16. "Ces éléments iconiques qui suffisent à désigner 'le moyen âge.'" Amy de la Bretèque, *Imaginaire médiéval*, 35 (my translation).

17. *Det Sjunde Inseglet (The Seventh Seal)*, directed by Ingmar Bergman (Svensk Filmindustri, 1957).

18. *La Passion Béatrice*, directed by Bertrand Tavernier (AMLF/Cléa Productions, 1987); T. S. Eliot, *Selected Poems* (London: Faber, 1961), line 19 of "The Waste Land," 51–67.

19. Barry Keith Grant, *Film Genre: From Iconography to Ideology* (London: Wallflower, 2007), 11.

20. "*Les Visiteurs* offers a cinematic variation of the Quixotic model with its own combination of cinematic, cultural and social satire." Will McMorran, "*Les Visiteurs* and the Quixotic Text," *French Cultural Studies* 19, no. 2 (2008): 164.

21. *L'Armata Brancaleone*, directed by Mario Monicelli (Fair Film/Vertice Film, 1965); Risi's film is *Le Bon Roi Dagobert*. The original quotation is "d'évoquer toute une série d'aspects religieux et sociaux du moyen âge, en démolissant par la force corrosive du rire les tabous et les valeurs traditionnelles." Pierre-André Sigal, "Brancaleone s'en va-t-aux croisades: Satire d'un moyen-âge conventionnel," *Cahiers de la Cinémathèque, Special edition, Le Moyen Âge au Cinéma*, 42/43 (1985): 152 (my translation).

22. Hans Robert Jauss, *Toward an Aesthetic of Reception* (Brighton: Harvester, 1982), 79.

23. *Ibid.*, 143.

24. Barry Grant, *Film Genre: From Iconography to Ideology* (London: Wallflower, 2007), 8.

25. See Grant, *Film Genre*, chapter 1; and Rick Altman, *Film/Genre* (London: British Film Institute, 1999).

26. Such as the winged and ornate helmets of Fritz Lang's Grail King and court in *Die Nibelungen* (1924), or of the Huns in *Aleksander Nevski*, a motif repeated in *Krzyzacy* (1960) among others.

27. Just one of several technical errors and anachronisms in Jerry Zucker's much-discussed *First Knight*; for a simple list of errors, see http://www.moviemistakes.com/film482. For critical analysis, some of the better material can be found in chapter 3 of Rebecca A. Umland and Samuel J. Umland, *The Use of Arthurian Legend in Hollywood Film: From Connecticut Yankees to Fisher Kings* (Westport, CT: Greenwood Press, 1996), especially 94–100; Robert J. Blanch and Julian N. Wasserman, "Fear of Flyting: The Absence of Internal Tension in *Sword of the Valiant* and *First Knight*," *Arthuriana* 10, no. 4 (2000): 15–32. See also Nickolas Haydock, "Arthurian Melodrama, Chaucerian Spectacle, and the Waywardness of Cinematic Pastiche in *First Knight* and *A Knight's Tale*," in *Film and Fiction: Reviewing the Middle Ages*, edited by Tom Shippey and Martin Arnold (Cambridge: D. S. Brewer, 2003), 5–38.

28. In *Braveheart*; for discussion of the ideological changes see A. E. Christa Canitz, "Historians ... Will Say I am a Liar': The Ideology of False Truth Claims in Mel Gibson's 'Braveheart' and Luc Besson's 'The Messenger' in Utz and Swan, *Postmodern Medievalisms*, 127–142.

29. When his literary predecessor is explicitly introduced as "a gode yeman," and therefore no people's champion and not the proto-class warrior of popular tradition. "A Lyttell Gest of Robyn Hode," 117A, line 3, accessed online at the Camelot Project at http://www.lib.rochester.edu/camelot/teams/gest.htm (Oct 2007), edited by Stephen Knight and Thomas H. Ohlgren, originally published in *Robin Hood and Other Outlaw Tales* (Kalamazoo: Medieval Institute Publications, 1997).

30. This "necessary invention" is broadly similar to the problem of "necessary anachronism" which arises in the domain of the historical novel. See Georg Lukács, *The Historical Novel*, translated by Hannah Mitchell and Stanley Mitchell (London: Merlin, 1962), 61 and ff.

31. Burkholder, "Popular [Mis]conceptions," 510 (my emphasis).

32. Kelly, "Beyond Historical Accuracy," 5.

33. "...en histoire comme au theatre, tout montrer est impossible, non pas parce qu'il faudrait trop de pages, mais parce qu'il n'existe pas de fait historique élémentaire, d'atome événementiel." *Comment on écrit l'histoire*, 37 (my translation).

34. Williams, "Medieval Movies," 4.

35. Paden, "I Learned it at the Movies," 92.

36. Airlie, "Strange Eventful Histories," 176.

37. Peter Burkholder, "Popular [Mis]conceptions of Medieval Warfare," *History Compass* 5 (2007): 518.

38. Robert A. Rosenstone, *History on Film/Film on History* (Harlow: Longman/Pearson, 2006), 38.

39. Robert A. Rosenstone, "The Historical Film: Looking at the Past in a Postliterate Age," in *The Historical Film: History and Memory in Media*, edited by Marcia Landy (New Brunswick: Rutgers University Press, 2001), 65.

40. William D. Paden, "I Learned It at the Movies: Teaching Medieval Film," in Utz and Swan, *Studies in Medievalism XIII*, 92.

41. Umberto Eco, *Travels in Hyperreality: Essays*, translated by William Weaver (London: Picador, 1987), 61–72.

42. Lindley, "The Ahistoricism of Medieval Film," unpaginated.

43. Helmut Nickel, "Arms and Armor in Arthurian Films," in *Cinema Arthuriana: Twenty Essays*, edited by Kevin J. Harty (Jefferson, NC: McFarland, 2002), 235.

44. Haydock, "Arthurian Melodrama," 29.

45. Natalie Zemon Davis, "Any Resemblance to Persons Living or Dead: Film and the challenge of authenticity," *Historical Journal of Film, Radio and Television* 8, no. 3 (1988): 271.

46. *Ibid.*, 272.

47. "L'image médiévale ne "photographie" jamais la réalité. Elle n'est absolument pas faite pour cela, ni dans le domaine des formes ni dans celui des couleurs." Michel Pastoureau, *Une Histoire Symbolique Du Moyen Âge Occidental* (Paris: Seuil, 2004), 118 (my translation).

48. Sabrina Mitchell, *Medieval Manuscript Painting* (London: Contact, 1964; 1965), 3.

49. For color symbolism in the Middle Ages, see Michel Pastoureau, *Une Histoire Symbolique*, 113–209. For more on the polysemy of blue in particular, see Pastoureau, *Bleu: L'Histoire d'une couleur* (Paris: Seuil, 2002), especially chapter 2, "Une Couleur Nouvelle," 43–71.

50. Muriel Whitaker, "The Illustration of Arthurian Romance," in *King Arthur through the Ages*, edited by Valerie Marie Lagorio (New York and London: Garland, 1990), 145.

51. *Ibid.*, 123–124.

52. Honorius of Autun, *Gemma Animae*, chap 132 (PL, 172, col. 586), quoted in Umberto Eco, *Art and Beauty in the Middle Ages* (London & New Haven: Yale University Press, 1988), 16.

53. "L'oeuvre d'art était affirmation de puissance." Georges Duby, *Art et société au Moyen Âge* (Paris: Seuil, 1997), 9 (my translation).

54. Umberto Eco, *The Aesthetics of Thomas Aquinas* (Cambridge, MA: Harvard University Press, 1970; 1988), 3.

55. "Nous ne considérons pas ces formes du meme regard que ceux qui les premiers les virent." Duby, *Art et société au Moyen Âge*, 7.

56. Ernst Robert Curtius, *European Literature and the Latin Middle Ages* (London: Routledge & Kegan Paul, 1953), 224, note 20.

57. Jacques Aumont, *L'Image* (Paris: Nathan 1990), 156–157; see also chapter 1, "The Role of the Eye," 5–52.

58. Whitaker, "The Illustration of Arthurian Romance," 128.

59. "La peinture, à la rigueur, mais discrète. Non point, en tout cas, le relief." Quoted in Duby, *Art et société au Moyen Âge*, 46.

60. Richard Kohler and Walter Lassaly, "The Big Screens," *Sight and Sound* 24, no. 3 (1955): 122. In a later continuation of this article he suggests, though not entirely in earnest, that the horizontal expanse explained the popularity of the Roman and Egyptian themes in widescreen epics, given their propensity to spend much of the screen time lying on low couches. See also my forthcoming research paper, "Reframing the Past: The Effects of Technology on Historical Films."

61. So that there existed five "feared trades" ("métiers craints") in particular, each with symbolic meanings. See Pastoureau, *Une Histoire Symbolique*, 87–88.

62. "Ce thème essentiel: Image-Public-Histoire"; Nathalie Carré de Malberg, "Image et Histoire," *Vingtième Siècle. Revue d'histoire* 12 (1986): 91. "Grille d'analyse pour passer du signifiant au signifié puis au référant." Malberg, "Image et Histoire," 90 (both translations my own).

63. Chrétien de Troyes, *Le Conte du Graal* (Paris: Flammarion, 1997), line 835ff.

64. Pastoureau, *Une Histoire Symbolique*, 88.

65. Gilles Deleuze, *Cinema 1: The Movement Image* (London: Athlone, 1992), 2.

66. Jeffrey Richards, *Swordsmen of the Screen, from Douglas Fairbanks to Michael York* (London: Routledge and Kegan Paul, 1977), 19.

67. Jean Baudrillard, *Simulations* (New York: Semiotext(e), 1983), 18.

68. Guy Debord, *Society of the Spectacle* (Detroit: Black and Red, 1983), 1.

69. Marcus Bull, *Thinking Medieval: An Introduction to the Study of the Middle Ages* (Basingstoke: Palgrave Macmillan, 2005), 2.

Chapter 8

1. Isaac of York in *Ivanhoe*, directed by Richard Thorpe (MGM, 1952).

2. David Williams, "Medieval Movies," *The Yearbook of English Studies* 20 (1990): 20.

3. Roland Barthes, *Mythologies*, translated by Jonathan Cape (London: Vintage, 2000), 26.

4. Susan Bassnett and André Lefevere, *Constructing Cultures: Essays on Literary Translation* (Clevedon: Multilingual Matters, 1998), 36. See also Marcus Bull, *Thinking Medieval: An Introduction to the Study of the Middle Ages* (Basingstoke: Palgrave Macmillan, 2005), 137–138.

5. François Amy de la Bretèque, "Une 'figure obligée' du film de chevalerie: le Tournoi," *Cahiers de la Cinémathèque, Special edition, Le Moyen Âge au Cinéma* 42/43 (1985): 21–26.

6. François Amy de la Bretèque, *L'Imaginaire médiéval dans le cinéma occidental* (Paris: Champion, 2004), 35.

7. Marnie Hughes-Warrington, *History Goes to the Movies: Studying History on Film* (London: Routledge, 2006), 36.

8. *Braveheart*, directed by Mel Gibson (20th Century–Fox, 1995).

9. It is, incidentally, a growing tradition among Arthurian films (though not their literary counterparts) to soften the adulterous relationship of Lancelot and Guinevere by widening the age gap between Arthur and the two younger

lovers. In this way, we can see a recent trend which results in a conflation of the hitherto quite disparate tales of *Tristan and Isolde* with the Arthurian saga.

10. *Lancelot and Guinevere* (aka *Sword of Lancelot*), directed by Cornel Wilde (Emblem Productions, 1963).

11. For an interesting and more in-depth reading of this same poster, see Nickolas Haydock, "Arthurian Melodrama, Chaucerian Spectacle, and the Waywardness of Cinematic Pastiche in *First Knight* and *A Knight's Tale*," in *Film and Fiction: Reviewing the Middle Ages*, edited by Tom Shippey and Martin Arnold (Cambridge: D. S. Brewer, 2003), 7–19.

12. In which, famously, Marc discovers the lovers sleeping in a state of perfect chastity divided by the unsheathed sword of Tristan. See Béroul, "Roman du Tristan," *Tristan et Iseut: Les Poèmes Français* (Paris: Livre de Poche, 1989), line 2010. The same motif had already been transferred to Lancelot and Guinevere in film by Boorman, in his 1981 *Excalibur*, which suggests that Zucker was making more use of film versions of the legend than literary antecedents.

13. For more on the lack of individuality in cinematic medieval peasantry, see chapter 6, section 3.

14. T. H. White develops his concept of using "might for right" in *The Once and Future King* (London: Fontana/Collins, 1939, repr. 1980), book 3: "The Queen of Air and Darkness," chapter VI, 244–245. See also chapter 3, section 2.1.

15. Haydock, "Arthurian Melodrama," 9.

16. *Ibid.*, 33 (footnote).

17. *Ibid.*, 18.

18. In *Sword of the Valiant*, directed by Stephen Weeks (Golan-Globus Productions, 1984); *Robin Hood: Prince of Thieves*, directed by Kevin Reynolds (20th Century-Fox, 1991); *Highlander* (1986); *The Name of the Rose*, directed by Jean-Jacques Annaud (Neue Constantin Film / ZDF, 1986), respectively. All of which roles, of course, have been played by Connery in previous "medieval" films. My reading of this film offers a marked similarity to the way in which the raw aggression of knighthood was to be tempered by codes of chivalry, discussed above in chapter 3.

19. Elizabeth S. Sklar, "Review of *Black Knight*," *Arthuriana* 12, no. 3 (Fall 2002): 139.

20. *A Connecticut Yankee in King Arthur's Court*, directed by Tay Garnett (Paramount Pictures, 1949).

21. *A Knight in Camelot*, directed by Roger Young (Rosemont Productions/Walt Disney Television, 1998).

22. Umberto Eco, *Travels in Hyperreality: Essays*, translated by William Weaver (London: Picador, 1987), 69.

23. As Huizinga rather poetically comments, "so violent and motley was life, that it bore the mixed smell of blood and roses." Johan H. Huizinga, *The Waning of the Middle Ages* (Harmondsworth: Penguin Books Ltd., 2001), 25.

24. Stuart Airlie, "Strange Eventful Histories: The Middle Ages in Cinema," in *The Medieval World*, edited by Peter Linehan (London: Routledge, 2001), 172.

25. *Merlin*, directed by Steve Barron (Hallmark Entertainment, 1998).

26. It is interesting to note here that the recent recognition of the alterity and "foreignness" of the Middle Ages has formed fertile grounds for the mystery/whodunnit genre: not knowing anyone there, we can no longer be certain in whom to place our trust, even at times suspecting the sleuth himself. Cf. *The Name of the Rose*; *The Advocate* (aka *The Hour of the Pig*), directed by Lesley Megahey (Miramax Films, 1993); *The Reckoning*, directed by Paul McGuigan (Renaissance Films, 2004); see also the series of mystery novels from Ellis Peters' *Cadfael* series to Michael Jecks' West Country novels, not to mention the medieval-inspired — though monumentally misinformed — *The Da Vinci Code* (2006) and the Harry Potter series of books and films.

27. In *Ivanhoe*; *A Knight's Tale*, directed by Brian Helgeland (Columbia Pictures, 2001); *Kingdom of Heaven*, directed by Ridley Scott (20th Century-Fox, 2005); and *Magnificat*, directed by Pupi Avati (Duea Film/Istituto Luce, 1993), respectively.

28. The Stranger's (Sam Elliott) prologue to *The Big Lebowski*, directed by Joel and Ethan Coen (Working Title Films, 1998).

29. Williams, "Medieval Movies," 17.

30. *The Vikings*, directed by Richard Fleischer (Brynaprod S. A./Curtleigh Productions, 1958).

31. See John Aberth, *A Knight at the Movies: Medieval History on Film* (New York and London: Routledge, 2003), 44; also 29–61 for discussion of Viking-themed films in general.

32. A useful summary of the Historical position can be found in T. D. Kendrick, *A History of the Vikings* (London: Methuen, 1930). For the purposes of a simplified prologue, however, it has been useful to refer to Johannes Brøndsted's more general overview, *The Vikings*, translated by Kalle Skov (Harmondsworth: Penguin, 1960, 1965).

33. Such as *Det Sjunde Inseglet (The Seventh Seal)*, directed by Ingmar Bergman (Svensk Filmindustri SF, 1957); *The Messenger: The Story of Joan of Arc*, directed by Luc Besson (Gaumont, 1999); or *The Navigator: A Mediaeval Odyssey*, directed by Vincent Ward (Arenafilm/NZ Film Commission, 1988).

34. For a far more in-depth demonstration of this argument than would be possible here, refer to A. F. Christa Canitz's work on False Truth Claims in Shippey and Arnold, *Film and Fiction*, 128–142.

35. See W. P. Ker, *The Dark Ages* (London: Nelson, 1955), 1–23; Fred C. Robinson, "Medieval, The Middle Ages," *Speculum* 59 (1984): 750, and above in chapter 2.

36. *Conan the Barbarian*, directed by John Milius (Universal Pictures, 1982). See also Philippe Bordes, "Moyen Âge ou Heroic Fantasy?" *Cahiers de la Cinémathèque* 42/43 (1985): 171–182.

37. Richard Burt, "Getting Schmedieval: Of Manuscript and Film Prologues, Paratexts and Parodies," *Exemplaria* 19, no. 2 (Summer 2007): 225.

38. The expression "the corridors of history" comes from *Les Couloirs du Temps: Les Visiteurs 2*, directed by Jean-Marie Poire (Canal+/France 3, 1998), the sequel to Poiré's *Les Visiteurs*.

39. I have discussed such peripatetic history in the context of the Vikings in "Time Out of Joint: Why Astérix fought the Vikings in *Astérix and the Vikings*," in *Reel Vikings: Cinematic Representations of Medieval Scandinavia*, edited by Kevin J. Harty (Jefferson, NC: McFarland, 2011).

40. *King Arthur's Disasters*, 2005 and 2006; see also *King Arthur, the Young Warlord*, directed Patrick Dromgoole (Westlake Entertainment Group, 1975); and *Siege of the Saxons*, directed by Nathan Juran (Columbia Pictures, 1963). While a relatively new phenomenon in Cinema Arthuriana, this is of course by no means unfamiliar territory when we bear in mind those Italian peplum films which pitted Hercules against a series of increasingly implausible foes, such as *Ercole contro Roma/Hercules Against Rome* (1964), *Maciste nell'inferno di Gengis Khan/Hercules Against the Barbarians* (1964), *Ulisse contro Hercole/Ulysses against Hercules* (1961), and *Ercole sfida Sansone/Hercules, Samson & Ulysses* (1963). See also Derek Elley, *The Epic Film: Myth and History* (London: Routledge & Kegan Paul, 1984).

41. Arthur Lindley, "The Ahistoricism of Medieval Film," *Screening the Past* 3 (May 1988): unpaginated.

42. In the prologue to the film version of *A Walk with Love and Death*, directed by John Huston (20th Century–Fox, 1969).

43. Williams, "Medieval Movies," 6.

44. Airlie, "Strange Eventful Histories," 164.

45. Richard Burt, "Getting Schmedieval."

46. See Pierre Sorlin, *The Film in History: Restaging the Past* (Oxford: Blackwell, 1980); Robert Brent Toplin, *History by Hollywood: The Use and Abuse of the American Past* (Champaign, IL: University of Illinois Press, 1996); Robert A.

Rosenstone, *History on Film/Film on History* (Harlow: Longman/Pearson, 2006).

47. Tom Shippey, "Fuqua's *King Arthur*: More Mythmaking in America," *Exemplaria* 19, no. 2 (Summer 2007): 310.

Chapter 9

1. A. Keith Kelly, "Beyond Historical Accuracy: A Postmodern View of Movies and Medievalism," *Perspicuitas* (February 2004): 4.

2. Derek Elley, *The Epic Film: Myth and History* (London: Routledge & Kegan Paul, 1984).

3. François Amy de la Bretèque, "Une 'figure obligée' du film de chevalerie: le Tournoi," *Cahiers de la Cinémathèque* 42/43 (1985): 21–26.

4. Michel Pastoureau, *Une Histoire Symbolique du Moyen Âge Occidental* (Paris: Seuil, 2004).

5. William F. Woods, "Authenticating Realism in Medieval Film," *The Medieval Hero on Screen: Representations from Beowulf to Buffy*, edited by Martha W. Driver and Sid Ray (Jefferson, NC: McFarland, 2004), 47.

6. In Hayden V. White, "Historiography and Historiophoty," *The American Historical Review* 93, no. 5 (1988): 1193–1199; Marc Ferro, *Cinéma Et Histoire* (Paris: Denoël, 1977), especially chapter 16; Peter C. Rollins, *Hollywood as Historian: American Film in a Cultural Context* (Lexington, KY: University Press of Kentucky, 1983). See also Robert A. Rosenstone, *Visions of the Past: The Challenge of Film to Our Idea of History* (Cambridge, MA: Harvard University Press, 1995), who devotes an entire section of his work to this very question.

7. Marnie Hughes-Warrington, *History Goes to the Movies: History on Film* (New York and London: Routledge, 2007), 12.

8. Robert A. Rosenstone, "History in Images/History in Words: Reflections on the Possibility of Really Putting History onto Film," *The American Historical Review* 93, no. 5 (1988): 1173–1185.

9. Natalie Zemon Davis, "Any Resemblance to Persons Living or Dead: Film and the Challenge of Authenticity," *Historical Journal of Film, Radio and Television* 8, no. 3 (1988): 277 (emphasis added), although credit must also go to Nickolas Haydock, whose excellent article on medieval films makes explicit this fundamental rift between our ways of approaching the texts. See Nickolas Haydock, "Arthurian Melodrama, Chaucerian Spectacle, and the Waywardness of Cinematic Pastiche in *First Knight* and *A Knight's Tale*," in *Film and Fiction: Reviewing the Middle*

Ages, edited by Tom Shippey and Martin Arnold (Cambridge: D. S. Brewer, 2003), 5–38.

10. Zemon Davis, "Any Resemblance to Persons Living or Dead," 271.

11. Hughes-Warrington, *History Goes to the Movies*, 104.

12. The iconograms are medieval signs which "vont assez souvent par paires cumulatives ou antagonists" ("often go together in cumulative or antagonistic pairings"). François Amy de la Bretèque, *L'Imaginaire médiéval dans le cinéma occidental* (Paris: Champion, 2004), 1071 (translation my own). He further elaborates this pairing along the lines of a "motif" and a "theme," providing us with a degree of semiotic similarity with the "two worlds" theory I am outlining here (personal correspondence, July 2008).

13. Zemon Davis, "Any Resemblance to Persons Living or Dead," 273, also quoted in Anthony Guneratre, "Cinehistory and the Puzzling Case of Martin Guerre," *Film and History* 21 (Feb 1991): 3.

14. Robert Brent Toplin, "Film and History: The State of the Union," *Perspectives* 37, no. 4 (April 1999): unpaginated.

15. Woods, "Authenticating Realism in Medieval Film," 47.

16. *Ibid.*

17. Mark E. Neely, Jr., "The Young Lincoln: Two Films," in *Past Imperfect: History According to the Movies*, edited by Mark C. Carnes (New York: Henry Holt, 1995), 127.

18. Hughes-Warrington, *History Goes to the Movies*, 104.

19. See the discussion of *The Patriot*, *Ibid.*, 105.

20. Jean Baudrillard, *Selected Writings* (Stanford: Stanford University Press, 1988), 168.

21. Woods, "Authenticating Realism in Medieval Film," 39.

22. David Williams, "Medieval Movies," *The Yearbook of English Studies, Special Number* 20 (1990): 7–8.

23. Norman N. Holland, "'The Seventh Seal': The Film as Iconography," *The Hudson Review* 12, no. 2 (1959): 268.

24. Pastoureau, *Une Histoire symbolique*, 335 (translation my own).

25. As Jauss contends, "the new text evokes for the reader the horizon of expectations and 'rules of the game' familiar to him from earlier texts, which as such can then be varied, extended, corrected, but also transformed, crossed out, or simply reproduced." Hans Robert Jauss, *Toward an Aesthetic of Reception* (Brighton: Harvester, 1982), 88.

26. Georg Lukács, *The Historical Novel* (London: Merlin, 1962), 61; Robert A. Rosenstone, *History on Film/Film on History* (Harlow: Longman/Pearson, 2006), 38.

27. Marcus Bull, *Thinking Medieval: An Introduction to the Study of the Middle Ages* (Basingstoke: Palgrave Macmillan, 2005), 40.

28. George Macdonald Fraser, *The Hollywood History of the World: From One Million Years B.C. to Apocalypse Now* (Columbine: Columbine Trade, 1989), xv.

29. Arthur Lindley, "The Ahistoricism of Medieval Film," *Screening the Past* 3 (May 1988): unpaginated.

30. For an excellent deconstruction of encoded agendas, see Kevin J. Harty, "Agenda Layered Upon Agenda: Anthony Mann's 1961 Film *El Cid*," in *Hollywood in the Holy Land: Essays on Film Depictions of the Crusades and Christian-Muslim Clashes*, edited by Nickolas Haydock and E. L. Risden (Jefferson, NC: McFarland, 2009), 161–168.

31. For a more in-depth reading of the 1950s epics along these lines, see Rebecca A. Umland and Samuel J. Umland, *The Use of Arthurian Legend in Hollywood Film: From Connecticut Yankees to Fisher Kings* (Westport, CT: Greenwood Press, 1996), especially chapter 4, "The Arthurian Legend as Forms of Propaganda," 105–128. See also Alan Lupack's impressive article, "An Enemy in Our Midst: *The Black Knight* and the American Dream," in *Cinema Arthuriana: Essays on Arthurian Film*, edited by Kevin J. Harty (New York: Garland, 1991), 29–40.

32. For a full discussion of this, see Nickolas Haydock and E. L. Risden (eds.), *Hollywood and the Holy Land: Essays on Film Depictions of the Crusades and Christian-Muslim Clashes* (Jefferson, NC: McFarland, 2009), especially the fascinating introduction, "The Unseen Cross Upon the Breast," 1–30.

33. *Robin Hood*, BBC TV, series 1, episode 6.

34. Vivian Sobchack, *The Persistence of History: Cinema, Television, and the Modern Event* (London: Routledge, 1996).

35. Woods, "Authenticating Realism in Medieval Film," 39.

36. William D. Paden, "I Learned It at the Movies: Teaching Medieval Film," in *Studies in Medievalism XIII: Postmodern Medievalisms*, edited by Richard Utz and Jesse G. Swan (Cambridge and Rochester: D. S. Brewer, 2004), 92.

37. Marc Ferro, *Cinema and History* (Detroit: Wayne State University Press, 1988), 163.

38. Williams, "Medieval Movies," 3.

39. I have written more extensively on this particular "ambientalism" in my forthcoming article on the same phenomenon, "Historical Spaces, *Gladiator*, and That Tent."

40. Philip Rosen, *Change Mummified: Cinema, History, Theory* (Minnesota: University of Minnesota Press, 2001), xxv.

41. Rosenstone, *History on Film/Film on History,* (Harlow: Longman/Pearson, 2006): 36.
42. *Ibid.,* 37.
43. *Ibid.,* 35.

Glossary

1. "Myth Today," in Roland Barthes, *Mythologies,* translated by Jonathan Cape (London: Vintage, 2000), see especially 295–299.
2. Natalie Zemon Davis, "Any Resemblance to Persons Living or Dead: Film and the Challenge of Authenticity," *Historical Journal of Film, Radio and Television* 8, no. 3 (1988): 269–283.
3. Quoted in Fritz Terveen, "Film as a Historical Document," in *Film and the Historian,* a combined reprint of *University Vision,* The Journal of the British Universities Film Council, Issue 1 (February 1968), and monograph "Film and the Historian," an edited transcript of the conference held at University College, London, April 1968 (BUFC, 1969), 22–25, quotations from pages 23 and 24 respectively.
4. Deanne Schultz, *Filmography of World History* (Westport, CT: Greenwood Press, 2007), xii.
5. Leger Grindon, "Analysing the Historical Fiction Film," in *Shadows on the Past: Studies in the Historical Fiction Film,* edited by Leger Grindon (Philadelphia, PA: Temple University Press, 1994), 2.
6. Marnie Hughes-Warrington, *History Goes to the Movies: Studying History on Film* (London: Routledge, 2006), 4.
7. See also my forthcoming paper "A Sign of the Times: The Historicon in Historical Films." "Ce qui permet de situer l'action au Moyen Âge, ce sont des *formes décoratives.*" from Amy de la Bretèque, *L'Imaginaire Médiéval,* 157.
8. Hayden White, "Historiography and Historiophoty," *American Historical Review* 93, no. 5 (1988): 1193.
9. Satish K. Bajaj, *Recent Trends in Historiography* (New Delhi: Anmol Publications PVT, 1998), 69.
10. Natalie Zemon Davis, *Slaves on Screen* (Cambridge, MA: Harvard University Press, 2002), 4.
11. François Amy de la Bretèque, "Le Regard du Cinéma sur le Moyen Âge," in *Le Moyen Âge Aujourd'hui: Trois Regards Contemporains sur le Moyen Âge: Histoire, Théologie, Cinéma,* edited by Jacques le Goff et Guy Lobrichon (Paris: Cahiers du Léopard d'Or, 1997), 284.
12. Erwin Panofsky, *Studies in Iconology: Humanistic Themes in the Art of the Renaissance* (New York and London: Harper & Row, 1972). See also W. J. T. Mitchell, *Iconology: Image, Text, Ideology* (London: University of Chicago Press, 1986); and Umberto Eco, *Il Segno* (Milano: Mondadori, 1980). Unfortunately, to my knowledge there has been no translation of this latter work into English, leaving what is to my mind the final word in semiotics more or less unspoken to Anglophone readers.
13. Thomas S. Kuhn, *The Structure of Scientific Revolutions,* 3rd ed. (Chicago and London: University of Chicago Press, 1962; 1996), 23.
14. Sergei Eisenstein, *Film Form: Essays in Film Theory,* edited and translated by Jay Leyda (New York: Harvest, 1949, 1977), 28–44.
15. Many of these ideas can be found in Amy de la Bretèque, *L'Imaginaire Médiéval dans le Cinéma Occidental;* my schematic representation of them comes from personal correspondence with its author. For a study of the iconograms specifically, see Amy de la Bretèque, "Le Regard du Cinéma," especially 295–296. A further source of purely semiotic analysis of the Middle Ages can be found in Gérard Chandes's excellent, though unpublished, thesis, "Sémiosphère transmédiévale: Un modèle sémiopragmatique d'information et de communication appliqué aux représentations du moyen-âge," accessible online (in pdf) at http://revues.unilim.fr/nas/document.php?id=1848.
16. "Ces éléments iconiques qui suffisent à désigner 'le moyen âge'...." Amy de la Bretèque, *L'imaginaire Médiéval,* 35 (my translation).
17. Marc Ferro, *Cinema and History* (Detroit: Wayne State University Press, 1988), 160.
18. David Williams, "Medieval Movies," *The Yearbook of English Studies* 20 (1990): 1.
19. For the first two works, see François Amy de la Bretèque, *L'Imaginaire Médiéval dans le Cinéma Occidental* (Paris: Champion, 2004); and Nickolas Haydock, *Movie Medievalism: The Imaginary Middle Ages* (Jefferson, NC: McFarland, 2008). For more on the notion of historical capital, see Pierre Sorlin, *The Film in History: Restaging the Past* (Oxford: Blackwell, 1980), 20; and for a full exposition of the notion of "symbolic capital," see Pierre Bourdieu and Randal Johnson, *The Field of Cultural Production: Essays on Art and Literature* (Columbia: Columbia University Press, 1993).

Bibliography

Historical Film

Aumont, Jacques. "L'histoire au Cinéma: Comment on écrit l'histoire." *Cahiers du Cinéma* (May-June 1972): 64–70.

Carnes, Mark C., Ted Mico, David Rubel, and John Miller-Monzon. *Past Imperfect: History According to the Movies.* London: Cassell, 1996.

Carré de Malberg, Nathalie. "Image et Histoire." *Vingtième Siècle. Revue d'histoire* 12, no. 1 (1986): 89–92.

Cook, Pam. *Screening the Past: Memory and Nostalgia in Cinema.* London: Routledge, 2005.

Doherty, Thomas. "Film and History: Foxes and Hedgehogs." *Magazine of History: Film and History* 16, no. 4 (Summer 2002): 13–15.

Elley, Derek. *The Epic Film: Myth and History.* London: Routledge & Kegan Paul, 1984.

Elliott, Andrew. "A Sign of the Times: The Historicon in Historical Films." Unpublished research paper.

_____. "Reframing the Past: The Effects of Technology on Historical Films." Unpublished research paper.

Ferro, Marc. *Cinema and History.* Detroit: Wayne State University Press, 1988.

_____. *Cinéma et histoire.* Paris: Denoël, 1977.

Fraser, George MacDonald. *The Hollywood History of the World: From One Million Years B.C. to Apocalypse Now.* Columbine: Columbine Trade, 1989.

Goimard, Jacques. "Le Film historique." *La Cinématographie française,* 2042 (December, 1963): 12.

Haworth, Bryan. "Film in the Classroom." In *The Historian and Film,* edited by Paul Smith, 157–168. Cambridge: Cambridge University Press, 1976.

Herlihy, David. "Am I a Camera? Other Reflections on Films and History." *The American Historical Review* 93, no. 5 (1988): 1186–1192.

Hochman, Stanley. *From Quasimodo to Scarlett O'Hara.* New York: Frederick Ungar, 1982.

Hughes, William. "The Evaluation of Film as Evidence." In *The Historian and Film,* edited by Paul Smith, 49–79. Cambridge: Cambridge University Press, 1976.

Hughes-Warrington, Marnie. *History Goes to the Movies: Studying History on Film.* London: Routledge, 2006.

Isenberg, Michael T. "A Relationship of Constrained Anxiety: Historians and Film." *The History Teacher* 6, no. 4 (Aug 1973): 553–568.

Nichols, Bill. "Historical Consciousness and the Viewer: *Who Killed Vincent Chin?*" In *The Persistence of History,* edited by Vivian Sobchack, 55–68. New York & London: Routledge, 1996.

Richards, Jeffrey. *Swordsmen of the Screen, from Douglas Fairbanks to Michael York.* London: Routledge and Kegan Paul, 1977.

Rollins, Peter C. *Hollywood as Historian: American Film in a Cultural Context.* Lexington: University Press of Kentucky, 1983.

Rosen, Philip. *Change Mummified: Cinema, History, Theory.* Minnesota: University of Minnesota Press, 2001.

Rosenstone, Robert A. "The Historical Film: Looking at the Past in a Postliterate Age." In *The Historical Film: History and Memory in Media*, edited by Marcia Landy, 50–66. New Brunswick, NJ: Rutgers University Press, 2001.

_____. "History in Images/History in Words: Reflections on the Possibility of Really Putting History onto Film." *American Historical Review* 93, no. 5 (1988): 1173–1185.

_____. *History on Film/Film on History.* Harlow: Longman/Pearson, 2006.

_____. "Oliver Stone as Historian." In *Oliver Stone's USA*, edited by Robert Brent Toplin, 26–39. Lawrence: University Press of Kansas, 2000.

_____. *Visions of the Past: The Challenge of Film to Our Idea of History.* Cambridge: Harvard University Press, 1995.

_____, ed. *Revisioning History: Film and the Construction of a New Past.* Princeton: Princeton University Press, 1994.

Schultz, Deanne. *Filmography of World History.* Westport, CT: Greenwood Press, 2007.

Smith, Paul. "Film and the Historian." *University Vision* 1, no. 2 (February 1968): 32–36.

_____, ed. *The Historian and Film.* Cambridge: Cambridge University Press, 1976.

Sobchack, Vivian. "'Surge and Splendor': A Phenomenology of the Hollywood Historical Epic." In *Film Genre Reader III*, edited by Barry Keith Grant, 296–323. Austin: University of Texas Press, 2003.

_____. "The Insistent Fringe: Moving Images and the Palimpsest of Historical Consciousness." *History and Theory* 36, no. 4 (December 1997): 4–20.

_____. *The Persistence of History: Cinema, Television, and the Modern Event.* London: Routledge, 1996.

Sorlin, Pierre. *The Film in History: Restaging the Past.* Oxford: Blackwell, 1980.

Terveen, Fritz. "Film as a Historical Document." In *Film and the Historian*, a combined reprint of *University Vision*, The Journal of the British Universities Film Council, Issue 1 (February 1968) and monograph "Film and the Historian," an edited transcript of the conference held at University College, London, April 1968 (BUFC, 1969): 22–25, quotations from pages 24 and 23 respectively.

Toplin, Robert Brent. "Film and History: The State of the Union." *Perspectives* 37, no. 4 (April 1999): unpaginated.

_____. "The Filmmaker as Historian." *American Historical Review* 93, no. 5 (1988): 1210–1227.

_____. *History by Hollywood: The Use and Abuse of the American Past.* Champaign: University of Illinois Press, 1996.

_____. *Reel History: In Defense of Hollywood.* Lawrence: University Press of Kansas, 2002.

Toplin, Robert Brent, and Jason Eudy. "The Historian Encounters Film: A Historiography." *Magazine of History: Film and History* 16, no. 4 (Summer 2002): 7–12.

Weinstein, Paul B. "Movies as the Gateway to History: The History on Film Project." *The History Teacher* 35, no. 1 (Nov. 2001): 27–48.

White, Hayden. "Historiography and Historiophoty." *American Historical Review* 93, no. 5 (1988): 1193–1199.

Zemon Davis, Natalie. *Slaves on Screen.* Cambridge, MA: Harvard University Press, 2002.

Zolov, Eric. "[Review] *Based on a True Story: Latin American History at the Movies.*" *American Historical Review* 105, no. 2 (April 2000): 515.

Medieval Film

Aberth, John. *A Knight at the Movies: Medieval History on Film.* New York and London: Routledge, 2003.

Airlie, Stuart. "Strange Eventful Histories: The Middle Ages in Cinema." In *The Medieval World*, edited by Peter Linehan, 163–183. London: Routledge, 2001.

Amy de la Bretèque, François. "Au 'temps des Cathédrales': En hommage à Georges Duby, historien, biographe, et … scénariste de film." *Cahiers de la Cinémathèque* 42/43 (1985): 27–58.

_____. "La Figure du chevalier errant dans l'imaginaire cinématographique." *Cahiers de l'association internationale des études françaises* 47 (May 1995): 49–78.

_____. *L'Imaginaire médiéval dans le cinéma occidental.* Paris: Champion, 2004.

_____. "Le Regard du cinéma sur le Moyen Âge." In *Le Moyen Âge Aujourd'hui: Trois Regards Contemporains sur le Moyen Âge:*

Histoire, Théologie, Cinéma, edited by Jacques le Goff et Guy Lobrichon, 283–302. Paris: Cahiers du Léopard d'Or, 1997.

_____. "Une 'figure obligée' du film de chevalerie: le Tournoi." *Cahiers de la Cinémathèque* 42/43 (1985): 21–26.

Aronstein, Susan. *Hollywood Knights: Arthurian Cinema and the Politics of Nostalgia*. Basingstoke, Hants: Palgrave Macmillan, 2005.

_____, and Nancy Coiner. "Twice Knightly: Democratizing the Middle Ages for Middle-Class America." *Studies in Medievalism* 6 (1994): 212–231.

Aste, Mario. "Zeffirelli's Personal Encounter with St. Francis: Brother Sun, Sister Moon." *Romance Languages Annual* III (1991): 1–17.

Attolini, Vito. *Immagini del Medioevo nel Cinema*. Bari: Edizioni Dedalo, 1993.

Austin, Greta. "Were the Peasants Really So Clean? The Middle Ages in Film." *Film History* 14 (2002): 136–141.

Blanch, Robert J., and Julian N. Wasserman. "Fear of Flyting: The Absence of Internal Tension in 'Sword of the Valiant' and 'First Knight.'" *Arthuriana* 10 (2000): 15–32.

Bordes, Philippe. "Moyen Âge ou Heroic Fantasy?" *Cahiers de la Cinémathèque* 42/43 (1985): 171–182.

Burt, Richard. "Getting Schmedieval: Of Manuscript and Film Prologues, Paratexts and Parodies." *Exemplaria* 19, no. 2 (Summer 2007): 217–242.

Canitz, A. E. Christa. "'Historians ... Will Say I am a Liar': The Ideology of False Truth Claims in Mel Gibson's 'Braveheart' and Luc Besson's 'The Messenger.'" In *Studies in Medievalism XIII: Postmodern Medievalisms*, edited by Richard Utz and Jesse G. Swan, 127–142. Cambridge and Rochester: D. S. Brewer, 2004.

Chandes, Gérard. "Sémiosphère Transmédiévale: Un Modèle Sémiopragmatique d'Information et de Communication Appliqué aux Représentations du Moyen-âge." *Nouveaux Actes Semiotiques*. November 22, 2007, http://revues.unilim.fr/nas/document.php?id=1848.

Day, David D. "Monty Python and the Holy Grail: Madness with a Definite Method." In *Cinema Arthuriana: Twenty Essays*, edited by Kevin J. Harty, 127–135. Jefferson, NC: McFarland, 2002.

Demby, Betty. "An Interview with Franco Zeffirelli." *Filmmakers Newsletter* 6 (1973): 31–34.

Driver, Martha W., and Sid Ray. *The Medieval Hero on Screen: Representations from Beowulf to Buffy*. Jefferson, NC: McFarland, 2004.

Durand, Jacques. "La Chevalerie à l'écran," *L'Avant-scène cinémathèque* 22 (February 1979): 29–33.

Edensor, Tim. "Reading Braveheart: Representing and Contesting Scottish Identity." *Scottish Affairs* 21 (1997): 135–158.

Eliot, Thomas S. *Selected Poems*. London: Faber, 1961.

Elliott, Andrew B. R., "Mr. Monk and the Medieval Monks." In *Mr. Monk and Philosophy*, edited by Dylan E. Wittkower. Chicago: Open Court Publishing, 2009: 169–80.

Ewan, Elizabeth. "Review: [Braveheart, Rob Roy]." *The American Historical Review* 100 (1995): 1219–1221.

Finke, Laurie A., and Martin B. Shichtman. *Cinematic Illuminations: The Middle Ages on Film*. Baltimore: Johns Hopkins Press, 2009.

Freedman, Paul. "Review: [Le Droit de Cuissage: La Fabrication d'un Mythe (XIIIe–XXe Siècle)]." *Speculum* 71 (1996): 696–698.

Freixe, Guy. "Approche du Décaméron de Pier Paulo Pasolini." *Cahiers de la Cinémathèque* 42/43 (1985): 143–151.

Guneratre, Anthony. "Cinehistory and the Puzzling Case of *Martin Guerre*." *Film and History* 21 (Feb 1991): 2–19.

Harker, Jonathan. "Review: [The Hidden Fortress]." *Film Quarterly* 13 (1960): 59.

Harty, Kevin J. *The Reel Middle Ages: American, Western and Eastern European, Middle Eastern, and Asian Films About Medieval Europe*. Jefferson, NC: McFarland, 1999.

_____. "Roll the Final Credits: Some Notes on Cinematic Depictions of the Death of Arthur." In *The Arthurian Way of Death: The English Tradition*, edited by Karen Cherewatuk and K. S. Whetter, 241–248. Cambridge: D.S. Brewer, 2009.

_____, ed. "Agenda Layered on Agenda." In *Hollywood and the Holy Land: Essays on Film Depictions of the Crusades and Christian-Muslim Clashes*, edited by Nickolas

Haydock and E. L. Risden, 161–168. Jefferson, NC: McFarland, 2009.

_____, ed. *Cinema Arthuriana: Essays on Arthurian Film*. London: Taylor & Francis, 1991.

_____, ed. *Cinema Arthuriana: Twenty Essays* (Jefferson, NC: McFarland, 2002).

_____, ed. *Reel Vikings: Medieval Scandinavia in the Cinema*. Jefferson, NC: McFarland, forthcoming, 2011.

Haydock, Nickolas. "Arthurian Melodrama, Chaucerian Spectacle, and the Waywardness of Cinematic Pastiche in *First Knight* and *A Knight's Tale*." In *Film and Fiction: Reviewing the Middle Ages*, edited by Tom Shippey and Martin Arnold, 5–38. Cambridge: D. S. Brewer, 2003.

_____. *Movie Medievalism: The Imaginary Middle Ages*. Jefferson, NC: McFarland, 2008.

_____. "Shooting the Messenger: Luc Besson at War with Joan of Arc." *Exemplaria* 19, no. 2 (Summer 2007): 243–269.

_____, ed. *Hollywood in the Holy Land: Essays on Film Depictions of the Crusades and Christian-Muslim Clashes*, edited by Nickolas Haydock and E. L. Risden. Jefferson, NC: McFarland, 2009.

Holland, Norman N. "The Seventh Seal: The Film as Iconography." *The Hudson Review*, 12, no. 2 (1959): 266–270.

Iversen, Gunnar. "Clearly, from a Distance: The Image of the Medieval Period in Recent Norwegian Films." *Scandinavica* 39, no. 1 (2000): 7–23.

Jewers, Caroline. "Hard Day's Knights: *First Knight*, *A Knight's Tale*, and *Black Knight*." In *The Medieval Hero on Screen: Representations from Beowulf to Buffy*, edited by Martha Driver and Sid Ray, 192–210. Jefferson, NC: McFarland, 2004.

Kelly, A. Keith. "Beyond Historical Accuracy: A Postmodern View of Movies and Medievalism." *Perspicuitas* (February 2004).

Kozlovic, Anton K. "Saint Cinema: The Construction of St. Francis of Assisi in Franco Zeffirelli's *Brother Sun, Sister Moon*." *Journal of Religion and Popular Culture* 2 (Fall 2002): 1–21.

Levy, Brian, and Lesley Coote. "The Subversion of Medievalism in *Lancelot du Lac* and *Monty Python and the Holy Grail*." In *Studies in Medievalism XIII: Postmodern Medievalisms*, edited by Richard Utz and Jesse

G. Swan, 99–126. Cambridge and Rochester: D. S. Brewer, 2004.

Lindley, Arthur, "The Ahistoricism of Medieval Film." *Screening the Past* 3 (May 1988): unpaginated.

Lupack, Alan. "An Enemy in Our Midst: *The Black Knight* and the American Dream." In *Cinema Arthuriana: Twenty Essays*, edited by Kevin J. Harty, 64–70. Jefferson, NC: McFarland, 2002.

McCabe, Bob. *Dark Knights and Holy Fools*. London: Orion Press, 1999.

McMorran, Will. "*Les Visiteurs* and the Quixotic Text." *French Cultural Studies* 19 (2008): 159–172.

Nayman, Michelle. "The Navigator: Vincent Ward's Past Dreams of the Future." *Cinema Papers* 69 (May 1988): 30–31.

Nickel, Helmut. "Arms and Armor in Arthurian Films." In *Cinema Arthuriana: Twenty Essays*, edited by Kevin J. Harty, 235–251. Jefferson, NC: McFarland, 2002.

Oms, Marcel. "Les Yankees à la cour du roi Arthur." *Cahiers de la Cinémathèque* 42/43 (1985): 61–69.

Ortenberg, Veronica. *In Search of the Holy Grail: The Quest for the Middle Ages*. New York & London: Hambledon Continuum, 2006.

Paden, William D. "I Learned It at the Movies: Teaching Medieval Film." In *Studies in Medievalism XIII: Postmodern Medievalisms*, edited by Richard Utz and Jesse G. Swan, 79–98. Cambridge and Rochester: D. S. Brewer, 2004.

Pileggi, Antonio. *Medioevo e commedia all'italiana: Indagine storico-critico sul film l'Armata Brancaleone*. Cosenza: Le Nuvole, 2001.

Pittaluga, S., and M. Salotti, eds. *Cinema e Medioevo*. Genova: Università di Genova, 2000.

Salo, David. "Heroism and Alienation through Language in *The Lord of the Rings*." In *The Medieval Hero on Screen: Representations from Beowulf to Buffy*, edited by Martha W. Driver and Sid Ray, 23–37. Jefferson, NC: McFarland, 2004.

Sanfilippo, Matteo. *Il Medioevo secondo Walt Disney: Come l'america ha reinventato l'età di mezzo*. Roma: Castelvecchi, 2003.

Sharp, Michael D. "Remaking Medieval Heroism: Nationalism and Sexuality in *Braveheart*." *Florilegium* 15 (1998): 251–266.

Shippey, Tom. "Fuqua's *King Arthur*: More Mythmaking in America." *Exemplaria* 19, no. 2 (Summer 2007): 310–326.

Sigal, Pierre-André. "*Brancaleone s'en va-t-aux croisades*: Satire d'un Moyen-Âge Conventionnel." *Cahiers de la Cinémathèque* 42/43 (1985): 152–154.

Six, Jean-François. "François d'Assise." *Cahiers de la Cinémathèque* 42/43 (1985): 29–35.

Sklar, Elizabeth S. "Review of *Black Knight*." *Arthuriana* 12, no. 3 (Fall 2002): 139–140.

_____, and Donald L. Hoffman, eds. *King Arthur in Popular Culture*. Jefferson, NC: McFarland, 2002.

Tesich-Savage, Nadja. "Rehearsing the Middle Ages." *Film Comment* 14 (Sept–Oct 1978): 50–56.

Umland, Rebecca A., and Samuel J. Umland. *The Use of Arthurian Legend in Hollywood Film: From Connecticut Yankees to Fisher Kings*. Westport, CT: Greenwood Press, 1996.

Williams, David. "Medieval Movies." *The Yearbook of English Studies* 20 (1990): 1–32.

Woods, William F. "Authenticating Realism in Medieval Film." *The Medieval Hero on Screen: Representations from Beowulf to Buffy*, edited by Martha W Driver and Sid Ray, 38–51 Jefferson, NC: McFarland, 2004.

_____. "Seeking the Human Image in *The Advocate*." In *Film and Fiction: Reviewing the Middle Ages*, edited by Tom Shippey with Martin Arnold, 55–78. Cambridge: D. S. Brewer, 2003.

Zeffirelli, Franco. *Franco Zeffirelli: The Autobiography*. London: Arena, 1987.

Zemon Davis, Natalie. "Any Resemblance to Persons Living or Dead: Film and the Challenge of Authenticity." *Historical Journal of Film, Radio and Television* 8, no. 3 (1988): 269–283.

Classical Antiquity on Film

Arenas, Amelia. "Popcorn and Circus: *Gladiator* and the Spectacle of Virtue." *Arion* 9, no. 1 (Summer 2001): 1–12.

Bertini, F., ed. *Il Mito Classico e il Cinema*. Università di Genova: Pubblicazioni del D.AR.FI.CL.ET, 1997.

Nisbet, Gideon. *Ancient Greece in Film and Popular Culture*. Exeter: Bristol Phoenix, 2006.

Winkler, Martin M., ed. *Classical Myth and Culture in the Cinema*. Oxford: Oxford University Press, 2001.

_____, ed. *Gladiator: Film and History*. Oxford: Blackwell, 2004.

Wyke, Maria. *Projecting the Past: Ancient Rome, Cinema and History*. New York & London: Routledge, 1997.

Critical Texts on Medieval History and Literature

Bakhtin, Mikhail. *Rabelais and His World*, translated by Helene Iswolsky. Bloomington: Indiana University Press, 1984.

Barber, Richard. *The Knight and Chivalry*. Woodbridge, Suffolk: Boydell Press, 1995.

Bishop, Morris. *Middle Ages*. London: Cassell, 1969.

Bloch, Marc. *Feudal Society*, translated by L. A. Manyon. London: Routledge & Kegan Paul, 1962.

_____. *La Société Féodale*. Paris: Michel, 1939.

Bloch, R. Howard. *Etymologies and Genealogies*. Chicago: University of Chicago Press, 1986.

_____. *Medieval French Literature and Law*. Berkeley: University of California Press, 1977.

Brøndsted, Johannes. *The Vikings*, translated by Kalle Skov. Harmondsworth: Penguin, 1960, 1965.

Brooke, Christopher. *From Alfred to Henry III: 871–1272*. London: Sphere Books, 1969.

_____. *The Saxon and Norman Kings*. New York: Macmillan 1963.

Burkholder, Peter. "Popular [Mis]conceptions of Medieval Warfare." *History Compass* 5 (2007): 507–524.

Burrows, Daron. *The Stereotype of the Priest in the Old French Fabliaux: Anti-clerical Satire and Lay Identity*. Bern, Oxford: Peter Lang, 2005.

Campbell, Emma. *Medieval Saints' Lives: The Gift, Kinship and Community in Old French Hagiography*. Woodbridge: Boydell and Brewer, 2008.

Cantor, Norman. *In the Wake of the Plague:*

The Black Death and the World It Made. New York: Pocket Books, 2002.

_____. *The Sacred Chain: A History of the Jews.* London: HarperCollins, 1994.

_____, ed. *The Encyclopedia of the Middle Ages.* New York: Viking, 1999.

Cayley, Emma. *Debate and Dialogue: Alain Chartier in His Cultural Context.* Oxford: Clarendon, 2006.

Coss, Peter R. *The Origins of the English Gentry.* Cambridge: Cambridge University Press, 2005.

Coulton, G. G. *The Medieval Scene: An Informal Introduction to the Middle Ages.* Cambridge: Cambridge University Press, 1960.

Cowling, David. *Building the Text: Architecture as Metaphor in Late Medieval and Early Modern France.* Oxford: Oxford University Press, 1998.

Curtius, Ernst R. *European Literature and the Latin Middle Ages.* London: Routledge & Kegan Paul, 1953.

Duggan, Anne J., ed. *Queens and Queenship in Medieval Europe.* Woodbridge: Boydell Press, 1997.

Eco, Umberto. *The Aesthetics of Thomas Aquinas,* translated by Hugh Bredin. Cambridge, MA: Harvard University Press, 1970; 1988.

_____. *Art and Beauty in the Middle Ages.* London & New Haven: Yale University Press, 1988.

Ferrier, Janet M. *Forerunners of the French Novel: An Essay on the Development of the Nouvelle in the Late Middle Ages.* Manchester: Manchester University Press, 1954.

Figgis, John. *The Divine Right of Kings.* Cambridge: Cambridge University Press, 1922.

Fink, Karl August. *Papsttum und Kirche im abendländischen Mittelalter.* München: Dt Taschenbuch Verl., 1994.

Finke, Laurie A., and Martin B. Shichtman. *Medieval Texts & Contemporary Readers.* Ithaca, NY: Cornell University Press, 1987.

Habig, Marion A. *St. Francis of Assisi: Writings and Early Biographies: English Omnibus of the Sources for the Life of St. Francis.* Chicago: Franciscan Herald Press, 1983.

Hahn, Thomas. *Robin Hood in Popular Culture: Violence, Transgression, and Justice.* Cambridge: D. S. Brewer, 2000.

Harper-Bill, Christopher, and Ruth Harvey, eds. *The Ideal and Practice of Medieval Knighthood III.* Woodbridge, Suffolk: Boydell Press, 1990.

Heer, Friedrich, *The Medieval World: Europe 1100–1350,* translated by Janet Sondheimer. New York: George Weidenfeld and Nicolson, 1962.

Henderson, E., ed. *Select Historical Documents.* London: Bohn, 1892.

Huizinga, Johan H. *The Waning of the Middle Ages.* Harmondsworth: Penguin Books, 2001.

Humphrey, Chris, and W. H. Ormrod, eds. *Time in the Medieval World.* York: York Medieval Press, 2001.

Jones, Terry, and Alan Eireira. *Medieval Lives.* London: BBC Books, 2004; pbk 2005).

Kaeuper, Richard W. *Chivalry and Violence in Medieval Europe.* Oxford: Oxford University Press, 1999.

Kantorowicz, Ernst H. *The King's Two Bodies: A Study in Mediaeval Political Theology.* Princeton: Princeton University Press, 1957.

Keen, Maurice. *A History of Medieval Europe.* London: Routledge and Kegan Paul, 1967.

Kendrick, T. D. *A History of the Vikings.* London: Methuen, 1930.

Ker, W. P. *The Dark Ages.* London: Nelson, 1955.

Le Goff, Jacques. *Intellectuals in the Middle Ages,* translated by Teresa Lavender Fagan. Cambridge, MA; Oxford: Blackwell, 1993.

_____. *Mediaeval Civilization, 400–1500.* Oxford: Blackwell Publishers, 1990.

Le Goff, Jacques, and Jean-Maurice de Montrémy. *À la recherche du Moyen Âge.* Paris: Éditions Louis Audibert, 2003.

Le Goff, Jacques, and Jean-Louis Schlegel. *Le Moyen Âge expliqué aux enfants.* Paris: Seuil, 2006.

Lewis, C. S. *The Discarded Image: An Introduction to Medieval and Renaissance Literature.* Cambridge: Cambridge University Press, 1964.

Lobrichon, Guy. "Les 'Moyen-Âge': Une histoire à refaire?," In *Le Moyen Âge Aujourd'hui. Actes de la Rencontre de Cerisy-la-Salle,* vol. 7, edited by J. Le Goff and G. Lobrichon. (Paris: Cahiers du Léopard d'or, 1997): 327–33.

Myers, A. R. *England in the Late Middle Ages.* Harmondsworth: Penguin Books, 1952; repr. 1965.

Pastoureau, Michel. *La Vie quotidienne en France et en Angleterre au temps des cheva-*

liers de la table ronde. Paris: Hachette Littérature, 1991.

Pirenne, Henri. *Medieval Cities: Their Origins and the Revival of Trade*. Princeton: Princeton University Press, 1925.

_____. *Mohammed and Charlemagne*. London: George Allen and Unwin, 1939; 1965.

Power, Eileen. *Medieval People*. Harmondsworth: Penguin, 1924; 1937; 1951.

Prendergast, T. A. *Medieval Heroes and Legendary Nations*. Ann Arbor, MI: UMI, 1995.

Rosenwein, Barbara H., and Lester K. Little, eds. *Debating the Middle Ages: Issues and Readings*. Oxford: Blackwell, 1998.

Sawyer, P. H., and I. N. Wood, eds. *Early Medieval Kingship*. Leeds: University of Leeds, 1977.

Schramm, Percy Ernst. *A History of the English Coronation*. Oxford: Clarendon Press, 1937.

Schenck, Mary Jane Stearns. *The Fabliaux: Tales of Wit and Deception*. Amsterdam, PA: John Benjamins, 1987.

Southern, R. W. *Making of the Middle Ages*. London: Hutchinson, 1967.

Thatcher, Oliver J., and Edgar Holmes McNeal. *A Source Book for Medieval History*. New York: Scribner's, 1905.

Tuchman, Barbara. *A Distant Mirror: The Calamitous Fourteenth Century*. New York: Alfred A. Knopf, 1978.

Unstead, R. J. *Story of Britain: In the Middle Ages*. N.p.: Corgi Children's, 1971.

Vauchez, André. *Sainthood in the Later Middle Ages*, translated by Jean Birrell. Cambridge: Cambridge University Press, 1997.

Zumthor, Paul. *Essai De Poétique Médiévale*. Paris: Seuil, 1972.

_____. *Toward a Medieval Poetics*. Minneapolis: University of Minnesota Press, 1992.

Cantor, Norman F., ed. *The Medieval Reader*. New York: HarperCollins, 1994.

Cawley, A. C., ed. *Everyman and Medieval Miracle Plays*. London: Phoenix, 1993.

La Chanson de Roland. Paris: Livre de Poche, 1990.

Chaucer, Geoffrey. *The Canterbury Tales*, edited by Thomas Tyrwhitt. New York: D. Appleton, 1855.

_____. *The Riverside Chaucer*, edited by Larry D. Benson. Oxford: Oxford University Press, 1988.

Chrétien de Troyes. *Le Chevalier au Lion*, translated by David F. Hult. Paris: Livre de Poche, 1994.

_____. *Le Chevalier de la Charrette*, translated by Charles Méla. Paris: Livre de Poche, 1992.

_____. *Perceval, ou, Le Conte du Graal*, edited by Jean Dufournet. Paris: Flammarion, 1997.

de Lorris, Guillaume, and Jean de Meung. *The Romance of the Rose*, translated by Frances Horgan. Oxford: Oxford University Press, 1999.

Geoffrey of Monmouth. *The History of the Kings of Britain*, translated by Lewis Thorpe. Harmondsworth: Penguin, 1966.

John of Salisbury. *The Statesman's Book of John of Salisbury: Being the Fourth, Fifth, and Sixth Books, and Selections from the Seventh and Eighth Books, of the Policraticus*. New York: Russell & Russell, 1963.

Marie de France. *Lais*. Paris: Gallimard, 2000.

Renaut. *Le Bel Inconnu*, edited by Michèle Perret. Paris: Champion, 2003.

Ross, James Bruce, and Mary Martin McLaughlin, eds. *The Portable Medieval Reader*. Harmondsworth: Penguin, 1949; repr 1977.

Medieval Literature

Béroul. "Roman du Tristan." In *Tristan et Iseut: Les poèmes français*. Paris: Livre de Poche, 1989.

Boethius. *Consolatio Philosphiae*, translated by W. V. Cooper. London: J. M. Dent, 1902.

Bryant, Nigel, ed. *The High Book of the Grail*. Cambridge, D. S. Brewer, 2007.

Modern Literature with a Medieval Setting

Bradley, Marion Zimmer. *The Mists of Avalon*. London: Sphere Books, 1982; repr. 1988.

Costain, Thomas B. *The Black Rose*. New York: Bantam, 1950.

Crichton, Michael. *Timeline*. London: Arrow, 1999; 2000.

Edwards, Rex. *Arthur of the Britons*. London: Universal-Tandem Publishing, 1975.

Eliot, George. *Romola*. Harmondsworth: Penguin, 1980.

Fo, Dario. *Mistero Buffo: Comic Mysteries*, translated by Ed Emery. London: Methuen, 1969; 1988.

Green, Roger Lancelyn. *King Arthur and His Knights of the Round Table*. Harmondsworth: Penguin Books, 1980.

Knowles, James. *The Legends of King Arthur and His Knights*. London: Frederick Warne, 1921; repr. Twickenham: Senate, 1995.

Koningsberger, Hans. *A Walk with Love and Death*. Harmondsworth: Penguin, 1961; 1966; 1969.

Peters, Ellis. *The Fourth Cadfael Omnibus*. London: Warner Futura, 1993; Sphere, 2007.

Scott, Walter. *Ivanhoe*. Harmondsworth: Penguin, 1994.

Steinbeck, John. *The Acts of King Arthur and His Noble Knights*. London: Pan Books, 1976; 1979, 1980.

Tremayne, Peter. *Our Lady of Darkness: A Celtic Mystery*. London: Headline, 2000.

White, T. H. *The Book of Merlyn*. London: William Collins Sons & Co/Fontana, 1978.

_____. *The Once and Future King*. London: Fontana/Collins, 1939, repr. 1980.

Film Theory

Altman, Rick. *Film/Genre*. London: British Film Institute, 1999.

Armes, Roy. *The Ambiguous Image: Narrative Style in Modern European Cinema*. London: Secker & Warburg, 1976.

Aumont, Jacques. *L'Image*. Paris: Nathan 1990.

_____. *The Image*, translated by Claire Pajackowska. London: BFI, 1997.

Bazin, André. *Qu'est-ce que le cinéma?* Paris: Du Cerf, 1994.

_____. *What Is Cinema?*, translated by Hugh Grey. Berkeley: University of California Press, 1967.

Bordwell, David. *Narration in the Fiction Film*. London: Methuen, 1985.

_____. "The Use of Montage in Soviet Art and Film.' *Cinema Journal* 11 (Spring 1972): 9–17.

Cawelti, John G. *The Six-Gun Mystique*. Bowling Green, OH: Bowling Green University Popular Press, 1975.

Cook, Pam, ed. *The Cinema Book*. London: BFI, 1985; 1995.

Deleuze, Gilles. *Cinema 1: The Movement Image*. London: Athlone, 1992.

Ebert, Roger. *I Hated, Hated, Hated This Movie*. Kansas City: Andrews McMeel Publishing, 2000.

Eisenstein, Sergei. *Film Form: Essays in Film Theory*, edited and translated by Jay Leyda. New York: Harvest, 1949, 1977.

Field, Syd. *Screenplay: The Foundations of Screenwriting*. New York: Dell Publishing, 1984.

Giannetti, Louis D., and Scott Eyman. *Flashback: A Brief History of Film*. Englewood Cliffs, NJ: Prentice Hall, 1986.

Grant, Barry. *Film Genre: From Iconography to Ideology*. London: Wallflower, 2007.

Handhart John G., and Charles H. Harpole. "Linguistics, Structuralism, and Semiology: Approaches to the Cinema." *Film Comment* 9, no. 3 (May–June 1973): 52–59.

Hudlin, Edward W. "Film Language." *Journal of Aesthetic Education* 13, no. 2 (April 1979): 47–56.

Johnson, Albert. "The Tenth Muse in San Francisco." *Sight and Sound* 24, no. 3 (1955): 152–156.

Kohler, Richard, and Walter Lassaly. "The Big Screens." *Sight and Sound* 24, no. 3 (1955): 120–126.

Lindgren, Ernest. *The Art of the Film*. London: Allen & Unwin, 1963.

Lotman, Juri. *Semiotics of Cinema*, translated by Mark E. Suino. Ann Arbor: Michigan University Press, 1976, 1980.

Metz, Christian. *Film Language: A Semiotics of the Cinema*. Oxford: Oxford University Press, 1974.

Mitry, Jean. *Semiotics and the Analysis of Film*, translated by Christopher King. London: Athlone, 2000.

Prince, Stephen, and Wayne E. Hensley. "The Kuleshov Effect: Recreating the Classic Experiment." *Cinema Journal* 31 (Winter 1992): 59–75.

Willemen, Paul. *Pier Paulo Pasolini*. London: British Film Institute, 1976.

Wollen, Peter. *Signs and Meaning in the Cinema*. London: Secker & Warburg, 1969.

Critical Theory

Althusser, Louis. "Ideology and Ideological State Apparatuses." In *Lenin and Philosophy*. London: Monthly Review Press, 1971.

Aristotle. *Treatise on Poetry*, translated by Thomas Twining and Daniel Twining, 2nd ed. London: Cadell & Davies, 1812.

Barthes, Roland. *Image, Music, Text*, translated by Stephen Heath. London: Fontana, 1977.

_____. *Mythologies*, translated by Jonathan Cape. London: Vintage, 2000.

_____. *The Rustle of Language*. Berkeley: University of California Press, 1989.

Bassnett, Susan, and André Lefevere. *Constructing Cultures: Essays on Literary Translation*. Clevedon: Multilingual Matters, 1998.

Baudrillard, Jean. *Simulations*. New York: Semiotext(e), 1983.

Campbell, Joseph. *The Hero with a Thousand Faces*. Princeton: Princeton University Press, 1968.

Debord, Guy. *Society of the Spectacle*. Detroit: Black and Red, 1983.

Dubrow, Heather. *Genre*. London & New York: Methuen, 1982.

Eco, Umberto. *On Literature*. London: Vintage, 2006.

_____. *Il Segno*. Milano: Mondadori, 1980.

_____. *La Struttura Assente: Introduzione alla ricerce semiologica*. Milano: Bompiani, 1968.

_____. *Travels in Hyperreality: Essays*, translated by William Weaver. London: Picador, 1987.

Eco, Umberto, and Thomas A. Sebeok. *The Sign of Three: Dupin, Holmes, Peirce*. Indiana: Indiana University Press, 1983.

Forster, E. M. *Aspects of the Novel*. Harmondsworth: Penguin, 1988.

Frye, Northrop. *Anatomy of Criticism: Four Essays*. Princeton & Oxford: Princeton University Press, 1957; 2000.

Genette, Gérard. *Palimpsestes: La Littérature Au Second Degré*. Paris: Seuil, 1982.

Giraud, Pierre. *Semiology*, translated by George Cross. London: Routledge and Kegan Paul, 1971.

Hegel, Georg. *Aesthetics: Lectures on Fine Art*, translated by T. M. Knox. Oxford: Clarendon Press, 1975.

Holub, Robert C. *Reception Theory: A Critical Introduction*. London & New York: Methuen, 1984.

Jauss, Hans Robert. *Toward an Aesthetic of Reception*. Brighton: Harvester, 1982.

Kepes, Gyorgy, ed. *Sign, Image, Symbol*. London: Studio Vista, 1966.

Lévi-Strauss, Claude. *Myth and Meaning*. London: Taylor & Francis Group, 2003.

Lukács, Georg. *The Historical Novel*, translated by Hannah Mitchell and Stanley Mitchell. London: Merlin, 1962.

Propp, Vladimir. *Morphology of the Folktale*. Austin: University of Texas Press, 1968.

Segal, Robert A., ed. *Hero Myths: A Reader*. Oxford: Blackwell, 2000.

Historiography

Ankersmit, F. W. *Historical Representation*. Stanford, CA: Stanford University Press, 2001.

Barraclough, Geoffrey. *History in a Changing World*. Oxford: Blackwell, 1955.

Black, Jeremy. *Using History*. London: Hodder Arnold, 2005.

Bloch, Marc. *The Historian's Craft*. Manchester: Manchester University Press, 1954.

Brooke-Rose, Christine. "Palimpsest History." In *Interpretation and Overinterpretation*, edited by Umberto Eco, 125–138. Cambridge: Cambridge University Press, 1992.

Bull, Marcus. *Thinking Medieval: An Introduction to the Study of the Middle Ages*. Basingstoke: Palgrave Macmillan, 2005.

Burger, Thomas. "Droysen's Defense of Historiography: A Note." *History and Theory* 16 (May 1977): 168–173.

Cantor, Norman. *Inventing the Middle Ages: The Lives, Works, and Ideas of the Great Medievalists of the Twentieth Century*. New York: William Morrow, 1991.

Carr, E. H. *What Is History?*, 2nd ed. Harmondsworth: Penguin, 1990.

Droysen, Johann Gustav. *Outline of the principles of history (Grundriss der Historik)*. New York: H. Fertig, 1967.

Georgianna, Linda. "Periodization and Politics: The Case of the Missing Twelfth Century in English Literary History." *Modern Language Quarterly* 64, no. 2 (June 2003): 153–168.

Ricoeur, Paul. *La Mémoire, l'histoire, l'oubli.* Paris: Seuil, 2000.

_____. *Temps et récit.* Paris: Seuil, 1991.

Robinson, Fred C. "Medieval, The Middle Ages." *Speculum* 59 (1984): 745–756.

Veyne, Paul. *Comment on écrit l'histoire.* Paris: Éditions du Seuil, 1971.

White, Hayden V. *The Content of the Form: Narrative Discourse and Historical Representation.* Baltimore & London: Johns Hopkins University Press, 1990.

_____. "The Modernist Event." In *The Persistence of History,* edited by Vivian Sobchack, 17–38. New York & London: Routledge, 1996.

Zumthor, Paul. *Parler Du Moyen Âge.* Paris: Les Éditions de Minuit, 1980.

Robin Hood

Kaler, Anne K. "Who Is That Monk in the Hood? Friar Tuck, Francis of Assisi, and Robin Hood." *Journal of Popular Culture* 30 (Spring 1997): 51–74.

Knight, Stephen. *Robin Hood: A Mythic Biography.* Ithaca, NY: Cornell University Press, 2003.

Nollen, Scott Allen. *Robin Hood: A Cinematic History of the English Outlaw and His Scottish Counterparts.* Jefferson, NC: McFarland, 1999.

Sanfilippo, Matteo. *Robin Hood: La Vera Storia.* Firenze: Giunti, 1997.

Joan of Arc

Blaetz, Robin. "Joan of Arc and the Cinema." In *Joan of Arc, a Saint for All Reasons: Studies in Myth and Politics,* edited by Dominique Goy-Blanquet, 143–164 and filmography, p. 165 and ff. Aldershot, Hampshire: Ashgate Publishing, 2003.

_____. *Visions of the Maid: Joan of Arc in American Film and Culture.* Charlottesville: University of Virginia Press, 2001.

Harty, Kevin J. "Jeanne au cinema." In *Fresh Verdicts on Joan of Arc,* edited by Bonnie Wheeler and Charles T. Wood, 237–264. New York: Garland, 1996.

Leprohon, Pierre. "L'Hagiographie à l'écran." *Études Cinématographiques* 18/19, no. 10 (Autumn 1962): 125–130.

Lerner, Gelda. "Joan of Arc: Three Films." In *Past Imperfect: History According to the Movies,* edited by Mark C. Carnes, 54–59. London: Cassell, 1996.

Maddox, Margaret J. *Portrayals of Joan of Arc in Film: From Historical Joan to Her Mythological Daughters.* New York: Edwin Mellen, 2008.

Margolis, Nadia. *Joan of Arc in History, Literature, and Film.* New York: Garland, 1990.

Rosenstone, Robert A. "The Reel Joan of Arc: Reflections on the Theory and Practice of the Historical Film." *The Public Historian* 25 (Summer 2003): 61–77.

Richards, Sylvie F. "Keeping Up with the Joans: The Maid of Orleans in Literature and Film." Morgantown: *West Virginia University Philological Papers,* 2000.

Iconography

Alexander, Jonathan. "Labeur and Paresse: Ideological Representations of Medieval Peasant Labor." *The Art Bulletin* 72 (1990): 436–452.

Doner, Janet R. "Illuminating Romance Narrative, Rubric and Image in Mons BU 331/206, Paris BN, fr. 1453, and Paris BN, fr 12577." *Arthuriana* 9, no. 3 (Fall 1999): 3–26.

Duby, Georges. *Art et société au Moyen Âge.* Paris: Seuil, 1997.

Mitchell, Sabrina. *Medieval Manuscript Painting.* London: Contact, 1964; 1965.

Mitchell, W. J. T. *Iconology: Image, Text, Ideology.* Chicago and London: University of Chicago Press, 1986.

Panofsky, Erwin. *Early Netherlandish Painting: Its Origins and Character,* 2 vols, vol. 1. Princeton: Princeton University Press, 1953.

_____. *Studies in Iconology: Humanistic Themes in the Art of the Renaissance.* New York and London: Harper & Row, 1972.

Pastoureau, Michel. *Bleu: L'Histoire d'une couleur.* Paris: Éditions de Seuil, 2002.

_____. *Une Histoire Symbolique du Moyen Âge Occidental.* Paris: Seuil, 2004.

Whitaker, Muriel. "The Illustration of Arthurian Romance." In *King Arthur Through the Ages,* edited by Valerie Marie Lagorio, 123–148. New York and London: Garland, 1990.

Secondary Sources

Curran, John R. *Pagan City and Christian Capital*. Oxford: Clarendon, 2000.

Dowden, Ken. *European Paganism: The Realities of Cult from Antiquity to the Middle Ages*. London: Routledge, 1999.

Fiala, Andrew. "Crusades, Just Wars and the Bush Doctrine." *Peace Review* 19 (April 2007): 165–172.

Fishwick, M. W. "The Cowboy: America's Contribution to the World's Mythology." *Western Folklore* 11 (1952): 77–92.

Kluger, Jeffrey. "Michael Moore's New Diagnosis." *Time Magazine*, May 17, 2007.

Moskowitz, Jennifer. "The Cultural Myth of the Cowboy, or, How the West Was Won." *Americana* 5, no. 1 (Spring 2006), unpaginated.

Sartre, Jean-Paul. *La Nausée*. Paris: Gallimard, 1962.

Sebald, W. G. *Young Austerlitz*. Harmondsworth: Penguin, repr. 2005.

Thucydides. *The Peloponnesian War*, translated by Rex Warner. London: Cassell, 1962.

Zimmerman, J. *Chivalry Is Not Dead, It Simply Rode West: The Medieval Knight and the Nineteenth Century American Cowboy as Archetypes of Nation*. Vermillion: University of South Dakota, 2002.

Filmography

Filmography

The Adventures of Robin Hood. Directed by Michael Curtiz. Warner Bros. Pictures, 1938.

The Advocate (aka *The Hour of the Pig*). Directed by Lesley Megahey. Miramax Films, 1993.

Alexander Nevsky. Directed by S. M. Eisenstein. Mosfilm, 1937.

Alfred the Great. Directed by Clive Donner. MGM British Studios, 1969.

American Beauty. Directed by Sam Mendes. Dreamworks SKG, 1999.

Andrei Rublev. Directed by Andrei Tarkovskii. Mosfilm, 1966.

L'Armata Brancaleone. Directed by Mario Monicelli. Fair Film/Vertice Film, 1965.

Becket. Directed by Peter Glenville. Paramount Pictures, 1964.

The Beloved Rogue. Directed by Alan Crosland. Feature Productions, 1927.

Berserker (aka *Berserker: Hell's Warrior*). Directed by Paul Matthews. PeakViewing Transatlantic, 2001.

The Black Knight. Directed by Tay Garnett. Warwick Film Productions, 1954.

Black Knight. Directed by Gil Junger. 20th Century–Fox, 2001.

The Black Rose. Directed by Henry Hathaway. 20th Century–Fox, 1950.

The Black Shield of Falworth. Directed by Rudolph Maté. Universal International Pictures, 1954.

Le Bon Roi Dagobert. Directed by Dino Risi. France 3/Gaumont, 1984.

Brancaleone alle Crociate. Directed by Mario Monicelli. Fair Film/O.NCI.C., 1970.

Braveheart. Directed by Mel Gibson. 20th Century–Fox, 1995.

Camelot. Directed by Joshua Logan. Warner Bros. Pictures, 1967.

Conan the Barbarian. Directed by John Milius. Universal Pictures, 1982.

A Connecticut Yankee in King Arthur's Court. Directed by Tay Garnett. Paramount Pictures, 1949.

Les Couloirs du Temps: Les Visiteurs 2. Directed by Jean-Marie Poire. Canal+/France 3, 1998.

The Court Jester. Directed by Melvin Frank & Norman Panama. Paramount Pictures, 1956.

The Crusades. Directed by Cecil B. de Mille. Paramount Pictures, 1935.

Il Decameron. Directed by Pier Paulo Pasolini. Produzioni Europee Associati/Artemis Film, 1971.

Det Sjunde Inseglet (The Seventh Seal). Directed by Ingmar Bergman. Svensk Filmindustri SF, 1957.

Dragonheart. Directed by Rob Cohen. Universal Pictures, 1996.

Dragonslayer. Directed by Matthew Robbins. Paramount Pictures, 1981.

Edward II. Directed by Derek Jarman. BBC/ Working Title, 1991.

El Cid. Directed by Anthony Mann. Rank/ Samuel Bronston, 1961.

Elizabeth. Directed by Shekhar Kapur. Polygram/Working Title, 1998.

Erik the Viking. Directed by Terry Jones. Svensk Filmindustri SF, 1989.

L'Éternel Retour. Directed by Jean Delannoy. Films André Paulvé, 1943.

Excalibur. Directed by John Boorman. Orion Pictures, 1981.

Il Fiore delle Mille e una Notte. Directed by Pier Paulo Pasolini. Produzioni Europee Associati, 1974.

First Knight. Directed by Jerry Zucker. Columbia Pictures, 1995.

Flesh and Blood (The Rose and the Sword). Directed by Paul Verhoeven. Impala/Riverside Pictures, 1985.

Fratello Sole, Sorella Luna (Brother Sun, Sister Moon). Directed by Franco Zeffirelli. EIA/Vic Films, 1972.

Gawain and the Green Knight. Directed by Stephen Weeks. Sancrest, 1973.

Giullare di Dio Francesco. Directed by Roberto Rossellini. Rizzoli Film, 1950.

Henry V. Directed by Laurence Olivier. Two Cities Films, 1944.

I, Racconti di Canterbury. Directed by Pier Paulo Pasolini. Produzioni Europee Associati, 1972.

I Tartari (aka The Tartars). Directed by Ferdinando Baldi. Uncredited. Dubrava Film, 1961.

If I Were King. Directed by Frank Lloyd. Paramount Pictures, 1938.

Ivanhoe. Directed by Richard Thorpe. MGM, 1952.

Jabberwocky. Directed by Terry Gilliam. Python Films/Umbrella Films, 1977.

Joan of Arc at the Stake. Directed by Roberto Rossellini. Cine Associazione/Franco London Films, 1954.

Jungfrukällan (aka The Virgin Spring). Directed by Ingmar Bergman. Svensk Filmindustri SF, 1960.

Just Visiting. Directed by Jean-Marie Poiré. Gaumont, 2001.

A Kid in King Arthur's Court. Directed by Michael Gottlieb. Walt Disney Pictures, 1995.

King Arthur. Directed by Antoine Fuqua. Touchstone Pictures, 2004.

King Richard and the Crusaders. Directed by David Butler. Warner Bros. Pictures, 1954.

Kingdom of Heaven. Directed by Ridley Scott. 20th Century–Fox, 2005.

Knight for a Day. Directed by Jack Hannah/Bill Peet. Walt Disney Productions, 1946.

A Knight in Camelot. Directed by Roger Young. Rosemont Productions/Walt Disney Television, 1998.

A Knight's Tale. Directed by Brian Helgeland. Columbia Pictures, 2001.

Knights of the Round Table. Directed by Richard Thorpe. MGM British Studios, 1953.

Krzyzacy (The Knights of the Teutonic Order). Directed by Aleksander Ford. Zespol Filmowy, 1960.

Ladyhawke. Directed by Richard Donner. 20th Century–Fox/Warner Bros., 1985.

Lancelot and Guinevere (aka Sword of Lancelot). Directed by Cornel Wilde. Emblem Productions, 1963.

Lancelot du Lac. Directed by Robert Bresson. Mara Films/O.R.T.F., 1974.

The Lion in Winter. Directed by Anthony Harvey. AVCO/Haworth, 1968.

Little Norse Prince. Directed by Isao Takahata. Toei Doga, 1967.

The Long Ships. Directed by Jack Cardiff. Avala Film/Warwick Film Productions, 1964.

The Lord of the Rings: The Fellowship of the Ring. Directed by Peter Jackson. Newline Cinema / Wingnut Films, 2001.

The Lord of the Rings: The Return of the King. Directed by Peter Jackson. Newline Cinema / Wingnut Films, 2003.

The Lord of the Rings: The Two Towers. Directed by Peter Jackson. Newline Cinema / Wingnut Films, 2002.

Magnificat. Directed by Pupi Avati. Duea Film/Istituto Luce, 1993.

The Magnificent Seven. Directed by John Sturges. Mirisch Corporation/Alpha Productions, 1960.

A Man for All Seasons. Directed by Charlton Heston. Agamemnon Films, 1988.

A Man for All Seasons. Directed by Fred Zinnemann. Highland Films, 1966.

Marie Antoinette. Directed by Sofia Coppola. Columbia Pictures, 2006.

Merlin: The Return. Directed by Paul Matthews. Peakviewing Productions, 2000.

Merlin. Directed by Steve Barron. Hallmark Entertainment, 1998.

The Messenger: The Story of Joan of Arc. Directed by Luc Besson. Gaumont, 1999.

Monty Python and the Holy Grail. Directed by Terry Jones, Terry Gilliam. Python Pictures/Michael White Productions, 1975.

The Name of the Rose. Directed by Jean-Jacques Annaud. Neue Constantin Film / ZDF, 1986.

The Navigator: A Mediaeval Odyssey. Directed by Vincent Ward. Arenafilm/NZ Film Commission, 1988.

La Passion Béatrice. Directed by Bertrand Tavernier. AMLF/Cléa Productions, 1987.

Perceval le Gallois. Directed by Eric Rohmer. Les Films du Losange/France 3, 1978.

Pope Joan. Directed by Michael Anderson. Big City/Command/Triple Eight, 1972.

The Prince of Jutland. Directed by Gabriel Axel. Les Films Ariane/Woodline, 1994.

Prince Valiant. Directed by Anthony Hickox. Constantin Film Production, 1997.

Prince Valiant. Directed by Henry Hathaway. 20th Century–Fox, 1954.

The Princess Bride. Directed by Rob Reiner. Buttercup Films, 1987.

Princess of Thieves (TV). Directed by Peter Hewitt. Granada Entertainment, 2001.

Le Proces de Jeanne d'Arc. Directed by Robert Bresson. Agnes Delahaie Productions, 1962.

Quentin Durward. Directed by Richard Thorpe. MGM, 1955.

The Reckoning. Directed by Paul McGuigan. Renaissance Films, 2004.

Le Retour de Martin Guerre (The Return of Martin Guerre). Directed by Daniel Vigne. Dussault/France 3, 1982.

Robin and Marian. Directed by Richard Lester. Columbia Pictures, 1976.

Robin Hood: Men in Tights. Directed by Mel Brooks. Warner Bros. Pictures, 1993.

Robin Hood: Prince of Thieves. Directed by Kevin Reynolds. 20th Century–Fox, 1991.

Robin Hood. Directed by John Irvin. 20th Century–Fox, 1991.

Robin Hood. Directed by Wolfgang Reitherman. Walt Disney Pictures, 1973.

Romeo & Juliet. Directed by Franco Zeffirelli. BHE Films, 1968.

The Saga of the Viking Women and their Voyage to the Waters of the Great Sea Serpent. Directed by Roger Corman. Malibu Productions, 1957.

Saint Joan. Directed by Otto Preminger. Wheel Productions, 1957.

Shane. Directed by George Stevens. Paramount Pictures, 1953.

Shichinin no Samurai (The Seven Samurai). Directed by Akira Kurosawa. Toho Company, 1954.

Siege of the Saxons. Directed by Nathan Juran. Columbia Pictures, 1963.

The Spaceman and King Arthur. Directed by Russ Mayberry. Walt Disney Pictures, 1979.

Stealing Heaven. Directed by Clive Donner. Amy International/Film Dallas/Jadran, 1988.

The Sword in the Stone. Directed by Wolfgang Reitherman. Walt Disney Pictures, 1963.

Sword of Sherwood Forest. Directed by Terence Fisher. Columbia Pictures, 1961.

Sword of the Valiant. Directed by Stephen Weeks. Golan-Globus Productions, 1983.

The 13th Warrior. Directed by John McTiernan. Touchstone Pictures, 1999.

Throne of Blood. Directed by Akira Kurosawa. Toho Company, 1957.

Timeline. Directed by Richard Donner. Paramount Pictures, 2003.

Tristan and Isolde. Directed by Kevin Reynolds. Scott Free Productions, 2006.

The Vagabond King. Directed by Michael Curtiz. Paramount Pictures, 1956.

The Vikings. Directed by Richard Fleischer. Brynaprod S.A./Curtleigh Productions, 1958.

The Virgin Queen. Directed by Coky Giedroyc. BBC Pictures, 2005.

Les Visiteurs. Directed by Jean-Marie Poire. Canal+/France 3, 1993.

A Walk with Love and Death. Directed by John Huston. 20th Century–Fox, 1969.

The War Lord. Directed by Franklin J. Schaffner. Universal Pictures, 1965.

The Warriors (The Dark Avenger). Directed by Henry Levin. Allied Artists International, 1955.

Willow. Directed by Ron Howard. MGM/Imagine, 1988.

Index